MANAGEMENT
AN INTEGRATED APPROACH

PAUL E. TORGERSEN
Dean, College of Engineering, and Professor of Industrial Engineering,
Virginia Polytechnic Institute and State College, Blacksburg, Virginia

IRWIN T. WEINSTOCK
Professor of Management, Fresno State College
Fresno, California

PRENTICE-HALL, INC., Englewood Cliffs, New Jersey

0-13-548396-4

Library of Congress Catalog No.: 71-162354

Printed in the United States of America

10 9 8 7 6 5 4 3 2 1

PRENTICE-HALL INTERNATIONAL, INC., London
PRENTICE-HALL OF AUSTRALIA, PTY. LTD., Sydney
PRENTICE-HALL OF CANADA, LTD., Toronto
PRENTICE-HALL OF INDIA PRIVATE LIMITED, New Delhi
PRENTICE-HALL OF JAPAN, INC., Tokyo

contents

iii

PART THREE
THE HUMAN ELEMENT:
INDIVIDUAL
AND GROUP PROCESSES

10 human motivation 187

preface

It is probably more difficult to write a basic text in management today than it was fifty years ago. Early theorists operated in a virtual vacuum of scientific knowledge. Their works necessarily consisted of common-sense logic, spiced with real world examples, the latter usually more anecdotal than scientifically generated. This is in no way meant to derogate their work, any more than one would deride a young child's first attempts to walk. Their problem was a paucity of knowledge, the absence of both extensive and intensive investigation into the nature and administration of human organizations. Early basic texts were syntheses of the works of others, and the "others" had only begun their task.

The sciences associated with the management discipline are still immature, but they are developing rapidly. Today's author faces a plethora of concepts, techniques, and theories competing for his recognition. Knowledge concerning the nature of human organizations is literally exploding; mushrooming, too, are the number and power of analytical tools, bulwarked by an expanding computer technology and growing sophistication in such fields as economics, statistics, operations research, and industrial engineering. Selecting and integrating from this mass of relevant behavioral and analytical studies are probably the most frustrating concerns of the authors of current basic management texts. Accordingly, this work is not meant to be encyclopedic but rather a selective presentation of the principal, and most generally useful, thrusts in modern management thought.

Despite our efforts to create a clearly modern text, we have conscientiously attempted to integrate new insights with valid classical theory. We have studiously resisted the tendency to present only the new, the *avant garde*. This work should reflect the concepts and tools that have survived the rigors of time, as well as the more recent developments.

We believe that the materials herein can be of value to managerial aspirants with a wide variety of backgrounds. Knowledge in the fields of economics, sociology, statistics, or political science will certainly enrich and quicken the reader's comprehension. We assume no such common background, however. The materials are presented so that the fundamental theories, tools, and concepts can be readily grasped by most college-level students. As one advances beyond this foundations level toward more sophisticated treatments of organization theory and operations research, a firmer basis in the behavioral and analytical disciplines becomes mandatory.

This book is a synthesis of the works of many others. Thus the chapter on communications is based on an original draft by T. W. Bonham, Assistant Professor of Management at Virginia Polytechnic Institute. Materials on organizational control were contributed by J. B. Nelson, Assistant Professor of Industrial Engineering and Operations Research at Virginia Polytechnic Institute. Original cases were contributed by W. E. Martin and Terry Riddle, and the Harvard Business School graciously consented to the inclusion of two of its copyrighted cases.

We are indebted also to the professors who strengthened the manuscript through their critical reviews. We thank professors Robert H. Doktor (University of Pennsylvania), Joseph L. Massie (University of Kentucky), and John Slocum (Pennsylvania State University) for this assistance. Mrs. Emily Holland typed the manuscript.

Finally, we recognize the inputs of the numerous scientists and practitioners whose works are cited in this book. They provided the basic substance and structure of our discipline, the foundation upon which this book stands.

PAUL E. TORGERSEN
IRWIN T. WEINSTOCK

introduction

1

Soap and education are
not as sudden as a massacre
but they are more deadly
in the long run.

MARK TWAIN

Like many of his animal counterparts, the human being has found it necessary to establish somewhat durable organizations for the satisfaction of his needs. Armies, police forces, churches, universities, factories, and supermarkets, diverse though they may be, have many characteristics in common. For example:

1. They are dynamic (changing) aggregations of capital and human inputs.
2. They are created to achieve identifiable objectives, and to develop procedures for achieving them, both of which may be modified over time.
3. They possess official and informal hierarchies of authority and responsibility.
4. They are components of a larger society and a total environment, to which they must adapt if they are to survive.

These are rather obvious attributes of human organizations. They are helpful, however, in describing the overall purpose and the approach of this book. Our aim is to share fundamental insights into the challenges, concepts, and techniques associated with the management of organizations. This necessitates an understanding of the nature of human organizations, including the bases for their existence, the elements of their composition, and the processes by which they establish goals, evaluate

1

alternatives, develop plans and procedures, and assess progress toward those goals.

We are most interested in the organization that is created to provide services for the larger society, rather than the club or other purely social entity, whose purpose is limited to the satisfaction of its immediate members. To be even more specific, we are particularly interested in the operation of business enterprises. It would be a great error, however, to ignore the vast similarities between the large, profit-oriented corporation and any other form of service-providing organization. They all require inputs; all must provide desired social outputs in order to survive; all possess hierarchies and official procedures; all are faced with logistical problems and various constraints; all require internal coordination; and all face varying degrees of internal conflict. Although there is much ado about the differences between private, profit-centered enterprises and publicly operated institutions, their similarities may well outweigh their differences. Insights into the nature of organizations and approaches to their effective management should be as valuable to the manager whose title is Sergeant or General as they are for the manager titled Foreman or Chairman of the Board. It is, therefore, not surprising to find that certain ideas and techniques common to business management were initially developed and applied in other kinds of organizations or that other administrative systems characteristic of business have been subsequently emulated elsewhere. It is the purpose of this book to collect and integrate such fundamental insights toward more effective management of business enterprises and human organizations in general.

Management: Art and Science

Some essays have been written in support of the management discipline as a *science*. "How can such a field be a science?" asks the novice—it is inexact, frequently dealing with unmeasurables; it lacks the rigorous controls of the laboratory; its practitioners (managers) are predominantly disposed toward practical results, rather than the development of knowledge. Management, others maintain, is solely an *art*, a set of skills and abilities developed through study and practice to attain a set of goals.

THE SCIENCE OF MANAGEMENT

Let us examine for a moment the concepts of science and art. We may define science as "systematized knowledge derived from observation, study, and experimentation carried on in order to determine the nature and principles of the subject under study." There appear to be three major components in this definition of science: (1) Knowledge is systematized; information is generated, stored, and classified. (2) The information may be gathered empirically through systematic observation of relevant phenomena, through controlled experimentation, or by inferences based on empirical data. (3) The purpose of the science is to develop understanding of the topic under investigation. The criteria of a science may be usefully elaborated, as in this list compiled by Berelson and Steiner.

1. The procedures are public: There is made available to the scientific community a minutely detailed description of the procedures and findings.
2. The definitions are precise: Each important term is clearly delineated, so that common meanings can be universally applied.
3. The data-collecting is objective: Regardless of whether data confirm or refute hypotheses or personal preferences, they are accurately measured and treated without bias.
4. The findings must be replicable: Other scientists must be able to reproduce the study and reach the same finding, before a hypothesis is generally accepted as validated.
5. The approach is systematic and cumulative: Ultimately the goal is to construct an organized system of verified propositions, a body of theory; individual research projects should be related to existing theory to achieve an overall theoretical structure; new studies may be indicated by gaps or apparent inconsistencies among findings.
6. The purposes are explanation, understanding, and prediction; the growth of understanding and certainty, the decisions concerning control, creation, or change of conditions are *applications* of a science; they become part of the science only as they assist in meeting the six criteria discussed herein.[1]

It is unlikely that the study of human organizations can ever be as precise and generally replicable as studies in the physical sciences. Moreover, it is probably more difficult to remain absolutely objective when studying one's own species. Nevertheless, there is a growing effort to develop a science of organizations and a related science of management. One needs only to consult some leading academic journals in these fields to perceive their current scientific thrust.[2] A body of knowledge and theory does appear to have been developed in these disciplines. If any-

[1] Bernard Berelson and G. A. Steiner, *Human Behavior* (New York: Harcourt, Brace & World, Inc., 1964), pp. 16–17.
[2] See, for example, *Administrative Science Quarterly, Academy of Management Journal, Journal of Applied Psychology, Journal of Sociology, Management Science,* and *Personnel Psychology.*

thing, this movement is accelerating. The wise manager will tap resulting insights to complement his initial "feel" for the situation.

THE ART OF MANAGEMENT

All of this is not to suggest that there is no room left in management for judgment, intuition, and personal skills. Management science is still in its youth. Many questions are still unanswered, and some findings are still controversial. Even if the science were more mature, the manager would still face the challenge of applying the knowledge gained from it. The physics-engineering analogy seems appropriate here. Given certain physical "laws" or principles, the engineer must create a feasible, workable design for his bridge, aircraft, or tape recorder. Science provides the constraints within which he must operate. Within those constraints, he may perceive an infinite number of approaches to the design problem. Here his knowledge of costs, consumer preferences, local conditions, available production facilities, his own fancy, and so forth help him to construct a preferred design.

The practicing manager is in much the same situation as the design engineer. Science may tell him certain facts concerning the general relationship between group size and productivity; between leadership style and job satisfaction; and between depreciation techniques and taxes. Beyond such insights, he must evaluate the actual situation facing him as he searches for an optimum or near-optimum decision. His choice must blend the requirements of the situation with the resources available. This implies sensitivity and the ability to synthesize complex, diverse information. The application of knowledge (scientifically derived or otherwise) toward the achievement of human objectives is an *art*. Management, therefore, may be described as a science and an art, the former seeking knowledge, and the latter applying it.

MANAGEMENT AS A PROFESSION

The professions enjoy high status within developed societies. A result of this prestige is a natural desire of individuals to join a profession, for example, medicine, law, or teaching. But what of management? Is it a profession? The question is not easily answered, for at least two reasons: (1) No single meaning of the term "profession" is universally accepted. (2) The roles of managers are extremely diverse.

Let us briefly examine the concept of the profession and then comment on its applicability to management.

A recent distillation of historical views by K. R. Andrews may be of value. Andrews holds that there are five important criteria for judging whether a field of activity is a profession. These are:

1. *Knowledge:* a substantial and expanding body of information, vigorously realistic.
2. *Competent application:* skilled and judicious utilization of knowledge, in the solution of complex, important problems.
3. *Social responsibility:* primarily motivated by the desire to serve others and the community.
4. *Self-control:* an established code of conduct enforced by the profession's membership.
5. *Community sanction:* a condition of high community respect, based upon society's recognition of the first four criteria.[3]

There can be no doubt that there exists a rapidly expanding body of knowledge underlying the management field. Developments in the behavioral sciences, mathematics, statistics, economics, and political science provide a vast fund of knowledge that is expanding at an accelerating rate. One cannot precisely judge the aptness with which this knowledge is being applied. Who is to set the standards? Information is progressively more available to managers and potential managers. Management books and journals have proliferated, as have management curricula in universities and management development programs in industry and universities. Organizations such as the American Management Association, Society for the Advancement of Management, and the Institute of Management Sciences foster comparisons of management techniques among organizations, presumably facilitating the spread of successful techniques.

Several management consulting firms offer to perform "management audits," evaluating managerial teams or individuals according to their ratings or management checklists.[4] There exist no universally accepted standards and criteria, however; and there is no generally accredited certifying agency. There are no equivalents of the American Institute of Public Accountants or the American Medical Association to establish and administer state or national standards of competence. It follows that there is also lacking the self-control criterion of a profession, for this requires a central control mechanism.

Whether caused by a growing community interest or by increased community vigilance and pressure, corporate managements in this and

---

[3] K. R. Andrews, "Toward Professionalism in Business Management," *Harvard Business Review,* XLVII (March–April, 1969), 50–51.

[4] For an expansive treatment of management audit approaches, see William T. Greenwood, *Business Policy: A Management Audit Approach* (New York: The Macmillan Company, 1967), pp. 46–148.

other countries do seem to be projecting an image of increasing social responsibility. Nevertheless, it would be difficult to demonstrate that corporate managers are primarily altruistic, rather than self-seeking. Company efforts in pollution abatement, aid to higher education, or honesty in merchandising can be viewed as attempts to achieve long-term selfish goals. Unquestionably, the motives of managers range from the noblest to the most base. Who is to compute the national average? For that matter, who measures these motives in lawyers, accountants, or engineers?

If material rewards are any criterion of community support, managers probably rate among the highest of professional groups. Presidents of corporations may well constitute the highest-paid group of "employees" in the United States. The mean total compensation of the presidents of 887 large corporations approached $400,000 in 1968.[5] In general, salaries are closely linked to rank within organizations.

There is also typically a positive correlation between one's rank and his status or prestige within the organization. This organizational status tends to effect the manager's status *outside* of the organization. Thus high-ranking managers of a corporation (or university or military unit) tend to be accorded high status by the other groups to which they belong. Management does appear, therefore, to meet this last criterion of community sanction, at least as well as most other activities recognized as professions.[6]

In summary, it would seem presumptious to classify management as a profession. It meets the criteria of knowledge and community sanction, but it cannot be demonstrated to generally satisfy the criteria of self-control, competent application, and social responsibility. This book focuses on the knowledge and application aspects of management. We shall leave to the student, the manager, and their societies any further debate over the degree to which management is a profession, or the desirability of seeking professional status for management.

Approaches to Management Theory

Organizations and their administration are extremely complex topics. Each topic possesses numerous dimensions, and each dimension can be

[5] "Presidents' Pay by Sales and Industry," *Business Management*, XXXVII, no. 5 (February, 1970), 17–22.

[6] A. L. Delbecq and J. Vigin, "Prestige Ratings of Business and Other Occupations," *Personnel Journal*, IL, no. 2 (February, 1970), 111–16.

studied endlessly. Researchers, acting somewhat independently of each other, have approached the study of management in a variety of ways. Entire "schools" of management theory have emerged, each claiming to provide momentous insights into the essence of the management discipline. As Harold Koontz puts it:

> There are the behaviorists . . . who see management as a complex of the interpersonal relationships and the basis of management theory the tentative tenets of the new and undeveloped science of psychology. There are also those who see management theory as simply a manifestation of the institutional and cultural aspects of sociology. Still others, observing that the central core of management is decision-making, branch in all directions from this core to encompass everything in organization life. Then, there are mathematicians who think of management primarily as an exercise in logical relationships expressed in symbols and the omnipresent and ever revered model. But the entanglement of growth reaches its ultimate when the study of management is regarded as one of a number of systems and subsystems, with an understandable tendency for the researcher to be dissatisfied until he has encompassed the entire physical and cultural universe as a management system.[7]

A comprehensive study of management theory must encompass all of the major approaches to the topic. Let us examine some of these "schools" of management thought, recognizing the contributions of each toward a fuller grasp of the discipline. As proposed by Koontz, we will call these the Management Process School, the Empirical School, the Human Behavior School, the Social System School, the Decision Theory School, and the Mathematical School.[8] To these, we will add still one more recently developing approach: the Comparative Management School.

THE MANAGEMENT PROCESS SCHOOL

The identification of the universal functions of the manager is the chief goal of the management process school. It is submitted that the functions of the manager remain essentially the same, no matter what is the nature of the organization (business, government, religious) or the conditions it faces. Once identified, these functions can be studied to develop a body of theory, upon which managers may then base their decisions. The functions provide the overall conceptual framework, around which knowledge can be accumulated and synthesized. Training

[7] Harold Koontz, "The Management Theory Jungle," *Academy of Management Journal*, IV, no. 3 (December, 1961), 174–75.
[8] Structured after Koontz, "The Management Theory Jungle," pp. 176–82.

of managers and evaluation of managerial performance could also be organized around these universal functions. This approach might, then, be suitable for the development of both the science and the art of management.

Probably the most influential early exponent of the management process school was R. C. Davis. He submitted that the three "organic functions" of the manager were planning, organizing, and controlling, defined as follows:

> *Planning:* "the exercise of creative thinking in the solution of business problems. It involves the determination of what is to be done, how and where it is to be done, and who shall be responsible."
>
> *Organizing:* "the process of creating and maintaining the requisite conditions for the effective and economical execution of plans. These conditions are principally concerned with morale, organization structure, procedure, and the various physical factors of performance."
>
> *Controlling:* "the regulation of business activities in accordance with the requirements of business plans." The control process included three principal phases: "(1) the assurance of proper performance as specified by the plan; (2) coordination of effort in conformity with the requirement of the plan; (3) the removal of interferences with proper execution of the plan." [9]

Others, following the process or functional approach, modified the structure proposed by Davis, usually by isolating other important functions and adding them to the list. Most frequently added were the terms "leading," "motivating," or "activiating," dealing with the activity of influencing others (usually subordinates) to perform in the desired manner. Koontz and O'Donnel, in all editions of their most successful text, consistently refer to "staffing" as a separate management function.[10]

In all instances, this approach attempts to describe the essential functions of the manager, to show their interrelationships, and then to introduce evidence or logic toward inferring how each function may be effectively performed. Criticisms of this "conventional approach" to management theory generally focus on the lack of scientific rigor of early writers or on topics not yet sufficiently investigated, rather than on the intrinsic merits of this conceptual framework. The functional approach is still very much alive, reflected to a greater or lesser degree in virtually

---

[9] Ralph C. Davis, *Industrial Organization and Management* (New York: Harper & Brothers, 1940), pp. 35–36. (Original edition published in 1928.) Davis was probably heavily influenced by the earlier work of the French theorist, Henri Fayol, *Administration Industrielle et Generale* (1916).

[10] H. Koontz and C. O'Donnel, *Principles of Management* (New York: McGraw-Hill Book Company, Inc., 1955).

every management fundamentals book.[11] It does provide a broad conceptual structure and it directs research into strategic aspects of the managerial role.

THE EMPIRICAL SCHOOL

Another approach to management theory, the empirical school, stresses the study of the real experiences of organizations and managers in order to arrive at principles. The best-known use of this approach is the case method of instruction, popularized and probably endowed with prestige by the Harvard Business School. The real-life experiences of an organization and its management are reported, based on some combination of interviews, questionnaires, examination of records, and direct observation of operations. Analyses of a large number of such cases, it is believed, can yield general insights into the nature of management's challenges, problems, errors, and opportunities. Using many such insights, a body of theory and techniques may be constructed.

Case study is ordinarily used along with a more structured exploration of management. In fact, rarely is any approach applied to the exclusion of all others. The close interrelationships among them should become apparent as each is discussed. The case method enjoys a peculiar advantage for the study of management, in that it retains direct contact with "the real world," permits the use of a variety of information in deriving techniques toward a comprehensive, unified grasp of situations, and combines the opportunity for analysis with a chance for recommending improvements in the reported system.[12] If used alone, however, with no attempt to structure and classify findings, the empirical approach yields only a set of individual findings derived from singular situations, certainly not compatible with the construction of a science.

THE HUMAN BEHAVIOR SCHOOL

Lawrence Appley, past president of the American Management Association, has often maintained that "management is personnel management." [13] Like many others, he envisions the essence of management

---

[11] See, for example, D. E. McFarland, *Management, Principles and Practices* (London: Collier-Macmillan, Ltd., 1970), pp. 73–305.

[12] The case study approach to organizational understanding is well defended in Peter M. Blau, *The Dynamics of Bureacracy* (Chicago: University of Chicago Press, 1963), pp. 3–5.

[13] L. A. Appley, *Management in Action* (New York: American Management Association, 1956), p. 323.

to be gaining the active cooperation of others in the pursuit of common objectives. The focal challenge for the manager, therefore, is to understand the determinants of human behavior in organizations, and then to convert these insights into a system of leadership that will yield maximum efforts by subordinates or by others whose inputs are required. He must construct a formal organization, a work flow, a system of rewards, and a communication network, all aimed at gaining a knowledgeable, coordinated, energetic effort from his human resources.

This approach examines closely the theories of human motivation, perception, and learning and is basically the application of psychology to the understanding of normal individual behavior determinants. It stresses also the behavioral dynamics of small groups, with attention to the processes of establishing group values, status structures, socially accepted standards of behavior, and enforcement powers of the group. Intensely scrutinized are conditions found to be compatible with high levels of worker satisfaction, together with high output aspirations within the group. The rapidly emerging science of social psychology provides increasing comprehension of small-group processes, with intriguing, though controversial, inferences concerning effective organization and leadership.

Moving a step further toward the macro-level of the behavior school is the study of relationships between groups, the question of interdepartmental cooperation, conflict, status, and communications. Investigated here are such matters as differences in the goals and perceptions of various interdependent departments, the effects of work flow on interdepartmental relationships and efficiency, and obstacles to effective communication among departments. Thus, the human behavior school approaches management theory by examining organizational behavior at the individual, group, and multigroup levels. Organizations are constructed for human purposes and are constituted primarily of human inputs. The behavioral sciences, according to this group, hold the key to management theory and practice.

THE SOCIAL SYSTEM SCHOOL

To the casual observer, the physical boundaries of the plants and offices of General Motors Corporation distinguish that organization from the rest of the world. The machinists, secretaries, and administrators on that company's payroll are viewed as the members of that organization. Perhaps the stockholders are also included. The social system school holds such a limited conception to be unrealistic and potentially dangerous to organizational survival. Rather, the organization is viewed as being composed of a great variety of inputs, which are controlled by diverse segments of society—the greater social system.

March and Simon present the most cogent conception of an organization as an input-output system.[14] Their principle postulates are as follows:

1. An organization is a system of interrelated social behaviors of a number of persons whom we shall call the participants in the organization.
2. Each participant and each group of participants receives from the organization *inducements* in return for which he makes to the organization *contributions*.
3. Each participant will continue his participation in an organization only so long as the inducements offered him are as great or greater (measured in terms of *his* values and in terms of the alternatives open to him) than the contributions he is asked to make.
4. The contributions provided by the various groups of participants are the source from which the organization manufactures the inducements offered to the participants.
5. Hence, an organization is "solvent"—and will continue in existence—only so long as contributions are sufficient to provide inducements in large enough measure to draw forth these contributions.[15]

Thus the viable organization is a social device for creating and distributing utility. This output (inducements) must be of greater value than the utility contributed by each person or group and be greater than the utility realizable through alternative use of the contributions. A potential employee will join and remain with an organization only if he perceives that the various satisfactions to be gained by participating are of greater utility than may be obtained by his alternatives (idleness or other employment). Moreover, he will participate in the organization where the *net* gain of utilities (inducements minus contributions) is perceived to be the greatest.

Although the necessity for labor and capital inputs is generally recognized, the other inputs required for organizational survival are not always so visible. The potential customer or client, whose inputs must be obtained, performs the same kind of analysis as the employee or stockholder. The same is true for suppliers of raw materials. Beyond these, the

[14] J. G. March and H. A. Simon, *Organizations* (New York: John Wiley & Sons, Inc., 1958), pp. 84–111.

[15] Taken, in turn, from H. A. Simon, W. Smithburg, and V. A. Thompson, *Public Administration* (New York: Alfred A. Knopf, Inc., 1950), pp. 381–82. The foundation for this theory is Chester I. Barnard, *The Functions of the Executive* (Cambridge: Harvard University Press, 1938).

organization requires the support of various levels of government. It is truly said that the power to tax is the power to destroy; similarly the power to subsidize, or otherwise treat preferentially, is the power to create and sustain. Government support is a necessary contribution. Taxes and obedience to regulations may be interpreted as inducements designed to assure that level of government support that is essential for organizational survival.

Even less apparent on superficial observation is the need for acceptance by society in general and by residents near plant facilities in particular. Public outcries against various polluting emissions are increasing in volume and impact, forcing reluctant managers to modify their processes or, in extreme cases, to discontinue operations. During the "inner city" riots of the late 1960s, some plants and stores were left untouched, while surrounding facilities were destroyed. Obviously the inducements to society (clean air, acceptable racial employment, and so forth) must be sufficient to warrant society's support if an organization is to live.

Management is another of the required inputs. More accurately, management is a subcategory of the labor input. Like other employees, managers supply their skills and efforts to the system so long as the inducements (remuneration, status, challenging work, advancements) remain superior to those offered by other organizations. The essence of the manager's role is to acquire and efficiently utilize all of the other inputs so as to satisfy divergent and frequently conflicting demands. He must assure the continued flow of an output mix that will induce the contributions of the needed input mix.

This social system school of management thought promotes a view of organizations as extremely complex entities whose diverse needs must be met by a balanced, integrated approach to management. This is a most demanding view of the management role, for the manager is seen as simultaneously serving many publics. His attempts to please one public are constrained by the requirements of the others. He is, therefore, as much the led as he is the leader. This approach to management theory is probably the most comprehensive and the most inclusive of all; it is probably also the most realistic.

THE DECISION THEORY SCHOOL

Management literature contains many descriptions of the manager as a decision maker. A consequence of this view is the development of a school of thought whose paramount concern is the study of (1) rational decision procedures and (2) the ways by which managers actually reach decisions. This school attempts to develop qualitative and quantitative models for application to appropriate problem categories. Highly structured problems, such as inventory control or production-line balancing, lend themselves to a standardized and analytical approach. Once a portfolio of these standardized solutions is developed, the knowledgeable manager need only match the correct procedure with his problem and "plug in" the analysis. Otherwise, each organization—indeed each department—would have to replicate the insights and the study of those who originated these techniques; each would, in its turn, have to reinvent the wheel. The decision theory school is referred to variously as "management science," "decision science," and "operations research." As previously suggested, the principal contributions of this school to the management process occur in problem areas where parameter relationships are quantifiable and clear and where parameters can be either directly measured or reliably estimated.

The second facet of the decision theory school, concern with actual managerial decision behavior, strongly resembles the human behavior school. Primary stress is accorded to the factors that influence one's perceptions of the problem, the alternative solutions that are likely to occur in his mind, and the personal values against which alternatives are evaluated. The research focuses on human motivation, perception, and conditioning, emphasizing one's set of personal experiences and the values of groups with which one identifies, to understand the individual's reactions to particular situations.

THE MATHEMATICAL SCHOOL

It is the view of some that no discipline should be described as a science unless it is highly quantified. Science must be expressible in the precise, measured language of mathematics. Although this view appears extreme and unjust and would place a field such as botany at a disadvantage, it does point to the potential value of model construction as a conceptualization of a system or a problem; it does indicate what dimensions need to be measured; and it can provide answers to some very complex problems. Thus mathematical emphasis can show us what to measure and why, and may then indicate how best to improve a system or solve a problem.

For the most part, mathematics is contributing to the *art* of management, rather than to the *science*. Together with the computer, mathematics is helping to solve extremely difficult problems quickly and economically; but the solution of problems is the domain of art; the generation of systemized knowledge is the challenge of science. It would appear that the science of management is still in its infancy. A sign of its continuing maturation will be a shift from emphasis on qualitative statements of untested, controversial, and at times unrelated hypotheses, to quantified statements of principles that are integrated into a comprehensive model of the management discipline. We are far from a mature science, but we are working in this direction, and the efforts of mathematicians are essential to the endeavor.

THE COMPARATIVE MANAGEMENT SCHOOL

Most recently receiving recognition is a school of management thought that seeks to develop generalizations from the study of management systems in diverse cultures. Efforts are made to determine in what ways managerial systems resemble each other in heterogeneous cultures, providing insights into possible universal management characteristics. Differences in management systems among cultures may also provide clues to the factors that underlie these systems.

The comparative management school seems to be an offshoot of the empirical school. The comparative studies may be performed in geographically remote parts of the world, but the techniques employed and the objectives sought are the same. The area of investigation has been widened. This is a beneficial development, for otherwise empirical findings could be criticized as being "culture bound," that is, valid only for the culture studied, and not true generalizations.

INTERRELATIONS AMONG SCHOOLS

The patient and thoughtful reader has certainly noted the interrelatedness of these schools of management thought. All can provide insights into the management process; none studied by itself can provide a comprehensive view of the discipline. Certainly individuals who are specializing in a given sector of investigation will tend to stress their own contributions and, perhaps, criticize other approaches. The mathematician censures the behaviorist for his lack of quantitative vigor; the behaviorist attacks the mathematician's tendency to simplify assumptions and to utilize hypothetical data in the place of real-world analysis. The empirical school criticizes the process school for its "unscientific" approach to understanding organizations, and so on.

The assumption of this book is that all of these fields have contributed to the science and the art of management. All should be and are represented in this text. More advanced texts may then build their intensive treatments of specialized approaches upon this broad base.

Plan of the Book

The first section of this book is concerned with the decision process. We begin with the premise that the manager is—first and foremost—a decision maker. We then study the decision process from the viewpoint of the practitioner of management, from the viewpoint of the behaviorist, and then, in more detail, from the mathematically oriented decision theory viewpoint.

From this latter perspective, we discuss measurement, probability, and expected value. We also introduce the concept of utility as a measure of the worth of an outcome. The last chapter in this section proposes a theory of decisions that permits a structuring of the decision situation into a payoff matrix.

The second section is concerned with planning. Through all levels in the organizational hierarchy, we must establish objectives and decide on the means of accomplishing these goals. The plan is seen as a necessary projection of tomorrow's activity. We begin this section with a discussion of the elements of planning. Then we examine in more detail the goals of the firm and the attending subdivision of purpose throughout the organization. As an aid to planning, we present an analysis of the firm in terms of the economics of production. We also review the investment decision. The section concludes with a general discussion of the "management science" approach along with a more specific introduction to three quantitative decision models.

Section III examines the human element of organizations. Heavily influenced by the behavior school, this section first presents modern theory concerning human motivation and perception, both of which play a dominant role in determining human behavior. We believe that the rational manager should understand his own needs and should reflect on the way his interpretations of the world affect his own behavior. He must possess a similar understanding of others in the organization if he is to influence their actions.

A necessary supplement to a basic grasp of human psychology is a fundamental comprehension of the processes underlying the behavior of small groups. Discussed here are the process of group formation, the establishment of group standards of behavior, and the power of the group to enforce its norms. Of pivotal interest are the factors that seem to generate group commitment to the goals of the larger organization, a commitment to produce and contribute.

This section also probes a variety of theories about effective leadership, applying our knowledge of individual and group behavior. The manager is perceived herein as one who must, in addition to his other roles, influence the behavior of others. Influence processes and techniques, therefore, are stressed in this chapter.

Effective management includes the rational structuring of resources toward the achievement of established goals and the task of establishing the organization form. Section IV, therefore, probes the challenges, theories, and techniques associated with the organization of efforts. Reviewed first are the changing concepts of organization, including the chief dimensions of authority and responsibility. Next is discussed the general basis for rational organization: the division of labor at the individual and departmental levels. Departmental size is the ensuing topic, for there appear to be factors that limit the productivity of too-small or too-large departments. Given a rational structure of specialized departments of appropriate size, decisions must be made concerning the degree to which control is to remain at the summit or be delegated to lower-level managers; this is the issue of centralization versus decentralization.

Finally, in this section, we discuss the role of communications in providing the information required for the sharing of objectives and the coordination of efforts. Problems limiting the effectiveness of communications efforts are probed and techniques for improving the sharing of information are presented. The rational organizational structure, therefore, is seen to involve a realistic conceptualization of organizations, the shaping of components to meet conditions and goals, the appropriate diffusion of authority, and a dependable system of communications.

The last section examines the control function. In order to insure that our actual results conform to the planned results, we must exercise control. We must establish standards, assess performance and compare it to what is desired, and then take corrective action if necessary.

We begin with a treatment of the control function. Then we introduce three classes of control systems: life-cycle controls, concerned with the control of the system itself; general controls, such as budgets, workmanship, and time, that extend across the life-cycle of the system; and finally, specific controls, such as production control, concerned with only one phase of the system's life cycle. The control funtion will be seen to be the mechanism whereby the firm can take corrective action to remedy mistakes and prevent their recurrence.

A set of discussion questions follows each chapter. Some of these questions are readily answered by direct reference to the text. Others are designed to excite broader or deeper thought about the subject, beyond the coverage in the book. Problems are presented where they are appropriate to chapter materials. Some of these require the application of quantitative techniques for solution; others require the diagnosis and solution of human and organizational problems through the application of behavioral insights. All of these materials are included to assist the reader to visualize and utilize the materials covered and to help place single concepts in a fuller perspective.

DECISION MAKING: THE ESSENCE OF MANAGEMENT

PART ONE

the nature of
decision making

2

An executive is a man who decides;
sometimes he decides right,
but always he decides.

JOHN H. PATTERSON
National Cash Register Company

A decision is the selection of a course of action. It is both an ending and a beginning. A decision may be the impetuous result of a hunch or the deliberate consequence of a careful evaluation; in either case, it is likely to be the beginning of an activity.

The manager has no monopoly on decisions. Nor has the student of management a monopoly on the study of the decision process. Everyone makes decisions. What school to attend, which job to select, whom to marry? At the time, these are all considered to be crucial decisions. What to eat for breakfast, which bus to catch to work, which page of the newspaper to read first: the sports or the comics? These are also decisions, perhaps of lesser consequence, but decisions that have to be made every day. People make decisions—sometimes well and sometimes poorly, and at the time of the decision the outcome may not be known with certainty. Nevertheless, decisions must be made.

Philosophers, theologians, economists, and psychologists are concerned with how decisions are made and why a particular alternative may be selected. So also are market research analysts, politicians, criminologists, and others concerned with the decision process. The philosopher may look at the decision process as the search by man for happiness, for the good life. The theologian may see the decision process as the choice between good and evil, between right and wrong. Each discipline that studies man and his behavior eventually comes to focus on the decision process. So as students of management, we too must focus on the decision-making capacity of the manager. Here we can approach the decision process from at least three perspectives: through the experiences and observations of the practicitioner of management, from the essentially experimental viewpoint of the social scientist (the behavioral approach), or from the rigorous and highly structured viewpoint of the mathematician (the decision theory approach).

In this chapter, we will limit our discussion to the first two of these three viewpoints. We will offer as an example of the wisdom of the practitioner some of the insights of Chester I. Barnard into the decision process.[1] We will also offer two examples of the contributions of the behaviorists to our understanding of the decision process. In the latter part of the chapter we will describe the manager as a decision maker and then discuss the requirement for creativity in decision making.

In the two subsequent chapters we will concentrate upon the third of these three viewpoints—the decision theory approach. This is quantitative. It is a highly structured viewpoint where the alternatives must be specified, the goals or objectives must be known, and the costs associated with each alternative must be definable and projected, at least in a probabilistic sense. Although it is obvious that many decision situations will not lend themselves to conceptualization in decision theoretic terms, at the same time there are decisions that can be quantified. More important, an understanding of the decision theory viewpoint may help the manager make better decisions, even if all facets of the decision situation cannot be conceptualized within the decision theory framework.

The Decision Process

Decisions are often made without any self-consciousness or awareness of the processes involved. To some extent, asking the executive how he makes decisions is like asking the halfback how he runs with a football. The problem of self-analysis may have been best summarized in an alleged statement of Yogi Berra, a former catcher for the New York Yankees. Yogi was asked to describe what went through his mind when

[1] In *Essentials of Management* (Englewood Cliffs, N.J., Prentice-Hall, Inc., 1964, p. 18), John L. Massie states, "Much of the modern development in management can be traced to the theoretical work of a practicing executive, Chester I. Barnard, [who] published a classic in management literature."

he was at bat. What did he think? His reply was: "I can't think and hit the ball at the same time!" The executive may be similarly hard-pressed to provide an explanation of how or why he made a particular decision.

A number of attempts have been made to conceptualize the decision-making process. The element of uncertainty, the influence of experience and judgment in decisions, and the vagaries of individuals have not made this easy. Uncertainty might enter the decision situation when the costs and results of a particular alternative can only be anticipated in probabilistic terms. Alternatives x, y, and z may each have different projected expenses and yield different likelihoods of success. These alternatives may represent drilling sites with the objective of discovering oil. The likelihood of finding oil at each location can only be expressed in probabilistic terms and as the result of some geological survey. The quantities that might be involved may also have to be expressed in probabilistic terms and as a result of the same survey. Also, the side effects or costs of each alternative are not known in advance. An added choice in each case may be "selling a piece of the action." A decision has to be made. What should be done? To which site, if any, should the drilling rig be moved?

Conceptualizing a process that is built upon individual experience and judgment is also difficult. The attribute of judgment is not easy to incorporate in a description of how or why a person decides to do something. The skill of judgment varies among people just as the ability to ice skate or play a piano will vary even after the same amount of practice. Judgment appears to improve with experience, but at the same time, innate ability is also required. No good manager should make the same mistake twice, but one manager may be better than another in profiting from analogous, if not identical, experiences.

An interesting question is, "Can judgment be learned in the classroom?" Analytical capabilities and numerical problem-solving techniques can be taught effectively; for example, the ability to review an accounting statement or formulate a queuing model. The acquisition of these skills by students can even be objectively measured. The teaching of judgment may be possible in the classroom, but it is not so easy to measure. The use of case studies and role-playing exercises may not be a substitute for business experience, but some appreciation for the appropriate judgment may be imparted to students. Also, there is some recent evidence to support the value of business games in the classroom environment.[2]

The apparent capriciousness of individual choice has not made it easy to understand the decision process. For example, in decision theory

[2] Robert C. Albrook, "How to Spot Executives Early," *Fortune,* July, 1968, p. 106.

some assumptions are made concerning the nature of man. It is believed that he is informed of all the meaningful courses of action and the consequences of each, that the choices are continuous and divisible functions, and that the individual is sensitive to these differences. It is also assumed that the individual is consistent, and further, that he can arrange choices along a scale and make a selection that maximizes (or minimizes) some utility function. As a corollary of this, if choice A is preferred to B, and B is preferred to C, then A will be preferred to C $(A > B, B > C$ $\therefore A > C)$. However, this simple requirement of *transitivity* is violated in the case of the bookmaker who lays odds that favor Notre Dame over the University of Southern California in a forthcoming football game when, earlier in the season, USC had beaten Purdue, and Purdue in turn had upset Notre Dame. In similar fashion, the business executive does not always make decisions "the way he is supposed to." He may not be aware of all the alternatives; he may not even be sensitive to differences among those that are before him. He may play a hunch one time and follow a more analytical reasoning process another. Under these circumstances, it is difficult to understand, to describe, and to predict how a decision has been or will be made. Nevertheless, it is possible to examine the decision process and to gain some insight.

The Wisdom of the Practitioner

Decisions are made by executives. They are made, and they are often made well, in spite of the difficulty in dissecting the mental processes that were involved. Chester I. Barnard was a competent executive and a successful author.[3] He is certainly not the first nor will he be the last executive who will attempt to pass on to the student of management some of the wisdom acquired through many years of experience. In particular, however, some of Barnard's contributions relate directly to the decision process.

REALITY, POLITICS, AND DECISION MAKING

Barnard has suggested that the decision-making process ultimately reduces to a search for that alternative, "the strategic factor," that gets the job done.

[3] Chester I. Barnard, *The Functions of the Executive* (Cambridge: Harvard University Press, 1938).

"The [strategic] factor is the one whose control, in the right form, at the right time and place will establish a new . . . set of conditions which meets the purpose. . . . If we wish to increase the yield of grain in a certain field and on analysis it appears that the soil lacks potash, potash may be said to be the strategic . . . factor. . . . If a machine is not operable because a screw is missing, the screw is the strategic . . . factor." [4]

In effect, Barnard implies that activity must take place in the present—under conditions and with means presently available—and that wishful thinking will not change the characteristics of the environment in which the objective must be achieved. The manager must be realistic; he must get the job done. If an increased price is the only meaningful alternative, it must be the one selected. If it is really necessary to discharge a troublesome employee, then that employee must be told to seek employment elsewhere.

In this same vein, the manager should not select alternatives that are not realistic and that will not get the job done. If we describe politics as "the art of the possible," then the manager must also have a political orientation. He must understand what he *can* do. In the most elementary of suggestions, Barnard has stated that the fine art of executive decision making consists . . . in not making decisions that cannot be made effective." [5] Perhaps one of the better pieces of advice that can be given a new manager is this suggestion that he refrain from issuing orders that either can not or will not be obeyed. The suggestion is probably too obvious to be given, but it is advice that will often be ignored.

The environment in which decisions must be made will likely include people—their opinions, their beliefs, and even their prejudices. An effective manager will be sensitive to this environment. One can argue that a specific department manager *ought* to see the big picture, *ought* to be more concerned with the company as a whole, and *ought* not be so oriented to the needs and interests of the people in his group. However, a decision based upon what that manager *ought* to think and not how he is *likely* to react would be naive.

THE REQUIREMENTS FOR DECISIONS

The occasion or opportunity for decision making will likely originate in one of three distinct fields; (a) from superiors (authoritative), (b) from subordinates (appellate), or (c) on the initiative of the deci-

[4] Ibid., p. 203.
[5] Ibid., p. 194.

sion maker. This last occasion may be the decision maker's best opportunity for initiative and creativity.[6]

A number of decisions will be delegated downward to the manager. He may be told by his superior to "let go" three employees and the decision as to which three are to be given notice is his choice (if it is not spelled out in a labor contract). The executive may be told to establish a *value analysis* program in his company if he expects to receive additional government contracts. Another manager may be asked to prepare recommendations in regard to the subcontracting of some work. In each case, the manager may make the requested decision or he may delegate downward to a subordinate the requirement to make the decision (or a part of it). However, even this latter choice requires a decision.

A second occasion is one that has risen in the organizational hierarchy. A manager may receive a request from a subordinate for time off with pay to serve on jury duty. Another employee may request a change in shift. An executive may have to serve as arbitrator in a dispute between a production department and the quality control group in regard to the acceptability of some production work. On such an occasion, the manager may also pass the decision situation up the line for advice or an answer.

These first two occasions often become routine. The third is the one that permits a display of the capacity for innovation. At the same time, this third occasion is where the manager is most likely to "rock the boat" by disrupting the status quo. Failure to decide in this third occasion is less likely to be evident or to be questioned. The research manager might undertake some developmental work with a new and previously untested material. If he is successful, he may be a hero. If he fails, he may be asked "why he didn't leave well enough alone." The employment manager might experiment with the hiring of some hardcore unemployed. If he is successful, he will be a visionary in the ranks of employment managers. If he fails, their response might be, "I could have told him it wouldn't work."

In discussing Barnard's third occasion for decision making, Eric Ashby, Master of Claire College, Cambridge University, notes with some humor the means that may have to be employed in the academic world in exercising initiative. Enterprise on the part of an administrator in industry is said to create confidence, but this is not necessarily true in academic circles. "In British universities naked enterprise on the part of a university president is viewed with suspicion, not to say alarm." [7]

6 Ibid., pp. 190–92.

7 Eric Ashby, "A University Presidency: What It Takes," *Saturday Review*, November 21, 1964, p. 77.

Ashby then continues with a description of how the president must unobtrusively interject his ideas into the informal organization. Then, with luck and if they are any good, at some later date his ideas may be returned formally to his desk for consideration and possible approval. At that time, he may voice his pleasure and express his affirmative decision.

The Contributions
of the Behaviorist

Some insights into the decision process may be acquired through experimentation and the collection of data, either in the laboratory or in the real world. The social scientist might be concerned with the influence of stress on decision making. He might seek to establish a relationship between personality traits of the individual and the selection of some alternatives over others in a choice situation. Perhaps anxiety levels can be assessed and then predicted in risk-taking situations. The psychologist might be able to predict bias in a given situation: the salesman who underestimates his expected sales or the production manager who is cautious in promising a delivery date. Rationalization may be seen in the individual who will attempt to convince himself after the fact that the selected alternative is even more attractive, in comparison to other possible alternatives, than it was at the time of the decision.

The preceding are all examples of the contributions (or possible contributions) of the behaviorists to our understanding of the decision process. The social scientist may work either in the laboratory, where conditions may be carefully controlled, or in the real world. We will offer as examples two studies—one in each setting.

THE LABORATORY

Social influence may have an effect upon the values, the judgment, and the resulting decisions of an individual. An interesting series of experiments designed to test the strength of the urge toward social conformity was undertaken by Asch in the early 1950s.[8] A number of stu-

8 The initial study was reported by Solomon E. Asch, "Effects of Group Pressure upon the Modification and Distortion of Judgment," in *Groups, Leadership, and Men*, ed. H. Guetzkov (Pittsburgh: Carnegie Press, 1951). The study was then replicated with a more elaborate design and published by the same author as "Studies of Independence and Conformity: A Minority of One Against a Unanimous Majority," *Psy-*

dents were placed one at a time in a simple decision situation. A measure was then recorded of either their correct but independent response or their incorrect but conforming reply. In effect, the issue was the extent to which a group and the unanimous decisions of all other members of the group would influence the decisions of the individual.

The experiment could be restructured as follows. It begins when a group of perhaps seven college students is assembled in a classroom for an alleged psychological experiment in visual judgment. The students are told they are to compare lengths of lines. They are seated in a row and two large white cards are then placed before the group. The cards might appear as follows:

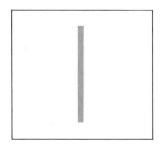 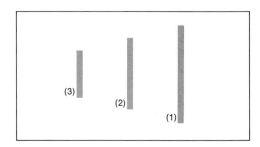

The students are told to indicate which of the three lines on the second card is of the same length as the single line on the first card. In a routine fashion, each student, in order across the row, verbally responds with the correct answer. Then, a second set of cards is exposed and the students again announce their answers in the order in which they have been seated. Again the group is unanimous. On the third trial something unusual occurs. The first respondent gives an incorrect answer. The second individual then gives the identical incorrect reply. In turn, each individual gives the same incorrect response until the last or the next-to-last student is asked for his reply. The reply of this last or next-to-last student is the focal point of the whole experiment. What this individual, the subject, does not realize is that he is the only member of the group who was not instructed in advance to give incorrect answers in unanimity at certain points. Will he join with the others and give the incorrect reply or will he disagree and answer correctly? The subject is given a total of 18 oppor-

chological Monographs, LXX, no. 9 (1956), 177–90. The results of this early work were also summarized in "Opinions and Social Pressure," Scientific American, CXCIII, no. 5 (November, 1955), pp. 31–35.

tunities to reply with the group to two sets of cards and on 12 in these instances, the majority response is in error. The differences in the lengths of the lines are such that in the absence of collusion less than 1 percent error would be reported. Nevertheless, under group pressure, the test subjects swung to accept the misleading but majority judgment in slightly over one third of their total selections.

Individual differences are even more significant. About one-fourth of the subjects were completely independent of the influence of the group. Some other individuals went along with the group in almost all instances. A third and larger group exerted their independence some of the time and yielded at other times. The reasons for these individual variations are difficult to identify. Asch suggests that the more independent individuals were not necessarily unresponsive to the majority; they simply had a large measure of confidence in their own judgment. Conversely, some of the yielding subjects viewed their difference from the majority as a sign of some deficiency in themselves, which they had to hide.

The unanimity of the majority and the size of the majority were two factors that were varied in subsequent experiments. In the first case, it was found that with the support of only one truthful partner the influence of the majority, regardless of its size, was reduced substantially; that is, subjects answered incorrectly only one fourth as often as when facing a unanimous majority.

The size of the majority itself was insignificant beyond a majority of 3. When the subject was confronted with 1 opponent, he was influenced only slightly. A majority of 2 did sway the subjects into some 10 to 15 percent error. A majority of 3 brought the error rate up to slightly over 30 percent and this did not change much with larger groups, even with groups that included 15 opponents. At least for the purpose of this experiment, social pressure begins with a group of 2 and has reached full force with the concerted reactions of 3.

The work of Asch, like much research, probably raises more questions than it answers. To what extent can these data be extrapolated to a more general setting? Why are some people more likely to conform than others? Is the manager more likely to be independent in his thinking? Perhaps the manager is less independent—his thinking may have to conform to the thinking of both his superiors and his subordinates. The leader may actually be adept at following his followers.

THE REAL WORLD

What does the manager actually do? What kinds of decisions must he make? Does he prefer certain types of decisions to others? Are some more difficult? These are interesting questions and they are the types of questions that are more likely to be answered in a real-world context.

Controls are difficult to establish in the real world. The virtue of the laboratory environment is seen in the ability of the researcher to nullify (or control) the effects of variables that are not of interest in the experiment. In the Asch studies it was possible to duplicate the setting with each replication of the experiment—the variables being the size of the group and the unanimity of their response from one subject to the next. At the same time, the laboratory environment is artificial and it is difficult to extrapolate from it into the real world. As a result, some data simply have to be collected "where the action is." The example to be described is of this latter variety.

Lower-level managers are expected to be both technical experts and supervisors. They often have to divide their time between task-oriented problems and strictly administrative matters. Shrode has defined five categories of recurrent decision problems facing the lower-level manager:

a. Functional or job-oriented
b. Sociopolitical or people-oriented
c. Economic or money-oriented
d. Informational or the exchange of relevant data
e. Other: remaining problems or highly related combinations of the first four.[9]

The first category reflects the task-oriented decision and the next three categories are subdivisions of the administrative-oriented decision. In collecting information concerning the manager's decision-making activities, both structured interviews and self-administered reporting were used.

Some of the findings may be summarized as follows:

1. Lower-level managers spend approximately half their time on task-oriented and half their time on administrative-oriented problems. Of the latter, a ranking of time allotments would be to information, people, and money problems, in that order.
2. People problems are considered the most difficult; money decisions are the least difficult to render.
3. People and task problems are considered the most important; money decisions are of least consequence.

[9] William A. Shrode, "An Analysis of Lower-Level Managerial Decision Making in an Industrial Firm," *AIIE Transactions*, II, no. 3 (September, 1970), pp. 214–21.

4. The preference of the lower-level manager, as one would expect, is to work upon the task-oriented decision problem.

This study, like the Asch study, raises more questions than it answers. What of the higher-level manager? How much information is considered adequate to make each of these types of decisions? Would the lower-level manager's judgment of relative importance agree with those of his superior? Some day these questions will also be answered—and it is likely that they also will be answered in a real-world context.

A Model of Management

The manager is a decision maker. The act of managing and the activity involved in making a decision are almost one and the same. Simon has suggested that these are actually synonymous terms.[10]

Much that is undertaken either through the existing organizational structure or to modify the organization itself is done to facilitate the decision-making process. As an example, a new computer-based management information system may be installed—to provide the manager with more complete, more reliable data and to permit more intelligent decisions. A reorganization occurs—perhaps to expedite the making of decisions. A cost control system is introduced—to enable the manager to detect and be able to respond to the out-of-control condition. Quantitative decision models may be interjected into the decision-making process to minimize guesswork and reliance upon the analogous (but never identical) earlier experience as the basis for decisions.

The activity of the manager, functioning as a decision maker, can be seen in the schematic model of Figure 2-1.[11] Not every specific decision situation is captured in all possible detail. Rather, a more or less idealized replica of the steps leading up to and following the decision event is presented.

The cycle begins with the requirement for a decision—a stimulus. A group of employees have indicated that they would like to be represented by a labor union and wish company recognition of the union as the collective bargaining agent. A machine has broken down. A district sales report has come in and it is far short of expectations. Each of these

[10] Herbert Simon, *The New Science of Management Decision* (New York: Harper & Brothers, 1960), p. 1.

[11] Adapted from William T. Morris, *Management Science* (Englewood Cliffs, N.J.: Prentice-Hall, Inc., 1968), pp. 5–8.

Figure 2-1

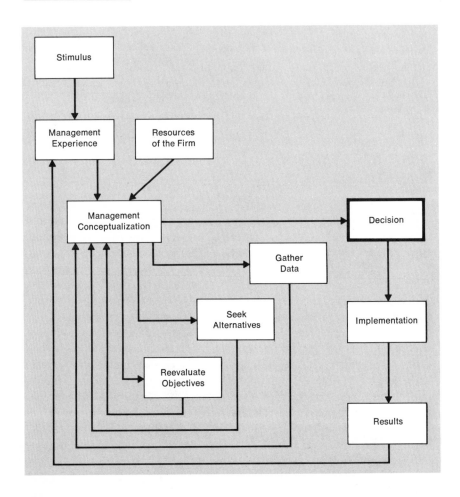

inputs may signal the existence of a problem or a potential problem. Each input may be seen as a decision situation.

Drawing upon his own experiences and possibly employing the information resources of the firm, the manager evolves a conceptualization of the decision situation. At this point, the objectives may be clear, the alternatives may be well defined, the uncertainty associated with each choice may be at a minimum, and it may be possible to make a decision. The manager is prepared to respond to the stimulus; he does so; he observes the consequences of his actions or the implementation of his choice, and the circle is complete when this activity and its attending results now become a part of the inventory of management experiences.

In some instances, the initial conceptualization may be hazy. The manager might not wish to risk a decision at this time. He may seek out additional information. Before deciding whether to repair or replace the machine that has broken down, he may wish more data on the history of the machine. Has it broken down often in the past and was it expensive to repair and maintain? How much did it cost to operate? What will the new asset cost in operation? The answers to these questions may permit a more solid conceptualization of the decision situation. Then, the decision may be made with more confidence.

As a second response, the manager may seek out additional alternatives. Neither replacement nor repair may appear satisfactory. Both choices may seem too expensive in that the machine, or its replacement, will still be idle a large proportion of the time. A third alternative may be sought and may be found in subcontracting out the work that had been done on the machine. This may prove to be the most economical choice of all.

The development of alternatives requires some technical competence along with an element of creativity. Failure to think of a unique alternative means that that alternative is not evaluated as a possible solution. An interesting question involves how long the search for alternatives or the collection of additional information relevant to these alternatives should take. Time spent in seeking additional inputs is time that cannot be spent on other decision situations. It is not likely that one can reduce the uncertainty associated with an alternative to zero, nor is it likely that one can discover all feasible choices. Eventually the choice must be made among the alternatives that have been delineated and with the evidence at hand. A satisfactory rather than an optimum solution may be the result.

A third response to an inadequate conceptualization may be one of value clarification: a reevaluation of objectives. What is actually to be accomplished? We tend to assume that the manager is purposeful, that the goals of the organization are well defined. This may not be true. A decision situation may point out the necessity for redefining goals. Sometimes the decision maker loses sight of his objectives and, to compensate, redoubles his efforts. We then confuse activity with progress toward the goal. Rather than repair or replace the machine, rather than consider the alternative of subcontracting this work, someone might ask the question, "Why is this part being made?" Does this fit into the objective or should the objective be changed?

The gathering of data, the seeking of additional alternatives, and the reevaluation of objectives are all undertaken to permit a more concise and better-defined conceptualization of the decision situation. This then leads to the decision itself, the implementation, and the observance of the results of the decision. All then becomes part of the management experience. Hopefully, the manager learns through this experience. He profits by his mistakes; he is reinforced in his judgement; he sharpens his intuition. The management process is also a learning experience.

Creativity in Decision Making

The decision-making process requires a solution to a problem; it requires an acceptable alternative to accomplish an objective. There is usually more than one solution to a given problem and more than one valid alternative. The search for the best solution or the most acceptable alternative is probably undertaken first within the framework of one's own background and second, in the experiences of others. Perhaps as a last resort, the search is made for a novel approach.

It is only natural for the manager to first search in his own experiences for a solution. A production scheduling problem may be analogous to a scheduling problem that was resolved last year. Perhaps the same approach will work a second time. Some allowances may have to be made for the unique features of the current problem. However, the previous approach was sound and possibly that solution can be modified so it will fit. Familiarity with a solution will make it attractive.

As a second choice, the executive may search for an acceptable alternative in the experiences of others.

How does Monsanto handle this situation?

What did Paul Hansen over in Union Bolt do with their vendor rating program?

Another, more deliberate means of exploiting the solutions of others is the use of professional and technical societies and trade meetings and their publications. Just as the medical doctor might read his medical journals and attend a regional or national medical convention to keep abreast of advances in medicine, the purchasing agent, the accountant, the personnel director, or the design engineer might subscribe to his respective journals and attend national meetings to learn how his colleagues are resolving professional problems.

There are times, however, when an answer cannot be found in one's own experience or in the experiences of others. Then, if a solution is to be found at all, it must be original and it must be creative. The creative process requires a new way of looking at what might be an old problem; it is a mental activity that was triggered by a specific requirement and results in a novel solution. The answer may, however, have an application or implication beyond its immediate requirement.

THE CREATIVE PROCESS

There does not seem to be an easy formula—a sure road—either to being creative or to understanding the creative process. At best, a sequence of overlapping mental activities can be observed and perhaps artificially categorized into four discrete steps. The process begins with the *perception of a problem.* The creative individual is more sensitive to problems. He "sees" something that can be improved. He is probably familiar with the setting within which the problem is found. He deliberates over this problem, notes relationships about different aspects of the problem, analyzes the total problem into constituent parts, and attempts to rearrange the problem in his mind. There may be a popular misconception that creative ideas appear quickly and almost by accident to a chosen few. Perhaps the chocolate-covered ice cream bar was discovered when an ice cream cone was accidentally dropped into a small vat of molten chocolate and perhaps Goodyear's discovery of the method for vulcanizing rubber occurred with the spilling of crude rubber on his kitchen stove; but these and a few other accidents are not typical of the search for new ideas. The discovery is usually preceded by a great deal of concentration upon and examination of the problem situation.

Following the recognition and understanding of the problem comes the *incubation* stage. In this step, the subconscious as well as the conscious thought processes come into play. During this development period, a solution may begin to germinate and take shape. The creative person wrestles with a problem, and if he is successful, an idea emerges as a result of his thoroughness in coming to see into the problem and his persistence in the search for a possible solution.

If the incubation step has been fruitful, it will be followed by a sudden *illumination.* An insight into the problem will exist where one did not exist only a few moments before. The idea—the solution—may indeed be a creative experience for an individual but he may subsequently learn to his chagrin that the idea was not new to others. He had simply "reinvented the wheel." This is not an uncommon experience. In any event, the illumination step is difficult to describe in physiological terms. Insight will initially occur at the subconscious level. A synthesis of many trains of thought will suddenly form a pattern that will rise to the level of consciousness. At this point, the solution will be illuminated.

The idea may still require some *accommodation* to make it work. To some extent, this is the "hammer and tongs" step, where a fit is achieved. Developing the details of the solution may not be as exciting as the illumination step, but just as the painter has to put his inspiration on canvas and the composer transfer the melody from his head to a musical score, so the manager must accommodate his idea to the reality of the situation. This will require time, patience, and persistence.

A discussion of the creative process would not be complete without mentioning the art of *serendipity*. A prospector who might be seeking gold and who stumbled upon a vein of silver ore might pass this vein with only the observation: "Whatever it is, it's not gold!" Serendipity is the gift of finding and recognizing valuable or agreeable things *not* sought for: the knack of uncovering unexpected discoveries.[12] Should the prospector recognize the worth of his find, he could be said to possess the gift of serendipity.

There is some question as to whether or not this art or knack is part of the creative process. The executive certainly cannot manage his firm by counting on unexpected discoveries. At the same time, the manager should be alert to the importance of accidental discoveries. To the extent that opportunities do occur, the creative manager will be perceptive to their occurrence and conscious of their value.

INHIBITIONS AND CREATIVITY

The capacity for creativity is not limited to a small portion of the population nor is it limited to the more intelligent. Some minimum level of intelligence is probabily a prerequisite in the problem perception stage of the creative process. However, almost anyone can have an original idea. A second misconception has already been suggested—that the new idea simply occurs. On the contrary, the creative process is likely to call for a lot of hard work.

If new ideas are the result of hard mental work and are not limited to a select few, are there other aids to creativity or restraints that can be removed? Can creativity be taught? In a sense, our educational process and our culture work against us and create barriers to individual creativity. Social pressure tends to inhibit the development of individualistic traits. The encounters one has with others are developed through social

---

[12] A word coined by Walpole in allusion to a tale, "The Three Princes of Serendip," who in their travels were always finding things they did not seek.

mores and within legal "dos" and "don'ts" and these place a payoff on conformity. The maverick is also the outcast. In addition, our educational system tends to reward the *proper* correct answer. The *novel* correct answer is not encouraged. As a result, curiosity is more likely to be found in children and then lost in adults. The individual also works against himself when he develops habits and routines that then become comfortable and hard to break. The creative process requires overcoming the habitual approach. To the extent that these society- and self-imposed psychological barriers exist, it will be more difficult to see a new approach.

As an example of the type of block one creates for oneself, consider the following:

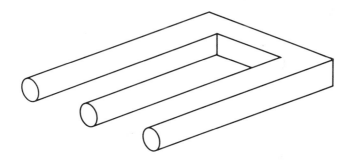

In looking at the right end of this sketch, one forms a preconceived image of how the left end should appear. But the left side doesn't fit this picture. Something is wrong. Actually, nothing is *wrong* with the sketch. It is simply not a three-dimensional drawing, no matter how much we want it to be.

Consider another sketch and a possible test for creativity. *Without moving your pencil from the paper, connect all nine dots with four straight lines.*

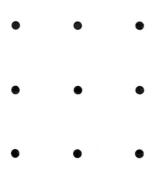

In attempting to comply with this directive, many people will add the self-imposed restriction that the lines should not extend beyond the periphery of the dots. However, this restriction was not stated in the problem and once it is realized that it does not exist—that one or more of the lines can extend beyond a dot—then a solution is possible. In a similar vein, we often impose restrictions upon our thinking and eliminate possible solutions from consideration. Most attempts to teach creativity are oriented toward making the individual aware of his self-imposed inhibitions in thinking.

GROUP CREATIVITY

Sometimes novel ideas have been developed in group-thinking or *brainstorming* sessions. Under favorable conditions, a group of people can reinforce each other in the generation of ideas and produce more good, creative ideas when working together than when working individually.

A brainstorming session is conducted for the specific purpose of generating ideas. A problem is posed and solutions or ideas are requested. All ideas are accepted and recorded no matter how far-fetched or ridiculous they may seem. There is no attempt to evaluate any idea until all have been collected. The advantage of this procedure is that someone's idea may trigger an extension or a divergent idea in the mind of another individual and this, in turn, may lead to the proposal of a really significant idea by a third or a fourth party. In summary, brainstorming is usually based on the following principles and procedures:

a. An initial goal should be "the more ideas the better." With more ideas, we are likely to discover a good idea.

b. Group ideation will be more productive than noninteractive but collective individual ideation. The reinforcement and sequential triggering of ideas is responsible for the multiplying effect.

c. The generation of ideas will be still more productive if immediate judicial judgment is withheld. "This does not mean that we forego evaluating our ideas. It simply means that if we [intersperse] the hot faucet of [proposals with] the cold faucet of judgment . . . we will get only lukewarm ideas." [13] Our education and experience has trained most of us to think judicially rather than creatively. We therefore tend to restrict our creative thinking when we evaluate each idea as it is proposed. We should wait

[13] M. O. Edwards, "Tips on Solving Problems Creatively," *Management Review*, March, 1966, p. 28, condensed from *Systems and Procedures Journal*, January–February, 1966.

until the train of ideas has been exhausted before beginning the evaluation process.

In recent years, executives have used brainstorming on a wide variety of problems. Although most suggestions will be trite or impractical and the cost of the collection of talent involved in a brainstorming session may be impressive, one or a few creative and significant ideas may easily make the session well worthwhile.

SUMMARY

Decision making *is* the essence of management. Other people may be called upon to make decisions and the duties of the manager may be defined in terms of other functions, but the decision-making capability of the manager will be a significant factor in the success of the organization.

The decision process is not an easy process to understand. We have elected to approach the decision situation from three distinct perspectives: (a) the viewpoint of the practitioner of management, who has had experience in making successful (and unsuccessful) decisions; (b) that of the behaviorist, who is basing his insights on controlled experimental inquiry; and (c) the more abstract and highly structured decision theory viewpoint of the mathematician. In this chapter, we have limited ourselves to the first two of these three perspectives. We have chosen the insight of Chester I. Barnard as representative of the "wisdom of the practitioner." For example, Barnard suggests that decisions have to be made in the present, under conditions and with means presently available, and that the decision maker ought to be aware of the realities of "the art of the possible." Barnard also delineates three requirements or opportunities for decisions. Of these, the third—the initiative of the decision maker—is described as the best opportunity for a display on the part of the manager of the capacity of innovation.

The behaviorists have made their contributions both in the laboratory and in the real world. The work done by Solomon Asch is cited as representative of laboratory experimentation and a very recent study by William Shrode is typical of a real-world experiment. The Asch study was concerned with the effects of social (group) influence upon the decisions of individuals. The Shrode study defined different categories of decision situations and then attempted to determine the amount of actual time spent by different levels of managers upon these categories of decisions. The study further ascertained the preference of managers for decisions in these respective categories and their consideration of the relative importance of each category of decision.

A schematic model of the manager functioning as a decision maker is also included in this chapter. This model traces the decision sequence, beginning with the requirement for a decision, through the filtering of management experience and the resources of the firm, to a conceptualization of the decision situation. Following this conceptualization, the decision may be made and implemented and the results made a part of the manager's experience. Alternatively, additional data, additional alternatives, and/or a reevaluation of objectives may be undertaken to redefine the conceptualization of the decision situation. The last section in this chapter deals with the requirement for creativity in decision making, the creative process, the effect of inhibitions upon creativity, and the opportunities for group creativity.

This chapter serves to introduce the decision process. The next two chapters are more specifically concerned with the quantitative aspects of the decision process. In the next chapter, we will establish a structure for decisions. Following the establishment of this framework, the decision process will be defined in matrix form under conditions of certainty, risk, uncertainty, and conflict. It will be seen that this approach will require a formalization of the decision situation.

QUESTIONS

1. List the two or three most important decisions that you have made to date.

2. List two or three decisions that you have already made today.

3. Describe a decision that you have not made, but that you need to make within the next few days.

4. Cite an example of an *authoritative* requirement for decision. An *appellate* requirement. A decision made on the initiative of the decision maker.

5. Give an example of the social conformity (Asch) effect in decision making.

6. Why might a lower-level manager have a preference for task-oriented decisions?

7. The manager should profit from his mistakes. Describe this process with an example and in the context of the schematic model of Figure 2-1.

8. What are the four steps in the creative process?

9. Discuss the relationship between inhibitions and creativity.

a structure for
decisions

3

*Beauty (as well as value) is in the eye
of the beholder.*

MARGARET WOLFE HUNGERFORD

The decision is made within some framework. A simple objective might have to be attained; a number of alternatives may be available so that comparisons are undertaken and the choice is made. But as we have already suggested, it is not always that simple. The decision situation can also be vague, ambiguous, and perplexing. The decision process can be hard work.

A structure within which the decision situation should be conceptualized would include at least two significant dimensions. The objective is one such dimension: Why make a decision? What are we trying to accomplish? The goals of the organization will be treated in a subsequent chapter. The second dimension to the decision situation comes in the evaluation of alternatives. How do we obtain alternatives? How do we compare them? How do we treat probabilistic outcomes? The manager may wish to quantify the degree of uncertainty associated with each choice and then work with *expected values* in contrasting alternatives. His evaluation of a course of action may be based upon (a) the value or worth of the outcome *and* (b) the attending probability that the outcome will be realized. He may then select the alternative whose expected value, the product, is greatest.

The manager may also modify the objective units of measurement included in each alternative to incorporate a personal value system. The *utility* of an outcome is the subjective worth placed upon that outcome. Utility is obviously a personal thing, but it can be included in the structure of the decision situation.

In this chapter and the next we will introduce a quantitative structure for and theory of the decision process. We will assume that the objective has been defined and the alternatives identified. We now simply wish to know which alternative should be selected.

Measurement

Comparisons and contrasts are of interest to practically everyone and of necessity in everyday affairs. Some people measure their intake of calories, students are likely to compare grades received on an examination, the new VW owner will check miles per gallon on his car, and the activities of the younger generation are contrasted against some standard of behavior set in an earlier era. A decision also requires that comparisons be made, and this must begin with the measurement process. When we do measure, we strive for *accuracy;* we may also require *precision.* Sometimes we speak of the *validity* and the *reliability* of our measuring instrument. These are criteria that should be of interest to the decision maker, because they are used to describe measurements in the evelution of alternatives and reflect upon the comparisons that are being made.

The measurement process requires the assignment of numbers to objects or events according to rules. It is possible to distinguish among four levels of measurement, each with separate rules. The lower levels have less restrictive rules, but at the same time, less can be done with these numbers in a manipulative sense. As one ascends the four scales, more restrictions are imposed, but one can then do more with the numbers that have been obtained.

In ascending order, the first level of measurement is the *nominal scale.* Here a number is used as a label for a category or a class. A number can be assigned to the first document when it is placed in a specific file, for example, 3,001. Another number can be assigned to the first document placed in a second file, for example, 5001, and so forth. Airline flights might be given numerical designations in accordance with some scheme, such as eastbound flights using even numbers. Football players are given numbers in accordance with the position they play, for example, centers are numbered in the fifties, guards in the sixties, tackles in the seventies, and so forth. After we have completed our numbering system, we can count the number in each category and obtain *frequencies.* The most populous class would be the *mode*. If objects are classified across two dimensions, it is possible to determine the independence (or lack thereof) of these two aspects by computing a *coefficient of contingency*. However, this is about the extent of the data analysis that is possible with the nominal scale.

The *ordinal scale* is a scale of rank ordering. The pleasantness of odors and the taste of food may be ranked; so also may the socioeconomic level of jobs and professions. The administrator may rank his preference for three outcomes as follows: signing a contract with the union as first, continued negotiations second, and a strike third. The implication is that along some scale of preference a hierarchy can be established. The ranked outcomes need not be equally spaced along this scale, but outcome one is preferred to outcome two and outcome two is then preferred to outcome three.

Not all states or events lend themselves to ranking. Color is difficult to rank. The position of an airplane is difficult to rank, although its anticipated arrival time can be contrasted to other arrival times on an ordinal scale. Also, the position of an airplane in a holding and landing pattern over an airport can be expressed as a rank-order position until landing.

In using an ordinal scale we require a dimension, but only one dimension. This can be preference in taste, or relative weight, or relative position in a holding and landing pattern. We cannot rank both position and aircraft weight along the same ranking scale. The permissible statistics are those of the nominal scale plus the calculation of *medians, centiles*, and *rank-order correlation coefficients*. However, we cannot add and subtract, nor can we calculate a mean; our manipulative restrictions are still quite serious.

The *interval scale* is the first scale that is quantitative in the everyday sense of the word. Numerically equal distances stand for empirically equal distances over the aspects in question. Almost all statistical measures are applicable unless a true and reference zero point is required. Measures of calendar dates, temperature (Fahrenheit and centigrade), and intelligence may be recorded on an interval scale. We may calculate the *mean* and *standard deviation* and, of course, we may add and subtract. The difference between 10 and 15 degrees on a Fahrenheit temperature scale is the same as the difference between 30 and 35 degrees. Note however, that because no true zero is required with this scale, it is meaningless to say that 80 degrees Fahrenheit is twice as warm as 40 degrees. Also, an individual with an IQ of 120 is not half again as intelligent as an individual with an IQ of 80.

The *ratio scale* is similar to the interval scale and has the added property of an absolute zero. Two pounds are twice as heavy as one pound. In traveling 120 miles, one has traveled half again as far as 80 miles. The ratio scale, as the name implies, permits the meaningful comparison of ratios. The ratio 20/15 is equal to 4/3 in that both stand for the same relation between two quantities. A ratio scale is possible when zero means none in the absolute sense. Along a weight scale, zero weight has a meaning of none. However, zero on a Fahrenheit temperature scale does not have this same meaning of none-at-all. There still exists some measure or quantity of warmth.

The decision maker who wishes to measure will have to employ a scale of measurement. In general, he should use as rich a scale as possible. If he can quantify outcomes along an interval or a ratio scale, he may be able to employ analyses not possible with only a ranking of preferences. Conversely, if he must resort to an ordinal scale, he should not assume that preference three is twice as desirable as preference six. Not only is the interval scale lacking in a hierarchy of preferences, but geometric comparisons are invalid without an absolute zero.

Numbers are employed in measurement. However, counting is the only empirical use of numbers where it is possible to be precise and accurate in an absolute sense. The measurement of any continuous dimension, such as time, distance, and/or weight is not precise and accurate in this same absolute sense.

Precision refers to the number of significant digits. We may measure a rod with a yardstick to the nearest one quarter of an inch. We may measure it again with a micrometer to the nearest 0.001 inch. The second measurement is more precise. However, it may not necessarily be more accurate. *Accuracy* refers to correctness or conformity to the truth. As an example, for some reason or other our micrometer may be improperly calibrated, and it may be reading an inch too long or an inch too short. Although the micrometer is still precise, the yardstick may now be providing more accurate information.

Reliability and *validity* are terms also used to describe the measurement process. However, they are more likely to be used to describe an aptitude or an intelligence test than a voltmeter or a pressure gauge. A valid test is one that measures what we presume it to measure. In dealing with physical things we are not usually concerned with validity. We can measure mass or electrical conductivity and we think we know what we are measuring. However, when we presume to measure fatigue, learning, or intelligence, we are not as certain of the validity of our results. Perhaps an improvement in performance should be attributed to maturation or to improved motivation, rather than learning, as we might assume. How then is a test ever validated? How do we know if we are actually measuring what we propose to measure? A test for mechanical aptitude is a valid test if the scores correlate highly with later individual proficiency. Unfortunately, this is determined only after the fact. Sometimes we would like to know in advance. The only answer is in the *face validity* of the test—does it seem to make sense, does it appear to measure that for which it was designed?

The *reliability* of a measuring instrument refers to its stability: the same "yardstick" applied to the same object yields the same value time after time, provided the object itself is not changing or being changed by the measurement process. A reliable measure is a consistent measure— a repeatable measure. The decision maker should be concerned with validity and reliability. He may, however, also confuse the two. The fact that a measure can be duplicated with the same result does not guarantee that we are measuring what we think we are measuring. Conversely, a valid measure that is not consistent may force us to take many measurements before we can place any faith in the results.

Likelihood and Probability

The manager must be oriented toward the future. He must anticipate; he must project; he must predict. In each case, he must face varying degrees of uncertainty. Without the element of chance, errors in decision making could only be attributed to the failure to consider a meaningful alternative or the failure to include all relevant information. Unfortunately, we do not live in a world where it is possible to forecast the future with certainty. As a result, we have employee turnover, unexpected equipment breakdowns, and material shortages; we turn out defective products, overproduce, and ship to the wrong market regions; we also have business failures.

Our desire to handle the element of uncertainty in decision making leads us to the concept of probability. Here we have a measure of certainty or of uncertainty. We have a means for mathematically expressing the possibility of an event or for quantifying the degree of assurance in an outcome. An event that is certain to occur will have a probability of one. An event that is certain *not* to occur will have a probability of zero. These extremes rarely exist in reality, but they establish limits between which measures of relative certainty may fall.

SOME DEFINITIONS OF PROBABILITY

Probability can rest upon an objective and/or a subjective foundation. An objective probability is one that can be established either on the basis of logic—the classical or *a priori* approach—or on the basis of past experience—the relative frequency approach. A subjective probability is based upon opinion and is an expression of a degree of belief.

The *classical* definition of probability suggests that if an experiment can result in N equally likely outcomes and n of these possess the attribute A then $P(A)$ (the probability of the occurrence of A) is:

$$P(A) = \frac{n}{N}$$

For example, if each of the sides of a six-sided die numbered consecutively from one to six is equally likely to land face up (a fair die) and we consider a success (the occurrence of A) to be a roll of a four, a three, a two, or a one, then the probability of success on the next roll would be:

$$P(4 \text{ or less}) = \frac{4}{6} = \frac{2}{3}$$

The key to this definition is the assumption of "equally likely outcomes." Had the die not been fair or, for example, if playing cards are not shuffled properly, probabilities developed from this definition would be in error.

The *relative frequency* definition of probability is also an objective approach, which suggests that if in N repetitions we denote the number of occurrences of A by n, then assuming N is large, $P(A) = \frac{n}{N}$.

For example, if we roll the six-sided die a large number of times, say 10,000 rolls, and we note that 6,650 times we have a four or less, then the probability of a four or less on the next roll is:

$$P(4 \text{ or less}) = \frac{6,650}{10,000} = 0.665$$

The key to this definition is two-fold: we need a reasonable amount of historical data before we can make any predictions about the next event (the probability is theoretically correct only in the case where N approaches infinity); and the collection of this data—the repetitions—must be done under similar conditions. We should not use data that have been amassed over a period of time during which the circumstances affecting the likelihood of an event have been changing. This latter requirement is often difficult to meet.

The *subjective* approach to probability may be thought of as individualistic and personal. The assessment of the likelihood of an event will be a measure of belief and will depend not only upon the specific experiences of the individual who is involved, but also upon his nature— his prejudices, his degree of optimism in the future, and so forth. The individual will weigh the evidence as he sees it and then express a probability as a degree of belief.

Most human decision making will incorporate a degree of uncertainty. Most probability will contain a subjective element. Personal experience, judgment and intuition will influence the assessment of the degree of uncertainty. Nor is this undesirable in the absence of objective, quantifiable data. However, the decision maker should lean upon the classical and the relative frequency definitions as far as possible in formulating his subjective probability. This might be seen in Figure 3-1.

Consider the bridge player who must decide whether or not to attempt a finesse. Relying upon the classical definition of probability, he can assume that the cards have been shuffled and dealt properly and that the "equally likely" requirement has been met in dealing each card. He can then calculate the probability of certain distributions or "splits," which will give him an objective probability. However, he can also review the bidding and, based upon his knowledge of his opponents and their

Figure 3-1

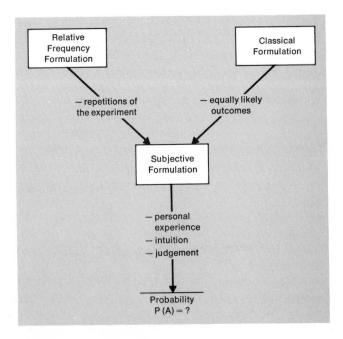

actual bidding patterns, he can modify the initial objective probability.

The decision maker is more likely to rely upon the relative frequency definition in formulating his subjective probability. He might realize that previous conditions were not the same as existing ones and use this initial information as a reference upon which to add the subjective element. The quality control manager might tabulate the percent of defective units received over time from a certain supplier, then modify this information to incorporate an apparent trend in quality improvement. A market forecast might be modified to reflect an unusual change in the activity of a competitor. The probability of success attached to a research proposal might be changed from the average figure to reflect the influence of the individual who will be directing the specific project. In each case, judgment will be used to modify the results of the more objective approach.

SOME THEOREMS OF PROBABILITY

Events or outcomes are said to be *mutually exclusive* if one and only one can occur at a time. Consider the tossing of a coin. The coin may land heads up or tails up. These outcomes are mutually exclusive. On any one toss of a coin, either heads or tails may turn up, but not both. Events are *independent* if the occurrence of one event has no effect upon the occurrence of a second event. Consider the tossing of two coins. The outcome of the second toss is independent of the outcome of the first.

The *addition theorem* states that the probability of the occurrence of either one or another of a series of mutually exclusive events is the sum of the probabilities of their separate occurrences. Thus, in tossing a coin, the probability of either a head or a tail would be:

$$P(H + T) = P(H) + P(T)$$
$$= \tfrac{1}{2} + \tfrac{1}{2} = 1$$

If the addition theorem is violated, some erroneous and often bizarre results may ensue. For example, assume that a college student is beginning a cross-country trip on some rather bald tires. He is told by a garage mechanic that the probability of each or any one tire having a flat before he reaches his destination is 0.3, or $P(T_1) = P(T_2) = P(T_3) = P(T_4) = 0.3$. Because he has four tires (and no spare), he is anxious to calculate the probability of having a flat on any tire and not being able to complete his trip. By using the addition theorem incorrectly, he would conclude:

$$P(T_1 + T_2 + T_3 + T_4) = P(T_1) + P(T_2) + P(T_3) + P(T_4)$$
$$= 0.3 + 0.3 + 0.3 + 0.3 = 1.2$$

DECISION MAKING: THE ESSENCE OF MANAGEMENT

This is not true, because the failure of tires (even bald tires) is not mutually exclusive.

The *multiplication theorem* states that the probability of occurrence of independent events is the product of the probabilities of their separate events. Thus, in tossing two coins, the probability of the occurrence of two heads would be:

$$P(H \cdot H) = P(H)P(H)$$
$$= (\tfrac{1}{2})(\tfrac{1}{2}) = \tfrac{1}{4}$$

The tire failure problem can now be resolved, because these events are independent. The probability of any tire, for example, tire number one, not failing is:

$$P(\overline{T_1}) = 1 - P(T_1)$$
$$= 1 - 0.3 = 0.7$$

Then the probability of no tire failing would be:

$$P[\overline{T_1} \cdot \overline{T_2} \cdot \overline{T_3} \cdot \overline{T_4}] = P(\overline{T_1})P(\overline{T_2})P(\overline{T_3})P(\overline{T_4})$$
$$= (0.7)(0.7)(0.7)(0.7) = 0.2401$$

And the probability of any tire failing, or one or more tires failing, would be:

$$P(T_1 + T_2 + T_3 + T_4) = 1 - 0.2401 = 0.7599$$

and it would appear as though the odds were three to one against the student's completing his trip without at least one flat tire.

The *conditional theorem* states that the probability of the occurrence of two dependent events is the probability of the first event times the probability of the second event, given that the first has occurred. Thus, consider the possibility of drawing two successive white balls from an urn containing three white and two black balls. We need to calculate the product of the probability of selecting a white ball times the probability of selecting another white ball, given that the first attempt has been successful. The probability of selecting a white ball initially is ⅗. Should a white ball be selected and not replaced, then the probability of selecting another white ball is ¾. Thus, the calculation is as follows:

$$P(W_1 \cdot W_2) = P(W_1) \cdot P(W_2 | W_1)$$
$$= (\tfrac{3}{5})(\tfrac{2}{4}) = \tfrac{6}{20} = \tfrac{3}{10}$$

The conditional theorem takes into account changes in probabilities between two successive events.

The decision maker should be able to profit from experience. He should be able to revise an estimate or modify a probability when he acquires additional information. One means of doing this—of calculating *a posteriori* probability—is with Bayesian statistics. Assume that an alternative has to be selected. The probability of selecting the correct one is determined on an *a priori* basis. Then additional information is obtained. The revised probability may be expressed as:

$$P(A|b) = \frac{P(b|A)P(A)}{P(b)}$$

where $P(A|b)$ is the revised or *a posteriori* probability of state A, given the occurrence of b; $P(b|A)$ is the probability of occurrence b, given state A; $P(A)$ is the *a priori* probability of state A; and $P(b)$ is the probability of occurrence b.

For example, assume that we have three urns—one containing four white balls and one black ball, a second containing three white and two black balls, and a third containing two white and three black balls—and that we do not know which urn contains which mixture.

State A (or B or C)

We now select one of the three urns. What is the probability that it is the one designated as State A and containing the four white balls and one black ball? Working with *a priori* probabilities:

$$P(A) = \tfrac{1}{3}$$

Now assume that we have the opportunity of reaching into the urn and selecting one ball. We do so and observe that the ball that was selected is black. Now, with this added information, what is the probability that we have selected State A?

$P(b|A) = \tfrac{1}{5}$, or the probability of selecting a black ball from the urn designated State A.

$P(A) = \tfrac{1}{3}$, or the *a priori* probability of selecting State A.

$P(b) = (\frac{1}{3})(\frac{1}{5}) + (\frac{1}{3})(\frac{2}{5}) + (\frac{1}{3})(\frac{3}{5}) = \frac{2}{5}$, or the probability of selecting a black ball.

And the probability we have selected State A:

$$P(A|b) = \frac{(\frac{1}{5})(\frac{1}{3})}{\frac{2}{5}} = \frac{1}{6}$$

The probability that State B or State C has been selected, given the occurrence of a black ball, would be:

$$P(B|b) = \frac{(\frac{2}{5})(\frac{1}{3})}{\frac{2}{5}} = \frac{1}{3}$$

and:

$$P(C|b) = \frac{(\frac{3}{5})(\frac{1}{3})}{\frac{2}{5}} = \frac{1}{2}$$

Note how the odds have changed from an *a priori* probability of $\frac{1}{3}$, $\frac{1}{3}$, $\frac{1}{3}$, for States A, B, and C respectively, to an *a posteriori* probability of $\frac{1}{6}$, $\frac{1}{3}$, and $\frac{1}{2}$. In similar fashion, odds may change any time additional information is acquired. The manager may not be able to define precisely *a priori* probabilities, quantify the influence of incremental information, and finally develop the revised or *a posteriori* probabilities. However, he does something similar to this continuously and extensively on an intuitive basis. We have seen that the management experience is a learning experience. Bayesian statistics describes how learning can contribute to the accuracy of probabilities and may assist in conceptualizing the decision-making aspect of the management function.

Expected Value

In choosing among alternatives, the individual is likely to attempt to establish some scale of preferences. The high school senior may be considering one of two or three girls to ask to the prom. The new college graduate may be considering four job offers. The manager must decide whether or not to risk a strike. In each case a scale of preferences may be attained through a rank ordering of desirable alternatives. If quantification is possible, the individual may attempt to place the alternatives upon an interval or ratio scale.

Consider the boy who can select one of two neighborhood lawns to cut during the summer. His parents have restricted him to one such outside job. He is offered $2.00 to cut the first lawn. The second lawn is about the same size and he is offered $3.00 to keep it cut. If a linear relationship may be assumed to exist between dollars and the boy's utility or preference for money, at least within the limits of the few dollars in this example, then the second job is half again as desirable as the first.

Now we interject a probabilistic element: The first job is a certainty—he can get it and he can keep it for the summer. The second job is not a certainty—there is a small possibility that the owner may sell the house and move, in which case there is no assurance that the new owner would want his lawn cut. The first opportunity would likely have been taken in the meantime by another boy. Which alternative should be selected? In part, the decision will depend upon the probability involved in the second case. In part the decision will also depend upon the tendency of the boy to "take a chance." If the probability can be established, then the alternatives can be contrasted on the basis of the *expected value criterion*.

The expected value (EV) of an alternative is the product of the probability (p) and the value or worth of that alternative (w). The first case was a certainty. Thus:

$$EV_1 = (1)(\$2.00) = \$2.00$$

Assume that the probability of the second job becoming and remaining a reality is 0.9. Then:

$$EV_2 = (0.9)(\$3.00) = \$2.70$$

These two expected values can now be contrasted and, because the second is larger, it may be selected. There is a fallacy in this comparison and choice, however. The expected value criterion defines the payoff or *expected value in the long run*. Thus, if many hundreds or thousands of boys were confronted with these identical choices, the average earnings of those who selected the second choice would be $2.70. However, no individual would receive $2.70. Some individuals (10 percent) would earn nothing. The remainder would earn $3.00. From the viewpoint of the individual examining a single choice situation, $3.00 at probability 0.9 plus no income at probability 0.1 is not the same as an expected value of $2.70. Nevertheless, the expected value criterion is a yardstick for contrasting alternatives. It is an especially useful measuring instrument where repeated incidents of an identical or a similar evaluation are required.

When an alternative may result in a number of possible outcomes, each of which has a numerical worth (w_1, w_2, and so forth) and a respective probability (p_1, p_2, . . . p_n), then the expected value of the alternative may be expressed as:

$$EV = p_1w_1 + p_2w_2 + \ldots + p_nw_n$$
$$= \sum_{i=1}^{n} p_iw_i$$

Assume that an individual is about to invest $1,000 in either some stock or in a bond. Three possible outcomes in the investment economy and their attending probabilities may be projected:

O_1—reduced growth ($p_1 = 0.20$)
O_2—continued growth ($p_2 = 0.50$)
O_3—increased growth ($p_3 = 0.30$)

An investment in a stock or a bond will likely result in subsequent stock or bond value, depending upon the investment economy, of:

	Stock	Bond
O_1	$ 900	$1,010
O_2	1,050	1,020
O_3	1,200	1,060

Which choice should be selected? We could hedge our bet by buying some of each. However, the expected value will be maximized by selecting one or the other. The expected value of the stock and of the bond are:

$$EV_{stock} = (0.20)(\$900) + (0.50)(\$1,050) + (0.30)(\$1,200)$$
$$= \$1,065$$
$$EV_{bond} = (0.20)(\$1,010) + (0.50)(\$1,020) + (0.30)(\$1,060)$$
$$= \$1,030$$

This comparison requires that the outcomes be mutually exclusive, thereby permitting our use of the addition theorem of probability. It is also required that the value of the outcomes and the respective probabilities be defined. If this is possible and we wish to use the expected value basis for choice then we would invest in stock. The expected value superiority of stock over a bond is $1,065 — $1,030 = $35. Note again, however, that if our outcomes are as defined then one of three things will occur in the single case. If we select stock over a bond:

1. We will lose a net of $110, if we experience reduced growth.
2. We will gain a net of $30, if the present growth rate continues.
3. We will gain a net of $140, if the growth rate increases.

In no instance will we experience an exact net gain of $35.

The expected value criterion can also be applied to gambling and to other situations where a loss may be experienced or a cost may have to be incurred to participate. In this instance, the "fairness" of the game may be ascertained. Assume that a six-sided die is to be rolled. If a six occurs, you win $600. However, if any other number comes up you must pay $150. Should you participate? The expected value of the game would be:

$$EV = (\tfrac{1}{6})(\$600) + (\tfrac{5}{6})(-\$150)$$
$$= +\$100 - \$125 = -\$25$$

If the game is played once you would either win $600 or lose $150 and the loss is far more likely. If the game were repeated 1,000 times, the expected loss would be $(1000)(-\$25) = -\$25,000$. This game is not fair to you in that the expected value is negative.

One might ask in regard to this game, what would be a fair price to pay in order to participate? In other words, at what cost does $EV = 0$?

$$EV = (\tfrac{1}{6})(\$600) + (\tfrac{5}{6})(-X) = 0$$
$$\$100 = \tfrac{5}{6}(-X)$$
$$X = -\$120$$

A charge of $120 to participate with a payoff of $600 at a probability of $\tfrac{1}{6}$ would be fair in that the game would favor neither participant. In most routine and repetitive gambling situations—racetracks, gambling casinos, lotteries—the odds usually favor the "house," but not to the extent that an individual cannot win sometimes and in the short run. In most raffles, on the other hand, where the objective is to raise money quickly, the odds greatly favor the house. Selling 10,000 tickets for $1.00 each on a car worth $2,500 is not uncommon.

A classic example of the difficulty in using the expected value criterion can be seen in the "St. Petersburg Paradox." In this gaming situation, one flips a coin and continues only until a tail lands up. Then the game is over. The payoff is in dollars and in the amount of 2 raised to the number of tosses, or 2^n dollars. Thus, if the first toss is a tail, the game is over and the player collects 2^1 or $2. Should a player flip one head and then a tail (whereupon the game must cease), he would collect 2^2 or $4. Should he be fortunate enough to have a string of heads, for example, four heads before the tail, he would win 2^5 or $32. The question is: How much should one be willing to pay to play this game? How much should it cost to have a fair game where $EV = 0$? Most people will see the $2 minimum payoff and the fact that it is also possible, if not probable, to win a large amount of money if one encounters an initial string of heads. As a result, typical bids or offers to play the game will run from $2 or $3, perhaps up to $10 or $20 for the more venturesome. The "paradox" of this game is that the payoff, as an *expected value in the long run*, is an infinite amount of money. This can be seen with the help of Table 3-1. We have an infinite series of $1s, because there is no guarantee that tails will first show before the one-millionth or one-billionth throw. Mathematically, the expected payoff is:

$$\sum_{i=1}^{\infty} p_i v_i = \sum_{i=1}^{\infty} 1 = \infty$$

Thus, any bid to play the game at less than ∞ would favor the participant. However, few people will spend more than $10. One can even add more insult to the illustration by changing the rule so that there will be no

Table 3-1

Sequence of Tosses	Probability (p_i)	Payoff (v_i)	$p_i v_i$
H	1/2	$ 2	$1
HT	1/4	4	1
HHT	1/8	8	1
HHHT	1/16	16	1
HHHHT	1/32	32	1
HHHHHT	1/64	64	1
.	.	.	.
.	.	.	.
.	.	.	.

payoff until 1,000 successive heads occur. The expected value is still infinitely large, because:

$$\sum_{t\,=\,1,001}^{\infty} 1 = \infty$$

Now it is unlikely that even a cent would be ventured for the privilege of playing the game.

In our reasoning to date, we have implicitly assumed that individuals have the same affinity for money and that a single individual's relative affinity for different amounts of money should be expressed as a linear function. In fact, these two assumptions may not be true. In a decision situation, probabilities may be preferred to expected value dollars.[1] A person may choose a p of 0.95 and a payoff of $100 [$EV = 0.95(\$100) = \$95$] over a p of 0.30 and a payoff of $400 [$EV = 0.30(\$400) = \$120$]. However, this same individual may then "contribute" a dollar on a long-shot car raffle, where 10,000 tickets are being sold on a car valued at $2,500 [$EV = 1/10,000(\$2,500) - \$1 = -\$0.75$].

In spite of the fact that individuals do not place equal value on dollar amounts and that a single individual does not always value $10 twice as much as $5, we may still work with the expected value criterion. We need only convert dollars to utility. We may then work with the expected utility in contrasting alternatives.

Utility

The decision situation can be conceptualized as the choice of that alternative possessing the greatest utility, where utility is defined as the power to satisfy human wants. In addition, in a choice situation where each alternative may have many possible outcomes, we can assume that the rational manager is also interested in that alternative with the maximum expected utility.

Consider the following two potential ventures. A manager could secure Contract A calling for an investment of $200,000. If he is successful in meeting the contractual requirements, and there is a probability of 0.5 that he will be successful, he will realize a profit of $400,000 plus the

[1] Ward Edwards, "The Reliability of Probability Preferences," *American Journal of Psychology*, LXVII (1954), 68–95.

return of his investment. If he is unsuccessful, he will lose his investment along with the potential profit. Contract B is more modest. The profit is $100,000, the investment is $40,000, and the chance of losing the investment is only 0.3. If only one contract can be selected, which one should it be? The expected value criterion clearly indicates a preference for the first contract:

$$EV_A = (0.5)(\$400,000) + (0.5)(-\$200,000)$$
$$= \$100,000$$

$$EV_B = (0.7)(\$100,000) + (0.3)(-\$40,000)$$
$$= \$58,000$$

However, the manager might reject Contract A on two counts. A venture with a possible loss of $200,000, at any odds, might be avoided simply because such a loss could put the company out of business. The criterion of expected value in the long run is meaningless if the company goes bankrupt in the short run. The manager might also select Contract B simply because the odds of being successful are greater (0.7 instead of 0.5).

With this rationale, a manager selecting Contract B appears to be making a reasonable choice, in spite of the expected value advantage of Contract A. The manager's judgment should not be considered illogical or irrational. In effect, the manager is selecting that alternative possessing the greater utility for him or for his company.

An insurance contract is another illustration of the inadequacy of the expected value criterion. If the probabilities of loss have been correctly ascertained, the purchaser of an insurance policy is always involved in a transaction of negative expected value. Still, insurance is big business. Why do people purchase insurance policies? The answer lies in the utility of the policy. Peace of mind and the guarantee of protection against a major loss, even when coupled with a low probability, are worth more than the cost of the premium.

Consider the company faced with the requirement of shipping $100,000 worth of finished goods to some part of the world where there is a serious risk that the goods will be lost or destroyed in transit. The probability of total loss is 0.05. An insurance firm is willing to insure the shipment against total loss for a cost of $8,000. The company accepts. Is this transaction advantageous to both parties? The answer may well be yes. The company could self-insure itself for $(0.05)(\$100,000)$ or $5,000; this is the premium at which $EV = 0$. However, an insurance firm, with large financial reserves, is set up to accept these types of ventures. It is structured to work with expected values in the long run. Its charge of $8,000 includes an expected value loss of $5,000 and an additional $3,000 profit plus cost of operation, such as calculating the probability of loss. If the firm's estimates of the probabilities are accurate and its capital reserves are adequate, it will continue to sell insurance. On the other hand, the company is more than willing to pay $8,000 to effectively raise the probability of success in shipment from 0.95 to 1.00. The utility of guaranteed delivery, or its equivalent, is greater than the $8,000 cost of that guarantee. Hence, the transaction has utility to both parties.

The concept of utility is of value in describing how and why decisions are made. An early scientist, Daniel Bernouilli, doubted the value of the expected value criterion because of its inability to treat the "St. Petersburg Paradox." In a paper written about 1730, he raised the question of how to assess the utility of money. Rather than attempting an experimental inquiry, he reasoned that the more money one has, the less the utility of another dollar. In effect, he reasoned that the utility of money is inversely proportional to the amount already on hand. Bernouilli then settled upon a logarithmic function to relate dollars and the worth of those dollars to the individual. In more recent years, the assessment of utility has taken an empirical approach. People have been placed in decision situations and their choices have been observed.

John von Neumann and Oskar Morgenstern have developed the ingenious *standard-gamble* method for determining an individual's utility for the outcomes associated with different alternatives.[2]

Earlier in this chapter, on an ordinal scale of measurement, we listed an administrator's ranking of preferences for three outcomes as follows:

a. Signing a contract with the union.
b. Continued negotiations.
c. Strike.

It might now be advantageous to obtain a measure of the utility of each outcome to this administrator. We are going to attempt to enrich this ranking of preferences up to ratio measurement, using utility as the measurement scale. We begin with the ranking and we tell the executive that we are going to ask him to make a choice between a contract at probability p and a strike at probability $(1 - p)$ *or* continued negotiations. In effect, after defining p, we give the executive the following two choices:

Choice 1	Choice 2
$p(\text{contract}) + (1 - p)(\text{strike})$	negotiations

[2] John von Neumann and Oskar Morgenstern, *Theory of Games and Economic Behavior* (Princeton, N.J.: Princeton University Press, 1947).

We might begin by letting $p = 0.5$. The executive has a choice of a 50-50 chance between a contract settlement or a strike, and the opportunity to continue negotiations. Perhaps he selects the continuation of negotiations. Then we change the probability so that $p = 0.6$. Now the administrator must select between the first choice, where a contract has a probability of $p = 0.6$ and a strike has a probability of $p = 0.4$ or the second choice— continued negotiations. Perhaps the risk of a strike is still too high and the second choice is selected. Again p is changed. Eventually a p is achieved where the decision maker is *indifferent* between the two choices, that is, he has no preference. Assume that in this case $p = 0.8$. We now assign a utility of 1 to the original preferred outcome of a signed contract, a utility of 0.8 to the second outcome of continued negotiations, and a utility of 0 to the strike. These utilities now give us much more information than the simple ranking. We know that, although a contract is to be preferred to continued negotiations, even this second choice is much more desirable than a strike. These relative preferences can possibly be transferred to subordinates, to help them guide their activities. In addition, we now have a much richer structure of the decision situation in case we should have to select an alternative that has one or more outcomes included in a probabilistic mode.

Utility can also be measured where there are a number of possible outcomes associated with each alternative. In the stock-versus-bond investment choice, each alternative had three possible outcomes and these six situations ranged from a return of $900 to a return of $1,200. If we assign a utility of 1 to the $1,200 return and a 0 utility to the $900 return, and then compare all other outcomes in turn, our investor might end up with the following:

Payoff	Utility
$1,200	1
1,060	0.85
1,050	0.80
1,020	0.70
1,010	0.75
900	0

Now, by developing the expected values of utility, EVU, the decision maker might conclude that the bond is to be preferred:

$$EVU_s = (0.20)(0) + (0.50)(0.80) + (0.30)(1)$$
$$= 0.70$$

$$EVU_B = (0.20)(0.70) + (0.50)(0.75) + (0.30)(0.85)$$
$$= 0.77$$

The concept of utility is interesting and valuable in describing the decision situation. At the same time, the determination of utility in a given choice situation is not as simple as the two preceding examples might have one believe. Utility will vary from one individual to another—some people are more cautious, others prefer risks. In addition, the same decision maker may change from one instance to another in his evaluation of risks and possible payoffs. One can readily see individual variations in any gambling situation or investment opportunity—some people purchase bonds, others invest in wildcat oil well drilling opportunities. Both investments must have utility in the value systems of the respective investors.

SUMMARY

The decision is made within a frame of reference. There must be an objective, at least two viable alternatives, and a setting within which the decision situation will occur. Perhaps one alternative is the choice not to make a decision at this time. Nevertheless, the manager will have to make comparisons in evaluating alternatives and he will have to do this prior to making the decision.

A comparison requires a measurement. We have distinguished among four levels of measurement: the nominal, the ordinal, the interval, and the ratio scales. We have also reviewed the necessity for accuracy and for precision in measurement and have discussed the validity and the reliability of measuring instruments, all of which bear upon the comparison that must be made.

The element of uncertainty in evaluating alternatives is introduced in the context of probability, which provides a means for including the element of chance in the decision process. Objective and subjective probabilities are defined and the addition, multiplication, and conditional theorems of probability are described. The use of Bayes' theorem is introduced as a means of profiting from experience, or modifying a probability, with the acquisition of additional information.

The product of the probability times the value of the outcome associated with that alternative is introduced as the expected value. Alternatives may be contrasted on the basis of the expected value criterion.

As we have suggested, however, the measure of this approach is found in the expected value in the long run. The St. Petersburg Paradox is cited as the classic example of the difficulty in using the expected value criterion for the single or short-term situation.

The expected value criterion is sometimes modified to interject the utility associated with an outcome, rather than the value of the outcome itself. It is suggested that the assessment of an individual's utility function is not a trivial matter. However, the standard-gamble method is described as an approach. With this description of measurement and the problems involved in measurement of probability and the basic theorems of probability, of the expected value criterion and its modification through the interjection of utility, we are now ready to propose a theory of decisions. This will be done in the next chapter.

QUESTIONS AND PROBLEMS

1. Give an example of the use of (a) the nominal scale, (b) the ordinal scale, (c) the interval scale, (d) the ratio scale.

2. An expression of preference implies a measurement. Which scale is being used?

3. Discuss the merits of assessing student performance by a short-answer versus an essay examination in terms of the possible validity and reliability of each.

4. Give an example of the likelihood of a future event, where that likelihood is based upon (a) an *a priori* probability, (b) a *relative frequency* probability.

5. Is it possible to discuss "hindsight probability"? For example, can one say that the probability is 0.8 that Caesar actually crossed the Rubicon on January 10, 49 B.C., sometime after breakfast but before the customary midmorning coffee break?

6. Might one consider the phrase "Guilty beyond a shadow of a doubt!" in probabilistic terms? If so, what subjective probability should be accepted to decide guilt?

7. List some events that are mutually exclusive and some events that are independent.

8. In selecting a card from a deck of 52 cards, what is the probability of obtaining a king? A king or a queen? A heart? The king of hearts?

9. In selecting two cards from a deck of 52 cards, what is the probability

of selecting two kings? A king and a queen? One heart? The king of hearts?

10. Four bridge hands are dealt to four people. Each person is given the opportunity of looking at his cards for only a short period of time and then must place them face down in a pile. The four piles are kept separate, but are moved about on the table so that each player can no longer tell which pile was his. One player remembers only that his hand contained three kings. He then specifies a pile as the hand that might have been his hand and is able to look at one card. If the card is a king, what is the probability that the hand was his original hand? If the card is not a king, what is the probability that the hand was his original hand?

11. The following news story reports an unlikely event:

MALONEY, WILSON PROVE ODDS OF 9,025 TO 1
BY PITCHING CONSECUTIVE NO-HITTERS

by Leonard Koppett

Our subject today, class, is no-hitters.

We will consider the following questions:

What are the odds against a no-hit game in the major leagues? And what are the odds against having two straight no-hitters in one ball park, involving the same teams?

Is it significant that three no-hit games were pitched during the first 25 days of this season? Especially after all the publicity given to lowering the mound and shrinking the strike zone to help the hitters?

When is a no-hitter not a no-hitter?

And, finally, what role does the no-hitter play in the complex cultural conflicts of our time?

Let us begin with the odds. There have been approximately 107,000 championship games played in six major leagues since 1876, when the National was recognized as the first major circuit. The record book lists 180 no-hit performances—that is, games in which a team was hitless for at least the first nine innings, even if there were hits later.

Divide 180 into 107,000 and you get 594.4. So the odds are 594.4 to 1 against a no-hitter—and 594 times 594 (352,836) to 1 against two consecutive no-hitters.

Right? No, not really.

DEFINING THE WORD "CONSECUTIVE"

You see, we have to make some definitions.

First: What we really want to know is how unlikely a pair of events Jim Maloney and Don Wilson produced at Crosley Field, Cincinnati, last week. Maloney held Houston hitless on Wednesday, and Wilson held Cincinnati hitless on Thursday. But these were not "consecutive" games in terms of all 107,000 ever played; they were only two of the 24 games played on two consecutive days.

We are really asking, therefore, for the odds against two no-hitters on consecutive days, since the games played on any one day cannot be put into any particular order. (They can, by noting the time each ended, but no one has bothered to do it and we don't intend to.)

Second: Even though this is baseball's Centennial Year and baseball history is being re-explored, comparisons lose meaning beyond certain limits. Rules about strikes, balls, pitching distance and other fundamentals differed radically from year to year during the 19th century. The present distance of 60 feet 6 inches was adopted only in 1894, and only in 1903 did both the American and National Leagues agree that fouls count as strikes up to two strikes.

So arbitrarily, we will take 1903 as our starting point for computing even roughly comparable figures.

Third: What we really care about is the chance of a pitcher—one man —pitching a no-hitter. There are two starting pitchers in every game, and two such opportunities. Let's weed out, then, all no-hitters that required more than one pitcher to complete.

Fourth: A no-hit game, strictly speaking, should be a complete game in which one team failed to get a hit. While it is nice to know that Maloney held the Mets hitless for 10 innings before Johnny Lewis led off the 11th with a home run back in 1965, one can't logically call it a no-hit game. Maloney's 10-inning 1–0 victory over Chicago a couple of months later, of course, was the purest of the pure among no-hitters.

Now we can proceed more rigorously.

From Opening Day, 1903, through last Friday night, the American and National Leagues played 84,152 games.

That meant 168,304 pitchers had a chance to pitch a no-hit game. Exactly 118 of them did. The odds: 1,427 to 1.

In the same period, there have been (approximately) 11,250 playing days—with no-hitters on 118 of them. That's a 95-to-1 shot that any given playing date will produce a no-hitter.

And two playing days in a row? That's 9,025 to 1.

But perhaps there is a trend. During the first 11,210 playing days, such consecutive no-hitters never occurred. In the last 40 playing days— last Sept. 17 at San Francisco, when Gaylord Perry and Ray Washburn did it, and last week's case—it has happened twice.

Does that mean that until last Sept. 17, the odds against it were infinite? And that since then, the odds against it are only 20 to 1?

You'll have to check with the mathematics department. For now, let's put those papers back into the files, sweep up the broken glass, move that pile of furniture away from the door and get out of the building before the police arrive.[3]

a. Which definition of probability is being employed in this discussion?

b. Are no-hitters mutually exclusive? Are they independent?

[3] *New York Times,* May 4, 1969.

    c. How would you answer the two questions posed in the next-to-last paragraph?

12. In a gambling situation, an individual is to roll a six-sided die. He is then to be paid the value, in dollars, of the side that appears face up. What would be a fair price to pay in order to participate?

13. Assume that you have $30 in cash and that you consider this ample for a date you have planned for the evening. Would you be willing to bet your $30 (double or nothing) on the flip of a fair coin?

14. A friend is considering the purchase of collision insurance for his automobile. He has three choices: "$50 deductible," "$100 deductible," or "$200 deductible." What advice would you give your friend?

15. A raffle ticket will generally have negative expected value, yet it may have positive utility. How is this possible?

a theory of
decisions

*But since the affairs of men
rest still uncertain,
Let's reason with the worst
that may befall.*

SHAKESPEARE
Julius Caesar

With the aid of the material presented in the last chapter, we will now develop a conceptualization of the decision process. Our approach will favor the decision situation that is readily quantified. For example, we are more likely to be able to help an investor develop a portfolio of stock than we are to assist that same individual in selecting a flavor of ice cream to bring home for dinner.

Our approach will require a structuring of the decision situation, which may not always be possible or practical. We will require an identification of future possible events or "states of nature"; we will have to delineate all the alternatives available to the decision maker; we will also have to ascertain the consequences associated with all combinations of alternatives and future possible states of nature. Faced with a matrix of information, the decision maker should then be able to select a desirable alternative. This approach will require that we be explicit. We will have to specify alternatives, future possible states of nature, and attending alternative state-of-nature consequences. This may not be easy. However, to the extent that explicitness is achieved, decisions can be reviewed by others, the decision process can be discussed and taught, and means of improving decisions may be sought. Many, if not most, decision situations will not lend themselves to evaluation in pure decision theoretic terms. Of those situations that do, the majority would probably call for the selection of an alternative that was obvious from the beginning. Nevertheless, the decision theory viewpoint permits an insight into the decision situation that is logical, consistent, and satisfying. It is this insight that is of value to the manager. And it is to gain this insight that the material in this chapter is presented.

We will begin by describing the payoff matrix—the vehicle for expressing the decision situation. Then we will review two categories of decisions: decision making under certainty (real or assumed) and decision making under risk. These have already been introduced in the preceding chapter, although not under these headings. A third category of decisions—decision making under uncertainty—will constitute a major portion of the chapter. In this section, we assume that there are two or more possible future states of nature and we either do not know or we are not willing to estimate the probabilities associated with the occurrence of each state. Nevertheless, and in the face of this uncertainty, a decision has to be made.

The last portion of the chapter is directed toward the requirement for decision making under conflict. Again, a matrix of the decision situation is constructed, but in this case an opponent is substituted for nature. The opponent is assumed to be a decision maker in conflict or in competition with us. His deliberate selection of an alternative replaces nature's more neutral inclination toward the occurrence of a state of nature in the matrix of the decision situation.

The Payoff Matrix

A formulation of the decision situation in decision theoretic terms rests upon a number of assumptions and requires the construction of a payoff matrix. Consider the following example of a decision situation: A man is about to leave for work. The weather is foggy and the forecast is somewhat indecisive. It might rain; then again, it might not. Should the man take his umbrella? A payoff matrix is quickly constructed.

STRATEGY	CONSEQUENCES	
	Rainy	*Clear*
Take umbrella	Dry	Foolish
Leave it home	Wet	Smug

First, consider the consequences associated with the two possible states of nature. If it rains, one of two physical consequences will result: the man will remain dry or he will get wet. If the weather should clear, one of two other consequences will result, both of which relate more to a state of mind: If the man takes his umbrella, he will feel foolish carrying it about all day when it is not needed. If he leaves it at home, he may derive some satisfaction from guessing the weather forecast correctly and from chiding his more cautious associates.

One might also view the same situation from the perspective of the two possible strategies. One strategy will result in either being dry or feeling foolish, the other in either being wet or feeling smug. Which alternative should be selected? Perhaps the decision will depend upon the relative value placed upon physical versus mental well-being. In either case, the construction of the matrix representing the decision situation rested upon some rather subtle assumptions.

1. There is a *decision maker* who is going to *select one strategy* or alternative from a known set of strategies.
2. The *consequence* will be able to be *specified* and will be dependent, in part, upon the strategy selected.
3. The consequence will also depend upon the occurrence of a state of nature. *One such state,* from a set of states, *will occur* and this will be independent of the strategy selected by the decision maker.

Returning again to our example, the decision maker is either going to take his umbrella or leave it at home. Within the restrictions of the matrix as constructed, there is no provision for buying an umbrella at lunch if it begins to rain during the day. The consequence associated with the two alternatives are assumed to have been stated completely and precisely. If the decision maker takes the umbrella and it rains, he will return home dry. There is no possibility of the umbrella being misplaced or stolen.

A number of contingencies like these could be incorporated into the matrix as additional alternatives and additional possible states of nature. However, further contingencies could also be expressed and it is likely that these can be thought of faster than the rows and columns can be constructed in the original matrix. In effect, we must stop somewhere short of reality in defining the alternatives available to the decision maker, the possible future states of nature, and the attending consequences.

The general format for expressing the payoff matrix is as follows:

| | States of Nature s_j | | |
Strategies a_i	P_1 s_1	P_2 s_2	P_m $\ldots .s_m$
a_1	$V(\Theta_{11})$	$V(\Theta_{12})$	$\ldots .V(\Theta_{1m})$
a_2	$V(\Theta_{21})$	$V(\Theta_{22})$	$\ldots .V(\Theta_{2m})$
.	.	.	.
.	.	.	.
.	.	.	.
a_n	$V(\Theta_{n1})$	$V(\Theta_{n2})$	$\ldots .V(\Theta_{nm})$

where a_i is the ith alternative out of a set of n alternatives.

s_j is the jth state of nature out of a set of m states of nature.

Θ_{ij} is the outcome associated with the selection of alternative i and the occurrence of the jth state of nature.

$V(\Theta_{ij})$ may be an expression of the value of this outcome in some common units, such as dollars or utility.

P_j may be the probability of the occurrence of state s_j.

In some instances, $V(\Theta_{ij})$ may be obtainable. In the preceding "umbrella illustration" this would not be easy. Also, in some cases the probabilities of the future states of nature may be available. In the preceding example, the weather forecast might have provided an estimate of each of the two states of nature.

We will now consider another illustration. Three investment opportunities are available, three economic conditions may occur, and the consequences are expressed in dollars of return.

| | | ECONOMIC CONDITIONS | | |
		s_1	s_2	s_3
	a_1	$\$5$	$\$3$	$\$0$
INVESTMENT OPPORTUNITY	a_2	4	2	0
	a_3	1	1	5

Which alternative would a decision maker select? The choice would be dependent on the method or principle of selecting a strategy. However, in no case should a_2 be selected; it is dominated by a_1. The *dominance principle* proposes that if for each state, the consequence of alternative a_1 is at least as desirable as the consequence of a_2, then a_2 should not be selected. In our example, regardless of the economic conditions, we can do at least as well, and in two instances better, by selecting opportunity a_1 over a_2.

The means of selecting an alternative from the payoff matrix will be dependent upon the category of decision required: decision making under certainty, under risk, under uncertainty, or under conflict. Each of these will now be discussed in turn.

Decision Making Under Certainty

There are a number of ways of classifying the decision process. We are relying upon the amount of information available to the decision maker concerning the likelihood of the occurrence of future states of nature. If there is only one relevant future occurrence, or if we wish to assume we have complete information and assume a given future state of nature, then we make a decision in the face of certainty.

We may consider either investing money in a business venture or purchasing a United States Government Bond. In the first case we are not likely to make a decision under certainty. We would have to establish a number of possible future states of nature, perhaps one of which would be the bankruptcy of the firm. In the second opportunity, however, we may place our faith in the fiscal soundness and in the future of the government and assume decision making under certainty. We are certain of the specified return on our investment.

If we assume only one future state of nature, the decision matrix includes only one column. The decision process then requires calculating the return or the payoff for each alternative and selecting the strategy that best satisfies the objective. The decision maker should be able to read down the one column and select the alternative with the largest payoff. It may be that simple; then again it may not. In a simple case, if we knew that it would rain tomorrow, the decision maker in our former example would be expected to take his umbrella. Consider a more complex case. Eight different assemblies are to be produced by eight contractors. Each contractor is to receive the contract for the production of one and only one assembly. The cost of each assembly will be determined by the bids submitted by the contractors. These bids are tabulated as follows:

| | | CONTRACTORS' BID PRICES | | | |
	A	B	C	....	H
1	$16	$19	$15	....	$22
2	37	35			:
ASSEMBLY :	:	:	:		:
:	:	:	:		:
8	29	25	24		25

The differences in the bid prices are due to differences in the work itself and preferences on the part of the contractors for certain assemblies. All of the above is a certainty; there is only one future state of nature. The decision maker would like to allocate assemblies to contractors so as to minimize the total cost. The first assembly can be assigned to one of eight contractors, the second to one of the remaining seven, the third to one of the remaining six, and so forth. The total number of possible assignments is 8! $(8 \times 7 \times 6 \times 5 \times 4 \times 3 \times 2 \times 1)$ or 40,320, one of which will be the minimum cost. This is also the number of alternatives available to the decision maker. A solution to the problem, that is, finding the minimum cost alternative, could be accomplished by enumeration—that is, listing all of the possible alternatives. However, one or more of the techniques of optimization would save the decision maker a great deal of time. In this case, the assignment model of linear programming could be used (see Chapter 9).

Decision Making under Risk

When there is more than one possible future state of nature *and* when a probability can be assigned to the likelihood of occurrence of each, then we face a decision under risk. We will handle this category of decision making under risk by using the expected value criterion (expected value in the long run) as the basis for choice.

We have already indicated that people may respond differently when confronted with the same decision situation, especially if there are a number of possible future states of nature. In the face of decision making under risk, some of the disparities in response may be attributed to differences in the subjective probabilities assigned to the possible future states of nature. Other disparities may be attributed to differences in the utility assigned to each of the consequences in the decision matrix. Within the framework of these differences, we will accept as the *expectation principle of choice* the assumption that the decision maker will always select that alternative that maximizes his expected utility. The expectation principle was actually illustrated in the latter part of the preceding chapter. In the example, investment in a bond permitted the larger expected value of utility ($EVU_b = 0.77$; $EVU_s = 0.70$) even though the expected dollar return favored the stock ($EV_s = \$1,065$; $EV_b = \$1,030$).

In some decision situations, the maximum expected profit (or minimum expected loss) may be used in the expectation principle of choice, thus eliminating the necessity for ascertaining utility. This substitution will prove satisfactory to the extent that one or the other of the following conditions is met:

1. The range between the most desirable and the least desirable consequence is not too great.
2. A large number of identical or similar decision situations are required.

In the first case, if the range between the largest and smallest possible profit (or largest loss) is not great, we can assume a linear relationship between dollars and utility.[1] In the second case, if our resources are not limited and many similar decisions have to be made, then the law of large numbers will come into play and our average actual return will converge upon our expected return.

Where the expectation principle of choice is not relevant because we do not wish to work with utility and where the substitution of dollars for utility is not feasible, one of two other principles may be considered. The *most probable future principle* suggests selecting the best alternative for that future state of nature most likely to occur. Consider the following

		OUTCOMES		
		1 *($P_1 = 0.1$)*	*2* *($P_2 = 0.3$)*	*3* *($P_3 = 0.6$)*
ALTERNATIVES	1	\$2	\$2	\$10
	2	5	6	8

example. The values in the matrix represent possible profits. Based upon the expected profits:

---

[1] Note that we only require an interval scale. We do not have to value a \$10 profit twice as much as a \$5 profit. Rather, the increase in a \$15 profit over a \$10 profit has to be valued as much as the increase in a \$10 profit over a \$5 profit.

$$EV_1 = (0.1)(\$2) + (0.3)(\$2) + 0.6(\$10)$$
$$= \$6.80$$
$$EV_2 = (0.1)(\$5) + (0.3)(\$6) + (0.6)(\$8)$$
$$= \$7.10$$

Alternative 2 would be selected. However, a decision maker might transfer this decision situation to decision making under certainty by assuming that the most likely future state would be the one to occur. Under this assumption, alternative 1 would be selected. The most probable future principle is not unreasonable if only one or a very few decisions are to be made and if none of the consequences could be catastrophic. In the previous illustration, outcome 3 *is* most likely to occur, and the selection of alternative 1 would most likely result in a profit of $10. The selection of alternative 1 might be unreasonable if one of the possible consequences, even if it were of low probability, resulted in a very serious loss. For example, should outcome 1—alternative 1 result in a loss of $20, this might be sufficient to abandon the principle.

The *aspiration level principle* might also be employed in decision making under risk. In a subsequent chapter we will introduce the concept of bounded rationality—the notion that the decision maker seeks a satisfactory rather than an optimum solution. This can also be utilized as a decision principle. If $6 were an acceptable profit in the most recent example, then the decision maker might select the second alternative over the first because the probabilities of realizing an acceptable profit are 0.6 and 0.9 respectively. If $5 were an acceptable profit, the selection of alternative 2 would insure this profit.

The aspiration level principle is often considered a substitute for the expectation principle, and a substitute that does not require the calculation of the exact utility of each outcome. Rather, utility is defined on a "yes" or "no" basis and an attempt is made to maximize the likelihood of achieving this "yes" utility. The aspiration level principle is especially appealing when the outcomes do not lend themselves to quantification, but can be classified as either "satisfactory" or "unsatisfactory."

Decision Making under Uncertainty

There are instances when it may be unreasonable or impossible to assign probabilities to the likelihood of future states of nature. A decision maker may object to assigning a probability to the possibility of a war or a depression, or the likelihood that a key executive will die or will leave the company. The decision maker may simply refuse to consider these possible future states of nature in probabilistic terms. In some instances no meaningful data or previous experiences may be available from which probabilities could be developed. Consider the plight of Columbus and his crew as they left the harbor of Palos in Spain in August, 1492, and sailed westward. Some rather dire consequences were predicted for their fate, including sailing off the edge of the world and/or being devoured by giant sea serpents. These may have been considered as possible future states of nature. However, it is unlikely that the maritime records of the day would have provided much insight into the probabilities associated with these states of nature.

When probabilities cannot be assigned to future possible states of nature, we are faced with the requirement for decision making under uncertainty. The decision situation may still be structured in a decision matrix and a number of principles may be considered in selecting an alternative.

Consider the example of a firm wishing to upgrade the quality of a product line. Four alternatives exist: a_1, a_2, a_3 and a_4, each respectively requiring increasing capital outlays, and each permitting increasing degrees of quality improvement. The marketing division anticipates that an upgraded product can be sold for a higher price, but this price and the possible profits will depend upon the reactions of the firm's competitors and public acceptance of the product. Three possible states of nature are projected. Under s_1, the public will be neutral, or perhaps mildly receptive to an improvement in product quality and other firms will not attempt to upgrade their product lines. Under s_2, the public will react very favorably to an improvement in product quality, other firms will improve their product quality, and all firms will be able to establish and secure some price increases. Under s_3, the public will also react favorably and, for one reason or another, other firms will not be able to or will not elect to upgrade their product lines.

The decision matrix, including the possible outcomes expressed in terms of expected annual profit for each alternative investment proposal, is as follows:

| | EXPECTED ANNUAL PROFIT (IN THOUSANDS OF DOLLARS) | | |
	s_1	s_2	s_3
a_1	$100	$150	$200
a_2	100	150	250
a_3	75	150	300
a_4	50	150	500

ALTERNATIVES

Which alternatives should be selected? Alternative a_2 dominates a_1 and for that reason, the latter can be eliminated from any further consideration. A selection from the remainder will depend upon what *principle of choice* one wishes to employ.

The *maximin principle* might be adopted by a pessimistic decision maker. This principle says to review the consequences associated with each alternative and then "pick the best of the worst" or "maximize the minimum." The minimum possible return of a_2, a_3, and a_4 are $100,000 $75,000, and $50,000 respectively. Then, we would select a_2 as the best of these and insure a return of at least $100,000.

The maximax principle is at least as optimistic as the maximin principle is conservative. This principle says "pick the best of the best." In reviewing our returns, the best are $250,000, $300,000, and $500,000, and we would select alternative a_4. If probabilities were to be ignored at the race track, this principle of choice would insure that we place our bests on the "long-shots." Conversely, if we employed the maximin principle at the race track and if "no bet" were included as one alternative, then our choice would always be "no bet."

A compromise between these two extremes—one that will permit us to place a decent bet at the race track—is the *Hurwicz principle.*[2] The decision maker selects an index α, from one to zero along a continuum of optimism-pessimism. With $\alpha = 1$, the same degree of optimism is selected as that expressed in the maximax principle, and with $\alpha = 0$, the same degree of pessimism is desired as that expressed in the maximin principle. In our upgraded product quality example, if the decision maker wished to be somewhere in the middle along this optimism-pessimism continuum, perhaps slightly favoring the conservative position, then he might specify $\alpha = 0.4$. The decision maker would then calculate H_i for each alternative, using the following formula:

$$H_i = \alpha[\max\ V(\Theta_{ij})] + (1-\alpha)[\min\ V(\Theta_{ij})]$$

where:

$H_i =$ the Hurwicz criterion for alternative a_1
$\alpha =$ the index of optimism-pessimism
$\max\ V(\Theta_{ij}) =$ the best outcome under a_i
$\min\ V(\Theta_{ij}) =$ the worst outcome under a_i

The alternative with the largest Hurwicz criterion would be selected.

[2] Named for Leonard Hurwicz, a contemporary econometrician, and proposed in Leonard Hurwicz, "Optimality Criteria for Decision Making under Ignorance," Cowles Commission Discussion Paper, *Statistics,* No. 370 (mimeographed, 1951); cited in Martin Kenneth Starr, *Product Design and Decision Theory* (Englewood Cliffs, N.J.: Prentice-Hall, Inc., 1963).

Alternative a_1 has been eliminated under the dominance principle. Calculations for a_2, a_3, and a_4 would be:

$$H_2 = 0.4(\$250,000) + 0.6(\$100,000) = \$160,000$$
$$H_3 = 0.4(\$300,000) + 0.6(\$\ 75,000) = \$165,000$$
$$H_4 = 0.4(\$500,000) + 0.6(\$\ 50,000) = \$230,000$$

Alternative a_4 would clearly be our choice.

The effect of α upon the value of the Hurwicz criterion and the selection of an alternative can be seen in the following diagram:

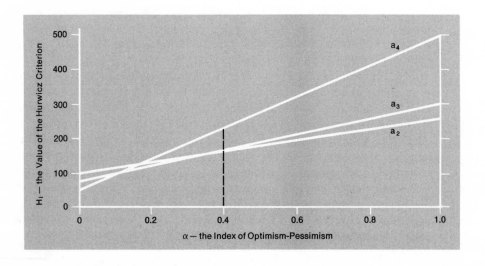

Note that alternative a_4 is superior to a_3 and a_2 over most of the range of α. It is only when the decision maker is quite pessimistic and α is less than 0.167 that a_2 becomes the preferred alternative.

A *minimum regret principle*, based upon the consideration of lost opportunity, permits the decision maker to "minimize the maximum possible regret." [3] What is the nature of regret in a decision? Savage

[3] L. J. Savage, "The Theory of Statistical Decision," *Journal of the American Statistical Association*, XLVI (March, 1951), 55–67.

suggests that after an alternative has been selected, and after a state of nature has occurred, the decision maker might contrast the resulting outcome with other possible outcomes had other alternatives been selected. The difference between the actual payoff and the best possible payoff, given the specified state of nature, can be considered a "regret."

Employment of the minimum regret principle requires the construction of a *regret matrix*. In this, each consequence is tabulated as a possible regret. For example, assuming state of nature s_1 occurs, if alternative a_2 is selected, there would be no regret. This is the maximum possible payoff, given s_1. Should a_3 be selected, we would have a regret of $100,000 - 75,000$ or $25,000. Similarly, the selection of a_4 would result in a regret of $50,000. The complete matrix would be:

		s_1	s_2	s_3
REGRET	a_2	$ 0	$0	$250,000
MATRIX	a_3	25,000	0	200,000
	a_4	50,000	0	0

Now, if we select alternative a_2, we could experience a regret as large as $250,000. The maximum possible regret of a_3 and a_4 are $200,000 and $50,000 respectively. The minimum of these three maximum regrets is $50,000. Therefore, we would select alternative a_4. The reasoning behind this choice and the use of the minimum regret principle is quite logical. A decision maker can reasonably be expected to wish to minimize his disappointment—to "hedge his bet." The selection of a_4 will provide this guarantee of a minimum of disappointment.

The last principle to be considered—the *Laplace principle*—rests on the rather dubious assumption that all future states of nature are equally likely to occur. Since we do not know or are not willing to assign specific probabilities (decision making under risk), we simply assume that one possible future state of nature is no more likely to occur than another. This argument, sometimes referred to as the *principle of insufficient reason*, is of questionable merit. However, it does permit the use of a maximum expectation criterion in selecting an alternative. We review each strategy as follows:

$$E(a_i) = \frac{1}{n}\Sigma V(\theta_{ij})$$

and then select the largest $E(a_i)$. In our example:

$$E(a_2) = \tfrac{1}{3}(\$100,000 + 150,000 + 250,000) = \$167,000$$
$$E(a_3) = \tfrac{1}{3}(\$\ 75,000 + 150,000 + 300,000) = \$175,000$$
$$E(a_4) = \tfrac{1}{3}(\$\ 50,000 + 150,000 + 500,000) = \$223,000$$

and alternative a_4 would be chosen.

If we use this expectation principle, we assign probabilities, at least by default. Then, it is more reasonable to at least undertake some educated guess in regard to the probabilities involved. Because the maritime records of Columbus' day were incomplete would be no reason to assume that "being eaten by giant sea serpents" was an *equally likely* fate to befall his crew. Perhaps some of the crew were actually convinced that this was a very real possibility. Even this judgment, however, would have rested upon some evidence in the form of rumors and stories concerning the fate of other crews. From these rumors, some guess could be made of the respective probabilities. To argue that two possible future states of nature are equally likely to occur because there are two states is to argue that when a man crosses the street he is equally likely to get hit by a car (or truck) as he is to make it safely across. The merit of the Laplace principle is that it is an expectation principle and it may lead one to consider a review of the probabilities involved and then to the case of decision making under risk.

The selection of an uncertainty principle will depend as much upon the decision maker as it will upon the decision situation. Our presentation has been descriptive—"it seems that some people think this way," rather than argumentative—"people should think this way." But how should a decision maker decide how to decide? He must decide whether to be bold or cautious or somewhere in between. He might prefer to minimize his possible disappointment. In each of these four cases, he will be working with only the largest and the smallest payoff associated with each alternative or with each state of nature. No consideration will be given to the number of intermediate payoff possibilities nor to their values, only to the best and the worst. With an expectation principle, one can at least consider all possible outcomes. However, the equal likelihood requirement of the Laplace principle is not intuitively sound. One must therefore decide for oneself how to decide. Each choice has something to be said for it and something against it.

Decision Making under Conflict

In evaluating alternatives, the decision maker sometimes faces an opponent rather than nature. We have already considered a number of decision situations that require a confrontation with nature. Another example would be one that might face a manufacturer of tire chains. The sale of tire chains could well be expected to depend upon the amount of snowfall. A winter with little snow might be considered one possible future state of nature. On a more optimistic note (if one sells tire chains), a winter that includes many heavy snowfalls might be considered another state of nature. Should probabilities be assigned to all the different possible states of nature, a decision under risk would be in order; otherwise a decision under uncertainty would be necessary. In each case, however, nature is assumed to be neutral. The occurrence of a state of nature is independent of the alternatives available to the decision maker and the associated consequences. When the decision maker faces an opponent, this is no longer true. The rational opponent is likely to give serious consideration to the alternatives available to *both* parties. If, in fact, a conflict situation exists, any opponent will likely make a deliberate attempt to frustrate the wishes of the other decision maker.

A conflict situation occurs in many settings. Chess and checkers are games of conflict. A football game requires decisions in a conflict situation. The study of decision making under conflict has produced the "theory of games." This complex and highly developed portion of decision theory is not limited to parlor games, nor is it restricted to athletic contests. The struggle between two political parties for seats in the state assembly might be described within a game theory structure. A contractor's bid on a section of highway in competition with other contractors is the selection of an alternative under conflict. The marketing policy of a major oil company in competition with other "majors" and with discount outlets might be described in game theoretic terms.

Game theory may be classified across at least two dimensions: the number of opponents involved and the extent of the conflict of interest. We shall restrict ourselves to the simplest case in each category: *the two-person, zero-sum game*. We will only consider competition between two opponents and the conflict will be complete in that what one opponent gains, the other loses.

Let us return to our example of a manufacturer of tire chains. In addition to the vagaries of the weather, our manager has expressed some concern about the possible actions of a competitor. Assume that the total market is shared between these two companies. Each company may elect one of a number of marketing strategies, relating to price, advertising effort, and so forth, in order to gain a larger share of the market. For illustrative purposes, assume that the competitor has three distinct alternatives and our manager has four alternatives. These are expressed in matrix form with the consequences representing increases (or decreases) in our share of the market. Because this is to be a zero-sum game, we will ignore the total market, or assume it to be a constant, and use percentage gains or losses in the matrix. Positive values will represent possible gains to the manager (and losses to the competitor).

Each party is assumed to have the following information before him and each party is assumed to want to maximize his winnings (or minimize his losses).

		COMPETITOR'S STRATEGIES		
		s_1	s_2	s_3
MANAGER'S STATEGIES	a_1	+5	0	−3
	a_2	+1	+1	+2
	a_3	−3	−2	+3
	a_4	0	−1	+2

Should the manager select a_1 and the competitor select s_1, the manager's company would gain 5 percent of the market. The competitor would lose this same 5 percent. Should the manager select a_3 and the competitor select s_1, or should the respective selections be s_3 and a_1, the competitor would gain 3 percent of the market. Other combinations fall between these payoffs. Which choice should be made by each party?

The first step in solving a game, and in selecting an alternative, is to test for dominance. Alternative a_4 is dominated by a_2 and can therefore be removed from consideration. The remaining three choices should then be tested for a *pure strategy*. The competitor will examine the three columns and designate his largest possible loss in each case. These are:

	STRATEGY		
	s_1	s_2	s_3
MAXIMUM LOSS	+5	+1	+3

The manager will examine his remaining alternatives and designate the smallest possible gain in each case (which may actually be a loss).

Alternatives	Minimum Gain
a_1	−3
a_2	+1
a_3	−3

If the smallest maximum loss is identical to the largest minimum gain (or in game theory terminology, if the largest of the row minima equals the smallest of the column maxima) then a *saddle point* is said to exist and each party would be well advised to select the alternative yielding that payoff. The competitor would designate s_2, the manager would select a_2, and the result would be a net gain to the manager's company of 1 percent.

When a saddle point exists and calls for the selection of a pure strategy by each party, any deviation from this policy will not result in a gain and may lead to a serious loss. For example, if the competitor in our illustration is perceptive and selects the pure strategy of s_2, and if our manager selects either a_1 or a_3, he will either receive no gain in the share of the market or we may even lose 2 percent, instead of gaining 1 percent.

If a game does not have a saddle point, then the optimal strategy for at least one player will not be pure. Rather, two or more alternatives will be selected in some fixed proportion (but not order). This will be a *mixed strategy*. The discovery of optimal mixed strategies can be complicated. However, the simple "two-by-two" case can be handled without too much difficulty. Consider the following example:

		RED	
		s_1	s_2
BLUE	a_1	4	1
	a_2	2	3

Note that the payoffs are all positive and represent losses to Red and gains to Blue. We first check for dominance, then for the existence of a saddle point. We find neither. A mixed strategy is in order.

We begin by calculating Blue's strategy.

a. For Blue a_1, find the absolute value of the difference between Red s_1 and s_2 (here we obtain $|4-1| = 3$) and call this result X.

b. Do the same for Blue a_2 ($|3-2| = 1$) and call this result Y.

c. The optimal mixed strategy for Blue is play a_1 with probability:

$$\frac{Y}{X + Y}$$

and play a_2 with probability:

$$\frac{X}{X + Y}$$

In our example, Blue would select a_1 with probability ¼, or in the proportion 1 to 3. Blue would select a_2 with probability of ¾. Following a similar procedure, Red would select s_1 and s_2, each with probability ½. The actual selection of an alternative should be done in some random fashion. For example, Blue might choose to flip two coins. If both coins land with a head up, $P(H \cdot H) = $ ¼, alternative a_1 would be selected. Otherwise a_2 would be chosen. This procedure would lead to the desired proportion of 1 to 3 without an established pattern of occurrences.

The strategies of Blue–1:3 and of Red–1:1 are *optimal* in that they maximize winnings or minimize losses in the long run. With a 2×2 game it is really only necessary that one of the two participants uses an optimal strategy. In this case, the *value of the game* is the expected payoff should one, or the other, or both players use this optimal strategy. We can calculate the value of the game by employing the optimal strategy of one party against either pure strategy of the other player. For example, employing Blue–1:3 against the pure strategy of Red s_1 yields:

Value to Blue
$$\tfrac{1}{4}(4) + \tfrac{3}{4}(2) = 2\tfrac{1}{2}$$

Alternatively, employing Blue–1:3 against s_2, yields:

Value to Blue
$$\tfrac{1}{4}(1) + \tfrac{3}{4}(3) = 2\tfrac{1}{2}$$

The use of Red's 1:1 against a_1 yields:

Loss to Red
$$\tfrac{1}{2}(4) + \tfrac{1}{2}(1) = 2\tfrac{1}{2}$$

And Red's 1:1 against a_2 yields:

Loss to Red
$$\tfrac{1}{2}(2) + \tfrac{1}{2}(3) = 2\tfrac{1}{2}$$

With games that are larger than 2×2, the failure to employ an optimal strategy places a party at a serious disadvantage. Larger games $(n \times n)$ may be solved with linear programming, but the special case of the $2 \times n$ game lends itself to graphic method of solution.

Game theory requires a highly structured decision situation. When one gets involved with more than two competitors, the computational procedures are quite formidable. Likewise, with non-zero-sum games, like those one might find in dealing with the utilities of two opponents, the approach is rather tedious. The value of game theory, like that of the other classes of decision processes, is in the insight it provides the manager. The concepts of pure and mixed strategies, of a saddle point, dominance, and the expected value of a game are concepts that may lead to an insight into a decision situation that may not otherwise be possible.

SUMMARY

Our conceptualization of the decision process requires a structuring of the decision situation that may not always be possible or practical. We require a matrix of alternatives, future possible states of nature, and attending alternative state of nature consequences. In decision making under certainty, these alternatives, states of nature, and resulting consequences are known. The decision process is straightforward and relatively simple unless the numbers of alternatives and/or states of nature are such that it is difficult to find the optimum choice or combination of choices. The techniques of optimization, such as linear programming, can then be used to advantage.

In decision making under risk, the outcomes or states of nature can be defined, but only in probabilistic terms. A number of principles of choice are available, including the expectation principle, which suggests selecting the alternative that maximizes expected utility; the most probable future principle, which suggests selecting the best alternative for that future state of nature most likely to occur; and the aspiration-level principle, which suggests accepting that alternative with the highest total probability of achieving some acceptable result. Decision making under uncertainty is similar to decision making under risk, except that the probabilities associated with the various states of nature are unavailable. Again, a number of principles of choice are relevant. The maximin principle, the maximax principle, the Hurwicz principle, the minimum regret principle, and the Laplace principle are available. The selection of one over the other would depend, among other things, on the relative pessimism or optimism of the decision maker.

The last category in this theory of decisions relates to decision making under conflict. In this instance, the decision maker is assumed to be confronting an opponent, rather than chance or nature. Alternatives are available both to the decision maker and to the opponent. The consequences associated with a decision are dependent on the alternatives selected by both parties. In the simplest case, the two-person, zero-sum game, there are only two parties in the conflict situation, and the losses of one party constitute the gains of the second. In this decision situation, the strategies developed may consist of the repeated selection of a single alternative—a pure strategy, or a mixed selection of two or more alternatives in some fixed proportion (but not order)—a mixed strategy. Decision making under conflict (game theory), even more than the other categories in this theory of decisions, is interesting in a conceptual sense but extremely difficult to structure in a real-world situation. Nevertheless, the concepts of pure and mixed strategies, of a saddle point, of dominance, and of the expected value of the game are concepts that are of value in assisting the decision maker in a general decision situation.

QUESTIONS AND PROBLEMS

1. A man is considering two land investment opportunities, each requiring an outlay of $100,000. A small tract of land on the edge of town may be purchased and later sold as a site for apartments. A larger tract, on the same side of town but further out in the country, can be purchased and subdivided for home building lots. Both opportunities should permit a return of the initial investment plus a reasonable profit within three years—a $60,000 profit on the small tract or a $50,000 profit on the large tract. Subjective odds of three to one are given on the above. There is a small chance that low-income housing developments may spread toward this section of town. Such an event would result in a $50,000 loss on the small tract, but would still permit a $40,000 profit on the large tract further out in the country. On a more optimistic note, higher-income developments may emerge on this side of town, leading to a possible $200,000 profit on the small tract or a $60,000 profit on the large tract. Although the odds are against these latter two eventualities, the odds are

two to one in favor of the low-income housing over the higher-income housing moving in the direction of these lots.

The decision must be made under risk. Assume that utilities are first developed as follows:

Profit	Utility
$200,000	1
60,000	0.85
50,000	0.80
40,000	0.75
−50,000	0

The payoff matrix of actual outcomes can be constructed:

ALTERNATIVE	OUTCOME		
	Low-Income Development $(P = \frac{2}{12})$	Normal Development $(P = \frac{9}{12})$	High-Income Development $(P = \frac{1}{12})$
Small tract, close in	−$50,000	+$60,000	+$200,000
Large tract, further out	+ 40,000	+ 50,000	+ 60,000

Which lot should be purchased:
  a. If we wish to maximize the expected profit?
  b. Under the expectation principle of choice?
  c. Under the most probable future principle of choice?
  d. Under the aspiration level of choice (if we wish a 10 percent return on investment, or at least $33,000 profit)?
2. Assume the following decision or payoff matrix with decision making under uncertainty:

	STATE OF NATURE			
STRATEGY	A	B	C	D
1	+$10	+$20	+$30	−$25
2	− 20	− 20	− 20	+ 40
3	0	0	0	+ 20

What strategy should be selected:
   a. Under maximax?
   b. Under maximin?
   c. Under Hurwicz α with $\alpha = 0.6$?
   d. Under minimum regret?
   e. Under the Laplace principle?
3. Assume the following football offensive plays and defensive alignments:

		DEFENSIVE TEAM	
		Stop Run	Stop Pass
OFFENSIVE TEAM	Run	+ 1 yard	+ 5 yards
	Pass	+ 20	− 10

What mixed strategy should be selected by each team and what will be the average gain? Discuss the weakness of using this approach in an actual football situation.

PLANNING:
ENDS AND MEANS

PART TWO

an introduction
to planning

5

*The best laid schemes o' mice and men
Gang aft a-gley.*

ROBERT BURNS
To A Mouse

The requirement for planning pervades any enterprise. Through all levels in the organizational hierarchy, objectives must be established and the means selected for accomplishing these goals. Planning requires answers to the following types of questions: What products will be added or services provided? What prices will be charged? What customers will be sought? Which parts will be purchased and which will be manufactured? What production methods will be employed? Will a dividend be declared? When and how much?

At a more restricted and specialized level in the firm, the following questions might also be asked: What inventory levels and reorder quantities should be used in the purchase of sheet metal? What replacement policy will be established for the presses in the stamping department? Which payback period should be used in accepting cost reduction proposals?

The answers to each of these questions (as well as the formulation of the questions themselves) require planning, or the anticipation now of what we may wish to do in the future. A plan is a forecast for accomplishment; it is a predetermined course of action; it is today's projection for tomorrow's activity.

Planning presupposes that someone will make a decision. The nature of the decision-making process has already been examined in the preceding chapters. Now we will focus on the planning function itself. In this introductory chapter we will first discuss the different forms that plans may take. We will examine the effects of both the time variable and the repetitiveness variable upon planning. We will also discuss the planning process in terms of an indication of effectiveness, that is, the measure of success of activity. Finally, we will introduce the concept of modeling and experimentation as aids to the planning process.

In subsequent chapters of this section we will discuss the objectives of the firm and describe the basic cost components relative to the level of the firm's operations. We will consider the dimensions of the investment decision in planning and conclude with a brief formulation of some quantitative decision models that may facilitate the planning process.

The Elements of Planning

Planning is the most basic of management functions and requires the designation of goals and the selection of alternatives throughout all levels and divisions of the organization. The structuring of the organization itself, the activation of the human resource within the framework of this structure, and the subsequent control process all require planning. When we plan, we decide in advance what must be done. The alternative to planning could only be something akin to random behavior with frequent shifts in direction and inconsistent activity. A lack of planning on the part of management would be seen in the requirement for excessive attention to immediate problems—putting out fires—and erratic and perhaps inconclusive decisions. Most organizations would be hard-pressed to survive under these conditions.

TYPES OF PLANS

Plans may be firm or flexible; they deal with goals and the means of achieving them. It is possible to designate one type of plan (or one form of planning) as that concerned with organizational direction or *objectives*. For example, the objective of a company may be to manufacture and sell garden implements at a profit. Within a department, an objective may be to purchase quality materials and parts at a reasonable price and in economic order quantities and by delivery dates that are compatible with inventory capabilities and manufacturing requirements. These objectives are plans for the future that will serve to provide direction for subsequent activity.

To accomplish the objectives, *policies, rules, procedures,* and *budgets* may be used. In a sense, these are all constraints or guides that border the path leading to the objective. They assist in selecting those alternatives that permit the attainment of the goal in as economical a fashion as possible.

Policies are likely to take the form of general statements or understandings that serve to channel activity toward the objective. A policy is a plan in that it establishes, in advance, some ground rules to assist in making decisions. A firm may have a policy of promoting from within. This would suggest that should a vacancy occur, the first review of prospects would be of existing employees to see if any of them can meet the job requirements. The relative rigidity of a policy can vary from one situation to another. Policy should be viewed as a means of assisting the decision maker, not as a restriction that ties his hands. At the same time, deviations from policy should come to be the exception and should require some extraordinary circumstances.

A *rule* is more rigid, and usually more specific, than a policy. "Injuries and/or accidents are to be reported immediately to the foreman!" does not leave much room for discretion. There may be some question as to what constitutes an injury or an accident, for example, a torn fingernail, but if this is defined or understood, the procedure is, or should be, clear-cut. A rule is designed to define in advance what alternative must be selected or what decision must be made. Rules should be decisive and will reflect a managerial intent to direct the decision-making processes of the individuals under the appropriate jurisdiction. For example, smoking in one area of the plant may constitute a fire hazard. A "no smoking" rule reflects the intent of the manager to restrict smoking in that area. This rule should govern the actions of all individuals who work in or pass through the area and in regard to their choice of smoking or not smoking. In effect, the rule dictates the way an activity is to be (or is not to be) done.

A *procedure* is a rule that usually incorporates a temporal element or requires sequential activity. A procedure might be the means of implementing a policy. For example, the shipping department may attempt to effect the policy of shipping all orders within 48 hours. The means of accomplishing this goal may consist of a sequence of steps that must be followed after the receipt of an order and that culminate in the final shipment of the items requested. These steps constitute a procedure. Another procedure might consist of the means of reporting and then reworking or scrapping defective production units.

A *budget* is a projection (and a plan) that defines the anticipated cost of attaining an objective. Budgets are usually established in dollars,

Figure 5-1

Some types of plans.

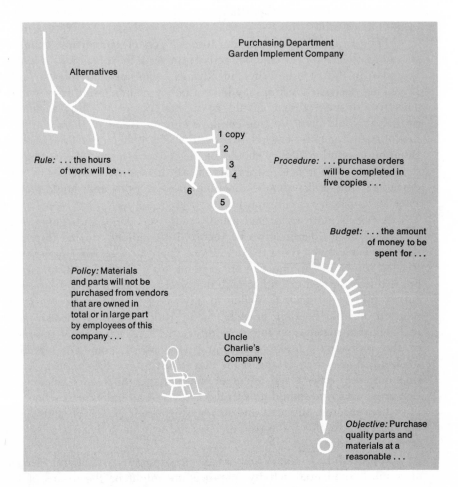

Purchasing Department
Garden Implement Company

Alternatives

1 copy
2
3
4
5
6

Rule: ... the hours of work will be ...

Procedure: ... purchase orders will be completed in five copies ...

Budget: ... the amount of money to be spent for ...

Policy: Materials and parts will not be purchased from vendors that are owned in total or in large part by employees of this company ...

Uncle Charlie's Company

Objective: Purchase quality parts and materials at a reasonable ...

but they might also be expressed in time, man-hours, or any other "cost" of achieving some goal. The budget may come to be used as a control device. However, the budget begins as a forecast and therefore requires planning.

THE RIGIDITY OF PLANS

Objectives—like policies, rules, procedures, and budgets—are likely to be established for all the divisions or departments of the enterprise.

These plans may be firm and inflexible or they may be easily and often changed. Plans are important to the organization in that they serve to establish a commitment to the economical attainment of an objective. But can they ever be changed? Can we violate company policy? How sacred is a budget? Do we ever exceed one? Do we ever permit rules to be broken or procedures to be circumvented? Do we ever change our objectives? The answer to each of these questions is "Yes, . . . sometimes," but under what circumstances and how often are difficult to express in unequivocal terms.

The relative *flexibility* of planning should involve a trade-off. Plans are always made with incomplete information and in the face of an uncertain future. As a result, plans should not be "set in concrete." Errors may have been made in the forecasting process and subsequent unexpected events may occur. At the same time, plans that are *too* flexible do not provide guidance and are not really plans at all; they are only points of departure. In regard to flexibility in planning, Koontz and O'Donnell have proposed "The Fexibility Principle" and "The Principle of Navigational Change."[1] In the first case, it is suggested that plans should be able to be changed and that this flexibility should be a major consideration in all planning. The second principle recommends that the planning process itself include a review process to ascertain if changes are needed. Periodically, the following question should be asked: "Are we going the right way and is this the best way of getting there?" Asking and answering this question will provide flexibility in the planning process.

BARRIERS TO PLANNING

All executives will agree that planning is a necessary management function. At the same time, adequate planning is not always undertaken. The failure to plan—to think ahead—can usually be attributed to some identifiable barriers. The planning process requires detailed, careful, and often analytical thought. This may not come easy for some managers. It requires dealing with intangibles, in the face of uncertainties. Finally, planning lends itself to a postponement until tomorrow, especially when confronted by the immediacy of an operational problem requiring a specific decision today.

The day-by-day job of the manager involves time pressures of three kinds, each of which is a barrier to the development and use of plans.[2]

[1] Harold Koontz and Cyril O'Donnell, *Principles of Management* (4th ed.) (New York: McGraw-Hill, 1968) pp. 104–6.

[2] James S. Hekimian and Henry Mintzberg, "The Planning Dilemma," *Management Review,* May, 1968, pp. 4–17.

There is usually a lack of time to get the immediate job done. The day is simply not long enough for the manager to be relaxed and reflective and to engage in necessary planning. In addition, the manager must be able to react to unanticipated and immediate problems. An accident in his department or the threat of a wildcat strike will be more pressing than the review of a plan related to next year's budget. Finally, the manager must be involved in making some decisions that cannot be planned in advance. He may have to seize an opportunity and make a decision that cannot be scheduled. For example, an employee may resign unexpectedly, and this may provide an opportunity to make some changes in the organizational structure.

The executive should place a high priority on the planning function, even when confronted with the barriers to planning already indicated. The following two such reactions to this dilemma have been reported:

> When Donald C. Burnham took over as President of Westinghouse Electric a few years ago, one of the first major changes he undertook was to reduce the number of subordinates reporting to vice presidents so that the latter would have more time for setting goals and formulating programs. And when more recently, another top executive, Robert S. Ingersoll, began revising the organization policies of Borg-Warner Corporation, one of his aims in realigning the divisions was to free himself and other top men in the company from supervisory duties so they could devote more of their time to planning and policy matters.[3]

The Time Span and Repetitiveness Variables

The length of the planning period—the time interval between the point at which plans are formulated and specified and when they are actually implemented and then carried through to conclusion—will have to vary a great deal from one situation to another. The time interval may involve a trade-off between the advantages to be gained from seeing into the future, including the relative uncertainty involved, and the costs (in time and efforts) involved in securing this perspective. The desired length will also vary with the planning area itself. To market a new product or restructure organizational responsibility will involve a more distant planning horizon than that involved in scheduling production or procuring of materials. Koontz and O'Donnell have proposed "The Commitment Principle" as an approach to establishing the time range for company

[3] David W. Ewing, "Corporate Planning at a Crossroads," *Harvard Business Review,* July–August, 1967, pp. 77–86.

planning. The principle states "that planning should encompass the period of time necessary to foresee [through a series of actions] the fulfillment of commitments involved in a decision." [4] In effect, the planning period should be long enough to project a recovery of the costs sunk into a course of action, recognizing that costs are not limited to dollars. If a plan is made to purchase a new machine tool, the analysis may be carried through to the expected life of that tool. If a new organizational structure is proposed, however, the planning period is not so easy to define.

Some of the problems involved in planning research activity relate to this difficulty of assessing the necessary commitment. In describing some experiences at Honeywell, McGlauchlin [5] points out that production information is usually available within a day or a week, financial feedback may be available each month, and sales data can usually be collected each quarter. However, the collection of historical data relevant to research activity might require 10 to 15 years. Obviously, research planning that requires historical data for projection purposes will pose some special problems. Two other difficulties unique to the planning of a research effort are the singularity of the effort itself—successful research activity, unlike successful production, does not have to be duplicated—and the uncertainties of schedules. The efforts of another concern may render work obsolete; research personnel usually resent having to "invent according to some plan."

The repetitiveness of plan usage—the extent to which a plan is developed and employed, and then used a second time, and then a third —will also vary from one situation to another. At one end of the continuum is the single-use plan, usually a program that includes a schedule and some special methods and is designed for a unique situation or set of circumstances. At the other end of the scale is the standing plan designed to be used again and again in routine and repetitive situations.

A standing plan can be a policy, a rule, a procedure, or even a budget. It may have simply evolved, like common law, and owe its existence and legitimacy to nothing more substantial than established practice and custom. An office procedure may have been initiated in the distant past by a secretary who has long since left the employment of the company. Although the procedure may have been modified and improved over time, it may never have been systematically reviewed in contrast to other possible alternatives. Nevertheless, the procedure may work reasonably well. It is more likely however, that a thoughtful and systematic analysis will lead to a well-established policy or procedure.

[4] Koontz and O'Donnell, *Principles of Management*, pp. 100.
[5] Lawrence D. McGlauchlin, "Long-range Technical Planning," *Harvard Business Review*, July–August, 1968, pp. 54–64.

One virtue of the standing plan is that it provides the manager with *relief from decision making.* Each repetitive situation is handled in accordance with a preprogrammed decision rule. Thus, for example, a request from an employee for a leave of absence to return to school may be routinely granted for a period of up to two years in accordance with company policy. The advantages and disadvantages of granting such a request were apparently weighed some time in the past, the decision was made, the policy was established, and this most recent request does not require the same careful review.

A second advantage of the standing plan is that it leads to *consistency* in handling like decision situations. An employee from one department receives the same response as an employee from another department to a similar request for an educational leave. Also, the response is identical to that which was given last year to a third employee. In like fashion, identical budget request formats make it easier to compare the funding required in different departments. Consistency in format will likely lead to an equitable evaluation.

The third advantage of the standing plan is in the possibility of *delegating* the decision problem downward in the organization. A standing plan that establishes inventory levels at two month's production and that sets up a procedure for calculating economic order quantities makes it possible for a clerk to decide how many of a part to order and when. Also, a leave of absence may be granted by a department head rather than by someone at a much higher level in the enterprise.

In spite of these advantages, some problems are inherent in the establishment of standing plans. The plan may become a crutch and remove the incentive to a careful evaluation of each decision situation. The standing plan requires an inflexible response when an imaginative reaction may be in order. Also, times and conditions change. The information contained in an accounting report may no longer be relevant. Nevertheless, the report continues to be developed and circulated. The inertial effect of the standing plan makes it advantageous to periodically review any existing procedure or policy. Also, there are times when exceptions must be made.

The single-use plan, in contrast to the standing plan, can be described in terms of the need for a singular effort. The acquisition of a new product line, a facilities expansion project, opening a new sales territory, or changing an organizational structure are not routine actions. Some aspects of these activities, at least in regard to timing, will require a unique approach. Such a plan is often referred to as a *program.* The development of a program first requires a specification of the *steps* that must be accomplished. In particular, attention should be given to activities that have to be undertaken in sequence. The start-up leading to the operation of a new plant may require that capital be raised, the plant shell constructed, production machinery ordered and installed, workers hired and trained, raw materials ordered, production begun, a sales effort organized, and sales activity conducted. Some of these steps must be completed in sequence. Production machinery may be ordered while the plant shell is being constructed. However, the shell will have to be completed before the machinery is installed. On the other hand, the organization of the sales effort may begin at any time.

Because the total program will include a temporal element—a beginning and an end that spread across time—each step should include a *time span*. In particular, close attention should be given to those steps that must be completed in sequence.

Finally, the program should specify the resources that will be needed to complete each step. Who or how many people will be needed? What will it cost to complete this step? What supplies and other materials will be required?

With the designation of the steps (sometimes best expressed in schematic form), the time element, and the resources required, the program is essentially complete. All that is necessary to accomplish the goal is now carefully spelled out in advance. Perhaps the only remaining part of the plan to be developed includes some contingency activities. Once implementation begins and if it becomes evident that changes are needed, for example, another step is required or more time is needed to complete a step, then a contingent action—spelled out in advance—may be used. In effect, plans may even include a response to the unexpected.

The Effectiveness Measure

Decisions are made toward some goal and within a purposeful framework. Implicit in the planning situation is the desire to *optimize* and to achieve the goal at least cost or select the alternative that yields the most of that which we are after. And yet in many cases it is not really necessary that we select, much less even consider, the alternative yielding the optimum payoff. We seek only a satisfactory solution.

Assume for the moment that it is possible to develop an effectiveness function in a decision situation. We are assuming that the decision situation lends itself to quantification. The effectiveness function is a mathematical statement formally linking a measure of effectiveness with two classes of variables: those that the decision maker can readily manipulate and those not under his immediate control. This relationship is usually expressed in the general case as

$$E = f(x_i, y_j)$$

Where E is the outcome, or measure of effectiveness; x_i are those variables under the control of the decision maker; and y_j are the variables not under his control.[6]

For example, consider the classical economic order quantity model. The manager would like to establish an inventory of some raw material, component part, or finished product. This inventory is maintained in order to satisfy a need. It can be seen as a reservoir between the source of supply and the demand for that item. A retail store may be described as an inventory system; so may a gasoline station. In a manufacturing operation, it may be necessary to purchase and then store a quantity of sheet metal as an input to the production process. A bank should have an amount of money on hand to cash checks on payday. In each case, it is usually necessary to order and receive into the reservoir in bulk quantities. Items are then usually drawn from the inventory on a per unit basis. How large an inventory is necessary? This can be a significant question. An inventory that is too large requires excessive storage facilities and represents an investment that might be better spent elsewhere. At the same time, with a small inventory we may get caught short and run out. A lost customer or a halted production line can be expensive. A balance is needed. We do not wish to run out or, at least, we do not wish to run out very often. At the same time, excessive inventory is expensive and a waste. The manager wishes to minimize the costs involved in the inventory system; this is the measure of effectiveness. The variables under his control are the order quantity and the order level. In effect, the two basic inventory decisions are:

1. How many to order at one time?
2. When to order this quantity?

The answer to the first question is in the determination of the *economic order quantity*.

Two classes of costs are relevant to the inventory system: (a) the

[6] A more complete discussion of this relationship may be found in C. W. Churchman, R. L. Ackoff, and E. L. Arnoff, *Introduction to Operations Research* (New York: John Wiley and Sons, Inc., 1957).

ordering costs, and (b) the carrying costs. The ordering costs are the costs of bringing a quantity of items into the inventory bank. They are incurred each time an order is placed and can usually be expressed as a dollar cost per order. Such costs would include those involved in placing the order, following it up if necessary, receiving the shipment of goods and placing them physically in inventory, and finally, paying the supplier. Salaries would be a major ordering cost and would be largely independent of the relative size of the order.

Carrying costs are dependent on order quantity. The value of the money tied up in inventory, perhaps expressed as an interest charge, can be a major carrying cost. Storage facilities, storage operations, and product obsolescence costs can be significant and are dependent on the inventory level and hence on the order quantity. In addition, taxes and insurance charges are costs that depend on the inventory level. All of the preceding costs, that is, order costs and carrying costs, are variables not under the immediate control of the decision maker. He can readily specify only the order quantity and reorder level. He will attempt to do so in such a fashion as to minimize the total cost for a given demand. He will attempt to develop an effectiveness function of the inventory system. This will yield the economic order quantity.

Consider the following simplified example. We will likely use some 10,000 pieces of sheet metal this coming year. We assume that the demand is known and a constant. We assume the same for the lead time (the elapsed time between placing the order and the receipt of the units for inventory). Neither of these assumptions is likely to be valid in a real-world case, but they permit the development of the basic "saw-tooth" inventory model. This can be seen in Figure 5-2. We let Q represent the order quantity. The number of units in inventory is Q immediately after receipt of an order. These units are then withdrawn from inventory at a constant rate until such time as the inventory is depleted. Fortunately, at that instant, another order of Q units arrives. The order had been placed the exact "lead time" prior to the date projected for inventory depletion. If the demand or the lead time has to be expressed in probabilistic terms, a safety stock would be included as a form of insurance. However, this will not be included in our example. Returning to our demand of 10,000 pieces of sheet metal per year—another variable in the effectiveness function not under the control of the decision maker—we need to determine how many orders to place to satisfy that demand. At the one extreme, we could place a single order for 10,000 pieces, that is, one tooth per year. At the other extreme, we could place 10,000 orders of one sheet each, a rather small-toothed saw. The economic order quantity, or that order

Figure 5-2

The "saw-tooth" inventory model.

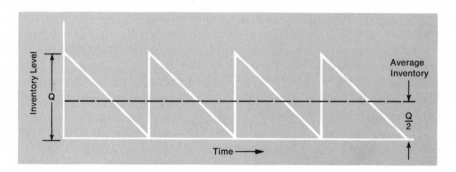

quantity that will minimize total cost, will likely fall between these two extremes. To determine the economic order quantity we need to ascertain (or estimate) the ordering and carrying costs. Assume that the ordering costs are $80 per order. This gives an annual ordering cost of ($80 $\times$ 10,000) $\div Q$. The carrying costs are likely to be calculated on the basis of $Q/2$, the average inventory level. If we assume that our carrying costs are 10 percent of the average inventory value and the unit purchase price is $4.00 per sheet, then the annual carrying costs would be ($4.00)(0.10) ($Q/2$), or $0.20Q$. The total annual cost, TC, would be:

$$TC = \frac{\$800{,}000}{Q} + \$0.20Q$$

This total cost function can be seen in Figure 5-3. The graphic solution yields an economic order quantity of 2,000 units and an attending inventory cost of $800 per year. We could also have effected a tabular and trial-and-error solution, that is, we could have calculated the total cost at different values of Q and searched for the minimum cost. Alternatively, we could have generated and used the economic order quantity formula.[7]

[7] In the general case:

$$TC = \frac{RS}{Q} + Q\frac{CI}{2}$$

where $R =$ the annual requirement
$S =$ the order cost
$C =$ the unit price, and
$I =$ carrying cost expressed as a per cent of average inventory.

We may obtain the economic order quantity, EOQ, by obtaining the first derivative of the TC equation with respect to Q, setting this equal to zero, and solving for Q as follows:

Figure 5-3

The inventory cost system.

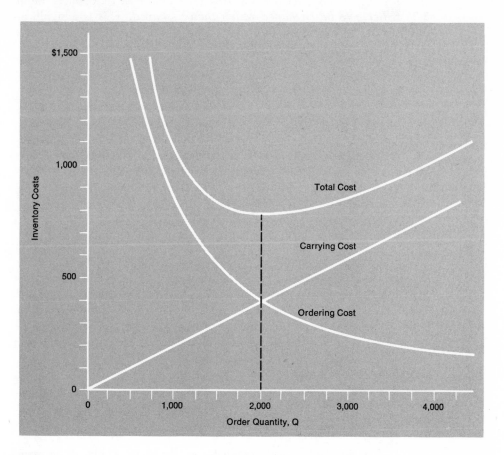

$$\frac{dTC}{dQ} = -\frac{RS}{Q^2} + \frac{CI}{2} = 0$$

$$EOQ = Q = \sqrt{\frac{2RS}{CI}}$$

and in our example:

$$EOQ = \sqrt{\frac{(2)(10,000)($80)}{($4.00)(0.10)}}$$

$$EOQ = 2,000 \text{ units, and}$$

$$TC = \frac{10,000($80)}{2000} + \frac{2000($4.00)(0.10)}{2} = $800$$

101

In any case, *the effectiveness function* (the total cost function in Figure 5-3) *is likely to be U-shaped rather than V-shaped.* This is a significant observation. In our example, had we designated $Q = 2,400$, an error of $+ 20$ percent from the EOQ, then:

$$TC = \frac{\$800,000}{2400} + \$0.20(2,400)$$

$$TC = \$813$$

an increase of only 1.6 percent over the minimum total cost. Had we been 20 percent below the EOQ, that is, $Q = 1,600$, then:

$$TC = \frac{\$800,000}{1,600} + \$0.20(1600)$$

$$TC = \$820$$

an increase of 2.5 percent. In effect, we need only "get in the ball park" and into the lower flat region of our U-shaped effectiveness function to have made a good decision. To be off a little from the optimum will not cause us much concern. As a matter of fact, our data, including our cost estimates, may make our search for *the* optimum only an academic exercise. Although we do wish to find a satisfactory solution, we do not need to find the best solution.

Consider another illustration. A company needs to find a replacement for the general manager who has left to become the president of another firm.

> The Assistant to the President was placed in charge of the search program. His instructions were to find the most highly qualified man in the industry, since this is a critical position in the organization. An executive search consultant was engaged to secure candidates from outside the firm. An intensive search was also begun in each of the divisions within the firm. Eventually the search narrowed down to seven candidates: five from outside the firm and two from within. These were each intensively interviewed by the President and given the opportunity of meeting some members of the Board of Directors. Eventually one of the candidates from another firm was selected.

How close might this choice be to an optimum solution? Almost certainly there were other people who might have had the necessary qualifications, but they were not considered. Of the number who were considered, did all those who were possibly qualified make it to the final evaluation and review process? Of the final seven, two or three might have been good choices. Was the best man selected? The answer to each of these questions is likely to be in the negative. It is probable that the "best" person in the country wasn't even contacted. Even though the stated objective was to secure the most highly qualified man for the position, the final decision would have been to select a satisfactory candidate.

Rationality in decision making requires consistency and implies the continued selection of those alternatives that maximize the desired result.[8] But there are limits to rationality. We may not be aware of all the alternatives, nor be able to afford the time to seek them out. In addition, we may not know the consequences of each choice, nor be able to readily secure all the information needed to evaluate each alternative. As a result, the decision maker (and the organization) usually becomes "concerned with the discovery and selection of satisfactory alternatives; only in exceptional cases is [he] concerned with discovery and selection of optimal alternatives."[9] Simon has expanded this concept into the *principle of bounded rationality*. According to this principle, the decision maker seeks a range of outcomes that would be good enough. Then he selects the one alternative that appears to be the best choice. The search for the best candidate actually becomes a search for some qualified candidates from which one of the most qualified will be selected. This is all possible because most effectiveness functions are rather flat near the optimum. The superiority of the best choice over the second or third best choice is usually rather slight.

Models and Simulation

A model is an abstraction of the real world. It is a simplified version of the complex state or event that we refer to as reality. The process of manipulating a model and of imitating a state or an event, is the process of simulation.

Managers were developing models and simulating reality long before we were "advanced" enough to describe this process in such sophisticated terms. The organization chart, the accountant's ledgers, and the Gantt chart are all models. At the same time, a great deal of progress has been

---

[8] I. J. Good, "How Rational Should a Manager Be?," *Management Science*, VIII, no. 4 (July, 1962), pp. 383–93.

[9] James G. March and Herbert A. Simon, *Organizations* (New York: John Wiley and Sons, Inc., 1958), pp. 140–41.

made in recent years in the development of models—particularly mathematical and statistical models—and in simulating more and more aspects of the business enterprise.

The manager, functioning in a planning capacity, would like to know as much as possible about the operations under his control. He may be able to gain an understanding of some of the relationships through the process of experimentation. What is the relationship between the level of production and the requirements for equipment repair and maintenance? What factors are contributing to the high turnover of sales personnel? What market penetration will we achieve with our new product line? Just as the scientist employing the scientific method will wish to experiment to better understand nature, so the businessman might wish to experiment to better understand the constituent parts of his world. However, direct experimentation implies the manipulation of reality and this can be expensive and time-consuming. It can also be disruptive of the system itself. The model permits indirect experimental inquiry that yields information in less time and at less expense. For example, a mathematical model that relates varying production levels to corresponding maintenance requirements permits the manager to select an optimum production-maintenance schedule without having to resort to an expensive and time-consuming trial-and-error approach. The use of simulation as an aid to decision making may be expected to continue to gain in significance in the business world as models are developed that capture essential elements of the business activity.

A CLASSIFICATION OF MODELS

When used as a noun, the word "model" implies a *representation*. A youngster may construct an airplane model or, in effect, a scale replica of the real thing. "Model" may also be used as a verb. In this case, we could have substituted the verb *to demonstrate*. A woman may model or demonstrate a new dress. Sometimes "model" is used as an adjective. A model child or a model student is an *ideal* child or student. The model that is constructed for the purpose of simulation retains each of these meanings. Such a model is a representation, it is used to explain or demonstrate relationships, and it is an idealized replica in that it only attempts to capture the salient features of reality.

Models may be categorized across a number of different dimensions. For our purposes, we will distinguish between physical, schematic, and mathematical-statistical models.

Physical models are probably most familiar to us. We are used to seeing dolls, toy trains, and globes. These are physical replicas of reality, although they are not usually manipulated in an experimental sense. However, a model aircraft may be placed in a wind tunnel and tested for different wing configurations. A model of a ship's hull may be tested in a water basin. A pilot plant may be built to test a new process for the purpose of locating operational difficulties. Two- or three-dimensional templates may be constructed and manipulated to achieve a good plant layout. In each of these latter examples, the physical model is constructed for the purpose of indirect experimentation.

Schematic models are achieved by reducing a state or an event to a chart or a diagram. A break-even chart, an organization chart, a Gantt chart or a PERT network, a man-machine chart, and a flow-process chart are all schematic models. In a similar view, a football play that has been diagrammed on the blackboard is a schematic model. It shows who is to block whom, and who carries or throws the football where or to whom. In effect, the execution of football play over a time domain is reduced to a diagram.

The schematic model may or may not look like the real-world situation it represents. Reality is described through a coding process inherent in the model and it is the idealized aspect of the model that permits an insight into the state or event so captured.

Mathematical-statistical models represent the ultimate in abstractions of reality. Although the symbols may be more difficult to comprehend, the model permits a great deal of precision. Because of the logic incorporated in this procedure, the model lends itself to easy manipulation. One can take the derivative of a mathematical function to ascertain a maximum or minimum. The mathematical model used in decision making relates two classes of variables: those under the control of the decision maker and those not under his control. The following model:

$$Q = \left(\frac{2C_pD}{C_h} + \frac{2C_pD}{C_s} \right)^{\frac{1}{2}}$$

describes the functional relationship in a deterministic inventory system between the minimum cost procurement quantity (Q) and the demand (D), the procurement cost (C_p), the holding cost (C_h), and the shortage cost (C_s).

Because many of the significant variables within an organization are not able to be described in direct causal relationships, probabilistic elements may be necessary in the model. Thus, for example, our designated unit price and resulting sales may have to be related in a probabilistic fashion. The number of stand-by production machines may have to be designated within some confidence level. The probabilistic element in the model permits the decision manager to capture reality and to make rational decisions even when faced with elements of uncertainty.

THE SIMULATION PROCESS

The scientific method is a method of controlled experimentation to discover relationships. In direct experimentation, the object, state, or event is subject to manipulation and the results are observed. For example, the housewife may rearrange the furniture in her living room a number of times until she achieves the layout she prefers. Although this activity may not be dignified by being called "scientific," it is direct experimentation. Simulation or indirect experimentation employs a model of reality and the model is manipulated. The problem of the housewife is approached in an industrial setting by constructing a model layout with templates, and these templates are moved about until a good layout is determined. Then the machinery is moved into position. In like fashion, the schematic and mathematical models may be manipulated until the relationships between significant variables can be established.

Models are used to describe, predict, or control, although only the latter two functions are likely to be manipulated in an experimental sense. An accountant's ledger may describe the cash flow within an organization, but it is not likely to be manipulated in itself. A forecasting model may be manipulated to establish that price-sales relationship that maximizes net profit. A control chart may be installed to monitor the proportion of defective units that are being produced, and this control model may also be manipulated.

The sequence of steps leading to the use of a model and the simulation process require first that the problem be defined, then that the model be formulated and manipulated, and finally, that the decision be made. The model will be only a partial representation of reality, but it will take the decision maker part of the way with an initial basis for comparison. Intuition and judgment may then be applied in the final selection by the decision maker.

SUMMARY

Planning attempts to answer the question, "Well, where do we go from here, what do we do now?" The requirement for planning—for answering this question—exists at every level in the organizational hierarchy. A plan requires the thinking through of an action well in advance of when it must be done. Plans are concerned with objectives as well as with the policies, rules, procedures, and/or budgets required to accomplish these objectives. Sometimes plans have to be changed. We have suggested that flexibility is needed in planning; at the same time, too much flexibility negates the advantages of this process.

The planning process requires decisions in regard to both the length of the planning period and the extent to which a plan will be repeated, that is, employed a second time, and a third, and so on. In regard to the time variable, the planning period should be long enough to recover the effects of the effort or dollars invested in the course of action. The repetitiveness of plan usage will be dependent on the situation, the advantages to be gained from "standing plans," and the disadvantages in being involved in an automatic program or procedure that is not likely to be subject to inquiry.

The concept of a measure of effectiveness and of the effectiveness function is introduced in this chapter. In the general case, the measure of the outcome is dependent on two classes of variables: those under the control of the decision maker and those not under his control. The significance of the effectiveness function, however, is seen in the shape of that function. In the region near that of the optimum solution, the effectiveness function tends to be rather flat. The implication of this generalization is that the near-optimum solution is almost as effective as the optimum solution. From the viewpoint of the decision maker, a satisfactory alternative will be adequate; the optimum alternative is not really necessary.

Models and the manipulation of models through the process of simulation are often used in planning. This indirect experimentation permits the manager a better understanding of the operations under his control. Physical, schematic, and mathematical-statistical models are employed as replicas of reality. Their manipulation in a controlled experimental fashion permits an inquiry that yields information in less time and at less expense than real-world trials.

Following this introduction to planning, subsequent chapters will be concerned with the objectives of the organization, the basic cost components and cost analysis of the firm, and the investment decision, including the treatment of depreciation models and evaluation procedures that may be employed in capital investment decisions. The last chapter will describe the management science approach and treat three of the more basic quantitative decision models: linear programming, waiting-line methods, and the manufacturing progress (learning) function.

QUESTIONS

1. What are the different types of plans? Give an example of each.

2. Why should plans be flexible? Why should they be firm? How may this conflict be resolved?

3. How would you reply to the manager who claims, "I can't find the time to do any serious planning"?

4. What must be defined in a program or single-use plan?

5. What are the advantages of standing plans?

6. What is an effectiveness function? What is the shape of this function?

7. Give an example of a physical model. A schematic model. A mathematical-statistical model.

8. Discuss the advantages of simulation in contrast to direct experimentation.

objectives

An objective can be a personal thing. It can also be the direction of a cooperative venture. Individuals are said to be purposeful, to have goals or objectives; so also must organizations be purposeful. An enterprise must have a service objective—a product or a service that it will provide to society. It must enjoy a *raison d'être*.

Identification of the service objective is the first step in the planning process. Someone must ask, "What shall we do? What product shall we make or what service shall we provide?" One company may focus on the manufacture and sale of garden tools. Another business may be formed to clean clothes. A third may collect and dispose of garbage. A fourth may produce and sell candy. The list could go on and on. After the goal is specified, other planning can then be undertaken. The total objective can be subdivided into component purposes, similar activities can be grouped together, and the organizational structure can be established. The enterprise can be staffed, direction can be provided to the personnel that now make up the organization, and control procedures can be introduced to monitor the progress being made toward the objective. All of these steps follow the designation of the objective.

Sometimes goals are easily found, other times they come about only after an exhaustive search. An enterprise must seek out an objective that is required by society and that it can offer with some competitive advantage. The formulation and statement of the purpose will affect the perspective of the organization. A company that will sell "grass seed" has a narrower viewpoint than one that will offer "lawn care" and provide the homeowner with garden tools, grass seed, bulbs, fertilizers, and other garden products. The outlook of "Hollywood" was changed with the realization that it was no longer merely in the "movie business," but rather in the "entertainment business" and that it could work with, rather than against, the television media. An example of the possible impact of an organizational goal can be seen in the intent of Henry Ford to make a car that could be sold to the average man for $500. The result was the development of the techniques of the assembly line, the growth of a great industry, and eventually, an entire nation on wheels.

Individual Goals and Organizational Goals

The word goal can have both an individual and an organizational connotation. People have goals; so do organizations. Sometimes these are quite similar; other times they are not. Sometimes the goal of an individual is accomplished within an organizational framework and under the umbrella of the organizational purpose; other times it is not.

Consider the stated goal of an educational institution: "The purpose of Virginia Polytechnic Institute, Virginia's Land-Grant University, is to provide the intellectual atmosphere, the scholarly guidance and the modern facilities for the education of men and women of the Commonwealth, the region and the nation." Now consider what we would hope to be at least one of the goals of a student—"to acquire a first-rate education." These two goals appear to be related. But what of some other possible individual motives within the university? The activities at one small college were described in a novel by Stringfellow Barr:

> There's no common purpose. The trustees want to prevent subversion and stay solvent. . . . [The president] wants to get publicity and, eventually, if it isn't too late, a bigger job somewhere else. The department heads want to raid each other for students, especially for majors, and thereby enlarge their departments. The professors want to publish, get promoted, get famous, and meanwhile stave off their creditors. . . . The wives of the professors . . . are socially ambitious and go in for cutthroat competition. The men students try to make fraternities, make athletic teams, avoid study, and then graduate somehow or other. The girls try to make sororities and find a husband. The parents of the students hope their offspring won't "get ideas." The dean of women hopes the

girls won't conceive anything more dangerous than a concept before they find husbands. And the alumni hope the teams will win, and hunt promising high-school athletes to send us.[1]

This description could be considered facetious, except that it contains too many elements of truth for us to brush it aside. However, it is not evidence of a lack of common purpose. Rather the description points out the wide variety of individual objectives that may be accommodated within a complex organization such as a university. Individual goals are diverse and they may or may not appear to be related to the organizational purpose. In either case, the distinction between individual and organizational goals is an important one. As early as 1938, Chester Barnard suggested:

> We have clearly to distinguish between organization purpose and individual motive. It is frequently assumed in reasoning about organizations that common purpose and individual motive are or should be identical. With the exception noted below, this is never the case; and under modern conditions it rarely even appears to be the case. Individual motive is necessarily an internal, personal, subjective thing; common purpose is necessarily an external, impersonal, objective thing even though the individual interpretation of it is subjective. The one exception to this general rule, an important one, is that the accomplishment of an organization purpose becomes itself a source of personal satisfaction and a motive for many individuals in many organizations.[2]

Although the motives of individuals may differ one from another, the organization consists of the coordinated activities of those individuals directed toward a common purpose. This may be depicted as follows:

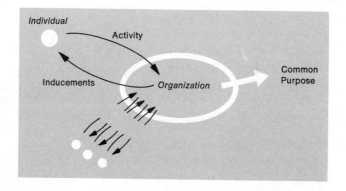

---

[1] Stringfellow Barr, *Purely Academic* (New York: Simon and Schuster, 1958), pp. 34–35.

[2] Chester I. Barnard, *The Functions of the Executive* (Cambridge: Harvard University Press, 1938), pp. 88–89.

If the above were a university, the service purpose could be as previously stated. The individuals, with their individual motives, would be the students, the faculty and staff, and so forth. The organization could also be the Ford Motor Company at the turn of the century. The service purpose would have been to "make a car that could be sold to the average man for $500." An employee working on the assembly line might have been initially attracted to the job and then been motivated, at least in part, by the wage of "$5.00 per day." On the other hand, Henry Ford would have fit Barnard's description—"the accomplishment of an organization purpose becomes itself a source of personal satisfaction." Perhaps some of the management personnel and even some of the hourly workers were similarly motivated, but to a lesser extent. It is doubtful, however, if these other contributors of activity to the organization were *primarily* motivated by the common purpose.

EFFECTIVENESS AND EFFICIENCY

An organization will have a service objective and the participants in the organization will be directed toward the attainment of that goal. It has already been suggested that both the designation of the objective and the development of any policy, procedures, rules, and/or budgets—any guide lines to the participants—are planning functions. Now it will be suggested that a measure of the success of the planning activity, and of the organization itself, can be seen in the effectiveness and the efficiency of the enterprise.[3] Effectiveness refers to the extent to which the cooperative system is successful in attaining its objective. Efficiency relates to the net costs to the participants, that is, the inducements received by the participants less any required contributions, physical or otherwise.

An organization ultimately exists to satisfy the motives of individuals. People benefit from the United States Post Office, from General Motors, and from The Garden Implement Company. If people were not benefiting, the organizations would not long survive. However, the motives of individuals can be satisfied because the organization achieves its service objective. The Garden Implement Company may exist "to manufacture and sell quality tools, supplies, and equipment for the

---

[3] These criteria, as measures of cooperative systems, were first proposed by Barnard, *The Functions of the Executive*, pp. 26–32, 55–59. They are cited in reference to planning in Harold Koontz and Cyril O'Donnell, *Principles of Management* (4th ed.) (New York: McGraw-Hill, 1964), pp. 83–84. They are discussed in more detail in Paul E. Torgersen, *A Concept of Organization* (Princeton: D. Van Nostrand, 1968), and James G. March and Herbert A. Simon, *Organizations* (New York: John Wiley & Sons, 1958).

garden." Stitzel-Weller, the distillery bottling *Old Fitzgerald,* claims as its intent, "We make fine bourbon . . . at a profit if we can, at a loss if we must . . . but always fine bourbon." A hospital may include the statement "to provide patient care." In each case, a rather specific product is being produced or service is being offered. This product or service can be seen as the objective of the organization. Attainment of the organizational objective must parallel if not precede any satisfaction of individual motives. Therefore, effectiveness can be used as a meaningful measure of the relative attainment of the organizational objective. An effective hospital is one that *is* providing patient care; Stitzel-Weller *is* effective if it is making fine bourbon.

Planning should lead to effectiveness in an enterprise. The objective must first be attainable and then the means of accomplishment, developed through planning, should lead to the objective. Lack of planning may be instrumental in the enterprise not reaching its goal.

Planning should also permit organizational efficiency. A plan is efficient when the positive gains to the participants exceed the negative costs; it is efficient when the unsought consequences are at a minimum. Efficiency is not limited to dollar assessments, although Stitzel-Weller will also be efficient if it makes fine bourbon *at a profit.* A hospital will be efficient if it provides patient care in an economical fashion. The Garden Implement Company will be efficient if it sells its products to satisfied customers, declares a dividend, and pays good wages. A company is likely to be efficient if its planning is thorough in that it considers and makes provisions for most contingencies. Plans that result in a minimum of unforeseen or unsought consequences will usually result in a favorable input-output ratio, an attractive efficiency.

The Goals of the Organization

Organizations are typically "born" with service objectives. A transit authority is created to transport people. A hospital is added to the community to provide patient care. The organization emerges as the vehicle to accomplish something—it is the means to an end, not the end in itself. Sears, Roebuck and Company came into existence at the turn of the century to sell to the farmer—to merchandise goods to an isolated market through the mail-order catalog on a regular and recurring basis. In the 1880s, under the direction of Samuel Gompers, the American Federation of Labor (AFL) was formed. The goal was a restricted one—"bread-and-butter" issues for a craft or trade union membership. Contrary to the example of earlier labor movements, there were to be no attempts at social reform and no attempts to organize the unskilled. With the simple objective of improved wages, hours, and working conditions, this federation of skilled craft unions was able to survive in spite of hostile labor legislation and generally unfavorable public opinion.

Both Sears, Roebuck and Company and the AFL had definitive goals. They were successful, in part, because of these goals. Any enterprise must secure an objective that will permit it an advantage in competition with other organizations. Society, or a part of it, must turn to the organization for its product or service. Something about the product or service itself, the means of manufacturing the product or offering the service, or the distribution and marketing of it must give the organization an advantage over other requests for the attention of the consumer. Failure to secure a unique advantage will make survival a struggle and the loss of a unique advantage may lead to the failure of the enterprise. The local grocery store may have to emphasize service, such as telephone orders and home delivery, if it is to compete with the variety and the lower prices of the new supermarket. The independent motel could be as economical and offer the same facilities as the new chain motel. However, to the passing motorist, it is of unknown quality and it is not able, though a larger network, to offer convenient advanced reservations. As a result, it may have to stress lower prices.

The search for goals can be seen as the search for a niche (or two or three) where the organization will be successful. We must match the requirements of the customer with our enterprise capabilities. The needs of the customer may be stable or unstable over time. They may be relatively elastic or inelastic. It may be possible to fill them with substitute products or services. In the same fashion, our own capability may be built upon product strength and reputation, upon manufacturing capability, or upon marketing strength. The search is for an area of intersection of customer needs and enterprise capability. When this has been found, we will

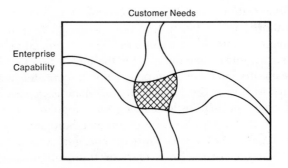

have our objectives. Failure to correctly identify the niche will lead to the selection of objectives that will cause the enterprise to operate at a disadvantage.

Organizational objectives should also be considered as dependent on time. The niche of objectives, where the enterprise is likely to be successful, will change over time. Customer needs change; the enterprise

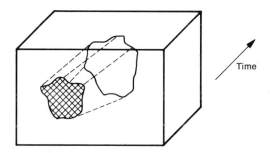

capability will change. As a result, the objectives should be reexamined at intervals and modified when necessary.

The objectives of Sears had to be modified after their initial formulation. By the mid-1920s, the farmer was not as isolated as he had been 25 years earlier. Roads and automobiles enabled him to go to town for some of his shopping. He was also not a rapidly expanding market segment. At the same time, in the cities a low- to middle-income group was developing that was outgrowing its subsistence standards. The group had some money and was in the market for goods. Sears set out to meet this new opportunity. It began to merchandise for the urban market as well as the rural one. In addition, it also included the retail store, as well as the mail-order outlet, to capture the emerging urban market. This change in objective was quite successful.

The American Federation of Labor was not as willing to be flexible in changing its objectives. By the mid-1930s, there existed a legislative environment more favorable to union activity. There also existed an opportunity for industrial unionism—unions of workers attached to a particular industry regardless of individual skills or lack of skills. But the AFL was not willing to respond. As a result, in 1935 a maverick Committee for Industrial Organization was formed within the AFL under the chairmanship of John L. Lewis "to encourage and promote organization of the workers in the mass production and unorganized industries. . . ." By 1936 this group had been expelled from the AFL and the Congress of Industrial Organizations (CIO) was formed. The CIO was successful in organizing as complete industries the automobile, steel, rubber, packinghouse, textile, and electrical industries. By the 1940s the CIO was almost on a par in membership with the AFL. Later, in 1955, these two groups were merged, but the effects of the earlier schism were felt long after the merger in jurisdictional disputes and in disagreements concerning the role of the labor movement in political activity and in social welfare legislation. Even today, the original AFL group tends to be "bread-and-butter" oriented, while the less conservative CIO element is willing to be involved in the broader affairs of society. It is interesting to speculate on the nature of labor movement today had the AFL been willing to broaden its objectives in the 1930s. Perhaps the makeup and outlook of the labor movement today would have been more homogeneous and consistent.

INDICES OF SUCCESS

It is not uncommon to hear people speak of profit as the *real* objective of an enterprise. Although the profit motive may be quite significant, it is not *the* objective of the enterprise. It may be a valid measure of success, but in some instances, it is not even the best measure of success. Profit is actually a surplus of earned income over expenditures. Most companies would like to make a reasonable profit, and they at least have to make some profit to stay in business. However, in a given situation and over a given period of time, the development of new ideas—new products or services—may be more important than a profit. Even in the long run, management may strive to increase the value of the enterprise rather than to secure immediate profits, especially under a tax situation where capital gains are taxed only when "realized" and then at a lower rate than profits or income. Finally, there are many instances where profit is simply not a realistic measure of success. In a hospital, the municipal police force, a transit authority, or a university, we may not expect earned income to exceed expenditures. The objective is service, and profit is not a requisite for success in accomplishing that objective.

Drucker has suggested that, in addition to profit, there are a number of other meaningful enterprise objectives (indices of success):

> There are eight areas in which objectives of performance and results have to be set: market standing; innovation; productivity; physical and financial resources; profitability; manager performance and development; worker performance and attitude; and public responsibility.[4]

[4] Peter F. Drucker, *The Practice of Management* (New York: Harper & Row, 1954), p. 63.

These eight areas might better be described as second-order objectives or indices of the health of the organization. With the possible exception of innovation in products or services, these are not objectives in themselves. Rather, they are measures of the success in the operation of the enterprise. The manager should be concerned with these indices. However, they are not independent of each other, nor are they universal. Innovation and productivity should affect market standing; both should also affect profitability; and all in turn should be dependent upon manager performance. Worker performance is not independent of manager performance, nor are physical and financial resources independent of profitability.

A second difficulty with such a generalization is the lack of universality. These eight "objectives" are not equally relevant to all organizations. Market standing is not a meaningful measure of the activities of a local telephone company. Public responsibility is not as likely to be of concern to the small stamping plant supplying parts to the automobile industry as it is to the automobile company using those parts. Innovation may be critical to the success of Mattel in the toy industry, and it may be important to Miles Laboratories in the pharmaceutical industry, but it is likely to be less important to Swift in the meatpacking industry. This is not to imply that an organization can ignore the advantages of change. Even the university and the church can sometimes profit from change. But for some organizations constant innovation is the only means to survive.

Indices of success, even if they overlap, are of some value. Measures of the extent to which the organization is effective and efficient are necessary. The measures should be those that are needed for the survival of the organization. The organization must be effective and it must be efficient if it is to survive.

The Division of Purpose

Objectives are usually accomplished in parts. The total purpose is likely to be subdivided and various portions assigned to divisions or departments; these are likely to be further subdivided and given to sections or individuals. Eventually a hierarchy of objectives is established. The goals of each subunit then contribute to the larger unit of which it is a part. Barnard suggests that "the effectiveness of cooperative systems depends almost entirely upon the invention or adoption of innovations of specialization; and . . . the primary aspect of specialization is the analysis of purpose or general ends into intermediate or detailed ends which are means to the more remote ends." [5]

Consider the individual who builds himself a birdhouse, then, upon request, builds one for a neighbor. Then a third one is built, this time at a price, for a friend of the neighbor. One step leads to another and eventually a small enterprise—the Birdhouse Company—is formed to build and sell birdhouses. The enterprise objective is the manufacture and sale of birdhouses. A partial listing of the steps necessary to accomplish this aim might be:

1. Order lumber—specify vendor.
2. Order screws—specify vendor.
3. Order paint—specify vendor.
4. Receive lumber.
5. Place lumber in storage.
6. Take lumber out of storage.
7. Cut to length.
8. Cut to width.
9. Assemble.
10. Paint.
11. Sell birdhouse.

The total objective can be subdivided a number of ways. On the one hand, each employee might be told to build and sell birdhouses and each employee might undertake each of the steps necessary to do so, finally culminating in the sale of the birdhouses he has built. It is more likely that similar activities would be grouped together, perhaps initially in divisions. One division might be responsible for manufacture, a second for sales, and a third for securing and maintaining financial resources. Within the manufacturing division, we might establish a purchasing department, a receiving and inventory department, a personnel department, and so forth. Each of these subunits would have an objective. The composite of the objectives should then permit the attainment of the total objective. If objectives are to be accomplished in parts, specialization is possible. Through specialization and the division of labor, unique individual talents and capabilities can be utilized. In addition, activity that is repeated is likely to be done better the second time, and the third, and so forth. The purchasing agent in our Birdhouse Company may have more of an aptitude for clerical work than for carpentry work. Also, with experience, he may become more proficient at predicting contractor de-

---

[5] Barnard, *The Functions of the Executive*, p. 132.

livery capabilities. Certainly, he would do a better job for the company in total than each employee would do for himself. The benefits and methods of specialization are treated in more detail in the chapters dealing with the nature and the structure of organizations.

SUBOPTIMIZATION

If objectives are to be accomplished through subobjectives, it is desirable that the latter contribute to the former. This is not always the case. A schematic of an objective and the attending subobjectives may be drawn as follows:

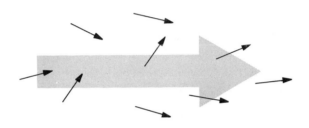

Hopefully, these subobjectives are approximately parallel (and not in opposition to each other) and add to the desired total objective. Conflicts may still occur. Consider the possible viewpoints of some departments in the Birdhouse Company in regard to inventory policy. The production department would prefer long uninterrupted production runs for each model. This would minimize set-up and tear-down costs and hence reduce total production cost. The end result would be a large inventory of a relatively few product models. The sales department would also prefer a large (or at least adequate) inventory of diverse models in order to maximize sales. A stable labor force, desired by the personnel director, would require production for inventory through slack sales periods. The finance department, on the other hand, would prefer to minimize inventory levels in order to reduce the capital investment and obsolescence. These preferences are partially in conflict.

Whenever a hierarchy of objectives is required, conflicts and suboptimization is likely to occur. Limited perception at subordinate levels, together with the desire to pursue immediate objectives effectively, may result in action that is appropriate for the subordinate objective, but suboptimum for the enterprise as a whole. A choice of operating policies for the overall economy requires consideration of how the segments of the whole are related.

Just as the enterprise objective is subdivided at a certain point in time into a hierarchy of subobjectives, it is also likely to be subdivided across a time domain. Long-range plans may extend over the next five years and include an immediate objective for the coming year. This type of planning is commonly used in personal decisions. An individual, perhaps a recent high-school graduate, may aspire to an executive position in industry. In order to successfully climb this ladder, he may set as a goal for himself a college degree from a business school in four years. Even this objective may be made more immediate by focusing on the goal of successfully completing the first semester of required academic course work.

An advantage of establishing an immediate objective is that it can be seen as an attainable goal for the foreseeable future. One can then measure progress against a meaningful and tangible benchmark. It is difficult on a day-by-day basis to assess the progress being made toward becoming a successful executive. One can, however, measure on a day-by-day basis the progress being made toward passing some academic course work.

Long-range goals should precede short-range goals in formulation if there is to be an integral relationship between the two. The long-range goal may be less precise and less certain than the immediate goal. However, the choice of short-range objectives must follow the designation of the more distant goal. For example, a company may aspire to the production and sale of a second product line some two years hence. It may then have to install some new production equipment within the next six months in order to have the facility to manufacture the product. Capital may have to be raised within the next three weeks in order to proceed with the facility expansion. These three objectives represent a sequence over time. The two-year objective was defined first, the six-month objective was second, and the three-week objective was last. They were established in this order, but must be accomplished in the reverse order.

Objectives provide the first step in the planning process. With the objective defined, the direction is established and activity can be undertaken in that direction.

SUMMARY

Identification of the objective of the firm is the first step in the planning process. Just as the corporation must have a goal, each division and department must also have a goal. A distinction is made between the purpose of the organization and the motives of individuals that make up that organization. Sometimes these are identical or at least parallel. At other times, there may be little relation between the goals of the organization and the inducements that the individual hopes to receive from his contribution to the organization. Within this framework, effectiveness is defined as a measure of the attainment of the organizational goal. Efficiency is then defined as a relative measure of the value received by the participant in the organization in comparison to the contributions required of that individual. Organizations must be effective before they can be efficient. The organization may ultimately exist to benefit people; however, in order to be able to do this on a continuing basis, it must have a more immediate objective and it must be effective in achieving that objective.

Some organizations have no difficulty in defining their objectives. Others must search for goals and the first step in the success of the organization will be its success in securing an objective that is compatible with the enterprise's capability and the needs of its potential customers.

The objectives of the organization are usually accomplished in parts. The subdivision of purpose and the attending specialization of activity in accomplishing these purposes is the essence of organization. However, at the same time, one of the problems of the organization is that of suboptimization—the optimizing of a subobjective at the expense of the accomplishment of the total objective. In addition to establishing a hierarchy of subobjectives at a point in time, the organization is likely to establish subobjectives over a time span. Some objectives will be immediate objectives; others will be long-range objectives. In general, long-range goals should precede short-range goals in formulation, if the latter are to contribute toward the attainment of the former. Objectives are the necessary first step in the planning process. With the objective defined, one can focus on the means of accomplishing that end.

QUESTIONS

1. With the exception of the federal mint and a few counterfeiting groups, money is not the objective of an organization. Explain.

2. What would be the goal of the business college? This course? You?

3. List the activities that might be required of a professor if specialization were not employed in the university.

4. Describe an organization. State its objective. Describe how you would measure its effectiveness and its efficiency.

5. Illustrate, using an example, how the niche of desirable organizational objectives may change over time.

6. Illustrate, using examples, why Drucker's eight indices may not be universal and why they may not be independent.

7. How is specialization achieved within an athletic team? Within the family?

8. Give an example of suboptimization.

9. What might be the long-range goals of a football team at the start of the season? What might be its immediate objective?

10. Because long-range goals are likely to be vague and to require an element of uncertainty, it might be suggested that they are a waste of time. Is this a realistic position? Is there a difference between guessing what the future will bring and planning for the future?

11. The more specific the objective, the more specific will likely be the activity. Discuss.

12. Objectives are sometimes considered the means to more remote ends. Give an example.

the production decision

7

*The trouble with people is not that
they don't know
but that they know so much
that ain't so.*

JOSH BILLINGS

The organization has been described as purposeful—as providing a service or producing a product.[1] It does so by accepting inputs of varying kinds and amounts and blending these in an economical fashion to achieve the desired output. The nature of the conversion process will vary from one firm to another and will be largely dependent upon the product or service to be provided. If we manufacture a product, such as a vacuum cleaner, a television set, or a fountain pen, the conversion processes may be somewhat different, but in each case it will be a manufacturing system. If we mine coal or raise turkeys, we still require inputs and provide products, but the conversion processes will have still different characteristics. Likewise, with a service industry, such as a commercial airline, we still require inputs and a distinctive means of blending them in order to offer the service.

In this chapter we will be concerned with the production decision. We will look at the inputs to the firm, as well as the different classes of costs that are likely to accrue in the conversion process. We will also attempt to answer the question: "What will be the economic implications

[1] Some of the illustrations presented in this chapter and in the next were adopted from W. J. Fabrycky and Paul E. Torgersen, *Operations Economy: Industrial Applications of Operations Research* (Englewood Cliffs, N.J.: Prentice-Hall, Inc., 1966), Chapters 4 and 6.

123

—the profit or costs—of possible decisions relative to the level of operation of the firm?"

Production Inputs

Literally tens of thousands of inputs may be required in the production of an automobile or an airplane. Even the inputs to a restaurant or a barber shop would require a lengthy listing. It is hardly possible and not practical to enumerate all the possible inputs to a firm. Rather, four classes of inputs will be defined and discussed. These are listed in Figure 7-1.

The firm must have a labor input. In a sense, the organization *is* the coordinated efforts of people. An airline requires pilots, stewardesses, baggage handlers, reservation clerks, and mechanics. It also employs accountants, attorneys, and computer programmers. These individuals, with their respective skills, provide the human service input.

Within the various types of organizations, different categories of labor inputs may be established. Within a university, we speak of faculty, staff, and administration. Sometimes we remember the students. In a manufacturing firm, it is not unusual to distinguish between direct and indirect labor, with the former capable of being measured and charged directly to the production units.

Materials are also required to meet the objectives of the firm. Like the labor input, we may wish to distinguish between direct and indirect material. In the first category would be the component parts, along with the raw materials that are physically altered and directly converted into

Figure 7-1

Production as an input-output system.

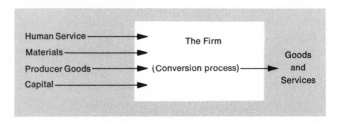

the end product. In the second category are materials that are consumed in the support of the production process.

Producer goods is a third class of input. These would include land and buildings, as well as the production facilities that are involved in altering the input materials. Most producer goods are consumed in the production process. Eventually they have to be replaced. This consumption of producer goods is another cost of the product or service that the firm provides.

Capital is still another necessary input. The cost of producer goods, as well as daily operating expenses, must be met with capital. Insufficient capital is a frequent reason for business failure. Like the other inputs of producer goods, materials, and human services, capital also costs money. An interest charge must be paid for the use of money and this interest is a cost of doing business.

A specific firm will likely require inputs from each of these classes, but of varying types and in different proportions. For example, the labor input into an urban mass transit system (a city bus company) may be close to 85 percent of the total cost of operation. If this same company is not able to realize a profit, it may become a municipal authority and pay no direct taxes. A petroleum refinery, on the other hand, may consist of an extensive investment in physical facilities and convert large quantities of a crude oil input into a number of products. The labor input may be rather minimal. In general, an input of extensive physical facilities may permit a reduction in the needed labor input.

Production Costs

The product or service that the firm provides should result in sales revenue. This income will likely be proportional to the quantity of the product that is sold or the amount of service provided. Each of the inputs in turn will cost money. To some extent, the quantity of inputs that will be required will depend on the desired level of output. Thus, the costs of inputs will be at least partially dependent on the level of operation of the firm.

The costs of operation will be classified in this section according to their independence of or dependence on the level of production. In the first class are fixed costs and in the second class are variable costs. In addition, costs will be viewed in the framework of cost extensions for added levels of production. This view leads to the concept of incremental (or marginal) cost analysis. Finally, the concept of unrecoverable or sunk costs will also be treated in this section.

FIXED COSTS

A cost thought to be fairly constant over a complete range of operational activity is considered to be *fixed*. For example, the expenses incurred in the rental of an insurance office for a month will be the same regardless of the amount of insurance sold that month. Cost items in this class are more or less fixed in amount for a time period, such as a year, regardless of the number of units produced or quantity of service offered. In general, managerial expenses, as well as sales and research inputs, are independent of production levels. The cost of the consumption of producer goods (depreciation), as well as rental expenses and the cost of some indirect materials, are also likely to be fixed. In addition, interest charges on capital will be a constant if the capital requirements do not change with the level of operations.

Fixed costs usually arise because of preparation for the future. Research activity is considered an investment in the future. A machine is bought now to reduce labor costs for some time to come. A sales effort is thought to extend beyond any immediate fluctuations in production.

We must recognize, however, that not all costs considered to be "fixed" are fixed in an absolute sense, nor are they "fixed" over the complete range of possible operational activity. For example, an expenditure for research may be curtailed somewhat in the event sales and production are less than expected. On the other hand, a bonus could be granted to management personnel after an exceptionally good year of operation. Either of these actions would modify the so-called "fixed costs of operation."

Costs may also remain relatively fixed within a range of operation and then change markedly when another range is entered. For example, if production in a manufacturing plant that normally operates on a two-shift, five-day-a-week basis were to increase so that three shifts were necessary, the additional supervisory personnel necessary to direct this third shift would be lead to a step-function increase in fixed costs.

VARIABLE COSTS

Other costs incurred by the firm are assumed to vary directly with output. These are *variable* costs. Direct labor and direct material are considered in this class. For example, each unit of production might require $1.80 in component parts and $1.70 in other materials. Under a piecework system, the labor cost per piece may be $2.50. This totals $6 per unit of variable costs. If 10,000 units are produced one month, the variable cost that month would be $60,000. Should production the second month be increased to 11,000 units, the variable cost the second month would be $66,000. The relationship between fixed cost, variable cost, total cost and the level of production can be seen in Figure 7-2.

Variable costs, like fixed costs, are not as easily defined in practice as they may be in theory. Increasing production from 10,000 to 11,000 units per month may result in more waste and more defectives, thus increasing the material cost per unit. Also, overtime work at time-and-a-half pay may even increase the unit labor cost.

In actual practice, most costs should properly be considered neither fixed nor variable in an absolute sense. Nevertheless, they may be placed in one class or the other, over a given range, if the approximation does not result in a great sacrifice in accuracy. Alternatively, some costs may be prorated with a portion assigned to one class and the remainder to the other. The advantage to be gained in cost-output analyses may warrant this classification system.

INCREMENTAL COSTS

The consideration of incremental (or marginal) costs in the analysis of alternatives includes more than the simple definition of another type

Figure 7-2

The fixed and variable portions of a total cost function.

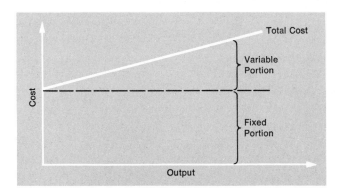

of cost; it represents a way of looking at an opportunity. The outcome of a course of action is estimated in terms of changes in revenue in comparison to changes in cost. With this reasoning, a decision is considered to be profitable if it increases revenue more than it increases costs. The measurement of an incremental cost is illustrated in Figure 7-3.

The added cost could be the cost to produce one more unit of output. In the event that the total cost function consists of a fixed and a variable cost, as seen in Figure 7-2, the incremental cost would be a constant from any one unit to another. On the other hand, there would be almost no incremental cost in carrying an additional passenger in an airplane that is only half full.

Incremental cost analysis can be useful, provided some care is exercised in its application. Consider the following example: The total cost of producing 400 units per year is $72,000. This results in an average cost of $1,800 per unit. The opportunity now presents itself for selling an additional 5 units for a total price of $7,500. At $1,500 per unit, this appears to result in a loss of $300 per unit or a total loss of $1,500. The total cost of producing 405 units has, however, been estimated at $78,500. Then, the incremental cost per unit of the extra units would be $\Delta C = \$78,500 - \$72,000 = \$6,500$, $\Delta Q = 405 - 400 = 5$ units, and

Figure 7-3

The incremental cost, ΔC, resulting from the incremental output, ΔQ.

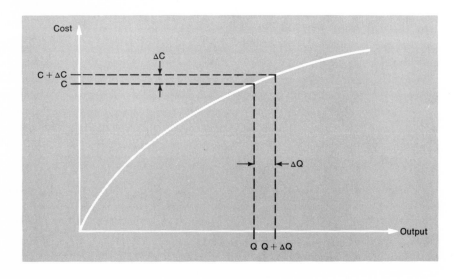

$\Delta C/\Delta Q = \$6,500/5 = \$1,300$. Thus, the sale of the extra 5 units would result in a profit of $1,000 ($200 per unit) rather than a loss of $1,500 ($300 per unit).

Some caution must be exercised in the use of incremental analysis. Although a decision is sound if it increases revenue more than it increases costs, the total effect of the decision cannot be ignored. In the preceding example, the original customers may learn of the dual price structure and resent paying the higher price for subsequent orders. Then the profit of $1,000 may turn out to be a rather expensive profit. Incremental or marginal analysis is actually a method of reasoning wherein receipts and expenditures that have already occurred are considered beyond our control. Subsequent receipts and expenditures are then evaluated in terms of the added amounts in each case. The decision is made on the basis of these added amounts and providing there is no effect upon the initial or base decision.

SUNK COSTS

Sunk costs are similar to incremental costs in that their acceptance and use represent an outlook rather than a simple definition. A *sunk cost* is an expenditure that has been incurred in the past and that is unrecoverable. The significance of a sunk cost is that it should be completely ignored in evaluating alternatives and in making future decisions. This is easy to say; it may be more difficult to do.

Consider another example: A machine was purchased one year ago for $60,000. According to our initial estimates of the machine life, it should now be worth $50,000. (We might assume that $10,000 has been recovered over the past year.) However, a new machine now on the market will do the same job much more efficiently. Should we decide to purchase the new machine, we will be given a $5,000 trade-in on our existing machine. The difference between our projected worth of the machine ($50,000) and the trade-in allowance ($5,000) is a sunk cost, if we go ahead with the purchase of the new machine. Should this $45,000 "loss" influence our decision? The answer is an emphatic "No!" We might consider the initial purchase a mistake, but the failure to purchase the second machine, if, in fact, it is more economical, would be a second mistake. A sunk cost should be recognized as such and accepted if necessary; it should not influence a future decision. In the next chapter we will consider the means of evaluating two alternatives. We will learn how to compare an existing machine with a new machine in terms of their respective earning potentials for the firm.

Breakeven Linear Analysis

The breakeven chart is a deterministic model that permits an analysis of the profitability of a firm at different levels of output. As the name suggests, the chart identifies that level of output where revenue equals cost, either for the firm as a whole or for an individual product or service. In addition, the amount of profit (or loss) can also be assessed at other levels of output.

In this first case, we will assume that a linear relationship exists for costs and income over the range of possible output. We will illustrate the breakeven chart schematically, but we will first define it in algebraic terms, thus facilitating mathematical manipulation of the model. Let:

Q = number of units made and sold each period
p = price per unit
$I = Qp$, the income per period
F = fixed cost per period
v = variable cost per unit
$C = F + vQ$, the sum of fixed and variable costs for Q units of product
$P = I - C$, the profit per period for Q units of product. A negative value of P represents a loss.

These algebraic relationships are illustrated schematically in Figure 7-4 in the context of an example. Assume the fixed cost, $F = \$20$; the variable cost, $v = \$1.50$ per unit; the price, $p = \$4$ per unit; and the production capacity is 12 units per period.

A number of situations may now be defined. The breakeven point occurs at that level of Q where income equals cost, or $Qp = F + Qv$, and solving for Q:

$$Q = \frac{F}{p - v}$$

$$= \frac{\$20}{\$4.00 - \$1.50} = 8 \text{ units}$$

The income (and costs) at the breakeven point may be found by substituting $F/(p - v)$ for Q in either $I = Qp$ or $C = F + Qv$. Using income:

$$I = \left(\frac{F}{p - v}\right) p$$

$$= \left(\frac{\$20}{\$4.00 - \$1.50}\right) \$4 = \$32$$

130

Figure 7-4

A breakeven chart.

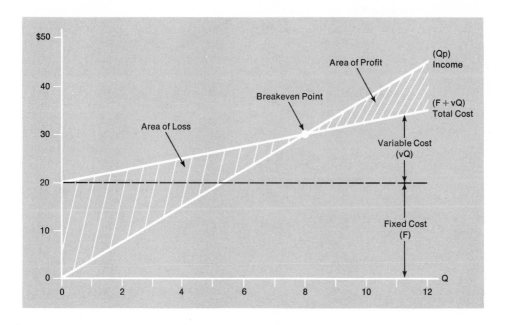

Since profit per period, P, is a function of Q, it may be useful to express this relationship as follows:

$$P = I - C$$
$$= Qp - (F + vQ)$$
$$= Q(p - v) - F$$

In the example, the profit at a capacity of 12 units would be $P = 12$ ($4.00 - $1.50) - $20 = $30 - $20 = $10. The profit at ten units would be $P = 10($4.00 - $1.50) - $20 = $5 and the loss (negative profit) at five units would be $P = 5($4.00 - $1.50) - $20 = -$7.50.

PRODUCTION ABOVE NORMAL CAPACITY

Assume in an extension of the previous example, that an output of 16 units is possible, but at a variable cost of $2.50 per unit for the extra 4 units of output. The price is still $4.00 per unit. Should the 16 units be produced? On an incremental basis, the added income per unit would be $\Delta I = \$4.00$ and the added cost would be $\Delta C = \$2.50$. Then, the incremental profit would be $\Delta I - \Delta C = \Delta P = \$1.50$ per unit or a total of $\$6.00$ in profit for the added 4 units.

The schematic model of this situation can be seen in Figure 7-5. Letting Q and v represent the units of production and variable cost per unit up to the normal capacity, we can designate the added units and the variable cost of output exceeding normal capacity as Q' and v' respectively. Then the total cost of production, including that in excess of normal capacity, becomes:

$$C = F + Qv + Q'v'$$

Figure 7-5

A breakeven chart for production above normal capacity.

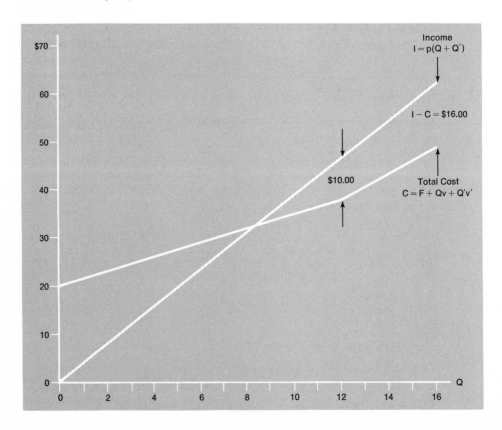

The total income is simply:

$$I = p(Q + Q')$$

And the total profit will be:

$$P = p(Q + Q') - F - Qv - Q'v'$$
$$= \$64 - \$20 - \$18 - \$10 = \$16$$

As long as the slope of the income function exceeds that of the cost function, production at extended capacity can be pursued with profit. This example could be one where overtime has to be scheduled for the added production. Although the extra units are more expensive, they can still be sold at a profit.

THE EFFECT OF DUMPING

In some instances, a constant unit price cannot be maintained over the total possible range of output. Perhaps the initial price can be realized for some of the output, but the remainder must be "dumped" at a lower price.

In our initial example, assume that 8 of the 12 units are sold for $4 each. The remainder can only be sold for $3 each. Schematically, this is shown in Figure 7-6. The cost of producing 12 units has not changed. Although the income for the first 8 units can be defined as $I = Qp$, the income for the remainder should be $Q''p''$ where Q'' is the last 4 units and the reduced price is $p'' = \$3$.

The income realized under dumping is:

$$I = Qp + Q''p''$$

The total profit will be:

$$P = Qp + Q''p'' - F - Qv - Q''v$$
$$= \$32 + \$12 - \$20 - \$12 - \$6 = \$6$$

Like production above capacity, dumping will be profitable if the "dumped" units are sold at a price that is greater than the variable unit cost. A danger exists only if the market price of the initial units is placed in jeopardy. For example, an airline can afford to fill up a partially loaded plane with passengers paying reduced fares. This is profitable, however,

Figure 7-6

A breakeven chart showing
the effect of dumping.

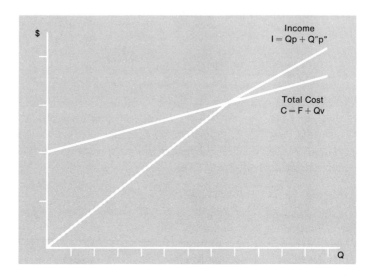

only if the subsequent ticket sales of the initial or original passengers
are not hurt by the practice.

Breakeven Nonlinear Analysis

The breakeven chart is applicable even when the firm's costs or revenue
are not linearly related to output and not easily described in algebraic
terms. Sometimes the unit price changes and continues to change with
the sale of additional units. At other times the variable cost may change,
perhaps increasing as more and more units are produced. It is even
possible that additional fixed costs have to be incurred beyond some levels
of output.

Consider the costs and income given in Table 7-1 for the varying
production and sale of from 0 to 12 units of output. In this example, the
fixed costs (Column B) are a constant. The variable costs (Column C)
increase, first at a decreasing rate and then, beyond unit 4, at an increas-

Table 7-1

INCOME AND COST DATA FOR VARYING LEVELS OF OUTPUT

Output, Q (A)	Fixed Cost (B)	Variable Cost (C)	Total Cost (B + C) (D)	Income (E)	Profit (E − D) (F)
1	$300	$ 100	$ 400	$ 140	−$260
2	300	190	490	280	− 210
3	300	270	570	420	− 150
4	300	350	650	560	− 90
5	300	440	740	700	− 40
6	300	540	840	840	0
7	300	650	950	980	+ 30
8	300	770	1,070	1,120	+ 50
9	300	900	1,200	1,255	+ 55
10	300	1,040	1,340	1,380	+ 40
11	300	1,190	1,490	1,490	0
12	300	1,350	1,650	1,580	− 70

ing rate. The unit sale price is a constant through the first 8 units of output. Beyond this, the unit sale price decreases and the income (Column E) increases at a decreasing rate. Two breakeven points can be identified —at units 6 and 11—and the profit (Column F) is apparently a maximum at unit 9 with income less total cost of $55. The data of Table 7-1 are illustrated schematically in Figure 7-8. Here we have a "picture" of the relationship between fixed cost, variable cost, income, profit, and the level of operation. It can also be observed that a range of profitable operation exists and this range is magnified to be able to ascertain the maximum possible profit.

The data of Table 7-1 can also be analyzed on an incremental basis. This is calculated in Table 7-2 and sketched in Figure 7-9. Note that the average income is a constant through 8 units and drops only slightly thereafter. The average cost drops quickly at first as the fixed cost is able to be prorated over more and more units. It is at a minimum at unit 9 and increases thereafter as the effect of the increasing variable cost begins to outweigh the reduction achieved through the prorating of the fixed cost. The average cost and average income are the same at unit 6 ($140) and at unit 11 ($135), the two levels of output at which breakeven is achieved. Although the difference between average income and average cost is the same at unit 8 ($140 − 134 = $6) as it is at unit 9 ($139 −

Figure 7-8

Breakeven chart for the data of Table 7-1.

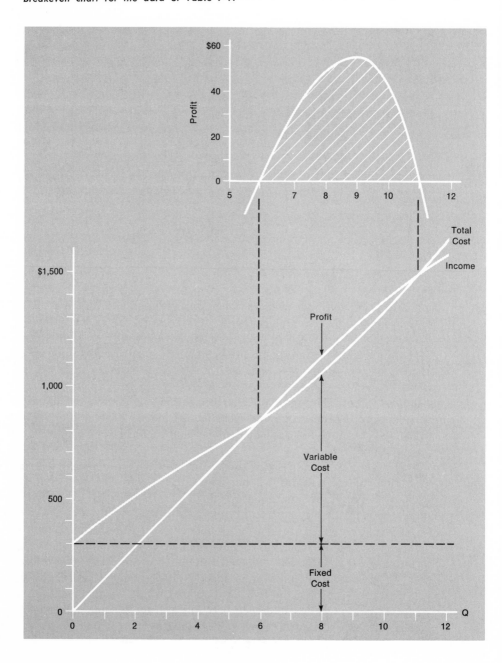

Table 7-2

AVERAGE AND INCREMENTAL VALUES FOR THE DATA OF TABLE 7-1

Output, Q (A)	Average Cost $(D \div A)$ (G)	Average Income $(E \div A)$ (H)	Incremental Cost $(D_Q - D_{Q-1})$ (I)	Incremental Income $(E_Q - E_{Q-1})$ (J)
1	$400	$140	—	—
2	245	140	$ 90	$140
3	190	140	80	140
4	163	140	80	140
5	148	140	90	140
6	140	140	100	140
7	136	140	110	140
8	134	140	120	140
9	133	139	130	135
10	134	138	140	125
11	135	135	150	110
12	137	132	160	90

$133 = \$6$), a larger profit is realized at an output of 9 units. In effect, the profit at 8 units of output is 8 units $\times$ \$6 average profit per unit $= \$48$ total profit. The profit at 9 units of output is 9 units $\times$ \$6 average profit per unit $= \$54$ total profit. Note that at 10 units the profit is reduced: 10 units $\times$ \$4 average profit per unit $= \$40$ total profit.

The incremental costs and income are also given in Table 7-2 and sketched in Figure 7-9. The incremental income is a constant through 8 units and then drops \$5, \$10, \$15, and \$20 respectively with the sale of the succeeding 4 units. The incremental cost increases from unit 4 through 12. In each case through the first 9 units, the incremental income exceeds the incremental cost. Unit 10 however, will result in an added cost of \$140 and an added income of only \$125. Thus, if profit is to be maximized, unit 9—the last unit where the incremental income exceeds the incremental cost—should be the last unit of output. Producing more than 9 units will result in a reduction in total profit.

Incremental analysis can be an aid in decision making. In some instances it may not be possible to accurately measure the total cost of or the total income from producing a number of units. It might be possible to assess the cost of producing and selling one additional unit with more confidence. If that unit can be sold at a profit, it should be produced. The only reservation in using this approach is that if there is a price break, the most recent sale must not jeopardize initial sales in future periods of time.

Figure 7-9

The data of Table 7-2.

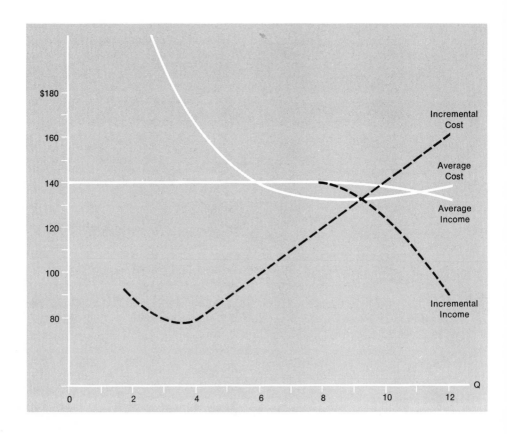

SUMMARY

The firm can be seen as a conversion process, accepting inputs of varying kinds and amounts and converting them to the goods and/or services that constitute the objective of the firm. We consider four classes of inputs: human service (or labor), materials, producer goods, and capital.

The product or service should result in sales revenue. The total income will depend on the quantity of output, which, in turn, will depend on the quantity of inputs. In analyzing the costs of the firm's operations, we can distinguish between fixed costs and variable costs. We may also review some decision situations in terms of the incremental costs. Sometimes we must recognize the occurrence of sunk costs. With the understanding of these different costs, we may proceed with a breakeven analysis of the level of the firm's operations. We can treat the linear and the nonlinear cases and observe the effect of incremental increases in production and/or the effect of the disposal of some quantity of our output at less than the standard price.

In the next chapter, we will continue with this analysis of the firm by examining the investment decision in more detail. We will examine the cost of capital, the effect of depreciation of producer goods, and a number of different evaluation procedures in replacement decisions.

QUESTIONS AND PROBLEMS

1. Specify a product-oriented firm and list its major inputs within each of the four classes presented in the chapter.

2. Specify a service-oriented firm and do the same.

3. Give some examples of fixed costs. Variable costs.

4. Give an illustration of the concept of incremental analysis.

5. What is a sunk cost? Why do you think it is so difficult for a person to recognize and accept a sunk cost?

6. Sketch the breakeven chart described by $F = \$1,000$, $v = \$15$ per unit, and $p = \$20$ per unit over the range of 0 to 250 units. Identify the breakeven point.

7. Solve for the breakeven point in Problem 6 by algebraic analysis. Calculate the profit at an output of 225 units.

8. In Problem 6, an additional 50 units could be sold at a variable cost of $18 per unit. However, the last 10 of those would have to be dumped at $15 per unit. Would this still be a profitable venture?

9. A firm has the capacity to produce 650,000 units per year. At present it is operating at 60 percent of capacity. Annual fixed costs are $100,000. The variable cost is $0.08 per unit. The selling price is $0.28 per unit.
    a. What is the profit at this level of operation?
    b. At what level of operation would breakeven be achieved?
    c. What would be the profit at 100 percent of capacity?

10. A market survey of towns X, Y, and Z reveals that it will be possible

to sell 10,000, 3,500, and 3,000 loaves of bread per day in each town, respectively, six days a week. At the present time two alternatives are under consideration to meet this demand. In the first, one plant with a capacity of 20,000 loaves could be located equidistant between the towns and produce at a fixed cost of $1,000 per day. The variable cost would be $0.08 per loaf. Alternatively, plants with a capacity of 12,000, 4,000, and 4,000 loaves respectively could be located in each town. The fixed costs would be $700, $350, and $350 respectively per day. Because of the reduction in trucking costs, the variable cost per loaf would be $0.06. If the market survey is correct, which alternative would be more desirable? If sales were to increase to production capacity, which alternative would be more desirable?

the investment
decision

"The cause of lightning," Alice said very decidedly,
for she felt quite sure about this,
"is the thunder—no, no!" she hastily corrected herself,
"I meant the other way."
"It's too late to correct it," said the Red Queen:
"When you've once said a thing,
that fixes it, and you must take the consequences."

LEWIS CARROLL
Through the Looking Glass

The firm, and particularly the firm responsible for producing a product, has been described as a conversion process. Inputs of varying kinds and amounts are acquired, processed through the firm, and *converted* to the product (or service) that constitutes the objective of the firm. For example, wheels and tires, appliances, doors and windows, plumbing supplies, lumber, aluminum siding, and other construction material may be the input to one firm; mobile homes may be the output. Crude oil may be the single input to a second firm; gasoline, kerosene, motor oil, and a host of petroleum by-products may be the output. Even a service industry will have some inputs that are directly consumed in providing the output or service.

Another class of physical inputs to the firm is largely responsible for this transformation. The plant itself, a warehouse, the production facilities, and materials handling equipment are also inputs, but inputs of a more durable nature. These inputs require an investment—a commitment of funds that the firm does not expect to recover during the current year or accounting period.

The selection of investment opportunities usually requires the selection of one or a few of a larger number of possible alternatives. Funds are always available in limited quantities and they must be ra-

141

tioned. This rationing and allocation of investment funds is called *capital budgeting*. Money spent for additional warehouse space is money that cannot be spent for a new fleet of delivery trucks.

An investment decision is one that is not easily reversed. If it has been a poor decision, profitability may be affected for some time. If the decision has been a wise one, the investment will be recovered, but it will be recovered over several years, and additional funds will be recovered as well. A successful investment is one that permits the recovery of the initial capital outlay plus a "return" on that investment.

The purchase of some capital goods may be required for expansion. Other purchases may be required to replace existing equipment that is worn out. A third investment decision may be one arising from innovation—the displacement of old technology by the new. The last decision will be the most difficult, because the existing equipment may still be functional. In this case, replacement will likely necessitate the acceptance of a sunk cost. The same evaluation is required in each of these investment decisions: Will the investment be recovered? When? What will be the "return"?

An evaluation of the investment opportunity should be undertaken within an objective and quantitative framework. However, this is not always possible. Even when it is possible, it is not always done. Subjective elements may seem to be more important than the amount of return that can be realized on an investment. The issues of prestige, morale, or safety may not lend themselves to quantification. Alternatively, an investment opportunity may be so important to the success and the future of the organization that a quantitative treatment is not necessary. Some opportunities appear more postponable than others. The major shortcoming of the nonquantitative approach is that it encourages the selection of the opportunity for which there is the most pressure. A project that is receiving less pressure and that is still postponable may be highly profitable. But it may never be seriously considered. The quantitative evaluation will not always replace the intuitive and the subjective consideration. However, if it is undertaken and if it accomplishes nothing else, it points out the cost of prestige or the sacrifice in yielding to the apparently immediate pressure.

The quantitative evaluation of investment opportunities will require an understanding of interest and interest calculations. Following a treatment of this subject, some different methods of evaluating alternatives will be presented. In addition, the concept of depreciation will be developed in order to properly quantify the costs involved in investment opportunities.

The Time Value of Money

Time and money are not independent. A dollar today is not equivalent to a dollar one year from now. The dollar today can be used today. It can earn money. The rent paid for the use of a building is essentially the same as interest paid for the use of money. The economics and the ethics of charging rent for the use of capital have been debated by economists as well as philosophers throughout the ages. Regardless of the moral implications of charging money for the use of money, the economic aspects of this practice cannot be ignored.

INTEREST AND INTEREST RATE

Money paid (or earned) for the use of money is referred to as *interest*. The lender can consider this a gain or a profit. The borrower is likely to think of interest charges as a cost. The *interest rate* is the ratio of the charge paid (or received) for the use of a sum of money over a specified period of time, usually one year. For example, if $8 is paid for the use of $100 for one year, the interest rate is 8 percent.

Consider an opportunity to earn money: an amount of $10,000 is to be invested in a project that will extend for a duration of four years and will pay an interest rate of 8 percent per year. If the interest earned each year is not withdrawn, but is reinvested in the project, then the total investment will increase each year. In effect, we will have a compounding of interest upon interest. The history of such an investment at 8 percent compound interest can be seen as follows:

Year	Interest Earned during Year	Amount of Investment at End of Year
1	$10,000.00 × 0.08 = $ 800.00	$10,800.00
2	10,800.00 × 0.08 = 864.00	11,640.00
3	11,640.00 × 0.08 = 931.20	12,595.20
4	12,595.20 × 0.08 = 1,007.62	13,602.82

At the end of four years, the $10,000 investment will be worth $13,602.82.

143.

To develop compound interest formulas for examples such as the preceding, let:

i = interest rate, expressed as a ratio
n = number of interest periods (usually years)
P = the present value of the investment
S = the sum that has accumulated over n interest periods
R = a series of n equal end-of-period payments.

Then, the example investment can be described as:

Year	Interest Earned During Year	Amount of Investment at End of Year
1	Pi	$P + Pi = P(1+i)$
2	$P(1+i)i$	$P(1+i) + P(1+i)i = P(1+i)^2$
3	$P(1+i)^2i$	$P(1+i)^2 + P(1+i)^2i = P(1+i)^3$
4	$P(1+i)^{n-1}i$	$P(1+i)^{n-1} + P(1+i)^{n-1}i = P(1+i)^n$

and:

$$S = P(1+i)^n$$
$$= \$10,000(1 + 0.08)^4$$

From the interest table compiled in the Appendix, $(1.08)^4 = 1.360$ and $S = \$13,600$. Thus, an investment of $10,000 today is "equivalent" to $13,600 four years from now at an annual interest rate of 8 percent.

We can also resolve the reverse of this general problem. Consider another investment decision: We wish to have $10,000 available for our use five years from now. We can invest some money today at 6 percent. How much should be invested? If:

$$S = P(1+i)^n$$

then:

$$P = S \frac{1}{(1+i)^n}$$

from the Appendix:

$$\frac{1}{(1+0.06)^5} = 0.7473$$

and:

$$P = \$7,473$$

In effect, we have determined that \$10,000 in five years at 6 percent interest is "equivalent" to \$7,473 today.

In some situations we either invest an amount P and then draw from this amount in equal amounts R, or we invest equal amounts R in an attempt to accumulate the sum S. In each case, R is an end-of-the-year amount.

An equal payment series can be seen as:

where:

$$P = R\frac{1}{1+i} + R\frac{1}{(1+i)^2} + R\frac{1}{(1+i)^3} + \cdots$$
$$+ R\frac{1}{(1+i)^{n-1}} + R\frac{1}{(1+i)^n}$$

The right-hand side of this equation can be simplified such that:

$$P = R\left[\frac{(1+i)^n - 1}{i(1+i)^n}\right]$$

It can also be shown that:

$$S = R\left[\frac{(1+i)^n - 1}{i}\right]$$

Assume that we intend to invest \$500 at the end of each year for 10 years. Our money will earn 5 percent interest. How much will we accumulate?

$$S = \$500\left[\frac{(1+0.05)^{10} - 1}{0.05}\right]$$

$$= \$500 \left[\frac{1.629 - 1}{0.05} \right] = \$500[12.54]$$

$$S = \$6{,}270$$

Consider a second example. A company has borrowed $100,000 at 6 percent interest. It must repay the loan in equal end-of-year amounts over the next eight years. How much must be paid each year? If:

$$P = R \left[\frac{(1 + i)^n - 1}{i(1 + i)^n} \right]$$

then:

$$R = P \left[\frac{i(1 + i)^n}{(1 + i)^n - 1} \right]$$

$$= \$100{,}000 \left[\frac{0.06(1 + 0.06)^8}{(1 + 0.06)^8 - 1} \right]$$

$$R = \$100{,}000 \left[\frac{0.06(1.594)}{1.594 - 1} \right] = \$16{,}104$$

In each instance, where P, S, i, and n; P, R, i, and n; or R, S, i, and n are involved, if three of the four factors are specified, the last factor can then be obtained. If either i or n is the unknown, it will be necessary to solve on a trial-and-error basis and then interpolate. For example, assume we are to invest $10,000 today. We would like our money to double in 10 years. What interest rate will we have to secure? We begin by defining:

$$S = P(1 + i)^n$$

$$\$20{,}000 = \$10{,}000(1 + i)^n$$

$$(1 + i)^n = \frac{\$20{,}000}{\$10{,}000} = 2$$

From our interest tables, for $n = 10$ years, if $i = 7$ percent:

$$(1 + 0.07)^{10} = 1.967$$

For $i = 8$ percent:

$$(1 + 0.08)^{10} = 2.159$$

And by interpolation:

$$i = 7 + (1)\frac{2.0 - 1.967}{2.159 - 1.967}$$

$$i = 7 + \frac{0.033}{0.192} = 7.17 \text{ percent}$$

EFFECTIVE INTEREST RATES

It is not uncommon to encounter problems that involve the time value of money and an interest period of other than one year. Interest intervals of less than a year, that is, monthly, quarterly, and semiannual periods, will be most often encountered. One type of problem will call for the use of the P, S, R, i, and n factors with i and n modified to account for the given interest rate and compounding period. For example, if $100 is to be deposited in a bank for five years and the conditions are specified as "4 percent nominal annual interest rate, compounded quarterly," this is the same as saying "1 percent per period for 20 periods (quarters)." Our $100 would become:

$$S = \$100(1.01)^{20}$$

$$S = \$100(1.220) = \$122.00$$

Note that this is slightly more than 4 percent, compounded annually:

$$S = \$100(1.04)^5$$

$$S = \$100(1.217) = \$121.70$$

Our 4 percent, compounded quarterly, is equivalent to an effective interest rate of slightly more than the 4 percent, compounded annually. This effective interest rate would be:

$$i = (1 + \frac{\phi}{c})^c - 1$$

where c is the number of interest periods per year and ϕ is the nominal annual interest rate. Thus:

$$i = (1 + \frac{0.04}{4})^4 - 1$$

$$= (1.01)^4 - 1$$

$$i = 1.041 - 1 = 4.1 \text{ percent}$$

In a few cases the interest rate may also be expressed in the period in which compounding will occur. Consider a finance charge of 2 percent per month (a 24 percent nominal annual interest rate). In terms of an effective interest rate, this amounts to:

$$i = (1 + \frac{0.24}{12})^{12} - 1$$
$$= (1.02)^{12} - 1$$
$$i = 1.268 - 1 = 26.8 \text{ percent}$$

Depreciation

The production of goods and services is usually dependent on the employment of large quantities of producer goods, often requiring a considerable investment. This may permit high worker productivity; however, the economy must be adequate to absorb the reduction in value of these facilities as they are consumed in the production process. In effect, the facilities must be made to pay for themselves.

With the possible exception of land, physical assets are likely to lessen in value with the passage of time. *Physical depreciation* results from wear and tear. The asset deteriorates from cracking, abrasion, or corrosion and the wear will likely be manifested in a lessening of the asset's ability to perform its intended service. Just as an automobile begins to burn more oil, requires increasing maintenance, and is no longer able to accelerate as it once did, so with a milling machine, the operator may no longer be able to achieve the tolerances that once were possible. The asset is simply wearing out.

Functional depreciation can also occur. There may be a change in the demand for the service rendered by the asset. Alternatively, the development of a new, perhaps faster, more economical machine or process may render the original asset obsolete. In either case, the asset itself may still be in a state of good repair. It is simply no longer needed.

The concept of depreciation is complicated because two aspects must be considered: First, the actual lessening in the value of the asset as it is consumed or becomes obsolete with the passage of time. This is actual depreciation. A second aspect is accounting for the depreciation. For financial purposes—the calculation of profit and the assessment of taxes—a record must be maintained of the value of the asset. This is a "book value." The actual value and the book value of an asset are likely to be the same when the asset is first obtained and put into service. There are some advantages to their being the same when the asset is eventually retired. There is little need for the two to be similar during the life of the asset.

Calculations involving depreciation as a cost of production are necessary both to establish this cost for profit and tax purposes and to evaluate alternatives. In the first case, we are more likely to be concerned with the book value. In the second case we are interested in the actual value and in the concept of capital recovery plus return.

DEPRECIATION MODELS

In considering depreciation as a cost of production, it is necessary to establish a value-time function. Any tangible property with a useful life of more than one year, excluding inventories and land, must be depreciated in computing taxable income. A life and a salvage value must be specified, along with a method of depreciation.

A general value-time function is illustrated in Figure 8-1.

The asset is assumed to have been acquired at a cost P. For accounting purposes, we assume it will last n years and have a trade-in or salvage value of L at the end of that time. During the period 0 to n it will have the book value as given in the value-time function. In computing taxes, it is desirable to select as short a life as possible and to depreciate the

Figure 8-1

A depreciation value-time function.

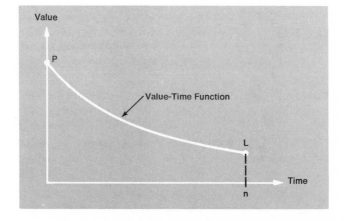

asset quickly. The tax laws do impose some restrictions, however. There is a limit to how soon and how rapidly an asset may be "written off" for tax purposes. The advantage of accelerated depreciation is seen in the time value of money. This can be demonstrated in the following illustration: Assume an asset is purchased for $9,000; it has an estimated life of four years, and a salvage value of $1,000. The asset will earn an annual income of $4,000 before taxes and depreciation. We will assume a tax rate of 50 percent. Consider the following three accounting systems: (1) straight-line depreciation over four years, (2) an accelerated depreciation schedule (sum-of-the-years model) over four years, and (3) straight-line depreciation over two years.

STRAIGHT-LINE DEPRECIATION [1]
(OVER FOUR YEARS)

Year	Earnings	Depreciation	Taxable Income	Tax
1	$4,000	$2,000	$2,000	$1,000
2	4,000	2,000	2,000	1,000
3	4,000	2,000	2,000	1,000
4	4,000	2,000	2,000	1,000
			Total Tax Outlay	$4,000

[1] The capital recovered (depreciation) each year is $(P-L)/n$.

SUM-OF-THE-YEARS DEPRECIATION [2]
(OVER FOUR YEARS)

Year	Earnings	Depreciation	Taxable Income	Tax
1	$4,000	$3,200	$ 800	$ 400
2	4,000	2,400	1,600	800
3	4,000	1,600	2,400	1,200
4	4,000	800	3,200	1,600
			Total Tax Outlay	$4,000

[2] If the number of years is added: $\Sigma n = 1 + 2 + 3 + \ldots + n$, then the capital recovered each year is $n/\Sigma n(P-L)$, $n - 1/\Sigma n(P-L) \ldots 1/\Sigma n(P-L)$.

STRAIGHT-LINE DEPRECIATION
(OVER TWO YEARS)

Year	Earnings	Depreciation	Taxable Income	Tax
1	$4,000	$4,000	$ 0	$ 0
2	4,000	4,000	0	0
3	4,000	0	4,000	2,000
4	4,000	0	4,000	2,000
			Total Tax Outlay	$4,000

Note that in each case the total tax outlay is $4,000. The improvement (if any) of one depreciation schedule over another is in the delay in paying these taxes. For example, with an interest rate of 10 percent, the present worth of the tax outlays would be:

Straight-Line Depreciation (over four years)

$$P = R\left[\frac{(1+i)^n - 1}{i(1+i)^n}\right]$$

$$= \$1,000\left[\frac{(1+0.10)^4 - 1}{0.10(1+0.10)^4}\right]$$

$$P = \$3,155$$

Sum-of-the-Years Depreciation (over four years)

$$P = S_1\frac{1}{(1+i)^n} + S_2\frac{1}{(1+i)^n} + S_3\frac{1}{(1+i)^n} + S_4\frac{1}{(1+i)^n}$$

$$= \$400\frac{1}{(1+0.10)^1} + \$800\frac{1}{(1+0.10)^2} + \$1,200\frac{1}{(1+0.10)^3}$$

$$+ \$1,600\frac{1}{(1+0.10)^4}$$

$$P = \$364 + 661 + 902 + 1,093 = \$3,020$$

Straight-Line Depreciation (over two years)

$$P = S_3\frac{1}{(1+i)^n} + S_4\frac{1}{(1+i)^n}$$

$$= \$2,000\frac{1}{(1+0.10)^3} + \$2,000\frac{1}{(1=0.10)^4}$$

$$P = \$1,503 + 1,366$$
$$= \$2,869$$

Under these conditions, and assuming each of the above were acceptable to the Internal Revenue Service, an accounting system that depreciated the asset over two years on a straight-line basis, would minimize the tax outlay—at least in present-worth dollars. There is another psychological advantage to an accelerated depreciation schedule. Should the asset actually depreciate faster than intended, perhaps due to functional depreciation, a smaller sunk cost would be incurred when the asset was replaced. If there is a disadvantage to an accelerated depreciation schedule, it is in the inaccurate profit picture. In the last case, for example, it would appear that no taxable income (profit) was being realized during the first two years. This is misleading.

CAPITAL RECOVERY PLUS RETURN

An asset is usually purchased with the intent that it will be able to pay for itself. The capital recovered over the life of an asset should be equal to the initial cost less any salvage or trade-in at the time of retirement. In addition to the recovery of the investment, a return should be earned on the unrecovered balance during the life of the asset. We need to recover our initial outlay. We should also earn money on the money invested in the asset.

In the evaluation of alternatives, we may have to consider one or more choices that involve a capital outlay. Consider the following two alternatives: First, we can complete a three-year drainage-ditch construction project with a labor cost of \$55,000 per year. Second, we can cut this labor cost in half by purchasing additional earth-moving equipment. The equipment will cost \$70,000, have a useful life of three years, and have a salvage value of \$10,000. If we are to consider money at an interest rate of 10 percent, is this a desirable investment? In effect, we are asking the question: Which is less expensive, (1) \$27,500 per year for three years in labor costs, or (2) a \$70,000 cost today, a salvage value return of \$10,000 in three years, with the time value of money calculated at 10 percent?

The equivalent annual cost of capital recovery plus return is given by:

$$(P - L)\left[\frac{i(1 + i)^n}{(1 + i)^n - 1}\right] + Li$$

THE INVESTMENT DECISION

In our example, we have an equivalent annual cost of:

$$(\$70,000 - 10,000) \left[\frac{0.10(1 + 0.10)^3}{(1 + 0.10)^3 - 1} \right] + \$10,000(0.10)$$

This is equal to \$25,127 per year.[3] In effect, at 10 percent, the earth-moving equipment will result in an annual saving of \$27,500 − 25,127 = \$2,273. At an interest rate of 15 percent, the capital outlay would result in an equivalent annual cost of \$27,779 and the investment opportunity would no longer be attractive.

The equivalent annual cost of capital recovery plus return is independent of the method of depreciation. With P, L, i, and n specified, the shape of the value-time function (Figure 8-1) will not affect this annual cost.

[3] The equivalent annual cost of capital recovery plus return can be seen for the example given, at 10 percent, in the following calculations. With a straight-line depreciation we hope to recover $(P - L)/n$ each year. Then, the capital recovery plus return each year would be:

Year	Unrecovered Capital (Beginning of Year)	Return on Unrecovered Capital	Capital Recovered during Year	Capital Recovery plus Return
1	\$70,000	\$7,000	\$20,000	\$27,000
2	50,000	5,000	20,000	25,000
3	30,000	3,000	20,000	23,000

The present worth of this capital recovery plus return is:

$$P = \$27,000 \frac{1}{(1 + 0.10)^1} + \$25,000 \frac{1}{(1 + 0.10)^2} + \$23,000 \frac{1}{(1 + 0.10)^3}$$

$$= 24,545 + 20,661 + 17,280$$

$$P = \$62,486$$

And the equivalent annual cost over three years is:

$$R = \$62,486 \left[\frac{0.10(1 + 0.10)^3}{(1 + 0.10)^3 - 1} \right] = \$25,127$$

The Evaluation

There is no single method of evaluation leading to the investment decision. Instead, a number of choices are possible. Some methods are more complex than others, but all attempt to answer the question: Will the firm be better off financially as a result of this investment opportunity?

Sometimes the evaluation is a choice between two (or more) alternatives. Should machine A be retained, or should machine B (or C) be purchased as a replacement? Other times, the evaluation is simply a question of accepting or rejecting a single investment opportunity. Should a company add an additional product line? The alternative would be simply not adding the product line, then selecting a second, perhaps more profitable product line. With either type of evaluation, we are interested in a comparison of incremental revenues and incremental costs. Our evaluation should take into account the cost of capital and the time value of money. Sunk costs should not be permitted to influence our decision.

We will treat three methods of evaluation:

1. Payback Period.
2. Present Value (and Equivalent Annual Cost).
3. Rate of Return.

The first of these is the simplest. Although the *Payback Period* does not consider the time value of money, it is widely used because of the ease of calculations.[4] The second and third methods are more complex, but they do meet our requirement that consideration be given to the time value of money. As we shall see, under some conditions they are equivalent.

THE PAYBACK PERIOD

As the name suggests, this approach requires the calculation of the length of time for an investment to pay for itself in savings realized through that investment. Savings can be based on either a "before taxes" or an "after taxes" basis. In either case, the savings are "before depreciation" in that we are concerned with how long it will take to recover the investment capital. The length of time it will take for the investment to pay for itself is contrasted to some standard. If the time is less then that

---

[4] J. Fred Weston, *Managerial Finance* (New York: Holt, Rinehart & Winston, Inc., 1962), p. 125.

standard, the investment is considered profitable. Otherwise the opportunity is rejected.

The computation of the time involved is

$$T = \frac{I}{S}$$

where:

$T =$ the length of time or payback period usually expressed in years

$I =$ the cost of the original investment

$S =$ the yearly savings before depreciation but after taxes [5]

We can illustrate this method with an example. A firm is considering the introduction of a conveyor-based materials handling system that would cost $40,000 installed. The annual labor savings are estimated at $8,000 and a reduction in breakage would likely permit another $2,000 annual materials savings. The economic life of the conveyor system is estimated at 20 years with no salvage value. Depreciation will be established on a straight-line basis over the estimated life of the asset, that is, $2,000 per year. We assume a 50 percent tax on earnings. If investments are expected to pay for themselves in 5 years, would this evaluation lead to an affirmative investment decision?

The total gross savings would be $8,000 plus $2,000 or $10,000 per year. Taxes would be calculated at 50 percent of gross savings less depreciation: $0.50($10,000 − 2,000) = $4,000$. Then S, the yearly savings before depreciation but after taxes, would be $10,000 − 4,000 = $6,000. And:

$$T = \frac{\$40,000}{\$\ 6,000}$$
$$= 6.6 + \text{years}$$

Based on this evaluation, the investment would not be undertaken.

Now consider a second possible conveyor system—one that would cost $30,000 rather than $40,000 and would last 10 years rather than 20 years. Assume the annual savings are the same. The annual depreciation

[5] We will treat the "after taxes" rather than the "before taxes" case. The former is slightly more complex and is usually based on a 50 percent tax of gross savings less depreciation. The "after taxes" approach is likely to have a larger standard or acceptable payback period.

by the straight-line method would be $30,000 ÷ 10$ years, or $3,000 per year. Taxes would be 50 percent of $10,000 − 3,000$, or $3,500. Then S would be $6,500. And:

$$T = \frac{\$30,000}{\$ 6,500}$$

$$= 4.6 + \text{years}$$

The second opportunity could be accepted.

Why is the second investment opportunity more attractive than the first? The second will apparently pay for itself in 4.6 rather than 6.6 years. But the second conveyor system has only half the expected life of the first. The explanation lies in the fact that the payback method does not consider the expected life of the asset in the evaluation process. The relevant criterion is how quickly the investment will be returned, and not how the total savings compare to the required investment. Excluding the time value of money, the first investment will pay for itself three times over. The second investment will only pay for itself slightly more than two times over. Nevertheless, the second will pay for itself in less than 5 years. The payback method also does not take into account *when* the savings are realized. If the savings are uneven from one year to the next, considering the time value of money, an investment that permitted larger initial savings would be preferred to one that deferred savings, even though both might pay for themselves in total over the same period of time.

In summary, although the payback period approach ignores the *total* savings and may not account for differences in the *timing* of savings, it is simple to understand and relatively easy to utilize. In addition, when the firm is short of capital and must realize a quick return on investments, there may be no meaningful alternative.

PRESENT VALUE

According to the present value criterion, we should accept an investment project that increases the net present worth of the firm. Where there are competing projects, we accept the project that increases the net present worth by the largest amount.

For example, a firm is considering the purchase of a $5,500 surface grinder. The machine should last four years and have a $500 salvage value at the end of that time. Savings as a result of the investment will amount to $1,500 per year. With an interest rate of 10 percent, is this a desirable investment? [6] The pattern of cash flow can be seen as follows:

End of year		0	1	2	3	4
Cash flow:	Machine	−$5,500				+$ 500
	Savings		+$1,500	+$1,500	+$1,500	+$1,500

The present value is:

$$- \$5,500 + \$1,500 \left[\frac{(1 + 0.10)^4 - 1}{0.10(1 + 0.10)^4}\right] + \$500 \frac{1}{(1 + 0.10)^4}$$

or:

$$- \$5,500 + \$4,755 + \$342 = - \$403$$

In effect, the investment would result in a reduction of present worth and should therefore be rejected.

The same decision would be made using the equivalent annual cost criterion, because the discounted annual cash flow is negative. This annual return would be:

$$- \$5,500 \left[\frac{0.10(1 + 0.10)^4}{(1 + 0.10)^4 - 1}\right] + \$1,500 + \$500 \left[\frac{0.10}{(1 + 0.10)^4 - 1}\right]$$

or:

$$- \$1,735 + \$1,500 + \$108 = - \$127$$

The present value criterion can also be established "after taxes." Using the same investment opportunity—the purchase of a $5,500 surface grinder with a four-year life and an estimated salvage value of $500—we also need to specify a tax rate and a method of depreciation. Assume a 50 percent tax and the straight-line depreciation schedule. The annual depreciation will be ($5,500 − 500) ÷ 4 = $1,250 per year. The annual taxes would then be 50 percent of gross savings less depreciation or

---

[6] We assume a specified interest rate. In actual practice the "cost of capital" to the firm may be more difficult to ascertain than our simple example would lead one to believe.

$0.50(\$1,500 - \$1,250) = \$125$. The net savings each year would then be $\$1,500 - \$125 = \$1,375$. The present value "after taxes" is now:

$$- \$5,500 + \$1,375 \left[\frac{(1 + 0.10)^4 - 1}{0.10(1 + 0.10)^4} \right] + \$500 \, \frac{1}{(1 + 0.10)^4}$$

or:

$$- \$5,500 + \$4,359 + \$342 = - \$799$$

Sometimes the decision situation requires a choice among a number of machines or other investment opportunities. Typically, the alternatives will render equal service and the choice is made on the basis of minimum cost, either in terms of present worth cost or equivalent annual cost. As long as the service lives of the assets are the same, either the present worth principle or the equivalent annual cost principle may be used. In decisions involving assets of different service lives, the equivalent annual cost principle should be used.[7]

If the alternatives are not equal in all respects except cost, it may still be possible to express some of the other differences in terms of cost. Perhaps a greater output capacity can be assigned a monetary value. If one machine is thought to be more reliable, this may be expressed as lower down-time and maintenance costs. If another machine will produce at a consistently higher level of quality, this can perhaps be translated into lower scrap and inspection costs. An attribute such as improved safety for the machine operator can probably not be expressed in dollars, but an economic evaluation can still be made and such intangibles as safety differences can eventually be contrasted to present-worth cost differences. At that point in the evaluation process, a judgment will have to be made. Someone will have to decide whether improved safety is "worth the price."

RATE OF RETURN

The rate of return criterion proposes that an investment should be accepted if the rate of return is greater than the cost (or value) of capital to the firm. A project usually involves an initial outlay of funds followed by a stream of subsequent outlays and incomes. The present value of such a project can usually be calculated using one or a number of different

[7] William T. Morris, *The Capacity Decision System* (Homewood, Ill.: Richard D. Irwin, Inc., 1967), p. 15.

interest rates. One interest rate will result in a present worth equal to zero. This interest rate is the rate of return on the project.

Consider the surface grinder proposal. An outlay of $5,500 was required, of which $500 would be recovered four years later in salvage value. The investment was expected to result in savings of $1,500 per year for four years. In effect, the proposal called for a net outlay of $5,000 and a return of $6,000. However, the outlay occurred early in the life of the investment and the return was then spread out over subsequent years. At what rate of interest would this outlay and income be equivalent? Our solution must be by trial and error. We will specify an interest rate and compare the present value of future receipts and disbursements to our initial outlay of funds. For 7 percent, this present value is:

$$\$1,500 \left[\frac{(1+0.07)^4 - 1}{0.07(1+0.07)^4} \right] + \$500 \ \frac{1}{(1+0.07)^4}$$

or:

$$\$5,081 + \$381 = \$5,462$$

This is less than the $5,500 initial outlay. At 6 percent, the present value is:

$$\$1,500 \left[\frac{(1+0.06)^4 - 1}{0.06(1+0.06)^4} \right] + \$500 \ \frac{1}{(1+0.06)^4}$$

or:

$$\$5,198 + \$396 = \$5,594$$

This is greater than the $5,500 outlay. Then, by linear interpolation:

$$i = 6\% + \frac{\$5,594 - \$5,500}{\$5,594 - \$5,462} \ \%$$
$$= 6\% + 0.7\%$$
$$= 6.7\%$$

The rate of return on the surface grinder is estimated at 6.7 percent. Note that this is not a profit of 6.7 percent. It is a return, and probably not a satisfactory return, on an investment of $5,500. It is calculated *before* the deduction of the cost of funds utilized. Had a rather modest 10 percent been established as a "satisfactory return," the proposal would have been rejected. Note that the decision in this case is the same as that reached with the present-value criterion.

The rate of return and the present-value criteria are equivalent for *simple* investments. They are not equivalent for *nonsimple* investments.[8] With a simple investment there is an initial outlay followed only by cash receipts. A nonsimple investment is one that is not restricted to only an initial net cash outlay. Other cash outlays are interspersed with cash inflows through the life of the investment. This may pose problems with the rate of return criterion, possibly even leading to multiple rates of return for a single investment opportunity.[9] As long as we are concerned with simple projects, however, the rate of return criterion provides an unambiguous measure of profitability.

THE DECISION

The investment decision will require an evaluation. There are advantages to a quantitative evaluation, particularly one that considers the time value of money. Nevertheless, it is unlikely that the decision will be made solely on the basis of a mechanistic quantitative review. First, the quantitative approach itself requires judgment. What value should be used to represent the cost of capital? What will be the life of the asset? What will be its trade in value? And what will be the dollar returns that will be realized each year? These answers will require some experience, some insight, and some judgment. Beyond that which can be quantified, it is likely that other relevant factors will be significant— factors that simply cannot be quantified. The human aspects—questions of morale, prestige, and even "empire building"—are not easily measured. Nevertheless, they may influence the investment decision.

SUMMARY

The investment decision is not easily reversed. The commitment of capital outlay funds is usually expected to be recovered, but over a rather extended time period. For this reason, the analysis preceding the deci-

[8] The terms *simple* and *nonsimple* investments were defined by D. Teichroew, A. A. Robichek, and M. Montalbanoin, "Mathematical Analysis of Returns Under Certainty," *Management Science,* January, 1965, pp. 395–403.

[9] A discussion of these problems is presented in James C. T. Mao, *Quantitative Analysis of Financial Decisions* (London: The Macmillan Company, 1970), pp. 192– 211.

sion may require consideration of the time value of money in addition to possible depreciation schedules.

Time and money are not independent. Money (interest) is usually paid or earned for the use of money that extends over time. A number of interest formulas are introduced to account for the interest that may be earned or paid in an investment situation. We distinguish among the present value of an investment, a sum that has accumulated over a number of interest periods, and a series of equal payments. We also distinguish between compound-interest calculations and effective-interest calculations.

Depreciation accounts for the lessening in the value of a physical asset. A number of different depreciation models are possible and the selection of a specific model may affect tax outlays. The concept of capital recovery plus return is introduced as a measure of the equivalent annual cost of an asset.

The investment decision may be preceded by one of a number of different methods of evaluation. The payback-period method is the simplest and does not take into consideration the time value of money. The decision is made after considering the annual savings resulting from the investment and the cost of that investment. The present-value and the rate-of-return methods do take into consideration the time value of money. These methods can be shown to be equivalent for simple investments, that is, investments involving an initial outlay followed by only cash receipts.

Following the evaluation, the investment decision should be made. It is likely that subjective elements, such as prestige and safety, may then be interjected into the evaluation process.

QUESTIONS AND PROBLEMS

1. What is a good *return* on an investment? What factors are relevant in answering this question?

2. What is the difference between functional and physical depreciation?

3. What is meant by capital recovery and return?

4. What are the essential parameters of a value-time depreciation function?

5. Why does the payback method of evaluation not use savings *after* depreciation?

6. What amount will be accumulated by each of the following investments?

    a. $500 at 5 percent compounded annually over 8 years.

    b. $1,200 at 8 percent compounded quarterly over 5 years.

    c. A year-end series of payments of $100 compounded annually at 6 percent for 10 years.

    d. $50 every 6 months compounded semiannually at 6 percent for 10 years.

7. How much must be invested to accumulate the following amounts?

    a. $1,000 in 10 years at 4 percent compounded semiannually.

    b. $500 in 5 years at 8 percent by equal year-end payments.

8. What interest rate compounded annually is involved if $5,000 results in $6,000 in 5 years?

9. What interest rate is necessary for a sum of money to double itself in 20 years?

10. An asset was bought for $4,800. It was estimated that it would last for 12 years and be worth $200 as scrap. After 5 years of operation, the unit was sold for $1,000. The interest rate was 6 percent.

    a. What was the anticipated equivalent annual cost of capital recovery plus return?

    b. What was the actual cost?

11. A prospective venture is described by the following receipts and disbursements:

Year End	Receipts	Disbursements
0	0	$800
1	$ 200	0
2	400	200
3	1,000	0

At an interest rate of 6 percent, describe the desirability on the basis of the present-worth criterion; the equivalent annual cost criterion.

12. A warehouse can be built for $80,000 and will have no salvage value. The annual value of storage space less maintenance and operating costs is estimated at $12,600.

    a. What rate of return is in prospect if the warehouse is used for 8 years?

    b. If the warehouse is used for 10 years?

13. A firm is considering an investment in computation facilities that will cost $200,000. The following information is relevant:

Annual savings in labor costs of $50,000.

Expected life of 10 years.

No salvage value.

Straight-line depreciation used over expected life.

Taxes estimated at 50 percent of profits.

a. Compute the payback period, ignoring taxes.
b. Compute the payback period with taxes.
c. At an interest rate of 10 percent, calculate the present value of the investment.
d. At an interest rate of 10 percent, calculate the equivalent annual cost of the investment.
e. What is the rate of return for the investment?

some quantitative
approaches

Figure as far as you can, then add judgment [1]

The manager must often plan in the face of an uncertain future. He may also have to make some comparisons when the unit of comparison— the scale of measurement—is not easily defined. Still, a decision may be required. The forward-looking manager is likely to realize that, although not all aspects of the decision situation lend themselves to a quantitative approach, it is still advantageous to carry the quantitative analysis as far as possible before adding the subjective elements. After drawing upon the results of quantitative analyses, some qualitative comparisons and judgments, and perhaps a little intuition, a sound decision can be made.

It is interesting to note that in dealing with the physical aspects of our environment, a substantial body of physical laws have been accumulated upon which to base comparisons and make a decision. How much fertilizer and how much water should be applied, and when, to a crop of lettuce? How large an electric motor should be used to turn a water pump of some specific capacity? The decisions will likely rest upon objective and quantitative information. This is due, in part, to the nature of the subject matter. It is also due to the method that has been employed

---

[1] H. G. Thuesen, and W. J. Fabrycky, *Engineering Economy* (3rd ed.) (Englewood Cliffs, N.J.: Prentice-Hall, Inc., 1964), pp. 190–92.

164

to study the many dimensions of the natural and physical world—the scientific method.

The method of science is a method of experimentation. Observation leads to the recognition and the definition of a problem. If a possible explanation is seen, this is proposed in the formulation of a hypothesis. The hypothesis is then tested through experimentation and either accepted or rejected. The criteria of the method of science include a number of standards that might best be described as ideals to be approximated, if not fully attained.[2] Objectivity or *intersubjective testability* is the requirement that the results be capable of test and confirmation by anyone. In effect, the "truths" that are only accessible to a privileged few, such as mystics, are not the "truths" that meet this standard. A second criterion is that of *reliability,* or sufficient degree of confirmation. *Precision* is also desired. Concepts and relationships should be clear and sharply defined. These same relationships should also be coherent and tie together into a *systematic structure.* A web of knowledge should be the result, rather than a collection of facts like a telephone directory. The fifth and final criterion is the requirement for *comprehensiveness* in knowledge. With the assistance of such devices as radio telescopes and electron microscopes, which permit us to extend the limits of our senses, we are able to acquire a more complete and detailed understanding of a subject area.

The Systematic Approach

The scientific method may have achieved its greatest successes in the natural and physical sciences. However, its use has not been limited to these areas. In the late 1800s, Frederick W. Taylor conducted and reported upon a number of careful experiments in the industrial environment.[3] Taylor's shovel study in a steel mill is an example of the controlled experimental approach. It had always been assumed that the largest shovel that a man could fill and carry was the best size in terms of maximum productivity. Taylor questioned this "reasonable assumption." After

---

[2] Herbert Feigl, "The Scientific Outlook: Naturalism and Humanism," in Herbert Feigl and May Brodbeck, ed., *Readings in the Philosophy of Science* (New York: Appleton-Century-Crofts, Inc., 1953), pp. 8–18.

[3] Frederick Winslow Taylor, *Scientific Management* (comprising "Shop Management," "The Principles of Scientific Management," and "Testimony before the Special House Committee") (New York: Harper and Brothers, 1911).

testing a number of variables, Taylor determined that the one significant variable affecting productivity was the combined weight of the shovel and its load. With too little weight, too many trips were required to move a given amount of material. With too much weight, the worker tired easily and moved slowly. The optimum load, at least for a "first-class" worker, was in the neighborhood of 20 pounds. Since the density of the materials in this steel mill varied greatly, a shovel was designed for each class of material. A small shovel was used to move iron ore; a much larger shovel was used to move rice coal. The result was a significant increase in productivity.

Taylor was responsible for a number of studies leading to increases in productivity. More important, he suggested a systematic approach to the study of such problems in an organizational setting. As a result of his work, Taylor is frequently credited with being the father of scientific management. His contemporaries in the movement include Henry L. Gantt, who was primarily concerned with methods of work-scheduling, and Frank and Lillian Gilbreth, who developed motion study in their search for "the one best way."

The past two to three decades have seen a significant increase in the use of the scientific method in organizational planning and in decision making. The initial application of the scientific method to military decision making was called *operations research* and was undertaken at the onset of World War II. Interdisciplinary teams of scientists, mathematicians, and engineers were formed, first in England and then in other parts of the world, to recommend courses of action relative to complex military operations. Problems studied were as diverse as (a) the development and coordination of Britain's early warning and anti-aircraft defense plans, (b) the deployment of merchant and escort ships within convoys to minimize losses from submarine attacks, (c) search patterns to be employed against submarines, (d) various strategic bombing patterns and their effectiveness, (e) the laying of mines in the Sea of Japan, and (f) evasive action to be taken by ships under kamikaze attack.

After the war, similar groups were established within many large corporations and civilian government agencies in an attempt to duplicate the military successes. Out of these groups—both military and civilian— evolved an aggregate of quantitative decision models. In more recent years, the area of specialized interest concerned with employing these models has also been referred to as *management science*. Not all quantitative decision models have been the product of interdisciplinary operations research groups and not all applications are classified within the realm of management science. However, many do fall in one or both of these categories, and in any case, the application of management science can be seen as a systematic and quantitative approach.

Applying Management Science

Management science can be considered in a general sense as the use of the scientific method to facilitate management planning and decision making. More specifically, it can be seen as the employment of certain quantitative decision models to solve problems. A systematic procedure to solve problems would include the following four steps.

DEFINE THE PROBLEM

Sometimes *the* major step has been taken with the recognition and the correct definition of the problem. Material and parts shortages may be an all-too-frequent occurrence, resulting in excessive production downtime. Customer complaints may reflect upon the reliability of a product. These problems are fairly straightforward and we can begin to think in terms of a solution. Other problems may not be problems *per se*—they may be only symptoms of problems that still have to be defined. Excessive labor turnover may appear to be a problem. More likely, it is an indication of a problem. The identification of the more basic problem then becomes an important first step toward a solution.

FORMULATE THE MODEL

The model is the idealized replica of reality. It relates, one to another, the significant elements that constitute the decision situation. The efforts of operations researchers have resulted in the identification and modeling of many recurrent processes. These models, in their aggregate, provide the analyst with a capability to resolve many problems. In some cases, it may be necessary for the analyst to modify an existing model. In other cases, it may be necessary to formulate a model unlike any that exist.

A useful by-product of the model formulation step is that the individual responsible for constructing the model will almost always gain a better understanding of the problem. Since the model must express the relationships among the significant variables, these relationships must be understood. Otherwise the model will fail to explain or predict results. The analyst is then forced to study further the important relationships in order to improve his model.

MANIPULATE THE MODEL

The next step is the manipulation of the model itself. We seek the values of the variables under our control that will yield an optimum or nearly optimum measure of effectiveness. In the deterministic inventory model of an earlier chapter, TC (total cost) was given as the measure of effectiveness, and it was related to:

R (the annual requirement)
S (the order cost)
C (the unit price)
I (the carrying cost) and
Q (the order quantity)

as follows:

$$TC = \frac{RS}{Q} + Q\,\frac{CI}{2}$$

This equation then constitutes our model. The order quantity is the only variable under our control. As a result, we will choose to manipulate the model by taking the first derivative of TC with respect to Q, setting this equal to 0, and solving for Q. We have:

$$Q = \sqrt{\frac{2RS}{CI}}$$

as that value of Q that will minimize total cost.

In addition to analytical manipulation of the model, we could have used a numerical or iterative approach, or simulated sampling. When the model is complex or where we must evaluate a wide range of operational possibilities, it may be desirable to use a digital computer.

MAKE THE DECISION

The model has likely taken us part of the way to the point of decision. Now we have to add judgment. If the model were a complete and accurate representation of reality, we would need to go no further, but this is not likely to be the case. In the inventory example, the decision maker may feel that the supplier of the part in question faces the possibility of a strike. The calculated economic order quantity may then be changed to reflect this added information.

Linear Programming

A basic and persistent problem facing the manager is that of resource *allocation*. Money, space, personnel, machines, materials, and even time are resources that are available, but always in limited quantities that must be judiciously distributed. A dollar can be spent for advertising or to improve the capital facilities or for a wage increase; it cannot be spent in all three places at the same time. In addition, men must be assigned to machines; salesmen must be assigned to sales territories. In-coming orders must be assigned to plants, then possibly to similar work centers, and even then to specific man-machine stations. Available stocks of materials, labor, and machines must be allotted among the various products that may be produced. In each case, the resources are likely to be available in a specific amount and this amount constitutes a limitation. (When all the men, or dollars, or materials, and so forth are allotted —there usually are no more.) These allotments are usually made toward some total objective, such as to maximize profits.

Linear programming is a method for finding the optimal solution to allocation problems. In general, it is applicable when there exists a large number of variables that are linearly related, interacting within boundaries or constraints that are also linear.

THE ASSIGNMENT MODEL

A special case of the general linear programming problem exists when it is necessary to assign each of a number of means to an equal number of requirements on a one-for-one basis. The assignment model could have been used to allocate jobs to different contractors on a one-to-one basis so as to minimize total cost (pages 70-71).

In the event the means are not equal to the requirements, we can still "force-fit" the problem into the assignment model by the addition of either dummy means or dummy requirements. Consider the following situation: A trucking firm has a surplus of trucks in cities, 1, 2, 3, 4, and 5 (one each) and a deficit in cities A, B, C, D, E, and F (again, one each). The distance between the numbered and the lettered cities are shown in Table 9-1.

Table 9-1

DISTANCE FOR MOVING VEHICLES (IN MILES).

		TO CITY					
		A	B	C	D	E	F
	1	13	11	16	23	19	9
FROM	2	11	19	26	16	17	13
CITY	3	12	11	4	9	6	10
	4	7	15	9	14	14	13
	5	9	13	12	8	14	11
	Dummy	0	0	0	0	0	0

Note that because there was one less means than requirement, a dummy city with a surplus truck was established.

An optimal assignment would be the movement of vehicles as follows: 1 to B, 2 to F, 3 to C, 4 to A, 5 to D, and Dummy to E. In effect, E would actually receive no vehicle and the total distance that trucks would have to be moved would be $11 + 13 + 4 + 7 + 8 + 0 = 43$ miles.

Near optimal if not optimal solutions to the preceding job-contractor and vehicle city-city assignment problems could have been reached with some common sense and a few trial and error attempts. However, in assignment situations, the number of possible combinations of assignments is n ! , or for the vehicle city-city problem, $6 \times 5 \times 4 \times 3 \times 2 \times 1 = 720$ combinations. With 20 or more means (or requirements), the number of possible assignments becomes too large to handle without assistance from a computational scheme such as the assignment algorithm.

THE TRANSPORTATION MODEL

The transportation model is a generalization of the assignment model, but still a special case of the general linear programming model. Again, we wish to allocate from means to requirements. Now however, only the total number of units at the origins must equal the total number of units required at the destinations. If this condition is not met, dummy units are introduced. More than one unit can be shipped from an origin or can be required at a destination. In addition, the number of points of origin may not have to equal the number of points of destination.

Assume that the same trucking firm in the earlier example also deploys trailers. At the start of the next week there will be a surplus of 6, 9, 7, and 5 trailers in cities 1, 2, 3, and 4, respectively. Cities A, B, and C will have a deficit of 8, 7, and 9 trailers, respectively. The cost of moving a trailer from a surplus city to a deficit city is given in Table 9-2.

Table 9-2

COST OF MOVING VEHICLES (IN DOLLARS).

| | | DEFICIT CITY | | |
		A	B	C
	1	26	32	28
SURPLUS	2	19	27	16
CITY	3	39	21	32
	4	18	24	23

The solution sought is one that will minimize the total cost of moving vehicles. In this example, and the earlier two, the assumption of linearity must be met. To move a vehicle from city 1 to city A would cost $26. To move two vehicles over the same route would cost $2 \times \$26$ or $52. There is no quantity discount for volume movements. Also, in the preceding three examples, either distance or cost was to be minimized. Effectiveness can also be expressed in terms of profit rather than cost and the solution can be in terms of maximizing an effectiveness function.

THE GENERAL LINEAR PROGRAMMING MODEL

The mathematical formulation, together with the *simplex method* of solution of the general linear programming model, was developed by G. B. Dantzig in the late 1940s. This method is significant because it is applicable to the general class of problems requiring the optimization of a linear effectiveness function, subject to linear constraints. The simplex method employs an iterative computational routine whereby successive solutions are developed in a systematic pattern until the optimal solution is achieved. The method may be used to solve *any* linear programming problem.

The general linear programming model can be illustrated in graphic terms. With two (or even three) variables the problem can be expressed and a solution achieved through graphic methods. Such a sample problem will be presented. However, the simplex method would have to be used for the more profound problems.

Assume that two products are to be manufactured. A single unit of product A requires 2.4 minutes of punch-press time and 5.0 minutes of assembly time. The profit from product A is $0.60 per unit. A single unit of product B requires 4.0 minutes of punch-press time and 2.5 minutes of welding time. The profit for product B is $0.70 per unit. The remaining available capacity of the punch-press department, the welding department, and the assembly department is 1,200, 600, and 1,500 minutes per week. All of these data are summarized in Table 9-3. How many units

Table 9-3

MANUFACTURING AND MARKETING DATA FOR PRODUCTS A AND B.

Department	Product A	Product B	Capacity
Punch-press	2.4 min.	4.0 min.	1,200 units
Welding	0.0	2.5	600
Assembly	5.0	0.0	1,500
Profit	$0.60	$0.70	

of product A and product B should be produced each week to maximize total profit?

In algebraic terms, we wish to specify the production quantities of products A and B in order to maximize:

$$TP = \$0.60 \ A + \$0.70 \ B$$

subject to:

$$2.4 \ A + 4.0 \ B \le 1,200$$
$$0.0 \ A + 2.5 \ B \le 600$$
$$5.0 \ A + 0.0 \ B \le 1,500$$
$$A \ge 0 \ \text{and} \ B \ge 0$$

The graphical equivalent of the above is shown in Figure 9-1. The three linear restrictions are the capacities of the punch-press, welding, and assembly departments. A solution, in the form of a product mix, must not exceed any of these restrictions. The shaded area constitutes the region of feasible solutions. For example, 200 units of product A and 100 units of product B would be a feasible solution in that none of the restrictions would be violated. The resulting profit would be:

$$TP = \$0.60 \ (200) + \$0.70 \ (100)$$
$$= \$120.00 + \$70.00$$
$$TP = \$190.00 \ \text{per week}$$

However, is this the optimal solution—the maximum profit? Not likely!

Figure 9-1

Maximizing profit for products A and B.

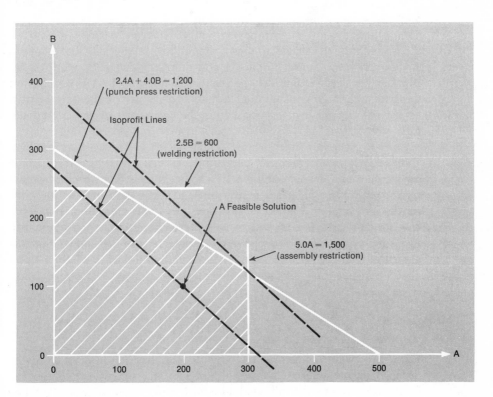

The optimal solution will be achieved where \$0.60 A + \$0.70 B is maximized, subject to the given capacity limitations. The relationship between products A and B is $B = 1.167\ A$. In effect, the profit realized on product B is 1.167 times that realized on product A. Any product mix that results in the same total profit can be sketched with an isoprofit line. Such a product mix would be achieved as follows: With every unit reduction in product B, there must be added 1.167 units of product A. An isoprofit line that yields a $TP = \$190.00$ is sketched in Figure 9-1. It includes the product mix of 200 A and 100 B; it also includes the mix of 83 A and 200 B.

It is possible to visualize in Figure 9-1 a family of isoprofit lines that are parallel to one another. We seek that single isoprofit line that still has at least one point in the region of feasible production quantity combinations and that is a maximum distance from the origin. The member that satisfies this condition is also sketched in Figure 9-1. It intersects the region of feasible solutions at the extreme point of $A = 300$, $B = 120$, and represents a total profit of $0.60\ (300) + \$0.70\ (120) = \$264.00$. No other production quantity combination would result in a higher profit and still satisfy the capacity limitations.

Alternate production programs with the same profit may exist when the isoprofit line is parallel to one of the limiting restrictions. For example, if the relative profits of product A and product B were $B = 1.67\ A$, the isoprofit lines would parallel the restriction imposed by the punch-press department. An optimal solution would then be any production quantity combination along that line and within the assembly and welding department restrictions.

The preceding illustration includes only 2 activities or products competing for scarce resources. Had there been 3 activities, we still could have achieved a graphic solution. With 30 activities this would obviously have been impossible. As a matter of fact, in the case of 4 or more activities, the simplex method will be necessary. This algorithm is an iterative process that begins with a feasible solution, tests for optimality, and proceeds toward an improved solution. It can be shown that the algorithm will finally lead to an optimal solution if such a solution exists.

Waiting Lines

A queue or waiting line may be found in a cafeteria, in front of a theater, or in the doctor's office. One may also be seen in a line of cars, buses, and trucks approaching the toll booth of a tunnel, in a stack of aircraft circling an airport, or in a fleet of barges waiting to be unloaded at a pier. Within the business and industrial environment, a queue may consist of stock orders waiting to be posted by a clerk, job programs waiting to be run on the computer, or the flow of items in process waiting at a machine center.

The queuing system begins with a facility that is maintained to meet a demand for service. It also includes the individuals or units that arrive to be serviced and form a waiting line in accordance with a predetermined queue discipline. The units then flow through the system in discrete steps. The queuing system is usually studied with a view toward determining the appropriate capacity of the service facility. This is done in the light of all relevant costs, the characteristics of the arrival pattern, and the queue discipline. The optimum service capacity is one that minimizes the sum of service associated costs and waiting associated costs.

A queuing system can be seen in schematic form in Figure 9-2. Note that units arrive, are serviced, and depart in discrete steps over a time span. The first unit arrived at time $t = 0$, entered the service facility immediately, required three minutes to service, and departed at $t = 3$ minutes. The second unit arrived at $t = 4$, entered the facility immediately, and left at $t = 6$ minutes. Note that the service facility was idle

Figure 9-2

A queuing system.

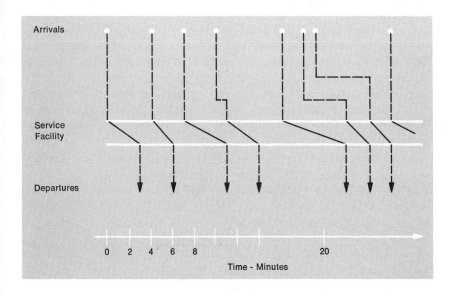

following the departure of the first unit and prior to the arrival of the second. The third unit was handled in routine fashion but the fourth unit arrived and had to wait one minute before it could enter the service facility. After 20 minutes, one unit was being serviced and two units were in a queue; these were then serviced on the first-come, first-served basis. Because of the randomness in arrival times and service times, an apparent contradiction is possible: The service facility is idle some of the time and at other times units are backed up awaiting work.

Sometimes a queuing system consists of a group of parallel facilities, such as the checkout counters in a supermarket. At other times, sequential service stages are necessary. A work piece may have to pass through a series of work stations, possibly waiting in turn at each station, before it is completed.

Queuing systems are customarily analyzed in the context of two classes of costs: a service facility cost and a waiting cost. When a unit joins a waiting line or is being serviced, a waiting cost is incurred. An aircraft circling an airport is consuming fuel; so is a bus waiting in a toll line. In addition, the airplane and the bus cannot be used for other activities. The aircraft crew and the bus driver may have to be paid additional wages for the extra time spent on the job. Also, the passengers are likely to become more and more irate as they wait in the queue, especially if the wait is unexpected. This last input may be the most difficult to measure, but it is also a cost of delay. Just as the customer in the supermarket might not return if the checkout lines always seem excessive in length, so the prospective customer may seek other entertainment if the line in front of the theater seems too long.

The service facility usually represents a capital investment plus operating and maintenance costs and wages for personnel. A larger facility may permit a faster average service time. Alternately, parallel facilities of the same capacity may be added. In each case, the service facility cost will increase. Since increasing the service capacity will lead to a reduction in the waiting time, it is appropriate to increase service capacity up to the point where the *sum* of the waiting costs and service costs is at a minimum.

The study of queuing systems necessarily involves the pattern of arrivals and service times. The most general and perhaps the simplest case assumes that both the arrival rate and the service rate are expected values from independent Poisson distributions. The arrival and service rates are independent of time, queue length, or any other property of the waiting-line system. With the above assumptions, and given specific arrival and service distribution data, one can easily calculate the average number of units in the system and the average waiting time; and, if the waiting costs and facilities costs are known, the least expensive service rate can be established. From this simple case, the study of queuing systems can become progressively more difficult. Other arrival and service distributions may be assumed. The arrival rate may not be independent of queue length. People may leave the queue. As the proposed model describing the real-world system attempts to become more and more accurate, its mathematical complexity increases. In the efforts to capture many of the subtleties of waiting lines, this mathematical modeling has been carried to as sophisticated a level of development as the study of any management decision situation.

Manufacturing Progress Functions

Many manufacturing operations are repetitive, but of low volume. A shipyard may secure a contract to build 2 tankers or an aircraft firm may be successful in its bid to produce 200 fighter aircraft. A firm in the machine tool industry may set up a production run for 100 surface grinders. Much of the work undertaken in any job shop is within the range of these production quantities.

It is not uncommon in instances of limited production quantities for the manager to expect, and even to plan on, reductions in the time necessary to manufacture successive production units. The manufacturing progress function is the graphic or analytical expression used to predict these manufacturing improvements; it is expressed as a predicted reduction in direct labor man-hours from one unit to the next. A number of other terms are also used to describe this same planning tool. The learning curve, the experience curve, the improvement curve, and the production acceleration curve all refer to the method of predicting a reduction in the direct labor man-hours necessary to accomplish a unit of work.

The empirical evidence in support of specific and predictable manufacturing improvements was first noted in the aircraft industry. It was observed that the direct labor man-hours necessary to complete a unit of product, for example, an airplane, would decrease by a constant percentage each time the production quantity was doubled. For example, a typical rate of improvement in the aircraft industry is 20 percent between doubled quantities. This establishes an 80 percent progress function. If the first production aircraft requires 100,000 direct labor man-hours, the second will require 100,000 (0.80) = 80,000 man-hours, the fourth will need 80,000 (0.80) = 64,000 man-hours, the eighth will require

64,000 (0.80) = 51,200 man-hours, and so forth. The progression shows why "follow-on" contracts in low-volume production are much more economical than the original contract and why low-volume military and commercial aircraft and spacecraft production is so expensive.

THE SHAPE OF THE PROGRESS FUNCTION

The initial formulation of the progress function was as a *cumulative average* rather than a *unit* model. The cumulative average time rather than the unit time was assumed to decrease by a constant percentage as production quantities were doubled. Both models will do essentially the same thing; but since the unit model is a more sensitive planning and control device, it is now most often used.

All unit models rest on the same assumption of a constant percentage improvement as the production quantities double. As a result, all progress functions will have the same general shape and any function can be defined if the number of direct labor man-hours required to complete the first unit is established and the subsequent rate of improvement is specified.

The number of direct labor man-hours required to produce the first production unit will depend upon three factors: First, the previous experience and the relevance of this experience. A firm with previous analogous experience should take less time on the first unit than a firm without this experience. Second, the amount of preproduction effort will influence the man-hours needed to complete the first unit. A firm that does a great deal of tooling-up in advance will take less time on early production units than a firm that tools-up during the production run. Third, and most obvious, the characteristics—the complexity and size—of the unit itself will have a direct bearing on the production time.

The rate of improvement following the completion of the first unit will also depend upon the preceding three factors. In addition, the effort put forth to achieve a reduction will affect the percentage improvement. In part this will also be dependent upon the opportunity for improvement. If the time required to manufacture the first unit is high, subsequent improvements may come rather easily. In effect, the time required to complete the first unit and subsequent improvements are not independent.

THE GRAPHICAL FUNCTION

A major reason for the initial acceptance and popularity of the manufacturing progress function is the relative ease with which it can be applied. Consider the initial illustration of a first production aircraft projected at 100,000 direct labor man-hours and subsequent improvements along an 80 percent progress function. On arithmetic paper, the projected man-hours are given in Figure 9-3. The unit times for the third or seventh aircraft can be read from the graph by interpolation.

On arithmetic graph paper, equal numerical differences are represented by equal distance. On logarithmic paper, the linear distance between any two quantities is dependent upon the *ratio* of those two quantities. As a result, if the progress function is plotted on double logarithmic paper, a straight line will result. This can be seen in Figure 9-4. The advantages of using log-log paper are the ability to use a straight line and the compression of the ordinate and abscissa. In the first case, the curve can be plotted from only two points or one point and the slope. Second, a large quantity of units can be presented on a single graph without losing the precision in the lower unit numbers, where the significant reductions are taking place.

The relative ease of using a double logarithmic graphical repre-

Figure 9-3

An 80 per cent progress curve with unit number 1 at 100,000 man-hours.

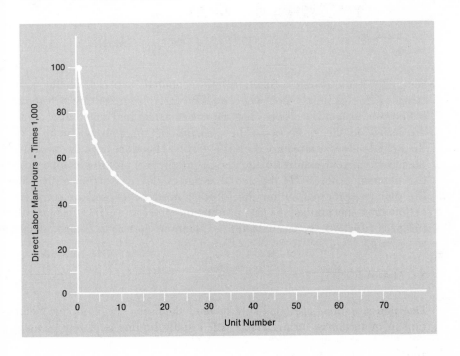

Figure 9-4

An 80 per cent progress curve with unit number 1 at 100,000 man-hours.

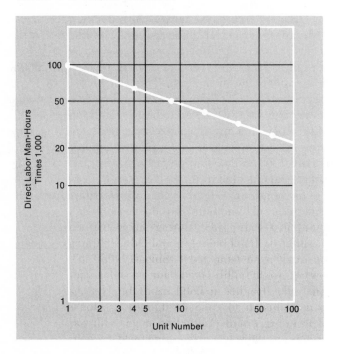

sentation of the progress function has accounted for much of the popularity of this planning tool. The progress curve, representing a forecast, is first established. Decisions that require financial and scheduling inputs are based on this projection. Then, as production units are completed, the actual values are recorded on the graph. This then provides a control device—a current exhibit of the actual production progress compared to the planned progress. If the actual progress deviates significantly from the planned progress, either the forecast must be revised or corrective action must be applied to the production process. In this fashion, the progress function serves to facilitate planning and as a control device.

SUMMARY

Decision situations are not likely to lend themselves to complete definition in quantitative terms. There will usually be one or a few elements

180

that can only be handled through qualitative comparisons and the exercise of judgment. Nevertheless, those elements that can be quantified should be handled in an objective fashion. A systematic procedure for applying management science would include the following four steps: define the problem, formulate the model, manipulate the model, and then make the decision. Three classes of quantitative decision models are presented in this chapter.

The allocation problem lends itself to solution through linear programming. The assignment model, the transportation model, and the general linear programming model are presented as means of allocating such resources as time, materials, machines, personnel, space, and money. The first two of these are special cases of the general linear programming model and are easier to resolve. In the general linear programming model, with three or more activities competing for scarce resources, the simplex algorithm must be employed. This algorithm is an iterative process that proceeds on a step-by-step basis toward an optimum solution.

The study of queuing systems (waiting lines) involves a pattern of arrivals, a service facility, and a pattern of service times. The service facility is likely to represent a capital investment plus some operating and maintenance costs and wages for personnel. Costs are also assumed to be incurred through delays in processing units as they arrive. A solution is desired that will minimize the sum of the waiting costs and the service costs. The service capacity is then established that will minimize the sum of these two costs.

In limited, low-volume production operations, it is reasonable to expect improvements from one unit to the second. The manufacturing progress function is a means of describing and predicting manufacturing improvements as a reduction in the direct labor man-hours necessary to complete each unit. The assumption is made that the direct labor man-hours will decrease by a constant percentage each time the production quantity is doubled. If this assumption is valid in a given situation, then the manufacturing progress function can be defined with the establishment of the time necessary to complete the first production unit and the subsequent rate of improvement between double production quantities. The function may be expressed both analytically and graphically. The latter approach is relatively simple to employ and explains the widespread popularity of this planning device.

This chapter concludes the section dealing with planning and planning tools. The next section will begin the behavioral treatment of the management functions. The individual will be treated first, then simple group processes. In the succeeding section, the organization will be introduced as the structure of individual and group activities within which the organizational objective must be achieved.

QUESTIONS AND PROBLEMS

1. List the criteria of the scientific method. Discuss these in the context of some "truth" of management, such as "Authority must equal responsibility" or "Orders should follow the proper channels of communication."

2. Obtain two or three definitions of *operations research* and *management science* and compare them.

3. List the steps in the systematic procedure for applying management science. Illustrate these in the context of some hypothetical management problem.

4. Define some allocation problems that might be resolved with the assignment model of linear programming. The transportation model. The general linear programming model.

5. What is a feasible solution? An isoprofit line? The optimal solution?

6. A queuing system is generally studied toward what objective?

7. Cite an example of a queuing system where the arrival rate or the service rate is likely to be a constant.

8. Cite examples of queuing systems where (a) parallel facilities may be added to improve the service capacity and (b) the single facility can be enlarged or expanded to improve the service capacity.

9. What must be defined to specify a manufacturing progress function?

10. Why might the extent of preproduction effort affect both the first unit man-hours and the subsequent rate of improvement?

11. Three customers in a certain sales territory have requested technical assistance. Three technicians are available for assignment, with the distance in miles from each technician to each customer being as follows:

		CUSTOMER		
		A	B	C
	1	470	580	410
TECHNICIAN	2	385	920	740
	3	880	550	430

On a trial-and-error basis, find the assignment that will minimize travel.

12. A small machine shop has capability in turning, milling, drilling, and welding. The machine capacity is 16 hours per day in turning, 16 hours per day in milling, 8 hours per day in drilling, and 8 hours per day in welding. Two products—A and B—are under consideration. Each will yield a net profit of $0.25 per unit and will require the following amount of machine time:

		PRODUCT	
		A	B
	Turning	0.064	0.106
OPERATION	Milling	0.106	0.053
	Drilling	0.000	0.080

Solve graphically for the number of units of each product that should be scheduled to maximize profits.

13.   How might waiting and service facility costs be ascertained in the checkout station of a supermarket?

14.   Sketch on arithmetic and on log-log paper the progress function for 100 units defined by a first unit of 10 man-hours and an 80 percent function. On the same graph paper, sketch the function requiring 8 man-hours for the first unit followed by a 90 percent function.

THE HUMAN ELEMENT: INDIVIDUAL AND GROUP PROCESSES

PART THREE

human motivation

10

*In this world there are only two tragedies.
One is not getting what one wants,
and the other is getting it.*

OSCAR WILDE

There are few topics as pivotal to effective management as human motivation. Unless individuals and groups are willing to strive toward organizational objectives, the efforts spent on establishing plans are largely wasted; meticulous organizational designs and control systems are also wasted, lacking the will of people to implement them. The importance of motivation is universal, being as significant for an army platoon, a church, a university, or a hillbilly band, as it is for a giant corporation or a small machine shop. Successful football coaches may pride themselves on getting their players "up" for the game; military offers strive to develop "morale," and corporate leaders work to generate in their subordinates a sense of involvement and an identification with or commitment to the organization's goals and problems. These are all variations on the theme of motivation, the recognized need to create or cultivate an internal need within individuals to perform.

As we shall see shortly, motivation is an extremely complex subject. For one thing, motivation, like human learning, cannot be directly observed and measured. Rather we infer its existence from observations of behavior, from interviews, and from a variety of projective techniques. We measure the *effects* of motivation and thereby reach conclusions about the person's motivational state. Since a given behavior pattern may be explainable in terms of several individual motives or combinations of

187

motives, erroneous conclusions about the person's motivation are quite common. For example, the inordinate intake of food by the obese is not always in response to bodily demands for nutrition. The destructive tendencies of children or adults may be a manifestation of the need for attention and recognition. The grim demand for a salary increase from an employee may be motivated by a desire for an increased sense of security or status rather than a sole desire for material rewards.

Examining the dynamics of motivation objectively is made even more difficult by the tendency to develop rigid subconscious motivation models. We have all observed human behavior and have all reached conclusions about underlying motives. This process of interpretation is frequently below the level of awareness, as are the conclusions themselves. That is, we do not realize that we are reaching these conclusions. Such subconscious feelings do not lend themselves to rational examination and modification. In fact the existence of such views may prevent subsequent inquiry into the causes of individual behavior. Once firmly established, subjective beliefs are usually slow to change. The student of management should attempt, therefore, to reflect consciously on his notions about the bases of human behavior in organizations. Research based on such questioning has shaken several very sturdy notions about human motivation and behavior.

Although there are an infinite variety of views about the human being as a worker, we shall examine three of the best known and documented. In historical order, these are: (1) Economic Man—Inferior Man, (2) Psychosocial Man, and (3) Ascendant Man.

Economic Man and Inferior Man

Throughout most of history, man was thought to be motivated by the bodily needs necessary for survival. Man worked for his sustenance, for food, for clothing, and for shelter. Work was the sacrifice made by the individual so that he and his dependents might live. The pleasures, if any, made possible by hard work were to be enjoyed outside of the workplace. Management attempted to obtain high productivity and general cooperation from its employees through its manipulation of economic rewards.

In order to develop a "feel" for the image of the worker that evidently predominated in the early twentieth century, two approaches to economic man are discussed below. Although they are presented separately for the sake of simplicity, *scientific management* and *paternalism* were often combined in real life.

Basing incentives on the prevailing conception of economic man, management theorists and practitioners in the early twentieth century created a variety of monetary reward systems that included time-saving bonuses, differentiated hourly wages, piece-rate systems, and profit sharing. Nor were these diverse pay systems the only managerial consequence of this economic man image. If man was inspired to produce by the promise of economic reward, then management owed it to workers, as well as stockholders, to provide conditions conducive to maximum output.

What might such conditions be?

1. Jobs simple enough so that their conceptual and physical contents could be mastered quickly.
2. High-speed, special-purpose machines.
3. High degree of standardization of components, tools, procedures, and working conditions.
4. Close supervision by experts.

The worker, it was thought, would respond positively to a workplace composed of highly specialized tasks, standardization, and overall close direction and control by management. Management was to manage and the workers to work.

Indicative of the worker's role in this scheme is the following incident reported by Frederick W. Taylor, the "father of scientific management":

> "Schmidt, are you a high-priced man?"
> "Vell, I don't know vat you mean."
> "Oh, yes, you do. What I want to know is whether you are a high-priced man or not."
> "Vell, I don't know vat you mean."
> "Oh, come now, you answer my questions. What I want to find out is whether you are a high-priced man or one of these cheap fellows here. What I want to find out is whether you want to earn $1.85 a day or whether you are satisfied with $1.15, just the same as all those cheap fellows are getting."
> "Did I vant $1.85 a day? Vas dot a high-priced man? Vell, yes, I vas a high-priced man."

"Oh, you're aggravating me. Of course you want $1.85 a day—every one wants it! You know perfectly well that that has very little to do with your being a high-priced man. For goodness' sake answer my questions, and don't waste any more of my time. Now come over here. You see that pile of pig iron?"

"Yes."

"You see that car?"

"Yes."

"Well, if you are a high-priced man, you will load that pig iron on that car tomorrow for $1.85. Now do wake up and answer my question. Tell me whether you are a high-priced man or not."

"Vell—did I get $1.85 for loading dot pig iron on dot car tomorrow?"

"Yes, of course you do, and you get $1.85 for loading a pile like that every day right through the year. That is what a high-priced man does, and you know it just as well as I do."

"Vell, dot's all right. I could load dot pig iron on the car tomorrow for $1.85, and I get it every day, don't I?"

"Certainly you do—certainly you do."

"Vell, den, I vas a high-priced man."

"Now, hold on, hold on. You know just as well as I do that a high-priced man has to do exactly as he's told from morning till night. You have seen this man here before, haven't you?"

"No, I never saw him."

"Well, if you are a high-priced man, you will do exactly as this man tells you tomorrow, from morning till night. When he tells you to pick up a pig and walk, you pick it up and you walk, and when he tells you to sit down and rest, you sit down. You do that right straight through the day. And what's more, no back talk. Now a high-priced man does just what he's told to do, and no back talk. Do you understand that? When this man tells you to walk, you walk; when he tells you to sit down, you sit down, and you don't talk back at him. Now you come on to work here tomorrow morning and I'll know before night whether you are really a high-priced man or not." [1]

The occurrence reported above may be an extreme instance of scientific management in operation. With a work force made up largely of immigrants, poorly educated and accustomed to domination by their superiors, this apparently crude treatment appears to have been extremely effective. The report does exemplify the managment assumptions that the dominant motivator of worker behavior is money. Note that all planning and controlling is performed by management, and there appears little concern for the worker's ego or for the potential value of the worker's ideas and suggestions.

Scientific management, as practiced by Taylor, was eminently successful in measuring worker output and wages. It should be noted, how-

[1] Frederick W. Taylor, *Principles of Scientific Management* (New York: Harper & Brothers, 1911), pp. 44–46.

ever, that Taylor's principles went far beyond concern for motivation. His insistence upon scientific worker selection and training, determination of the best way to do each job, and his general stress upon objectivity, measurement, and analysis in place of "seat-of-the-pants-management" all probably contributed to the success of his system. It may well be, moreover, that the typical worker in the early 1900s was primarily motivated by subsistence needs. Thus Taylor's emphasis upon greater financial rewards for high output could have been the most effective incentive possible for those workers and at that time. On the other hand, it appears unwise to construct general and lasting conclusions about human motivation from the early consequences of scientific management.

PATERNALISM—INFERIOR MAN

The paternalistic school of management thought, which seemed to peak in the 1920s, stressed management's responsibility to provide a broad variety of economic benefits for employees. Largely as a reaction to a growing union movement in the United States, management began to show concern over workers' general economic welfare. Thus businesses began to provide housing, medical services, insurance programs, education for dependents, food and clothing at reduced prices at company-owned stores, athletic programs, and so forth. These again were largely economic benefits designed to appeal to economic man.

The typical approach was to provide for workers what the manager believed was good for them. Again the manager made the decision and the worker passively accepted it. As "paternalism" implies, the relationship established was that of father and child, superior and inferior, benevolent tyrant and serf. Such an approach carries with it certain (usually implicit) assumptions about the nature of man:

1. His motivation is primarily economic.
2. He needs and desires help in caring for himself and his dependents.
3. He tends to be grateful for the gifts of benefactors. If treated "properly", he will be more productive, will not join labor unions, and will be generally cooperative.

The general validity of each assumption is open to serious question. This should become evident as we progress through the more modern conceptions of human motivation.

Unique and most publicized of such plans was that devised by The Ford Motor Company in 1914. Henry Ford, after announcing a minimum wage for all Ford workers of five dollars per day, created a "sociology department." The task of this department was to assure that the high wage (more than double the previous minimum) was paid only to those deserving it. Investigators were sent to each employee's home, there to question the employee about his views, ethnic background, health, economic status, and so forth; meanwhile the investigator was to observe the condition of the home and neighborhood. Workers could be disqualified (placed on probation and ultimately discharged, unless they reformed) for "excessive use" of liquor, for gambling, for any malicious practice derogatory to good physical manhood or unmoral character, for a dirty household, for an unwholesome diet, for housing boarders, or for "excessive expenditure on foreign relatives," for example.[2] Perhaps predictably, this program lasted only a short time.

Unlike the incentive scheme of scientific management, the paternalistic system did not tie rewards to output. The assumption that management concern about the employee's off-the-job condition would be repaid by an increased motivation to produce has never been established as valid. To the contrary, there are documented instances of worker hostility resulting from an overly indulgent management.[3]

Further insight into the nature and possible consequences of paternalism in international affairs is reflected in the following passage:

> I shall never forget a sad and embittered moment after the war when the Dutch leaders in Java realized for the first time that the desire of the Indonesians to see them leave those lovely emerald islands of the East was no passing emotion and that their empire, the third largest in the world, was tumbling down about them. I remember the governor-general turning to me and saying, "I cannot understand it. Look at what we have done for them. Look at the schools and the hospitals we have given them. A hundred years ago the population was only a few millions, today it is nearly sixty millions. We have done away with malaria, plague and dysentery and given them a prosperous, balanced economy. Everyone has enough to eat. We have given them an honest and efficient administration and abolished civil war and piracy. Look at the roads, the railways, the industries—and yet they want us to go. Can you tell me why they want us to go?" And I felt compelled to say, "Yes, I think I can: I'm afraid it is because you've never had the right look in the eye when you spoke to them."
>
> It may sound inadequate, but just think, for one moment, of the light that is in the eye of a human being when he looks at another human being he loves and respects as an equal. Then remember the look in the eye of the average European when he is in contact with "a lesser breed without the law," and you will understand what I mean. The difference

[2] Alan Nevins, *Ford* (New York: Charles Scribner's Sons, 1954), pp. 551–62.

[3] L. R. Sayles and George Strauss, *Human Behavior in Organizations* (Englewood Cliffs, N.J.: Prentice-Hall, Inc.), pp. 141–43.

between the two, I believe, is the explosive that has blown the Europeans out of one country after another during our time.[4]

Human Relations: Psychosocial Man

In November, 1924, a study was undertaken at the Hawthorne Plant of the Western Electric Company to investigate "the relation of quality and quantity of illumination to efficiency in industry."[5] To the surprise of the researchers, they could find no simple and consistent effect of light variations upon worker output. In the first of three departments studied, output "bobbed up and down without direct relation to the amount of illumination." Output tended to increase in the other two departments as the experiments proceeded, even at times when illumination was reduced.

A second set of experiments again failed to indicate any conclusive association between illumination and productivity. The third group of experiments eliminated natural light from windows by locating two groups of workers in rooms having solely artificial lighting. Once again, the illumination-output hypothesis was unconfirmed, as reported by one of the researchers:

> After the level of illumination in the test group enclosures changed to a lower value, the efficiencies of both the test and control groups increased slowly but steadily. When the level of illumination for the test group finally reached 3 foot-candles, the operatives protested, saying that they were hardly able to see what they were doing, and the production rate decreased. The operatives did maintain their efficiency to this point in spite of the discomfort and handicap of insufficient illumination.[6]

RELAY ASSEMBLY TEST ROOM

Attributing the illumination test results to psychological factors previously considered insignificant, the researchers undertook a new study. Six female relay assemblers were selected for intense observation on the job, plus frequent interviews. Their production was recorded for

[4] Laurens Van Der Post, *The Dark Eye in Africa* (New York: William Morrow & Co., Inc., 1955), pp. 116–17.

[5] F. H. Roethlisberger and W. J. Dickson, *Management and the Worker* (Cambridge: Harvard University Press, 1941), p. 15.

[6] Ibid., p. 16.

two weeks at their usual workplace, and they were given a physical examination before being transferred to a new work room, apart from the much larger group doing similar work. The girls were told of the illumination tests and were informed that this was a new experiment to test the effects of physical conditions on output. They were asked to produce at a comfortable pace and to forward any suggestions for improving their working conditions. All the girls expressed their willingness to participate.

One of the researchers was assigned to the test room as an observer. Supervision was permissive, in place of restrictive atmospheres prevailing in the plant. The research group established a group piece rate for this team, which replaced the group piece rate based upon the output of the 100 relay assemblers in the plant. The girls periodically underwent interviews and physical examinations. Otherwise they worked at their own pace while certain experimental changes were introduced in working hours, rest pauses, and similar variables. Although the research group was again attempting to relate physical conditions to output, they hoped to obtain other insights into the bases for human behavior at work through intensive study of this work group.

These experiments were continued for more than five years. Rest pauses were introduced, then varied in frequency and duration; midmorning and afternoon light lunches were tried; working hours were decreased, then increased. Once again the experiment failed to yield any consistent relationship between physical conditions and output. "The only apparent uniformity was that in each experimental period, output was higher than in the preceding one." What, then, was happening in the relay assembly test room?

Various explanations are offered to interpret the constant increase in the group's productivity. The girls found this new permissive atmosphere enjoyable and comfortable, particularly the new-found freedom to converse while working. Perhaps it was the girls' commitment to an important experiment, a feeling of participation and involvement. The development of a closely woven social group or team with its own spontaneous leadership may also have influenced group output. Evidently the group had committed itself to high productivity and had found ways within itself to attain this objective—virtually regardless of physical working conditions, fatigue, and the absence of expert supervision.[7]

Prevailing views of the worker as economic man, rational man, inferior man now had to be revised. Evidently the worker's feelings, emotions, social needs, beliefs, and attitudes could significantly expand or contract his productivity. The worker's sense of commitment, his feel-

[7] Ibid., pp. 19–127.

ings toward the organization, his ability to organize into productive teams without close supervision were seen as important facets of effective management systems. The "human relations" movement had begun.

BANK WIRING OBSERVATION ROOM

A final Hawthorne study further substantiated the complexity of individual and group motivation. A crew of 14 men who assembled telephone exchange terminal banks were relocated to a new room and a researcher was assigned to them as observer. Nothing else was changed. During the seven months duration of this study, the workers became accustomed to the observer's presence, gradually becoming candid in their discussions with him.

Despite an incentive system designed to reward high group output and high individual output, it was observed that both as individuals and as a group there was purposeful restriction of output. These men had their own idea of a normal day's work, which amounted to wiring two "equipments" per day. As soon as this goal was nearly reached (frequently by noon), the men would begin to slow down and "nurse" the remainder. Those workers considered overly productive by the group were punished by isolation, invective, or by "binging" (being struck on the upper arm by the clenched fist of co-workers).

Other violations of company policy were standard practice within the group. Men frequently traded jobs, which was strictly forbidden. There was substantial informal assistance given some men by others, thus distorting output ratings for individuals. Output records were often distorted in other ways by workers. For example, output late in a given day might not be reported until the next day, or might not be reported at all! Interestingly the man in charge of the group—the group chief— was well aware of these variations from company expectations, yet saw fit to ignore them. He had to "live" with these men from day to day, and their output was considered quite satisfactory by higher echelons. How much was he likely to gain by attempting to strictly enforce company policies? [8]

THE HAWTHORNE IMPACT

The Hawthorne studies had a profound effect on management theory and practice during the 1940s and 1950s. It became increasingly clear that the worker had been viewed in too narrow a light, that motivation

[8] Ibid., pp. 379–548.

was much more complex than previously believed. In particular man's social needs and social forces at the workplace now took center stage. Compare, for example, Elton Mayo's conception of human motivation with that of economic man, as summarized by Edgar Schein.

1. Man is basically motivated by social needs and obtains his basic sense of identity through relationships with others.
2. As a result of the industrial revolution and the rationalization of work, meaning has gone out of work itself and must therefore be sought in social relationships on the job.
3. Man is more responsive to the social forces of the peer group than to the incentives and controls of management.
4. Man is responsive to management to the extent that a supervisor can meet a subordinate's social needs and needs for acceptance.[9]

Although economic man was certainly not laid to rest, there was new emphasis on the worker's other dimensions. Thus managers became more concerned with the feelings and attitudes of workers. Morale and job satisfaction took on added significance, since they were believed to influence productivity. Efforts were made to assure social compatibility among individuals who made up work groups. Employee grievances and suggestions received more sympathetic attention. In fact employee ideas were now frequently requested *before managerial* decisions were made, in order to engender in workers a feeling of involvement and a greater sense of value to the organization. Through efforts such as these, management hoped to marshall the group's social forces toward a commitment to the needs and goals of the organization, rather than the restriction of output or mere passive acceptance of existing systems.

Ascendant Man

As we have seen, historical conceptions of man have tended to focus on certain elements of human motivation. Scientific management stressed economic needs. Paternalism incorporated man's apparent need for a sense of security and stability. To these, the human relationists added their emphasis on the human need for meaningful social relationships, and for treatment as thinking, feeling individuals. Still other limited views

---

[9] Edgar H. Schein, *Organizational Psychology* (Englewood Cliffs, N.J.: Prentice-Hall, Inc., 1965), p. 51. See Elton Mayo, *The Human Problems of an Industrial Civilization* (Boston: Harvard University Press, 1946).

of human needs exist, but have had much less impact upon management theory.

THE ROLE OF NEEDS

Probably today's most widely accepted view of human motivation sees man as being driven by a variety of needs, with the dominating needs shifting in a generally predictable fashion. This theory recognizes man as a complex, changing organism, constantly adapting to his own physical and mental inner states and to his perceptions of the environment.

Before we examine these needs, we should probe the role of needs as behavior determinants. Let us picture an individual who has a need for water. This need is communicated to the brain (consciously or subconsciously) through a sense of discomfort—the mouth and throat feel dry. This discomfort is, of course, unpleasant and the individual seeks relief. He examines his environment and his own perceived abilities, and then decides on an approach designed to satisfy his "thirst." If he is successful, he can forget about the now satisfied need and move on to satisfaction of other needs. Other needs also make themselves felt by stimuli that cause a state of tension within the individual, as indicated by the general model of the motivation mechanism in Figure 10-1. He then attempts to respond in a manner designed to relieve the tension. If the stimulus indicates a need for human association, the individual goes through some process of seeking and of evaluating his alternatives, and then deciding how best to satisfy the perceived social need. The reader may now wish to ask himself how an individual, or a dog, or any other animate organism would behave if all of his needs were completely satisfied? How productive would such a worker be?

In general, as a need stimulates the individual into a motivated state, he may first become restless and uneasy; as the need intensity increases, thoughts and behavior become more purposeful and goal-directed. Beyond a point, however, continued intensification of a need may cause such frustration as to precipitate disorganized or even destructive behavior.

Figure 10-1

A model of the motivation mechanism.

Need ⟹ Stimulus ⟹ Tension ⟹ Instrumental Behavior

Tension rises to such a level that it inhibits rational and creative thought or smoothly coordinated actions. If long-lasting, such severe tension may cause physical and mental illness. It is not quite correct, therefore, to say that the most highly motivated person will be the most productive. The combination of goal-oriented behavior that is flexible, rational, and coordinated is more likely to result from a condition of moderate tension.

A. H. Maslow, originator of the theory developed below, states that human needs generally tend to develop in a certain sequence. He believes that as an existing need is satisfied, another need becomes activated in the individual. Certain needs are seen as basic; they must be satisfied to a degree before higher-level needs are activated. The term "prepotent needs" is used to describe a need more basic than another. Thus Maslow envisions man as having a series of latent needs, each need growing in urgency as other, prepotent needs are to some degree satisfied. That is, each man, and man in general, possesses a "hierarchy of needs," a latent set of needs ranging from the most fundamental to the most advanced.[10]

PHYSIOLOGICAL NEEDS

The most basic of human needs, according to Maslow, are the physiological needs: food, water, oxygen, shelter, and so forth. These are the needs of the body, and they are essentially the same for man or animal. Unless these needs are largely satisfied, they remain the prime determinants of the individual's behavior. Where hunger, for example, is a chronic and critical condition, it is highly unlikely that an individual (or a society) will be much concerned with art or status or grandeur.

> All capacities are put into the service of hunger-satisfaction, and the organization of these capacities is almost entirely determined by the one purpose of satisfying hunger. The receptors and effectors, the intelligence, memory, habits, all may now be defined as hunger-gratifying tools. Capacities that are not useful for this purpose lie dormant, or are pushed into the background. . . . For the man who is extremely and dangerously hungry, no other interest exists but food. He dreams food, he remembers food, he thinks about food, he emotes only about food, he perceives only food and he wants only food.[11]

Nor does such privation affect only one's current actions. The individual experiencing such a long-standing condition structures his long-

[10] This discussion of Abraham Maslow's motivation theory is derived primarily from his article, "A Theory of Human Motivation," *Psychological Review*, L, 1943, 370–96. See also his *Eupsychian Management* (Homewood, Ill.: Richard D. Irwin, Inc., 1965).

[11] Maslow, "A Theory of Human Motivation," p. 370.

term aspirations around this currently critical need. Thus the chronically starving person begins to conceive of Utopia or Heaven as a place where no one is hungry, where food is plentiful and sumptuous. His entire philosophy will revolve around food. Such a man does live "by bread alone." Such a condition is not to be confused with one's appetite for food in an affluent society. Here, with the sources of gratification all about, the hunger sensation is more a signal for anticipated pleasure, rather than crisis. It is thus probably very difficult for the unhungry of the world to fully understand the critically hungry—and vice versa.

SAFETY-SECURITY NEEDS

Although there are some Americans who continuously lack adequate physiological satisfactions, most of our society is reasonably well fed, clothed, housed, and so forth. That is, their physiological needs are typically satisfied. When a need is largely satisfied, that need ceases to exist and thus ceases to influence behavior. A new need now swells in potency and directs the individual towards its gratification.

According to Maslow, the second most prepotent need is the need for safety or security. Having satisfied the bodily survival needs, the individual now seeks to assure that such satisfactions will continue to flow tomorrow and beyond. This becomes his dominant goal, his constant preoccupation, and in the neurotic, an obsession. Some manifestations of this concern about tomorrow in a wealthy society include increasing expenditures for medical insurance and retirement systems, as well as union drives for seniority provisions and the preference of individuals for positions with tenure.

Frequently human behavior that seems irrational has as its basis the preservation of the individual's existing position. For example, consider the executive who refuses to accept a promotion because it involves moving to a new city. At least two security-oriented motives may underlie this decision: (1) This man is comfortable in his current social surroundings and doesn't wish *risking* a move to a less satisfying social environment. (2) The executive may feel *uncertain* that he can handle the new position: the perceived consequences of possible failure outweigh the opportunity for growth. Such a decision, then, may well be based upon a need for security, a desire to preserve the status quo.

The manager who refuses to delegate authority may also be a victim of a strong security need. Could it be that he fears the rapid development of his subordinates, lest they challenge his position? Could it be that he does not want his subordinates to be too visible to higher-level executives, that he fears the comparisons that can be made? It may also be that errors will be made by subordinates to whom substantial authority is delegated, errors that may be attributed to the superior by still higher-level executives, again threatening his established position.

The more physical side of the security need results in locks on doors, pistols in bedroom drawers, seat and shoulder harnesses in automobiles, the fire department, and a plethora of other safeguards. One may expect such safety consciousness to expand as the fundamental needs of immediate survival are increasingly satisfied.

SOCIAL NEEDS

When the individual is physiologically satisfied and feels reasonably secure, he begins to yearn for close social relationships. He feels the need to love and be loved, to become an integral part of a group and its endeavors. The old cliché that man is gregarious, that he possesses the "herd instinct," is supported, but only after the prepotent needs are substantially gratified.

Thus among the most brutal of punishments in many prisons is solitary confinement. At work, the penalty for violation of group norms is often isolation of the offender—completely ignoring his presence. Work groups tend to form social cliques spontaneously and to communicate among themselves, even where the plant layout and management discourage them. Evidently, then, there is a great latent need for acceptance, for communication, for a sense of contribution, for joint work or play. Consequently existing social satisfactions at work are believed to be strong incentives to remain with an employer and to minimize absenteeism, while an unpleasant social milieu has the reverse effect.

ESTEEM NEEDS

Closely related to the need for love and affiliation are the needs for status and respect. The individual desires a positive self-image. He wishes to consider himself strong, able, competent, moral (by his own standards), or generally worthy.

Self-esteem, however, is somewhat influenced by the esteem that others show for the individual. Thus one desires the high regard of others for its own value and also because the high esteem of others helps him to justify high self-esteem. A position of high status and respect within the group reflects upon his capability and his likeability. Thus, having attained physiological satisfaction, a feeling of security, and a sense of belonging, the twin esteem needs emerge into prominence.

Status levels exist in all human groups and have been observed in animals. The well-recognized "pecking order" among chickens is an example. When one wishes to "move up," to "get ahead," he is frequently referring to his status position within the group as well as the economic satisfactions that accompany "success." An employee's request for a wage increase may reflect more than his desire for material benefits. One's wage level is a status symbol indicating one's value and role within the organization. Similarly, an employee may well hesitate to leave a job when he holds high status within the work group, even when the wages or the conditions seem better elsewhere.

GROWTH NEEDS

Assuming substantial satisfaction of the physiological, security, social, and esteem needs, a new need is said to emerge, termed "self-actualization." This refers to man's desire to grow, to develop to his fullest potential, to become what he is capable of becoming. Reflections of this need might be one's desire to upgrade skills or to take on increased responsibilities. More extreme examples might include the artist's need to paint, the author's need to write a better novel, the inventor's need to create the more sophisticated machine.

This last set of hypothesized needs is probably the most difficult to understand and thus the least well accepted. Strong support for the existence of the self-actualization or growth needs is offered by Chris Argyris. Looking at the human being from the point of normal personality development, Argyris sees man tending to develop in the following ways:

1. From passive acceptors to initiators.
2. From dependence to independence.
3. From limited behavioral capacities to diverse capacities.
4. From shallow, fleeting interests to deep sustained interests.
5. From a short time perspective to a lengthy one.
6. From a subordinate position to an equal or superior one.
7. From little self-awareness to great self-awareness and self-control.[12]

He maintains that traditional management—stressing worker-specialization, restrictive rules, and close supervision—frustrate this normal development, resulting in worker hostility and restriction of output.

[12] Chris Argyris, *Personality and Organization* (New York: Harper & Row, Publishers, 1957), pp. 49–53.

The need for self-actualization may be reflected in a drive for achievement. David McClelland provides some intriguing insights here.[13] Using a projective technique, wherein subjects write a story about each of several pictures presented to them, McClelland finds that the stories written by middle-level executives contain more references to achievement than do stories by lower-level managers and top executives. He hypothesizes that an intense achievement motive helps to propel the manager into the middle-management level, and then to top management, at which point the executive's need for achievement eases. This, he says, tends to be the case in large organizations. In small organizations, the top officers tend to be more achievement-oriented than their subordinates.

McClelland holds that society has misinterpreted the meaning that profit has for the achievement-oriented manager. He states:

> If not only the Marxists, but Western economists, and even business-men themselves, end up assuming that their main motive is . . . a quest for profit, it is small wonder that they have a hard time holding their heads high in recent years.
>
> But now research that I have done has come to the businessman's rescue by showing that everyone has been wrong, that is *not* profit per se that makes the businessman tick but a strong desire for achievement, for doing a good job. Profit is simply one measure among several of how well the job has been done, but it is not necessarily the goal itself.[14]

NEED HIERARCHY IN PERSPECTIVE

In contrast to early views on human motivation, which stressed one or a few human motives, Maslow's theory incorporates a diverse group of human motives. Moreover, this theory stresses the tendency of human motives to shift along a generally predictable sequence, rather than seeing man as unchanging and single-tracked (see Figure 10-2). As stated previously, Maslow's theory of human motivation has attained broad acceptance in management circles. This is not to say that the theory is beyond criticism or that we should accept it at face value.

Some often stated reservations include the following:

1. Do needs develop in the indicated sequence? Even Maslow admits wide variations here, although he maintains that his hierarchy is the predominant one.

2. Is security really a distinct need, applying solely to the physiological

---

[13] D. C. McClelland, "Business Drive and National Achievement," *Harvard Business Review*, XL (July–August, 1962), 99–112.

[14] Ibid., p. 100.

Figure 10-2

Hierarchy of needs.

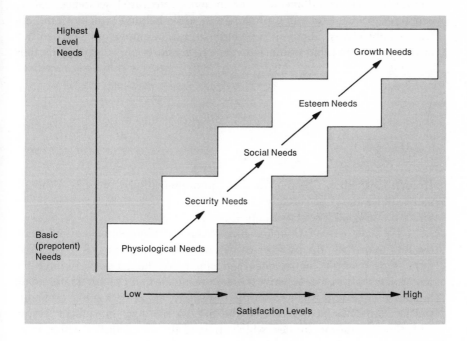

realm? Or is security probably associated with each need? For example, an individual who has attained high status within a group becomes concerned lest he *lose* this existing satisfaction. He may be willing to sacrifice the chance for higher status, rather than risk the loss of existing status.

3. As previously mentioned, the "self-actualization" need is not universally recognized.

Despite all of the reservations, there is currently strong acceptance of Maslow's basic tenets of a plural, shifting need structure. Also accepted is the notion that each individual does have a need hierarchy, although it may be somewhat at variance with that generalized by Maslow. The significance of such a theory to management practice is profound. It means that management must not assume that economic rewards (or any other form of reward) will always lead to high productivity, even though such rewards have been effective in the past. It means that management at all levels must be sensitive to the changing needs of the subordinate groups and individuals in order to provide the best atmosphere for productivity and stability. It means that provision must be made for an upward shift in employee motives with the passage of time. The challenge to management becomes the creation of an organization in which employees may simultaneously, or in some integrated sequence, satisfy economic, social, ego, and growth needs, while helping to achieve organizational objectives. There must be in the minds of employees a recognition of a dependable relationship between their efforts and the rewards they seek. Otherwise, why produce? Indeed, why remain with the organization?

SUMMARY

Human motivation is one of the keys to organizational success. Although motivation cannot be directly observed, we are able to make some rather pointed and confident statements about it.

We have moved from the time when the physiological needs were thought to provide the basic drive within the human being, as in the early days of the scientific management movement. We have passed through the era of paternalism, when many leaders presumed that the key to obtaining human cooperation was to offer them security, along with other economic satisfactions. We have traversed the human relations movement, begun with the Hawthorne studies, which stressed the social forces within man. We stand currently in a period that recognizes human motivation as a dynamic force, with multiple kinds of drives shifting in potency as satisfaction levels change and aspiration levels evolve.

The focus is on the human needs and tensions that inspire activity. According to A. H. Maslow, human needs tend to become activated in a generally predictable order, moving from the most basic (the physiological needs) to the needs for security, affiliation, esteem, and self-actualization. This theory is generally accepted. The self-actualization needs are confirmed and further defined by both Chris Argyris (writing on the natural development of the human personality) and David McClelland (on the need for achievement).

No theory of human motivation is accepted without reservations. Maslow's theory is no exception. It appears to be the best framework available for understanding human motivation and for developing systems designed to yield high satisfaction and productivity.

Closely related to motivation is the subject of human perception. This factor heavily affects aspiration levels. The next chapter examines human perception. It then discusses the process by which needs, perceptions, and aspirations are converted by the individual into behavioral decisions.

QUESTIONS

1. Wages and salaries are considered to be extremely important to most employees in the United States. Is this consistent with your understanding of human motivation? Explain.

2. Under what conditions might paternalism be most effective? Least effective?

3. How do you explain the increasing productivity in the Relay Test Assembly Room?

4. The pay system in the Relay Test Assembly Room was altered from a group incentive in which each girl's earnings were determined by the output of over 100 other girls, to a group incentive based on the output of the 7 girls in that room. How does this fact affect your answer to Question 3?

5. What do you consider to be the principal contributions of Maslow's motivation theory?

6. What reservations do you have concerning Maslow's theory?

7. What is self-actualization? Can this overall concept be broken down into component parts? Explain.

8. What is the motivated state?

9. What is a latent need?

10. Explain the concepts of (a) prepotency and (b) activation.

11. What features can be built into jobs so as to offer potential satisfactions for each level of human needs?

12. What are the differences between work and play?

perception and
performance

11

The first umpire said, "Some's balls and some's
strikes and I calls 'em as they is."
The second umpire said, "Some's balls and some's
strikes and I calls 'em as I sees 'em."
While the third umpire said, "Some's balls and some's
strikes but they ain't nothing till I call 'em."

Motivation theory helps to explain only one facet of human behavior. Were motivation the only determinant, human behavior would be much easier to predict than it is. Several other variables complicate such prediction. Assuming that an individual feels (through internal stimuli) a certain need, he is likely to initiate some internal process for deciding how to satisfy that need. He will probably consider the nature of the environment from which these satisfactions may be gained. And he will reflect on his own abilities to win these satisfactions from the environment. Based upon this analysis, the individual reaches a decision to attain certain objectives—such as a pay increase, a promotion, a new job, further education—that are felt to be instrumental in obtaining the satisfactions sought. The objectives that an individual establishes for himself, then, are based on his needs, his perception of the environment, and his perception of himself (self-image). Having examined human needs in the last chapter, let us now turn to the factors that influence human perception in organizations. From these insights, we will construct a theoretical model of human behavior, which should prove of great value in establishing and operating an effective work system.

The Perception Mechanism

Among other things, the human being is a sensor and processor of information. Thus, to a degree, he can sense variations in heat, light, momentum, and other environmental conditions. That is, he possesses receptors that are capable of sensing such stimuli and a communications network for transmitting sensory information to his nerve centers.

It is important, however, that we differentiate between the act of receiving stimuli through our sensory system, and the act of giving meaning to sensory inputs. Thus, we define *stimulus* as a unit of sensory input, such as a light beam activating receptors in the retina. The *meaning* that is attached to such a stimulus is, as we shall see, influenced by several factors. Basically the human being attempts to organize his sensory inputs in such a manner as to result in an understandable image of the environment. It is this overall process of sensing and organizing sensory data into meaningful images that we term perception. For example, when we look at a "beautiful" girl, we are relating the size, form, color, and complexion that we see to a preexisting set of standards. The concept "girl" (as well as "beautiful") is the result of our experience with our environment, through direct observation as well as through the eyes of others. The same may be said for our concepts of democracy, thunder, light bulb, or pen. That is, we learn to translate certain configurations of sensory inputs into meaningful classifications of events or objects. Having done so, we can use the information to decide on the behavior designed to satisfy our needs.

There is obviously much chance for error in perception. Sense organs and internal communications systems are imperfect. More important, perhaps, the process of interpreting, of assigning meaning to sensory inputs, often leads us astray.

The following experiment, conducted many years ago, provides an excellent medium for gaining insights into the perception process and some bases of erroneous perceptions.[1] A professor of law decided to impress upon his students the unreliability of eyewitness testimony. Toward this end the professor carefully staged an incident that would test the capacity of his students to perceive and report a complex series of events. In confidence, he asked 4 of the 75 students in the class to perform a set of actions in a predetermined sequence, upon receiving their cue from him. During an otherwise typical class session, the professor flashed the

---

[1] Taken from M. C. Otto, "Testimony and Human Nature," *Journal of Criminal Law and Criminology*, IX (1918), 48–104, as presented in W. V. Haney, *Communication Patterns and Incidents* (Homewood, Ill.: Richard D. Irwin, Inc., 1960), pp. 14–16.

signal as he collected some papers from students seated in the first row. As planned:

> (1) A suddenly hits B with his fist, and B retaliates by striking A with a book, and the two fall to quarreling very loudly; (2) at the same time C throws two silver dollars into the air, permits them to fall to the floor, and scrambles after them as they roll away from him, and picks them up; (3) the instructor now orders A, B, and C from the room; (4) as he does so, D simply gets up and walks from the room at a normal gait; (5) as A, B, and C are preparing to leave, the instructor glances at his watch, writes "9:45" on the blackboard, erases it, and writes it again; (6) A, B, and C leave the room.

Figure 11-1

The experimental classroom.

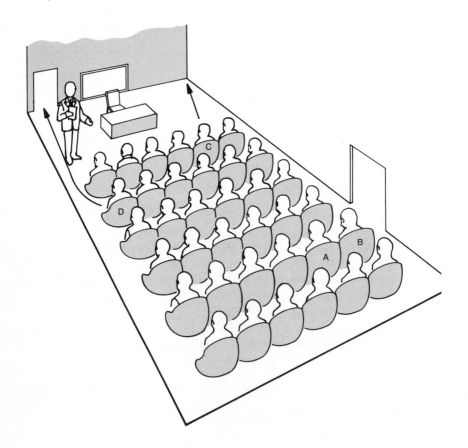

The professor then requested each remaining student to report what he had just observed, for the testimony of these eyewitnesses would probably determine the disciplinary actions resulting from the incident. Together the professor and his students composed a series of questions for all to answer. Following are some of the questions jointly developed and a tally of the student reports:

> *Q:* Where was the instructor when the disturbance began?
>
> Twenty-two of the students reported that he was near the front of the room; 20 that he was about in the middle; and 21 that he was in the rear. A number of students scattered all over the room said they would have testified under oath that the instructor was at his (the student's) desk collecting his paper!
>
> *Q:* Where was the instructor and what was he doing when the boys left the room?
>
> Only 5 of the 75 reported the "9:45" business with any accuracy. Only 6 said they did not know.
>
> The others gave very definite testimony. Three said the instructor was holding the door open for the students to pass through. One said he was standing in the middle of the room muttering, "I'll break this up, or know the reason why." Three remembered him sitting dejectedly at his desk with his face buried in his hands. The consensus of the remaining students was that he was sitting at his desk nervously toying with, variously, the papers he had collected, class cards, his watch chain, a piece of chalk, etc. He appeared "as if not knowing what to do," and "his face wore an expression of embarrassment and uneasiness."
>
> *Q:* What did C do?
>
> Some students reported that either A or B, in their fighting, had dropped some money; that these coins had rolled to the front of the room; and C had scrambled to pick them up. Other students said an adjustable desk arm from one of the classroom seats had been broken off (and A, incidentally, had tried to poke B with it) during the fighting; the little ratchet-ball inside had fallen out and had rolled to the front. It was this ball that C had rushed to pick up. The student sitting next to C, ironically enough, insisted he had seen a little steel ball come rolling out between C's feet and that C grabbed it and put it in his pocket.
>
> *Q:* How did A, B, and C look as they left the room?
>
> The reports corresponded directly with the observer's attitude toward the instructor's action. If the student felt the instructor had been fair and justified in sending the boys from the room, then they tended to look "embarrassed" and "ashamed." If,

however, the student thought the instructor too severe, the boys looked "angry," "injured," and "abused." C's neighbor, referred to previously as perceiving C do nothing more heinous than pocket a steel ball, reported that C had looked "very angry," while A and B appeared "sheepish."

Q: What did D do?

This question was quite accidental. While the class was deciding the questions to be answered for their reports, one student asked: "Are we to include the fact that D rushed from the room at the beginning of the disturbance?" The instructor replied noncommittally: "Please report what you saw as completely as you can, but report no more." The suggestion of the student's question plus the obvious fact that D was now absent was apparently enough to convince over 85 percent of the students that they *had* seen D leave, and most of them were quite confident about the specific manner in which he left—saying, variously, that he had "rushed," "hurried," "bolted," or "made a wild dash from the room."

These students were evidently reporting the "facts" of an incident that they had just "eye-witnessed." They were telling the truth as they saw it. How could they testify to occurrences so distant from reality? Although several psychological mechanisms may be involved, let us examine two of them.

SELECTIVITY

At any particular moment, one's attention is focused on an object or an event of interest; one is *selective.* The individual is much less conscious of other aspects of his environment. For example, assuming that the reader is engrossed in the material he is now reading, he is probably unaware (or much less aware) of many things around him, until they are brought to his attention. Let him stop reading, and he will become aware of a variety of sounds, temperature sensations, visual images, and so forth, all of which help orient him to his environment. At any point in our existence we focus on some phenomenon of interest, while the rest of our surrounding serves as backdrop to be sensed only peripherally. Obviously, we cannot see in all directions at once or hear and understand several simultaneous conversations. We are continuously making perceptual choices from among the infinite events or objects surrounding us, choices based on our needs, our expectations, and the intensity of the environmental stimuli.

Should two students begin a loud fight toward the rear of a filled classroom, how likely is the class to notice one student in the front of the room throw two coins in the air? And how many would pay close attention to the activities of the instructor at this moment? Or to the movements of a fourth student? One might expect much of the class to be unaware of these activities. Indeed the erroneous nature of much evidence given indicates that these activities were not closely observed. Yet, many of these "eye-witnesses" were willing to give contradicting testimonies about what they had "seen" C, D, and the instructor do.

Besides being focused "where the action is," perception is channeled toward those aspects of the environment that appear as satisfiers of activated needs. One's internal states influence his sensitivity to events around him. This phenomenon may be termed "selective vigilance," and described as follows:

> In any given situation, the organism singles out what it considers to be the environment's most relevant aspects. . . . What is singled out will be accentuated. Presumably a hungry man will single out cues leading to food. A rat in a maze will . . . single out cues which will get him out of the maze and into the food box. . . . We are never more aware of geographical environment than when walking in the dark over unfamiliar and potentially dangerous terrain. Under such conditions, we grow almost painfully aware of every rut and hummuck in our path, ones which we might never have noticed while traversing the path in the safe daylight.[2]

CLOSURE

Although we cannot sense equally intensely all that is happening around us, we nevertheless attempt to interpret our sensations so that they "add up" to an understandable situation. That is, we try to fit events together so that they constitute a logical, reasonable picture. Our life experiences teach us that events occurring closely in space or time are generally related, and that each sensed event helps to explain others. Thus we seek the drawstrings, the relationships among events, so that we may pull them together into a meaningful pattern. Psychologists have termed this overall, integrated perception of events a "*gestalt*" (German for form or configuration).

Although our senses do inform us of ongoing events, our subjective organization of the environment tells our senses what to look for. That is, existing *gestalts* influence selectivity and the subsequent process of interpretation. Our given understanding of the world controls our senses, just as our senses, in turn, help determine our understanding of the world.

[2] J. S. Bruner and L. Postman, "Tension and Tension-Release as Organizing Factors in Perception," *Understanding Human Motivation*, ed. C. L. Stacey and M. F. DeMartino (Cleveland: Howard Allen, Inc., Publishers, 1963), p. 415.

The relationship of senses and *gestalt* appear circular; they influence each other.

How does this *gestalt* theory apply to our experiment? While A and B are fighting, C (out of the vision of most of the class) throws two silver dollars in the air and goes after them as they roll along the floor. Students nearby probably hear metal striking the floor and rolling. Some may see C move and pick something up. How do these sensory inputs fit with the fight in the rear? Coins might have fallen from the clothes of the combatants. The steel ball in the movable desk arm might have broken loose. These events would "make sense." They would fit well into an understandable pattern of events.

The same, of course, is true of the instructor's supposed behaviors. The witnesses may well have imputed to him the behavior that they anticipated from their past subjective beliefs about him. The descriptions of D's exit can be interpreted similarly. Since he was gone, he must have exited in a manner which would add up, given D's perceived character and the rest of the situation. The observer's mind fills in the gaps and constructs the *gestalt*. This process of providing subjective elements to complete the integrated, related structure of events is termed *closure*. The mind decides what must have happened. Moreover, the individual may later be unable to differentiate between phenomena actually observed and those filled in subjectively. The *gestalt* is constructed as a whole, as though all parts of it had been directly observed. It is quite possible (even probable?) that a group of individuals witnessing a complex set of events will reach contradicting pictures of what "happened," both because their physical viewpoints vary and their initial mental positions differ.

The process of selective attention, filling in the gaps, and constructing meaningful images of the environment proceeds throughout human life. As the process progresses over a period of years or decades, the individual develops overall conclusions about his community; the managers, fellow workers, and procedures at work; ethnic groups; politics; and all other facets of his environment. Once established, these perceptions are slow to change. They become the base from which to interpret new sensory inputs. If one's foreman is envisioned as a "company man," not interested in the welfare of subordinates, then his actions will be interpreted in that light. Should he punish a worker for violating a "no-smoking" rule, the action may be seen as a cold, impersonal ("by-the-book") enforcement of policy, instead of real concern for the safety of fellow workers. Introduction of a piece-rate system may be translated as an attempt by management (perceived as self-centered) to exploit the work force, rather than as a desire to reward in accordance with an individual's merit. Such interpretations tend to reinforce existing perceptual organizations.

Over time, one develops an emotional attachment to his way of seeing the world. There is even evidence that information contradicting one's perceptual organization will be avoided or distorted in order to preserve the status quo. It is easy to see why opinions and attitudes, once formed, are so difficult to change.

SOCIAL INFLUENCE

Many of our impressions are influenced by the actions and statements of others. A worker usually receives more information from fellow workers than from management. He is taught the group's sentiments, its value system, its logic. He is informed of the group's behavior code, along with a feeling for the emotions and reasons underlying it. The group, then, helps to determine how the worker perceives his work, his superiors, and the overall system. As discussed in Chapter 4, experiments demonstrate that stated group opinions can actually affect an individual's visual perception, causing him "to see" objects less realistically than he would if unaffected by the group opinions; or the group may cause him to doubt his own sensory capacity and accept the group consensus even though he sees things differently.

Thus the group influences an individual's perceptual organization, his attitudes, his beliefs, and his behavior. When it is considered that small groups and individuals are exposed most to information of a specialized, job-related nature, it can be seen that different groups may develop somewhat different perceptions of the environment. Given a problem, different groups may well interpret it in widely varing ways; they may come up with different sets of alternative solutions and their own evaluations of the consequences associated with each alternative. The interests of the groups may be a factor here, but so are the singular set of perceptions that each group brings with it.

SELF-IMAGE

We have seen that an individual's perceptions of the environment will influence his goal-oriented behavior and that perception of one's surroundings is affected by several variables. Still another determinant of human behavior is the individual's impressions about himself. This self-image may have many facets, among them the following:

1. Physical appearance: height, weight, color, and so forth.
2. Intelligence.
3. General education.

4. Special skills and abilities, as well as weaknesses.
5. Moral code.
6. Potential for growth.
7. Aspirations.

All of these factors, and others, affect the behavioral decisions that an individual will make when faced with a choice situation. It should be noted that our views of ourselves are strongly influenced by the responses of others to us, as well as our subjective comparisons of ourselves with others. Our self-image, then, is socially determined to a great degree. To comprehend the basis for an individual's self-image, we must consider the groups with which he identifies. This may include his standing and experiences within his family, his current work group, community organizations, and so forth. Together such groups provide the feedback that helps the individual to evaluate himself and to adjust his aspirations.

Should an opening occur in a high-level position, he will probably attempt to compare his attributes (as he sees them) with those that he perceives to be relevant to success in the position. Is his appearance such that he will be seriously considered if he applies? Can he do the job? Do any aspects of the position conflict with his moral code? Does the position involve development in the direction of his aspirations? He will attempt to determine how well the position would satisfy his current needs. He will also compare his attributes (as he sees them) with those perceived by others to be relevant to success in the position.

He will probably examine his environment to ascertain the alternative positions available as well as the competition for them. Having consciously and subconsciously analyzed the situation, the individual makes his decision. He establishes a goal, which we will call an instrumental objective designed to achieve need satisfaction within the perceived environment. The model presented in Figure 11-2 traces the major relationships among needs, self-image, and environmental perceptions, as discussed above.

CLOSING THE LOOP

The need-perception-decision process presented above is still relatively incomplete as a description of human behavior. Let us attempt to fill in a more complete picture. Assume that an instrumental objective has been selected in an attempt to satisfy some need(s), given certain perceptions of self and environment. The decision must now be implemented. That is, some action must be taken to achieve the objective. Should the individual decide that he wants the high-level position pre-

Figure 11-2

A partial decision model.

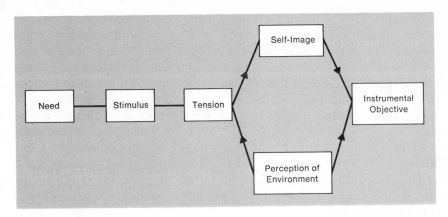

viously mentioned (instrumental objective), how should he go about obtaining it? This involves another decision, at the level of implementation: the means to be used to gain the end. Should he ask directly for the job? Should he subtly begin to "politic," perhaps by inviting the boss home for dinner? This "means" or "implementation" decision again rests on perceptions of self and environment.

Let us assume that the "means" decision is made. That is, the individual has decided upon the instrumental behavior designed to achieve the instrumental objective. This behavior will be, to some degree, successful: anywhere from 0 to 100 percent! The extent of success will result in need satisfaction, again to some degree, and a new pattern of needs now emerges. The process continues unabated, as depicted in Figure 11-3. Needs develop, tensions shift, perceptions occur, decisions are made, and so on, as long as life continues.

The effects of success or failure go far beyond the immediately resulting degree of satisfaction achieved. Success tends to improve one's self-image, and his view of the environment becomes more positive. Consistent failure, however, gradually deflates the ego, while the environment takes on a gloomy or even hostile appearance. Thus success and failure play strategic roles in determining aspiration levels by affecting one's view of his own potential and environmental conditions. Degrees of success resulting from given behavior patterns will also determine whether that behavior will be selected again in the future. Behavior that is followed closely by rewards (success) is reinforced, whereas unre-

Figure 11-3

A model of human behavior.

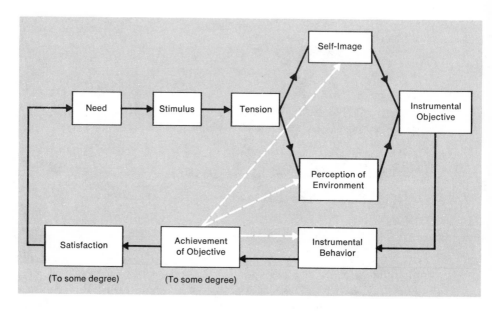

warded or punished behavior (failure) tends to occur less and less frequently. That is, one's behavior is *conditioned* by its consequences. It is, therefore, difficult to overemphasize the impact of success and failure upon subsequent behavior, for this factor heavily influences behavior indirectly through the self-image, the environmental image (see the broken lines in Figure 11-3), and directly by affecting the willingness to act in specific ways.[3]

DEFENSIVE MECHANISMS

Our perceptions of ourselves are subject to distortions, as are our images of the environment. It is natural to desire a high evaluation of one's self, to protect the ego from potentially damaging evidence or ideas. Evidence conflicting with high self-evaluation may well be ignored or

[3] For further elaboration of the effects of success and failure, see T. W. Costello and S. J. Zalkind, *Psychology in Administration* (Englewood Cliffs, N.J.: Prentice-Hall, Inc., 1963), pp. 64–78.

distorted in order to retain a positive self-concept. A variety of mechanisms exist for preserving a positive image, including the following:

1. Rationalization: finding acceptable reasons for acts or impulses when recognition of the actual reasons would endanger self-esteem.
2. Projection: attributing one's unacceptable subconscious desires and characteristics to others.
3. Repression: inability to consciously recognize one's unacceptable traits or desires.
4. Displacement: redirection of subconscious hostility away from self or from an object perceived as invulnerable toward a more vulnerable object— believed to be a prime factor in discrimination toward minority groups.

Human decisions, then, are based on somewhat distorted images of self and environment, as well as on changing patterns of needs. Is it any wonder that human behavior is often so difficult to predict and explain? And is it surprising that managers, when designing a production system or a leadership style, have tended to oversimplify their behavioral assumptions about workers?

IMPACT OF SATISFACTION

The theory of behavior that stresses the principles of motivation and perception has important implications for management. Some of those lessons have only recently been learned. During the 1940s and early 1950s, for example, there was great emphasis on keeping employees satisfied. Job satisfaction was seen as essential to the maintenance of a loyal, stable work force. Moreover, there seems to have developed a general belief that satisfied employees tended to be more productive employees, much as contended cows gave more milk. This satisfaction-productivity link was generally accepted until some doubtful social scientists began to study the relationship during the mid-1950s. Their findings were astonishing to many. Study after study indicated that there was no clear, general relationship between job satisfaction and output.[4] Many grossly dissatisfied individuals were found to be highly productive, while others who expressed great job satisfaction were low producers. This is not to imply a negative correlation; rather, no simple correlation was typical.

---

[4] An inventory of such studies may be found in H. Herzberg, et al., *Job Attitudes: Review of Research and Opinion* (Pittsburgh: Psychological Service of Pittsburgh, 1957).

The Decision to Produce

Our model of human behavior may be used to resolve this apparent puzzle. Let us examine a hypothetical employee who is found, through an attitude study, to have a high index of job satisfaction. Further study then indicates that this employee has a record of low productivity, possibly ascertained from actual production records, merit ratings of his foreman, or other measures. Why the disparity between job satisfaction and output? Overall job satisfaction presumably results from a set of specific satisfactions derived from the job. Assume for a moment that the individual's job is secure, perhaps because of a strong union or civil service tenure provisions. Assume, furthermore, that this employee fits in well with his coworkers; they have ample opportunity for conversation and are socially compatible, with similar interests. The work process may, however, interfere with such social interaction, and may be looked upon as an evil to be tolerated in order to obtain the social and economic rewards flowing from it. Continuation of his economic and social reward flows may be perceived by the worker to require only a minimum output level on his part. Once so perceived, that minimum output level may become his goal each day. In short, where the individual perceives that his needs are satisfied given a certain level and kind of behavior (or productivity), he has no reason to behave otherwise.

But what about the worker who is paid according to his level of output, perhaps on a piece rate? Might he, too, lack the motivation for hard work? Again this depends upon his current need structure and his perceptions. Suppose he produces at a consistently high rate and achieves high earnings. Might the time standards be tightened by management, resulting in less pay for more work? Would fewer workers now be required to do that kind of work, thus threatening his and his coworkers' economic security? Might he be classified as a "rate-buster," and rejected by the other workers?[5] Many managers have been chagrined by the apparent irrationality of the worker who refuses to put forth strong effort to produce even when on an incentive wage. Who is the irrational one, the worker or the manager? If the worker perceives that he can best satisfy his needs by restricting his output, he would be acting irrationally by doing otherwise.

Reversing the situation, let us look at the case of the dissatisfied but productive worker. Imagine an employee who dislikes his work, despises his boss and his coworkers, feels underpaid, and finds working

[5] A penetrating analysis of employee responses to incentive wages is provided in W. F. Whythe, *Men at Work* (Homewood, Ill.: Dorsey Press, Inc., 1961), pp. 98–120.

218

conditions unsatisfactory. Clearly he represents an extreme case of job dissatisfaction. Under what conditions may he nevertheless be highly productive? The first requirement is a feeling on his part that he needs this job, unsatisfactory though it is. He may feel immobile for a number of possible reasons:

1. A perceived lack of transferable skills and abilities.
2. A low level of demand for labor in the marketplace, perhaps associated with a general business recession or local conditions.
3. A strong vested interest in his current job, such as retirement rights or other seniority privileges that would be lost should he quit his current employer.
4. A fear of the unknown. Even though this job is bad, the alternative may be worse.
5. An awareness that changing jobs involves added effort to learn new systems, to recognize new faces.
6. A risk of failure and resulting damage to the ego, as well as economic loss.

An individual may thus possess powerful subjective (perhaps subconscious) reasons for remaining in his current job, despite being unhappy in it. His immobility, based on his self-image and his perceptions of the labor market, may cause him to strive for high output. Should such an employee sense that his productivity is being measured and that his continued employment is dependent on management's satisfaction with his output level, then he is likely to put forth great effort to produce.

Consider, for example, the following actual case of several physically handicapped or otherwise immobile workers in an automobile parts factory.[6] The plant was run by an autocratic management, which refused to mechanize the system or to improve poor working conditions. Wages were minimal, work demands were high. Those who did not meet production standards were discharged, though most turnover was caused by "quits." In this situation, the nonhandicapped workers quickly left, while the handicapped workers remained and were highly productive. Evidently the "normal" workers perceived a more favorable set of alternatives in the marketplace than did the handicapped. The latter employees may well have been deeply dissatisfied and resentful of their lot, but they stayed and they produced. The physically handicapped worker may appear to be an extreme example of job immobility, but his position is perhaps not much different from that of many unskilled workers or high-tenure, middle-aged employees or many other employees

[6] W. F. Goode and I. Fowler, "Incentive Factors in A Low Morale Plant," *American Sociological Review,* XIV, no. 5 (1949), 618–24.

in time of general economic slowdown. Moreover, personal pride may dictate against inferior performance by a worker who wishes to retain the image of competence and dependability.

The foregoing situations of high job satisfaction–low productivity and deep dissatisfaction–high productivity should help explain why there is not a simple relationship between individual contentment and motivation to produce. Rather the motivation to produce appears to be determined by:

1. The nature and strength of the individual's needs and aspirations.
2. The perceived existence of substantial satisfiers for strongest needs.
3. The recognition of a direct relationship between output and the flow of relevant satisfiers.

Thus an individual with strong unsatisfied needs who believes that his efforts and the rewards he most desires are closely tied together will strive to produce. The willingness to produce, then, is based on *anticipated* satisfactions, not on the degree of current satisfaction. Expectations influence output, and *rewards currently being received are important to motivation only as they affect those expectations.*

SATISFACTION AND STABILITY

Although there may be no simple, general relationship between an individual's satisfaction and his motivation to produce, a high level of job satisfaction may well contribute to the long-term productivity of the organization as a whole. Over a long period of time, low levels of satisfaction among a work force are likely to bring about high employee turnover. At some level of dissatisfaction, workers will overcome their tendency to remain. Their search for superior alternatives will intensify, and those other jobs that are visible will appear increasingly attractive. The rising number of "quits" means an infusion of replacements, who, even if they are skilled and motivated workers, must learn the particular system, language, and people at their new workplace. Coordination becomes more difficult to achieve because individuals find it harder to predict each other's behavior where the group composition keeps changing. The situation may resemble that of a highly trained and coordinated football team that must suddenly substitute two or three new men at various positions. Skilled and talented though the newcomers may be, team efficiency will probably suffer—even though all team members are highly motivated.

It may be useful to consider resignation from a job as an extreme case of withdrawal by an employee. Lesser forms of withdrawal may also appear with low levels of job satisfaction.[7] For example, rising absenteeism often results from an unrewarding or unpleasant workplace. The same is true for chronic tardiness. The work situation may be regarded by the employee as something to be avoided, although he cannot afford to permanently terminate his employment there. The frustrations and tensions associated with the job may be so severe as to precipitate various psychosomatic disorders, such as ulcers and heart disease. Thus, as a result either of a natural avoidance of unpleasant conditions or of declining health, the employee withdraws to the extent possible without quitting. Absenteeism and tardiness may play havoc with work systems and schedules, again reducing organizational effectiveness. Such unreliable employees may work very hard when present, to maintain their positions, but their frequent absences partially offset their contributions.

There are other, more subtle forms of withdrawal among workers, which we will classify as limited cooperation. An employee may perform his own work satisfactorily, but may ignore opportunities to help others. He may refuse to contribute his ideas for improving systems or product. He may resist changes proposed by management. He may support a strong labor union as a negative response to existing conditions. In short, the employee may refuse generally to commit himself to the goals and conditions established by management.

To summarize, then, low job satisfaction levels may take their toll on organizational performance by producing various forms of withdrawal from organizational affairs by employees. Withdrawal may take any of several forms, as listed below:

1. High turnover rates
2. Absenteeism
3. Tardiness
4. Limited cooperation

Each form of withdrawal reduces organizational effectiveness. Therefore farsighted management must remain concerned over the satisfaction levels of its subordinates. Satisfaction may not motivate the individual to produce. But general, long-standing dissatisfaction could render high group output very unlikely over time.

[7] Further discussion of withdrawal and dissatisfaction may be found in B. M. Bass, *Organizational Psychology* (Boston: Allyn and Bacon, Inc., 1965), pp. 36–45.

Fortunately there is growing evidence that management can create work systems that combine the motivation to produce with long-term stability in the work force. Motivation may be based on unsatisfied needs, but the current lack of satisfaction is not tantamount to dissatisfaction. The latter develops when the individual cannot see a reasonable means for gratifying his needs. Should the relevant satisfactions appear too distant or too difficult to obtain, then he becomes disgruntled and resentful. This is the essence of frustration, which underlies the withdrawal symptoms discussed above. In contrast, the employee who perceives the desired rewards to be attainable through reasonable effort takes a positive view of his work and of his superiors. The work activity itself may contribute satisfactions, as may the social relations and recognitions that constitute a total work environment. There can be much truth in the statement, "Getting there is half the fun."

SUMMARY

Although motivation impels human activity toward desired satisfaction, perception channels activity toward the most promising satisfiers. Perception consists of receiving stimuli (sensing) and attributing meaning to them (interpreting). Perception may be incomplete or distorted as a result of *selectivity,* the process of focusing on some events while ignoring others. It is also affected by the fact that few events are sensed in their entirety, requiring that the perceiver fill in the unsensed events to achieve a *gestalt,* a unified, consistent understanding of the phenomena observed. This filling-in process is termed *closure.*

Important facets of perception are the development and protection of one's self-image and of his environment. The motivated individual evaluates himself and his environment to determine what the opportunities are for satisfaction, what the obstacles are, what he *can* do and is *willing* to do to obtain the relevant satisfactions. Based on this conscious analysis and various subconscious processes, he selects an instrumental objective, then a plan of instrumental behaviors. To the extent he is successful, his need is satisfied and a new need structure emerges.

Beyond current satisfaction, the degree of success also influences the individual's evolving self-image and his perception of his environment. Success engenders a more positive perception of each and a willingness to take on greater challenges later. Failure may have the opposite effect, except that defensive mechanisms will probably protect the ego from too great and too sudden a deflation—a useful distortion, but a distortion nevertheless.

Despite many studies, there has not been found any simple relationship between job satisfaction and productivity. It appears that the motivation to produce is a function of *unsatisfied* needs, the perceived existence of potential satisfiers, and the recognition of a direct relationship between output and one's receipt of relevant satisfiers. There *is*, however, a strong relationship between satisfaction and organizational stability. Where stability contributes to productive capacity, job satisfaction may well be of great concern to management. Enlightened leadership, as we discuss later, may well achieve the benefits of motivation and stability within the organization.

QUESTIONS

1.   What is meant by perception?

2.   What factors importantly influence perception?

3.   What is meant by closure? By *gestalt*?

4.   Is conformity related to perception? How?

5.   Explain how perception affects the selection of the instrumental objective.

6.   Explain how feedback from the achievement of an objective influences subsequent behavior.

7.   Comment on the following excerpt from the writings of Diogenes Laertius: "When Thales was asked what was difficult, he said, 'To know one's self.' And what was easy, 'To advise another.'"

8.   How might perception influence the worker's willingness to produce?

9.   Indicate how perception and motivation are related.

10.   Does the old proverb "Contented cows give more milk" apply to the output of humans? Explain.

the work group

12

*What is distinctly human
comes from the fact that man
lives his life in groups,
with other people.*

BERELSON AND STEINER

Contained in the preceding discussions of motivation and perception are several references to the effects of groups on individual behavior. The Hawthorne experimenters stressed the impact of group controls over worker output; Maslow recognized affiliation as a major class of human needs; and it was noted that the perceptions, beliefs, and attitudes of individuals are strongly influenced by the groups of which they are members. Group phenomena, therefore, are considered to be important determinants of organizational behavior and effectiveness. The effective leader, whether at the lowest or highest level in the hierarchy, must understand the basic dynamics of group behavior. At a lower level, the leader must help to create a group that is internally compatible, coordinated, and devoted to goals consistent with those of the leader and a larger organization. As one climbs the management hierarchy, the leader becomes more responsible for establishing a total system within which a large number of diverse groups will contribute their joint efforts toward common goals. Such a system involves many facets, including work flows from group to group, communications networks, reward systems, authority relationships, and control techniques. All of these facets of the total system may affect group behavior toward, or away from, system goals. It thus behooves management at every level in the organization to grasp and apply current knowledge of group processes.

Group Formation

Groups do not just happen. Their formation and evolution are somewhat predictable, and even controllable. The key factors in group formation seem to be location, values, and interests. In a typical work situation, employees are officially assigned to a department and a work station. The new man may find himself within comfortable conversational distance of one or a few workers. It may be that interaction is a job requirement, as is true of a riveter and his assistant, a tool-bin clerk and tool users, a football quarterback and the center.[1] The need for coordination requires interaction. But interaction rarely stops at the level required. Rather it is expanded as a means of gaining social acceptance, to obtain information (work-related and otherwise), or as a means of diversion.

Mere proximity, although providing the opportunity for social interaction, is not sufficient in itself to support the formation of a stable, durable group. Other ingredients must be added to provide the cohesiveness that separates the group from the crowd. Should a set of newly interacting individuals find that they share similar backgrounds, values, sentiments, and beliefs, they will be attracted to each other. Should they, furthermore, sense that they share a set of goals that can best be achieved through concerted action, they will become even more cohesive. Those who do not share the values and interests of a given group may form other compatible groups, perhaps even sub-groups or "cliques" within a larger group.

The very membership in a group leads to increased frequency of contact, development of strong friendships, exchanges of favors, and a growing sense of identity, as described below:

> Once these groups have been established . . . , they develop a life of their own that is almost completely separate from the work process from which it arose. This is a dynamic, self-generating process. . . . Increasing interaction builds favorable sentiments toward fellow group members. In turn, these sentiments become the foundation for an increased variety of activities, many not specified by the job description: special lunch arrangements, trading of job duties, fights with those outside the group, gambling on paycheck numbers. And these increased opportunities for interaction build stronger bonds of identification. Then the group becomes something more than a mere collection of people. It develops a customary way of doing things—a set of stable characteristics that are hard to change. It becomes an organization in itself.[2]

[1] An interaction is any contact that links the activities of two or more persons. It may take the form of conversation, signals, cues, or other action that begins a programmed sequence of actions.

[2] L. R. Sayles and G. Strauss, *Human Behavior in Organizations* (Englewood Cliffs, N.J.: Prentice-Hall, Inc., 1966), p. 89.

Group Controls

A most important characteristic of the group is the development of an internal system of thought governing the sentiments and behavior of its members. Thus the group will typically share certain *values.* As new members join, they are exposed to these values and persuaded to accept them. Values refer to ideals and preferred states. They are not likely to be quantified, serving as ultimate standards. Examples of values that might be held important within work groups are honesty, equality, freedom, economic security, rewards based on merit (or tenure), mutual assistance, and high quality workmanship. Whatever the prized values of the group, the new member is expected to internalize them, to make them part of himself. At the very least he must appear to accept them.

Values may serve as informal and broad guides to individual thought and behavior, but most groups develop more specific controls called *norms.* A norm is a group expectation concerning appropriate thought and behavior of its members. Norms are vehicles designed to attain the group's values. Thus if a group of women value feminine modesty, they might devise norms prohibiting the wearing of miniskirts or "peekaboo" attire. Should a group of workers desire to avoid increases in production standards, they might establish output norms for their members. Such output norms could be high enough to satisfy management, but not so high as to cause a review of existing formal standards. Other common workplace norms might include sharing of relevant information with group members, respectful treatment of high-status members, assistance to group members when they request it, and refraining from too close a relationship with management or rival groups.

Output norms are of greatest concern to management. All too frequently, groups establish productivity norms well below the expectations of management and far below their capacity. Consider the following conversation between sociologist Donald Roy, acting the role of a naive new employee, and one of the senior members of the work group, Jack Starkey. Roy has been told by a personnel clerk he can expect to earn about $1.25 per hour, since that is the average for radial drill operators on piece work.

> *Jack Starkey:* Averaging, you say! Averaging?
> *Donald Roy:* Yeah, on the average. I'm an average guy, so I ought to make my buck and a quarter, that is, after I get on to it.
> *Starkey (angrily):* Don't you know that $1.25 an hour is the *most* we can make, even when we *can* make more? And most of the time we can't even make that. Have you ever worked on piece work before?
> *Roy:* No.

> *Starkey:* I can see that! Well, what do you suppose would happen if I turned in $1.50 an hour on those pump bodies?
> *Roy:* Turned in? You mean if you actually did the work?
> *Starkey:* I mean if I actually did the work and turned it in.
> *Roy:* They'd have to pay you wouldn't they? Isn't that the agreement?
> *Starkey:* Yes, they'd pay me—once. Don't you know that if I turned in $1.50 an hour on these pump bodies tonight, the whole damn methods department would be down here tomorrow? And they'd retime the job so quick it would make your head swim! And when they retimed it, they'd cut the price in half, and I'd be working for 85 cents an hour instead of $1.25.[3]

Thus Roy is introduced to the group's logic for limiting individual productivity. When Roy subsequently reaches the capacity to exceed the output norm, and he turns in $10.01 in an eight-hour day, he is immediately confronted by other members of the work group. One advises, "Don't let it go over $1.25 an hour, or the time-study man will be right down here. And they don't waste time, either. They watch the records like hawks. I got ahead, so I took it easy for a couple of hours." Starkey follows with, "What's the matter? Are you trying to upset the apple cart?"

Nor are such controls limited to nonmanagers. Groups of managers also collaborate informally to achieve common goals that may be incompatible with those of higher-level administrators. Thus Dalton points out how a group of managers cooperated systematically to hide surplus parts from inspection teams sent from headquarters.

> Notification that a count was under way provoked a flurry among the executives to hide some of the parts. Motor and hand trucks with laborers and skilled workers who could be spared were assembled in a given department. Then the materials not to be counted were moved to: (1) little-known and inaccessible spots in the plant; (2) basements and pits that were dirty and therefore unlikely to be examined; (3) departments that had already been inspected and that could be approached circuitously while the counters were en route between the official storage areas; and (4) areas where other materials and supplies might be used as camouflage for parts.
> As the practice developed, cooperation among the chiefs to use each others' storage areas and spare parts became well organized and smoothly functioning. And joint action of a kind rarely, if ever, shown in carrying on official activities enabled the relatively easy passage of laborers and truckers from one area to another.[4]

Thus informal expectations seem to control individual behavior throughout organizations. Wherever a group perceives mutual interests

---

[3] Donald Roy, "Quota Restriction and Goldbricking in a Machine Shop," *The American Journal of Sociology*, LVII, no. 5 (March, 1952), 431.

[4] Melville Dalton, "Managing the Managers," *Human Organization*, XIV, no. 3 (Fall, 1955), 8.

and has the opportunity to organize, one may anticipate the emergence of a set of informal behavior patterns designed to promote those interests. It should not be concluded, however, that such informal systems are always designed to circumvent or thwart formal systems. Groups frequently *improve* upon work procedures, speed up and fill out communications networks, and offer a flexibility to respond to unique conditions that assists in making the formal system operative. That is, the norms may call for sharing ideas, for making the job easier, for quick relaying of work related information, and for assisting one's "buddy" when one is ahead on his own job or possesses special skills. Where groups identify with the larger organization and its goals, a *norm of high productivity* may result, with pressure being applied to "slackers" and "goldbricks." Rather than fight group controls, then, the formal leader might better ask himself how to utilize them by demonstrating the common interests among organizational groups at various levels.

Group Power

Given that groups do exercise substantial control over the behavior of individuals, the question arises as to the powers possessed by groups that permit such control. Why do individuals permit the group to influence their behavior?

A most important element of group control is the factor of *internalization:* the tendency of an individual to adjust his system of thought toward that of the group. Constant, long-termed associations with a set of coworkers helps to shape one's perceptions, beliefs, and attitudes. The individual who senses that his background and interests are similar to those of fellow group members is especially open to group influence. He senses a resonance, a mutual sympathy that probably lowers his defenses to control by the group. Once the group's values, logic, and norms have become part of him, the individual conforms as a matter of routine. Why behave otherwise?

Although internalization is probably the broadest basis for conformity, it is not the sole control device. The new member may fail to adopt the "code." Indeed, many workers never do accept the group's system of thought and behavior. Here the processes of group pressure and sanctions emerge. The "deviant" individual becomes the target of much persuasion by affected members, as they attempt to indoctrinate him. Failing in this, threats are levied at the wayward workers. Finally, a series of punishments is available to force the deviant toward the desired behavior, and to serve as an object lesson for other potential deviants. Let us examine the nature and potency of these group sanctions.

A punishment may be defined as the withholding of a satisfaction currently being received or the infliction of pain or other unpleasantness. Our analysis, then, must encompass the satisfactions that a group can offer or deny, as well as the suffering it can inflict. Since satisfactions are related to human needs, Maslow's need structure provides an appropriate framework for our analysis. We shall ascend his need hierarchy and indicate the group's powers to satisfy each need or to frustrate attempts at satisfaction.

PHYSIOLOGICAL NEEDS

The use of physical violence to enforce group norms is probably very limited in "advanced" civilizations. Although the *cosa nostra* may feel obliged occasionally to "liquidate" a deviant brother, most work groups abhor violence. The practice of "binging" (punching a deviant on the upper arm) observed during the Hawthorne studies, and similar physical acts, are probably designed more as a symbol of disapproval than an attempt to injure. More frightening are acts of sabotage against the automobiles and homes of those who report for work during strikes and the anonymous threats to the deviant and his family. Again, however, these appear to represent rare extremes in the day-to-day life within typical work groups.

ECONOMIC SECURITY

The informal group may have much to offer toward helping the individual to feel a sense of job security. Group members are frequently assisted when they are feeling poorly or are faced with especially difficult tasks. Work-related ideas and special tools devised by innovative members are shared with the group. Thus the individual member in good standing may feel better able to meet forthcoming work challenges and contingencies than he would were he to rely solely on his own resources.

Moreover, membership in a strong, cohesive group may provide a sense of control over one's environment, including management. The leader, it is felt, will not disregard the wishes of such a group when he is deciding the fate of one of its members or when it is considering important changes in policy. Feelings of stability, predictability, and localized control may contribute heavily to an overall feeling of security on the job. In many situations, the reports of one's coworkers influence management's evaluations of a worker—or manager. To assure that these reports will be positive, an individual may well find overall group acceptance necessary.

Thus the work group can affect an individual's feeling of job security in several ways. Should he be security-motivated and should he perceive these potential benefits of full membership, he will probably develop strong internal pressure to accept the group's system of thought and behavior.

SOCIAL NEEDS

Perhaps the most obvious satisfaction offered by group acceptance is of a social nature. If there is a basic need for meaningful and positive human associations, one place to enjoy them might well be the workplace. Most jobs present many opportunities for social interaction, such as casual conversation, horseplay, or cooperation in job-related endeavor. The "coffee-klatsch" and lunchtime poker games are additional examples of social activities that seem important to most people. The feeling of acceptance, the opportunity to exchange views and information, the emotional attachments, all contribute to the fulfillment of social needs.

Recognizing the potency of social needs, groups use their power to frustrate social gratification to help enforce norms. Referring again to Donald Roy's study, we note the conversation between two workers concerning a third worker who is considered to be a "rate-buster," that is, one who consistently exceeds the group's output norms.

> *Mike:* He's ruined every job on that machine. They've cut him down to the point where he has to do twice the work for half the pay. A few more like him would ruin this shop.
> *Ed:* It's guys like that who spoil it for the rest of us. Somebody ought to take a piece of Babbitt and pound some sense into his thick skull. That's the only kind of treatment a guy like that understands.
> *Mike:* We're handling him the best way as it is. The only way to handle those bastards is not to have a thing to do with them. That guy doesn't have a friend in the place, and he knows it. You can bet your life he thinks about that every time he comes to work.[5]

The anticipation of eight or nine hours per working day of ostracism spiced with various forms of verbal abuse (swearing, jibes, criticism) might well persuade a potential deviant to conform—or to leave the job altogether if group pressures, management directives, and his own preferences are too incompatible.

[5] Roy, "Quota Restriction and Goldbricking," pp. 430–31.

It is most difficult for an individual to maintain a favorable self-image if he is constantly berated by others. In contrast, one who reflects the group's values, logic, and norms receives positive feedback that helps to support the desired self-image. Thus the individual, in his efforts to enhance his own view of himself, may well seek the approval of his fellows.

Not only does he seek the "member in good standing" position; he may desire to achieve high status, perhaps even a leadership role. One's status is defined as his rank within a group as determined by the degree to which he personifies that group's values. To the extent that his personal characteristics, abilities, performance, and values approach the values of the group, he is assigned high status. His perception of his status position indicates to him his "worth," in the eyes of the group. Their evaluation of him is an important determinant of his self-perception, especially if he respects the group members. To attain this high status, he may well attempt to adopt the group's sentiments and behavior and to "be" what the group values.

GROWTH NEEDS

It is conceivable that the informal group can, if it wishes, facilitate individual self-actualization. Acceptance by the group may open the way for training by senior group members beyond that offered by formal training programs. Group members frequently agree to switch jobs, despite official prohibitions, offering the individual a chance to expand his skills as well as his grasp of the relationships among jobs. Group approval of an individual may enhance his opportunities for advancement, since managers are often influenced by the evaluations of one's coworkers. Not only do such informal evaluations reflect upon the worker's technical skills and potential, but they also indicate his ability to "fit in," to become a member of a working team.

Limits of Group Power

Strong and varied though group powers may be, it should not be concluded that the group can always control the thoughts and behavior of individuals. The strength of group control is determined by a number of important situational factors. One pivotal determinant of group control is the degree to which the individual identifies with the group. Should his perceptions, logic, and interests lie distant from those of the group, he may feel that membership is too "costly," that group expectations are too distant from his own to permit easy adaptation. When such feelings are reinforced by strong identifications with outside groups (such as church, family, or clubs), the desire to be accepted by a given group may not be very strong. Moreover, some individuals see their current work locations as temporary, perhaps anticipating early transfer or promotion to supervisory positions. Their reference points lie beyond the group and their behavior develops accordingly.

Another factor that can limit group control over the individual is the technical structure of the workplace. Some processes are highly standardized with each step programmed to allow very little variation in performance. The work pace may be mechanically determined, with work-in-process brought to work stations by conveyor and then moved inexorably onward after permitting the standard interval for each programmed work unit. Individual performance may be readily observed and measured by supervision. Under these circumstances, the group's informal powers to control work-related behavior may well be more limited than it might be given a less structured, less standardized situation.

The most obvious constraint on group control is the power of formal leaders to reward, punish, or otherwise influence behavior. Thus the power to promote, to discharge, to transfer, to formally recognize, and the like can be extremely strong persuaders. Again the direction of identification may be significant. Some persons may identify with a strong, competent, authoritative leader, looking to him for their ideals and directives.[6]

The Productive Group

We have seen that the group can strongly influence the willingness of an individual to produce, at least under certain circumstances. Given such control, what determines whether a group will establish high or low output norms? Beyond this, what factors underlie a group's *ability* to produce at high levels, should it so desire? As with many other questions about human behavior, there are few universally accepted answers. Objective research in small group behavior does, however, provide valu-

[6] The powers of the leader are discussed in Chapter 18.

able insights to the aspiring manager. This section examines some of the existing evidence and logic concerning (1) the group's willingness to produce, and (2) the group's capacity to produce.

THE WILL TO PRODUCE

Under somewhat stable conditions, most groups establish conceptions of an appropriate day's work for the group as a whole and for each component task. Unfortunately there are often compelling reasons for purposely restricting output. In many instances these reasons do not reflect reality, but it is not always reality that governs logic and behavior. Among possible reasons for restricting productivity are the following:

1. Dislike for the work itself.
2. Dislike for the formal leader, the organization as a whole, or the goals currently being pursued.
3. The fear that jobs will be lost if output is high, because the volume of work is limited.
4. The fear that management will raise its standards of acceptable work loads, causing a loss of leisure and a reduction in the opportunity for social activities on the job.
5. The desire to protect slower group members from management action.
6. A general feeling that workers must protect themselves from inevitable attempts by management to exploit them.

Should the weight of group sentiments be similar to those above, one could predict low production norms. Such feelings need not, and frequently do not, prevail. Let us construct the positive pole, the sentiments leading toward high output norms. These include:

1. Work that is intrinsically satisfying.
2. A sense of trust and respect for leaders.
3. The belief that organization goals are worthwhile.
4. The feeling that satisfactions are closely related to group productivity.
5. The belief that jobs are threatened more by low output than by high output.
6. A general feeling that management has the welfare of workers as a primary goal.

With these sentiments, the group may well support high individual output by further training slower members, by offering mutual assistance where needed, by informally improving upon the procedures of production, and by generally urging each other on. Under these circumstances, the nonproducer is not protected by the group from management action. The group may encourage such action or make the workplace so unpleasant for him that he will leave voluntarily.

THE CAPACITY TO PRODUCE

It is conceivable that a group that is powerfully motivated toward high output will nevertheless be relatively unproductive. Group productivity depends on skills, communications, and coordination, as well as on motivation. Picture, for example, a football team whose first-string quarterback is suddenly injured during a game. Assume that his replacement has played and practiced very little with the starting team. What are some possible consequences? He probably calls signals at a different cadence from his predecessor, perhaps causing a lineman to jump offside or to hesitate before carrying out his assignment. This quarterback hands the ball off a bit higher or lower than did the other, and at a slightly different angle, increasing the likelihood of a costly fumble. Thus even if he is as capable as the starting quarterback, problems of communication (signal calling) and coordination may prevent effective team performance. If, in addition, the substitute is not quite as able as his predecessor, the team's problems are multiplied.

Few work situations require as much coordination as the football team. To some degree, however, coworkers must be able to communicate and to predict each other's behavior. It helps if each is aware of the others' special skills, weaknesses, and ways of doing things. Such an awareness can only result from repeated observations and interactions. Even the highly skilled machinist, accountant, or draftsman must, on newly joining an organization, learn the procedures, the language, the locations of tools and people, before he can perform to his full potential.

Stability, therefore, is prerequisite to highest group effectiveness, especially where the activities of workers are closely interwoven. Stability influences group capacities, although to a lesser extent, even where close coordination is not required. This ignores the possibility that replacements may lack the skills required for high *individual* output, in which case, of course, group capacity would plummet.

A number of studies have been conducted to ascertain the conditions most conducive to high output norms. It appears that the very structure of work groups and tasks can inhibit or enhance both stability and norms. A most comprehensive set of conclusions is presented by A. K. Rice as a result of two separate experiments with two groups in a weaving operation.

1. Irrespective of wages and working conditions, a work group will derive satisfaction from the efficient organization and performance of the task for which it has been organized and an inefficient organization or performance will diminish the chances for satisfaction.

2. Since task completion is believed to be an important source of satisfaction, a work group should be of such a size that its members can experience, so far as practicable, the completion of the "whole" task.

3. When individual tasks performed by members of a work group are interdependent, the relationships between those performing the tasks will have important effects on productivity. A work group should therefore provide its members with satisfactory interpersonal relationships.

4. Since practical self-government can provide satisfaction for group members, a work group should have control over its own day-to-day work and organization; that is, its "governing system" should be internally structured.

5. The coincidence of obvious physical and activity boundaries enables a work group to identify itself with its own "territory"; and, as a corollary, groups of workers "owning their territory" are more likely to form internally structured, stable, and cohesive group relationships than those in indeterminate or overlapping territories.

6. The range of skills required of group members should be such that all of them can comprehend all the skills and . . . could . . . aspire toward their acquisition.

7. The fewer differences there are in work-group status (and pay) consistent with offering opportunities for promotion, the more likely is the internal structure of a group to stabilize itself and the more likely are its members to accept internal leadership.

8. When individual members of small work groups become disaffected to the extent that they can no longer fit into their work group, they need, if group stability is to be maintained, to be able to move to other small groups engaged in similar tasks.[7]

[7] A. K. Rice, "The Experimental Reorganization of Non-Automatic Weaving in an Indian Mill," *Human Relations,* VIII, no. 3 (1955), 399–428.

Rice's findings are generally supported by other researchers. Berkowitz found that among self-governing groups the more cohesive groups were more productive than the less cohesive ones. For example, bomber crews rated as highly effective typically socialized more "off the job" than those rated as less effective.[8]

Others have confirmed the finding that groups composed of socially compatible persons tend to be more productive, as well as more stable, than randomly constituted groups. Schutz found this true in an experiment with 12 groups of college students over a six-week period.[9] Another study concluded that the pairing of carpenters or bricklayers according to the men's preferences resulted in lower labor cost per housing unit, lower materials cost, and much lower labor turnover than was true when pairings were done by management.[10]

Another important determinant of group output and stability appears to be the reward structure. Frequently the individuals within a work group are made to feel that they are compared with their coworkers, and that individual rewards are dictated by these comparisons. Under such a system the sharing of valuable work-related information or the rendering of assistance may be perceived as detrimental by the potential contributors. Each person tends to become self-oriented and disinterested in group and organizational goals. Needless to say, such an orientation can spell disaster for total group performance.

The effects of reward structure were well demonstrated in another classroom experiment. Two sets of groups were created, with each group assigned the same problem. This problem required communication and coordination for fastest solution. One set of groups was told that each *individual* would be graded upon his performance as compared with others in his group. The other set of groups was told that each *group* would be graded and that each member would receive the grade achieved by his group as a unit. This second set of groups performed more effectively in terms of both speed and quality of solutions and reported much better interpersonal relationships than did the groups of competing individuals.[11]

A somewhat similar experiment was conducted among 23 coordinating committees of a large business firm. The experimenters concluded:

[8] L. Berkowitz, "Group Norms among Bomber Crews," *Sociometry,* XIX (1956), 141–53.

[9] W. C. Schutz, *FIRO: A Three-Dimensional Theory of Interpersonal Behavior* (New York: Holt, Rinehart and Winston, Inc., 1958).

[10] R. H. Van Zelst, "Sociometry Selected Work Teams Increase Productivity," *Personnel Psychology,* V, no. 3 (1952), 175–85.

[11] Morton Deutsch, "An Experimental Study of the Effects of Cooperation and Competition Upon Group Process," *Human Relations,* II (1949), 129–52, 199–231.

Unfortunately in most industrial organizations specific rewards are almost always given on an individual basis. Rewards for collaboration and for helping others are generally more symbolic or elusive, e.g., informal signs of appreciation or respect. This may account for the general lack of concern for the welfare of one's associates observed in many organizations. To the extent that a functional interdependence exists among organized members—such that coordination or collaboration is required rewards may also serve as a detriment to organizational effectiveness.[12]

Possibly the most important overall determinant of group stability and output is the extent to which the group identifies its interests with those of the organization. Where officials throughout the hierarchy are believed to be sincerely concerned with the welfare of the group, the group may well reciprocate. In the long run, such beliefs are based on managerial actions. High group attainment must be followed by appropriate rewards. The informal group must feel that it is supported, rather than threatened, by officials. There should be no hint that increased productivity and earnings will be followed by higher output standards and lower piece rates. The group should feel influential in helping to establish and modify work systems. In these ways and others, a group can be made to feel an integral part of the total organization, working within a system that the group helped to create, a system that rewards high performance and permits free informal associations to help satisfy the broad spectrum of human needs.

SUMMARY

Informal work groups form as a result of proximity, similar backgrounds, and mutual interests. Once formed, groups move to control the behavior of their members. Group members share certain values. These values, together with the group's perception of the work environment, form the bases for group norms, specific behavioral standards. Output norms are, perhaps, the most important of these.

The group's power to enforce norms can be great, for the group may possess the ability to satisfy the whole spectrum of member needs or to deprive the member of those satisfactions. At times, this power exceeds that of management. In other instances, the group lacks effective

[12] Alvin Zander and Donald Wolfe, "Administrative Rewards and Coordination among Committee Members," *Administrative Science Quarterly,* IX, no. 1 (1964), 68–69.

power over at least some of its members. This occurs where members do not strongly identify with the group, where work processes are readily observed and measured by management, and where formal leaders possess great power to reward and punish.

Group productivity is affected by the *will* to produce and the *capacity* to produce. The former is affected by attitudes toward the work itself and the management, by perceptions of the labor market place, and so forth. The capacity to produce is determined partially by the group's skills, internal communications efficacy, and ability to coordinate activities. These are clearly the result of long histories of work interaction. Stability is pivotal here.

Studies of productive groups indicate that self-governing, cohesive, socially compatible groups are both highly productive and satisfying to their members. Group-based rewards are found to be most compatible with a sense of teamwork, as well as with smooth social relationships. Finally, the group that senses that management supports its existence and desires to satisfy its full range of needs is likely to establish high productivity norms and to achieve the high stability so basic to effective coordination.

QUESTIONS

1. Describe the process of group formation.
2. What is meant by group cohesion?
3. Differentiate between norms and values.
4. It has been said that the powers of formal leaders are often illusory. Is this true? Explain.
5. What powers might the informal group apply to control individual behavior?
6. What is meant by internalization?
7. In many cases the group finds itself unable to control individual behavior. Under what conditions is this likely?
8. What are the principal determinants of group productivity?
9. When will a group discourage high output? When will it encourage high output?
10. What is the effect of stability on group output?
11. Explain how the reward structure may encourage or inhibit coordination.

the leadership role

13

*A leader is best when people
barely know that he exists*

WITTER BYNNER

We began this book with a description of an organization as a system
with required inputs, outputs (inducements), and a transformation
process whereby the former are converted into the latter. It was emphasized that no organization could continue to exist without at least a
minimum level of support by the providers of *all* of the required inputs,
and that such support decisions are based on the conclusion that a particular allocation of these resources results in a benefit to the provider
that exceeds the opportunity cost. This is as true of the corporate financier
as it is for the client, the employee, or the local resident, among other
system participants. All such participants, or potential participants, may
be *influenced* by other persons toward a certain behavior, such as investing capital, buying a product, accepting a position, accepting the plant
and its personnel in the locality, and so forth. The process of influencing
the behavior of any type of system participant can be viewed as an act
of leadership. From this viewpoint, it is no less a leadership act for the
dean to "motivate" a business firm to financially support his college than
it is for him to motivate his faculty toward more effective classroom performance. *It is influence that identifies the leader*, not the type of person
influenced.

    Most treatises on leadership, nevertheless, stress the superior-sub-
ordinate influence process, ignoring the role that the fellow employee

239

(be he a titled manager or an informal leader) plays in directing the behavior of other employees. In a systems context, this is a narrow and limited approach. It can be justified only as an expedient to reduce an extremely broad topic to manageable proportions, leaving other leadership efforts to disciplines directly concerned (marketing, finance, public relations, and so forth). Moreover, the astute reader may well be able to transfer his grasp of leadership principles from one domain to another without benefit of further instruction. Accordingly, the following discussion of leadership centers on the influence relationship among employees, both managerial and operative.

Organizational Impact

To comprehend the impact that leaders have upon organizations, it is useful to examine the various kinds of inputs that leaders can contribute. Certainly the treatment by a leader of his followers is a key input to the system, and this factor is discussed later in this chapter. Other vital inputs must also be examined. The formal leader, for example, may be conceived as a device for gathering, interpreting, and communicating information for the system. He is, moreover, a decision maker. The way in which he performs these roles can profoundly influence the goals established for the organization and the means utilized for their attainment.

THE SENSING DEVICE

The human being has been characterized as an information sensing and processing device. If he is to adapt rationally to his constantly changing environment, he must be constantly receiving external stimuli and converting them into meaningful, realistic *gestalts*. The same is true for the internal stimuli that signal his bodily and mental states. Upon combining these information flows, the individual reaches behavioral decisions designed to adapt himself to his environment and/or to adapt the environment to himself.

The same basic process applies to organizations, although there are some significant differences. Like the individual, the organization requires that information relevant to its survival and growth be available for use by its decision centers. Of concern again are external conditions (interest rates, competitive activities, and so forth) and internal states (the firm's financial status, inventory levels, personnel turnover rates, and so forth).

Typically, the formal leader is in a strategic position to observe some combination of these conditions. He may use such information to help him to make reality-oriented decisions, as well as communicating it to other parts of the organization.

The key point here is that the leader is, among other things, a sensing device, a receiver of the kinds of information that may be necessary for organizational effectiveness. His sensitivity to both internal and external stimuli helps to determine the organization's adaptability. Clearly some leaders are more sensitive than others. One will perceive subtle shifts in employee attitudes, while another remains blind to them. One will notice gradual changes in product demand or customer makeup that are below the perceptual threshold of another.

It should be recalled that perception involves both the receipt of stimuli and a subjective organization of those stimuli that gives them meaning. Just as sensitivity to stimuli varies, so do individuals' abilities to synthesize from them a set of realistic conclusions about what those stimuli "mean." It is these conclusions, or inferences, that will determine the leader's decisions. Moreover, these inferences, rather than the stimuli underlying them, are the informational inputs that he provides to others in the organization. "Morale in my unit is high," is an interpretation of the information processed by the speaker and is not necessarily true. Nevertheless the leader acts as thought it is fact and communicates it as fact.

THE COMMUNICATIONS LINK

Having perceived certain events or conditions, the leader may initiate a flow of information to others in the organization to whom he believes this information is germane. This flow may be in any direction:

1. Upward, to those establishing objectives and policies.
2. Horizontally or "diagonally" to peers or others with interests similar to his.
3. Downward to subordinates to better inform them about organizational objectives, policies, and conditions pertinent to their performance.

In this manner, his perceptions may be disseminated through the organization as "facts." He also communicates his attitudes and opinions, not to mention some possible conscious distortions of reality and strategic omissions. All of this represents information inputs that may influence the decisions made by others within the organization.

Not only does the leader initiate information flows, but he also serves as a formal communications link between the levels of the hierarchy. Much information passes through him in all directions. He provides a voice for his subordinates at the higher levels of management and he represents management to his subordinates. But he is not limited to strictly vertical communications. The fidelity with which he relays this information may also affect the organization's behavior. It should be noted here that the receipt of any communication is a special case of perception and subject to all of the distortions involved therein. The sounds of a spoken sentence are stimuli to which meanings are assigned by the receiver, meanings that may be far from the intent of the sender.

THE DECISION MAKER

By now it should be amply clear that the leader plays a key role in determining organizational behavior through his functions as a sensing device and a communications link. Also to be considered is his role as a decision maker. Not only does he influence the decisions made by peers and superiors; he must also take actions to *implement* the policy decisions reached higher in the organization. Directives reaching him are typically broad, leaving to him the task of working out the details, that is, converting overall objectives and policies into operational programs of action. Rarely is a plan so highly defined by high organizational level that there is no room for interpretation and elaboration by lower-level leaders. This process of program interpretation and elaboration seems characteristic of all levels of organizations.

A high-level decision to expand production capacity by 10 percent during the ensuing year, for example, would require a great deal of program elaboration by lower-level decision makers. One individual (or group) might be assigned the task of ascertaining additional plant and equipment requirements and of costing out the alternatives. Another leader might be assigned similar responsibilities for personnel, still another might be concerned with the appropriate distribution network for the newly expanded firm, and so on. These decisions having been made, lower-level managers might accept the responsibility for making them materialize. In the personnel case, for example, a recruiting plan might be established, along with a plan for training current employees for greater responsibilities. Further downward, someone might be finally responsible for supervising the actual recruiting and training activities. At each step, from the broad statement of objectives and policy through the performance of the final operations that make a plan come alive, the plan has been further defined and elaborated and perhaps even altered where elements have been found unfeasible.

One may consider this process to be a means-end chain. Objectives (ends) are established at a high level and communicated downward. Each concerned subordinate manager and his unit provide the means to accomplish that end. The task accepted by each unit becomes the objective or end for that unit, which divides the responsibility among its subunits. The process of delegation and acceptance continues until the locations are reached where the means (tasks) need no longer be subdivided. That is, the tasks are operational; they can be performed at a given level without further delegation. This, then, is the lowest stage of program definition and elaboration.

The leader's elaboration and implementation may have several facets. He may be concerned with how best to organize his subordinates for smooth, coordinated effort, how best to motivate individuals and groups to put forth great effort toward the group's task, how best to measure progress and quickly correct deviations from the desired paths, and so forth. In short, his decisions may pervade the entire scope of his group's operations. Thus the leader's role as a decision maker, when combined with his other functions as a sensing device and communications link, has a profound influence on ultimate organizational behavior and effectiveness.

Leadership Attributes

Leadership has probably been the subject of human curiosity since the dawn of organizations. Among the most intriguing inquiries has been the question of the traits that distinguish the leader from the follower. Nevertheless, little progress has been made toward the identification of traits that are universally associated with leadership promise. That is, no single leadership type has been discovered. Leaders come in all sizes, shapes, colors, intellects, and personalities. Such a finding is not without value, for it avoids a stereotyped approach to the selection of leaders or the prediction of leadership success. This is not to deny the superiority of one individual within a particular situation. In fact, it seems that the situation and the nature of the followers are the primary determinants of leader choice and success.

It is entirely possible that more than one leader will serve the group, each with a set of traits most useful for particular situations. Thus one man with great experience, intuition, and charisma may generally lead the group's routine work efforts. Another leader might emerge under emergency conditions, such as fire, riot, or natural disaster, perhaps because of his quick perception and decisiveness. Still another possessing an adventurous, imaginative spirit may lead the group (or a subgroup) in recreational activities.

Leadership Skills

The search for traits that identify potential executive performance has been largely unrewarding. Thus one authority states:

> The assumption that there is an executive type is widely accepted, either openly or implicitly. Yet any executive presumably knows that a company needs all kinds of managers for different levels of jobs. The qualities most needed by a shop superintendent are likely to be quite opposed to those needed by a coordinating vice-president of manufacturing. The literature of executive development is loaded with efforts to define the qualities needed by executives and by themselves these sound quite rational. . . . But one has only to look at successful managers in any company to see how enormously their particular qualities vary from any ideal test of executive virtues.[1]

Although a few insights have been garnered through the study of leadership traits, it would be dangerous to select leaders generally on this basis. Moreover, the trait approach to leadership offers little in the way of *developing* leaders, since the traitist assumption seems to be that leaders are born, not made.

It may be more productive to inquire into the *skills* basic to effective leadership rather than the physical and mental traits. It is, after all, one's abilities that determine his success as a leader. Moreover, abilities and skills may be learned, whereas one's height, physiognomy, intellect, and personality are usually rather stable characteristics. A most persuasive classification system for leadership consist of three basic types of skills: technical, human relations, and conceptual.[2]

TECHNICAL SKILLS

In many situations, particularly at the lower levels of an organization, the leader finds it necessary to have a firm grasp of the processes

[1] Perrin Stryker, "The Growing Pains of Executive Development," *Advanced Management*, August, 1954, p. 15.

[2] The following discussion is abstracted from Robert L. Katz, "Skills of an Effective Administrator," *Harvard Business Review*, January–February, 1955, pp. 33–42.

and techniques with which the group is concerned. Relevant skills are a most important consideration at this level for both informal selection by the group and official promotion by superiors. Lacking such abilities and knowledge, the aspiring leader is hobbled in his efforts to personally assist, develop, and motivate subordinates. From a broader perspective, he finds it difficult to establish goals, procedures, and elaborate plans or to implement those devised by higher echelons. The informal leader is a device through which the group hopes to attain its goals, just as the formal leader is appointed to help achieve higher-level objectives. From either viewpoint, perceptions of a candidate's ability to translate aspirations into reality govern leader selection. It would be difficult to imagine a machine shop foreman, a supervisor of a nuclear experimentation lab, or a department store buyer who lacks intensive knowledge of the operations.

HUMAN RELATIONS SKILLS

Central to a leader's ability to influence the behavior of others is his ability to understand and communicate with them. The effective leader must accurately perceive, for example, the activated needs of his subordinates, peers, and superiors. Furthermore, he must be able to sense *their* perceptions of the human and technical factors relevant to the situation. He is likely to possess a sensitivity to the sentiments, beliefs, attitudes, and the informational frameworks that affect human reactions to instructions, work loads, objectives, or other organizational directives and conditions. If he is to help create a harmonious, coordinated work team, he must be aware of his group's social relationships and of the ways to improve them. He must be able to develop a work environment that supports high productivity alongside of worker satisfaction.

The leader must, then, be sensitive to human needs, social relationships, informational frameworks, attitudes, and so forth. He must transform his awareness into the decisions necessary to achieve long-term output and satisfaction. Helpful in developing accurate perceptions is the ability to communicate effectively. This requires more than a facility in the use of words and other symbols. It involves the creation of an atmosphere in which ideas and feelings are readily shared, where both human and technical information flow unhindered by fear or hostility.

Unlike technical skills, human relations skills appear to be vital to leadership effectiveness at all organizational levels. This importance is probably most obvious at the lowest supervisory level. The decisions of higher-level leaders, however, establish the ground rules upon which subordinate leaders base their own practices. Thus the formal organization structure is established at the summit, as are the overall reward structure and the "tone" of the hierachy. An ability to understand the human element, to reach appropriate decisions, and to communicate effectively is, therefore, extremely important at all levels.

CONCEPTUAL SKILLS

Of growing importance to a leader as he moves up the organizational hierarchy is his ability to see the enterprise as an integrated, complex unit. This involves a recognition of the multiple interdependencies among the subunits that make up the system. Instead of dealing with individuals and localized problems, he becomes concerned with the task of integrating the efforts of diverse skills and interest groups into a coordinated drive toward objectives. Not only must he obtain and blend the goal-oriented efforts of employees, both operative and managerial; but he becomes more and more involved with obtaining the other inputs necessary to organizational survival and achievement. Thus he requires skill in dealing with investors, various levels and agencies of government, the local and remote public, major clients and suppliers, and so forth.

At the summit of large organizations, the task of developing a structure capable of satisfying the interests of all required inputs is probably the leader's greatest continuing challenge. It is a challenge that requires a high order of conceptual skill. The ability to broadly conceptualize and integrate is not as strategic at low leadership levels. The typical foreman deals with a technically limited task and a somewhat specialized work group. His chief function is typically to implement stated goals within a system that has been created elsewhere in the organization. Thus his options are limited, as is the scope of his responsibility. Generally speaking, as he advances to higher leadership positions, both the scope of his concerns and the degree of discretion permitted him broaden, requiring increasing exercise of conceptual skills.

The Bases of a Leader's Power

The lack of general agreement over leadership traits does not necessarily prevent us from successfully predicting one's ability to influence the behavior of others in a particular situation. Why does one person do what another commands or recommends? Under what circumstances will such directives be disobeyed?

Perhaps the most comprehensive explanation of a leader's power is offered by the social psychologists, French and Raven. Leaders, it is proposed, possess five important types of power that may help them to influence the thought and behavior of others. The types of leader power are (1) reward power, (2) coercive power, (3) legitimate power, (4) referent power, and (5) expert power.[3] Each of these is now examined, along with some of their interrelationships. To aid in this discussion, let us designate as L an individual who is attempting to influence the behavior of F, a potential follower.

REWARD POWER

If behavior is motivated by the desire to satisfy a particular set of needs, then the ability of L to offer such satisfaction may be an effective means to influence the behavior of F. More precisely, F may permit L to influence his activities to the extent that F perceives that receipt of sufficient desired rewards will result. This issue, then, becomes one of assessing the L's power to reward *and* his propensity to reward, given F's obedience. The actual receipt of rewards following approved behavior tends to strengthen the leader-follower relationship through the process of reinforcement. That is, F becomes conditioned to obey through the strengthened association in his mind of approved behavior and need satisfaction.

Obviously, satisfactions that are derived regardless of obedience do not contribute to L's reward power. Such satisfactions may, in fact, reduce L's reward power by decreasing need levels in F. For example, L's power to offer job security is virtually nil in many cases, perhaps due to seniority provisions in the union contract or tenure policies in civil service organizations. F's perception that he can easily move from his current job to another may also weaken L's power to offer a meaningful increment of job security to F.

Much the same limitations may apply to the leader's power to offer substantial additional satisfactions of other needs. Wage levels may be set in the collective bargaining agreement or at higher management levels. Social needs may be most readily satisfied by F's working peers or even outside of the work situation. The need for other esteem (status, prestige, respect) is often most readily gratified through recognition by one's closest associates. One's greatest esteem satisfactions probably derive

<hr>

[3] J. R. P. French and G. Raven, "The Bases of Social Power," in *Studies in Social Power*, ed. Dorwin Cartwright (Ann Arbor, Mich.: Institute for Social Research, 1959), pp. 150–67.

from the groups with which he identifies, such as his work group, close associates within his profession, other friends, and family. Although leader recognition should not be ignored as a possible motivator, neither should it be overemphasized. It takes a sensitive, knowledgeable leader to ascertain his reward portfolio and to decide which incremental rewards can serve as true incentives to enhance organizational output and health.

COERCIVE POWER

In one sense, coercive power may be viewed merely as the other side of the coin from reward power. The power to coerce by threatening to *withhold* existing satisfactions (wages, security, recognition, and the like) is closely related to the power to offer such satisfaction; and the power to coerce by threatening pain or tension is closely related to the power to alleviate them. Exercise of these powers, however, may produce sets of repercussions so different that they warrant separate treatment.

It is clear that L's power to punish (withhold satisfactions or render pain) can serve as a potent motivator. However, the psychological consequences of such coercion have consequences beyond their immediate effect. Whereas the promise and receipt of rewards may cement the bond between L and F, the threat and application of punishment tend to weaken that bond. In general, coercion is only effective as long as F perceives no better alternative locations or leader. Continued coercion by L leads to increasing search by F for a new leader and, perhaps, for a new locus. The more intensive the search, the greater is the probability that acceptable alternatives will be found. And the more acceptable the alternatives, the less effective are the threats of punishment. Actual or threatened punishment, therefore, reduces F's tendency to identify with the leader and the organization, whereas such identification may be strengthened through rewards. Both may be effective influence devices in the short run, but their broader, long-term impacts must be recognized.

LEGITIMATE POWER

Not all behavior is based on the prospect of imminent reward or punishment to be dealt out by a leader. After one has worked in an organization for some time, he becomes accustomed to being directed by individuals who occupy certain official or informally accepted positions. Thus F will customarily accept general work directives from his supervisor, as well as a more limited range of directives from such specialists as the safety officer or the plant's chief accountant. Directives issued by persons who have the perceived authority to give such order are more likely to be followed than those lacking authoritative backing. This develops in F's mind a propensity to accept the orders of given persons as being rightful exercises of authority. Moreover, F evolves a subjective framework concerning the kinds of directives that he should accept from each L, based on his conception of his role and the legitimate role of others. This ability of L to influence the behavior of F because of their respective roles is termed legitimate power. It is the kind of power that is symbolized by uniforms, titles, and large offices. Such symbols are used to assure the recognition of the authority vested in a position and in the person occupying it.

Legitimate power, then, is based on a sense of obligation to follow the rightful orders of acknowledged leaders. Such power results from an internalization of an operating code on the parts of both L and F. L becomes accustomed to influencing certain individuals (or role incumbents) in certain ways, while F grows accustomed to accepting such influence. This power is limited, however, to F's perception of L's sphere of authority. Thus commands by a methods analyst to require the use of a particular work method by operating personnel may well meet with resistance or overt hostility, if he is seen to be overstepping the boundaries of his authority. By the same token, insistence by a dean for the use of certain classroom procedures may be deemed a violation of academic freedom and therefore an illegitimate exercise of authority, to be ignored or circumvented.

REFERENT POWER

Probably the most commonly recognized example of referent power is the influence that a young boy's "idol" has over him. Without necessarily knowing it, Joe Dimaggio, Willie Mays, and other sports heroes have been used as models by countless fans. The emulation does not end with batting styles, but frequently extends to dress, attitudes, speech, and other forms of behavior. It is said that when Clark Gable removed his shirt in the movie *It Happened One Night* and was seen to be wearing no undershirt, the sale of men's undershirts immediately plummeted. The public acceptance of hair and dress styles also seems to be largely based upon the emulation of respected social luminaries. These examples testify to the (often unknowing) behavioral and attitudinal impact of respected and prominent individuals. This ability of an individual to cause another to identify with him and to emulate him is termed referent power.

Many leaders are highly respected by their followers. Subordinates may aspire not only to a leader's position, but to *be* like him. Consequently, the leader's views are studied, as are his mannerisms, his skills, and his background. He may exercise a strong influence upon the thoughts and actions of his followers. Yet neither the leader nor the follower may consciously suspect the basis of this influence.

Referent power should not be confused with reward or coercive power. The latter two are based on the desire for favorable treatment by L, while referent power is based upon F's desire to become more like L. Certainly the exercise of reward power can strengthen the bond between L and F. Recognition by L of F's high performance or potential is an exercise of reward power, which may in turn enhance L's image in F's mind, making the identification even stronger.

EXPERT POWER

An appearance of intensive knowledge and analytical competence in a given subject can enhance one's ability to influence others on matters relevant to that expertise. If L is considered an authority on the topic, he is enabled to affect F's thoughts and actions in that area. Here is an instance where technical skill and knowledge contribute to leadership effectiveness. Thus the leader who "came up from the ranks" holds an advantage of having done similar work and solved similar problems. The person who can demonstrate his skill at the relevant tasks, be they manual or intellectual, has a built-in ability to influence.

The formal leader in a hierarchy usually possesses certain unique knowledge as a result of his position. Examples include knowledge of objectives, policies, procedures, and specific action being considered by higher echelons. He may be aware of interdepartmental matters of which his subordinates are ignorant. F's perception that L is uniquely vested with such knowledge increases L's influence. Should L also be seen as an authority on important intradepartmental processes, he would possess substantial expert power.

It should be noted that expert power is related to referent power in that knowledge is a respected characteristic in most cultures. It is possible for a leader to exercise expert power, however, even where he is disliked. The marine drill sergeant may be thoroughly despised, but his obvious expertise on the care and feeding of an M-16 rifle will heavily influence his recruits on that topic. Many a student has been heard to say of a professor, "He's a vain, cocky, conceited ————, but he really knows his ————." Of course, the opposite is also heard of the manager who is "a helluva nice guy" but "doesn't know beans" about the operation.

We have seen that the potential leader can exercise influence through a variety of powers that he may possess. Some of these powers are provided by the organization to strengthen his influence. In fact, the organization, besides bulwarking him with certain reward and coercive powers, can provide him with legitimate power (title, support by higher level managers, clear statement of authority, and so forth); with referent power (by proper placement and leadership training); and with expert power (placement, technical training, and flow of relevant information).

The formal leader competes for influence with the group's informal leaders and with the group itself, as well as with such external influences as staff officials, union leaders, higher level leaders, and so forth. These sources of influence also possess the powers discussed above in varying combinations. The leader's control of group behavior may be seen as a condition of moving equilibrium, a balancing of his changing powers with those of competing influences. Many managers exercise little or no leadership; frequently other men, lacking official titles, are the real influencers of thought and action in the work situation. An analysis of the powers discussed above may explain such apparent inconsistencies.

Leadership Style

> . . . All men when they are spoken of, and chiefly princes . . . , are remarkable for some of these qualities which bring them either blame or praise; and thus it is that one is reputed generous, another rapacious; one cruel, one compassionate; one faithless, another faithful; one effeminate and cowardly, another bold and brave; one affable, another haughty; one lascivious, another chaste; one sincere, another cunning . . . but [these characteristics] can neither be entirely possessed or observed, for human conditions do not permit it.[4]

So wrote Niccolo Machiavelli more than four centuries ago in *The Prince*, a treatise concerning the relationships that should exist between a ruler and his subjects. Among his most intriguing pronouncements are those dealing with the love and fear of the ruler by his followers:

> Upon this a question rises: whether it be better to be loved than feared or feared than loved. It may be answered that one should wish to be both,

[4] Niccolo Machiavelli, *The Prince* (London: J. M. Dent & Sons, Ltd., 1948), p. 118.

but, because it is difficult to unite them in one person, it is much safer to be feared than loved . . . for love is preserved by the link of obligation which, owing to the baseness of men, is broken at every opportunity for their advantage; but fear preserves you by a dread of punishment which never fails.[5]

Although the modern free-world administrator does not have life-and-death power over his subordinates, he too must decide on a leadership strategy. This strategy, or style, will be partially determined by his beliefs about the nature of his subordinates. If he sees them as "base," stupid, lazy, and driven predominantly by the desire for economic gain, he will design a work system very similar to that formulated by the scientific management movement in the early 1900s. Quite another leadership strategy would result from a view of the worker as industrious, imaginative, ambitious, and generally possessed of great potential. This latter view seems to be gaining strength among leading management theorists. Let us examine these views more closely, using as our medium the ideas of Douglas McGregor.

INTEGRATIVE LEADERSHIP

The writings of Douglas McGregor have recently had a profound influence on leadership theory and practice. McGregor postulates that conventional superior-subordinate relationships are based on a set of unrealistic assumptions about the nature of man as a worker. This set of assumptions, labeled *Theory X*, visualizes the worker as inherently lazy, passive, and unambitious, as follows:

1. The average human being has an inherent dislike of work and will avoid it if he can.
2. Because of this human characteristic of dislike of work, most people must be coerced, controlled, directed, threatened with punishment to get them to put forth adequate effort toward the achievement of organizational objectives.
3. The average human being prefers to be directed, wishes to avoid responsibility, has relatively little ambition, wants security above all.[6]

The assumptions carry with them some obvious leadership implications: they call for close supervision, emphasis on money and security

[5] Ibid., p. 131.
[6] Douglas McGregor, *The Human Side of Enterprise* (New York: McGraw-Hill Book Company, Inc., 1960), pp. 33–43.

rewards, the creation of narrow, highly specialized, fully programmed jobs; decisions regarding policies, procedures, objectives, and the like are to be made solely by management and staff specialists (the worker must work, management must manage). Thus the leadership practices attributed to the "scientific management" disciples are thought to be based on the *Theory X* set of assumptions.

As McGregor states, the validity of *Theory X* is, at best, questionable. The concept of inherent laziness contradicts clear scientific and "common-sense" evidence that physical and mental activity are sought out and are, indeed, *necessary* to human health. The simplistic notions of human motivation conflict with current motivation theory. It is suggested, furthermore, that the frequently observed worker inertia, lack of ambition, and avoidance of responsibility *result* from management systems based on *Theory X* and are not inherent human traits. Why should a worker show initiative, and innovativeness, and organizational concern within a *Theory X* management environment? How could he do so if he desired? Perhaps, then, he is taught to behave in the manner expected of him in the first place by the *Theory X* manager. Apathy, inertia, and even hostility are said to be the predictable results of a system in which the worker is restricted to simple, repetitive tasks with a minimum of opportunity to influence work procedures and the reward structure.

In place of the *Theory X* assumptions, McGregor proposes a new set of premises, which he terms *Theory Y*. The principle elements of *Theory Y* follow:

1. The expenditure of physical and mental effort in work is as natural as play or rest.
2. Man will exercise self-discretion and self-control in the service of objectives to which he is committed.
3. Commitment to objectives is a function of the rewards associated with their achievement. The most significant of such rewards, e.g., the satisfaction of ego and self-actualization needs, can be direct products of effort directed toward organizational objectives.
4. The average human being, under proper conditions, learns not only to accept but to seek responsibility.
5. The capacity to exercise a relatively high degree of imagination, ingenuity, and creativity in the solution of organizational problems is widely, not narrowly, distributed in the population.[7]

Man is seen herein as the possessor of various physical and mental energies that can readily be channeled toward organizational objectives

[7] McGregor, *The Human Side*, pp. 45–57.

ego and growth needs are thereby also satisfied. The leadership
enge is to create a system in which the satisfaction of one's activated
occurs as an integral part of the process of achieving the firm's
goals. The operative, the manager, and the organization are seen as mutually supportive. The success of a leader is ultimately tied to the development, motivation, and complete utilization of his followers. Such an
approach to leadership may sound idealistic and impractical, yet there is
growing evidence that this theory can be made operational, as indicated
by the following practices.

PARTICIPATION

In many cases, workers possess knowledge and specific analytical
skills that their managers lack. Moreover, workers are frequently more
deeply concerned about formal systems than are their superiors. Work
methods, conditions, and rewards are cases in point. The manager who
recognizes this valuable pool of knowledge, skills, and interest may well
seek to tap it in his efforts toward highest overall productivity and satisfaction. He seeks to create an atmosphere of *mutual influence,* wherein
all who are capable and concerned play an important role in making decisions. The leader refutes the role of the demigod ruling from on high.
He sincerely seeks assistance when it is available and renders assistance
when he can, all toward the achievement of the multiple goals of the
operatives, the organization, and, of course, the leader himself.

A strategic by-product of participative management is thought to
be an increased *involvement* on the part of all subordinates. Having contributed to the establishment of objectives, workers become more personally committed to their attainment. Having helped to create systems and
procedures, workers feel more inclined to make them work. The worker's
ego is engaged. Success of the endeavor means he was "right." The very
process of being consulted in the making of important decisions is ego-
gratifying. One may be made to feel of high personal worth—a person
with experience, information, talents, and viewpoints—rather than a pair
of hands to be attached to a machine.

The subordinate may also experience a sense of personal growth in
that he receives more information than he does under an authoritarian
manager. He feels more knowledgeable and more influential. He is asked
not only to "feel," but to articulate constructive ideas to help make policy
decisions. He may be asked to respond to problems of significance beyond
his primary workplace. Thus through participation, it may be possible
particularly to satisfy both ego and self-actualization needs, while improving the resulting decisions.

Another technique for satisfying ego and growth needs is termed general supervision or permissive leadership. This is a conscious effort to permit lower-level personnel to perform their functions in their own way, without constant or close supervision. Once objectives are established, workers are permitted to organize themselves in a manner designed (hopefully) to be functional as well as satisfying. Centrally devised standard operating procedures are deemphasized, the belief being that those who perform work can and will devise effective procedures and methods to ease their tasks.

Such permissiveness is thought to yield greater employee involvement with the problems of the organization. In addition, there is the clear implication that workers are capable of making substantial intellectual contributions to evolving work systems. A medium is thereby provided through which the worker may, to a greater degree, satisfy his ego needs in the course of a normal day's work. He finds himself the object of trust and confidence in the mind of management. This in itself is ego-satisfying. Presumably the worker experiencing such freedom and opportunity to contribute will strive to retain these privileges through his constructive efforts. Should these efforts yield recognizable benefits for his work group or the organization as a whole, further ego rewards would be forthcoming from peers and managers.[8]

CLIENT-PROFESSIONAL STAFF ASSISTANCE

The role of staff specialists has changed dramatically during recent decades. Staff personnel were conceived only as advisors to superior line officers. Staff men were to provide expertise that might help line officers to make decisions or to assume some of the line manager's routine functions, thus permitting him to focus his attention on urgent matters, unexpected developments, and major problems.

From this classic function of upward assistance, the staff role has evolved to the monitoring of lower echelons and the issuance of directives downward in the organization. Staff officers are frequently considered by lower-level managers and operatives as spies, who investigate operations at these levels and then report departures from policy and accepted practice to higher line officers. In addition, the exercise by staff officers of command authority may be viewed as an invasion of the prerogatives of

---

[8] An excellent discussion of leadership and organizational performance is found in Rensis Likert, *New Patterns of Management* (New York: McGraw-Hill Book Company, Inc., 1961), pp. 5–25.

lower-level managers. Consider, for example, directives flowing from a scheduling department or a work methods department to a line foreman or plant manager or district director. The line officer is answerable to his superiors for results. But he must also adhere to the directives initiated by a host of staff specialists who are *not* directly responsible for results. Two questions logically arise in the manager's mind: (1) If I am responsible for results, must I not be vested with the authority to achieve these results? (2) What is happening to the status of my position as staff specialists assume a greater and greater role in running my operation?

Nevertheless, there is good reason for the intensified use of staff competencies in an increasingly technical and rapidly changing environment. The contributions of highly trained specialists may be necessary to assure that operations keep pace with technology and other changing conditions. Some suggest that staff assistance can be effectively applied without jeopardizing the integrity of line positions. It is agreed that staff expertise should be available to lower-level line officers. This need not signify that each staff officer is an added superior. Rather, line officers at any organizational level should possess the authority to *request* information or advice from appropriate staff offices and personnel. The relationship should be one of client and professional. If a staff officer can render valuable assistance, then managers should be informed of this potential service. Should a manager require help, he should request it. The resulting reports and recommendations should be directed to that line official only, not to his superiors.[9]

Under such an arrangement, staff departments are viewed as resources to be tapped upon demand, not as an espionage system or a threat to line authority. It is assumed (perhaps optimistically?) that the true value of such expertise will be recognized and exploited by the line officer who knows that he alone is responsible for his unit's success. True individual responsibility and position integrity offer the promise of ego and growth rewards to the line official. His continuous challenge is his judicious use of available resources toward the achievement of organizational goals. He is not "force fed" by numerous insistant authorities. He decides his needs; he decides how best to use available assistance; and he reaps the consequences.

Staff officials, too, may better satisfy ego needs through this system of requested staff assistance. The staff units or individuals whose expertise is found valuable by line personnel will be in great demand. Those who are avoided, because of technical or human relations weaknesses, will be forced either to improve the quality of their service or leave the organization. The situation may again be likened to the client-professional rela-

[9] McGregor, *The Human Side,* pp. 145–75.

tionship. The "good" dentist will probably develop the thriving practice, with all of the associated rewards. Why should not the same be true of methods analysts, safety officers, and labor relations officials?

MANAGEMENT BY OBJECTIVES

Perhaps the ultimative in integrative leadership is an approach called management by objectives. This system blends participation, general supervision, and client-professional line-staff relationships. Under this system, each manager asks his direct subordinates to develop a set of reasonable and appropriate goals to be achieved within a specified time period. Thus the general manager of a manufacturing plant may establish goals for that plant covering the next year. Areas covered by such goals may include reductions in raw materials waste, increases in output per dollar of labor costs, reduction of employee turnover, a lower inventory-output ratio, and so forth. These objectives are stated in quantitative, readily measurable terms, so that progress can be easily determined.

Besides such performance goals, the manager may be encouraged to set objectives for his own development. He discusses his own perceived shortcomings and ways of overcoming them. He then presents a plan for strengthening his abilities to perform at his current level and indicating the positions to which he aspires. Discussions about performance and development may be involved and lengthy. But the final result is a set standard for each member of management, which he has participated in establishing and which he agrees is reasonable.

With the passage of specified time intervals, each manager submits terse reports of his progress toward his objectives. Should it appear that certain goals were set too high (or too low!), brief explanations are attached. At this point, objectives may well be modified in the light of new knowledge. It should be stressed that objectives are always based on premises or assumptions about the future. Should these premises prove inaccurate, it would be foolhardy to insist on objectives built on them. Thus a company-wide strike or a severe general labor shortage might well call for a revision of objectives and plans.

Thus management by objectives provides for intense participation in goal-setting and planning by every management level. It usually also involves a minimum of detailed, day-to-day supervision from above, including a minimum of staff control. It is for the individual manager to achieve his stated objectives with a minimum of external interference. Should he require and request the assistance of staff departments or his superiors, every effort is made to comply. The responsibility, and the accompanying rewards for achievement, remain with the individual.[10]

The principal hypothesis of integrative leadership is that all of the major kinds of human needs can be somewhat satisfied at work and that the very activity of contribution for organization success can be highly rewarding to the worker. Thus it is believed that an employee's needs can be tied to those of the organization, whether he be an operative or a manager. Let us take another look at Maslow's need hierarchy and indicate how these needs can be satisfied at work.

Need Classification	*Possible Satisfier*
1. Physiological	Working conditions Safety precautions Remuneration
2. Economic security	Seniority privileges Job or income guarantees Recognition by management Insurance and retirement systems
3. Social	Compatible work groups Small work groups Permissive leadership–group self-control Group work goals Competition between groups
4. Esteem (self-esteem and other esteem)	Participation in goal setting and planning Recognition by peers Recognition by management Achievement of challenging objectives Minimal supervision Formal training programs General status within group
5. Self-actualization	Participation in goal setting, planning, and achievement reviews Advancement to higher positions Increased opportunity to exercise discretion in current position Formal training programs Day-to-day learning through observation, informal coaching, practice, and so forth

[10] Much is being written about the philosophy, techniques, and limitations of management by objectives. Examples include D. D. McConkey, *How to Manage by Results* (New York: American Management Association, 1965); A. P. Raia, "A Second Look at Goals and Controls," *California Management Review* (Summer, 1966), pp. 49–58; H. L. Tossi and S. J. Carroll, "Managerial Reactions to Management by Objectives," *Academy of Management Journal*, XI, no. 4 (December, 1968), 415–26.

Current attempts at integrative leadership have, predictably, attracted many critics. The attacks basically come on two fronts: (1) the nature of the human being as a worker, and (2) the nature of work in complex organizations.

It is said that many persons are not psychologically prepared for the higher levels of individual responsibility and freedom associated with integrative leadership. Some people are "stuck" at the security need level or the social need level. They neither desire nor feel ready to cope with a *Theory Y* system. Some feel generally inadequate or inferior. Such people, it is held, want strong leadership and routine, stable jobs. Their performance might suffer, as would their satisfaction levels, should they be expected to assume more responsibility and discretion.

Other workers are so accustomed to autocratic leadership that they would question the sincerity, indeed the sanity, of a permissive, democratic approach. They might, initially at least, consider this new system as a trick, a ruse designed for unspecified ulterior motives. Still other workers may be only temporarily and casually associated with the organization. How likely are they to desire a role in decision making, challenging objectives, and the responsibility of helping to shape the system?

Even Maslow, upon whose motivation theories much of *Theory Y* is based, expressed serious doubts about the widespread application of this system, stating:

> . . . The truth is that we don't really have exact and quantitative information on the proportion of the population which does in fact have some kind of feeling for workmanship, some kind of desire for all the facts and all the truth, some sort of desire for efficiency. . . .
>
> What proportion of the population is irreversibly authoritarian? We don't even know what proportion . . . are psychopaths or paranoiac characters or overdependent or safety motivated, etc.
>
> We don't know how many people . . . would actually prefer to participate in managerial decisions, and how many would prefer not to have anything to do with them. . . .
>
> All of this then is an experiment . . . which is based upon a scientifically unproven assumption: namely that human beings like to participate in their own fate, that given sufficient information they will make wise decisions . . . , that they prefer freedom to being bossed, that they prefer to have a say in everything which affects their future, etc. . . .
>
> After all, if we take the whole thing from McGregor's point of view of human nature, a good deal of the evidence upon which he bases his conclusions comes from my researches and my papers on motivation, self-

actualization, etc. But I of all people should know how shaky this foundation is as a final foundation.[11]

Many individuals, it is believed, are much more interested in security and stability than in status or growth opportunities. Many prefer dependence on strong, competent leadership and perhaps lack self-confidence and fear failure. Furthermore, those who have experienced a lifetime (youthful though they may be) of taking orders from parents, teachers, dictatorial bosses, and so forth would be unable to adjust readily to a suddenly permissive system. Some employees, it is said, work primarily for money. Their real interests lie outside of the work place. Thus workers may respond to *Theory Y* treatment in a variety of ways: disinterest, tension, distrust, and incompetence among them.[12] Even those who are interested and confident may lack the information or the intellect to make a real contribution to the system.

Further limitations on permissive management are imposed by the nature of work processes. For example, it is difficult to apply participative leadership in an assembly-line situation or other highly structured technical system. Time constraints may limit the degree of consultation permissible.

THE FIEDLER MODEL

Perhaps the most telling argument against the general application of integrative leadership derives from the research of F. E. Fiedler. He suggests that the relationship between group performance and leadership style is determined by a number of important factors. Specifically, Fiedler hypothesizes that the effectiveness of the human-relations-oriented or task-oriented leader is affected by (1) existing leader-member relations, (2) the degree to which the group's tasks are structured, and (3) the official powers possessed by the leader. Fiedler's extensive studies indicate that under certain circumstances, group performances tend to be superior under a task-oriented leader, as listed in Table 14-1. Thus the task-oriented leader is found more effective where leader-member relations are good, task structure is high, and leader position power is either high or low. In contrast, as shown in Table 14-2, the human-relations orientation may be

---

[11] Abraham H. Maslow, *Eupsychian Management* (Homewood, Ill.: Richard D. Irwin, Inc., 1965), pp. 54–56.

[12] See, for example, George Strauss, "The Personality vs. Organization Theory," in *Organizational Behavior and the Practice of Management,* ed. Hampton, et al. (Glenview, Ill.: Scott, Foresman and Co., 1968), pp. 261–70.

Table 14-1

SITUATIONS ASSOCIATED WITH SUPERIOR PERFORMANCE UNDER
A TASK-ORIENTED LEADER

FACTOR	CONDITIONS			
	A	B	C	D
Leader-member relations	Good	Good	Good	Poor
Task structure	High	High	Low	Low
Leader position power	High	Low	High	Low

SOURCE: Fred E. Fiedler, A *Theory of Leadership Effectiveness*
(New York: McGraw-Hill Book Company, 1967), pp. 133–53.

Table 14-2

SITUATIONS ASSOCIATED WITH SUPERIOR PERFORMANCE UNDER
A HUMAN-RELATIONS-ORIENTED LEADER

FACTOR	CONDITIONS			
	A	B	C	D
Leader-member relations	Good	Poor	Poor	Poor
Task structure	Low	High	High	High
Leader position power	Low	High	Low	High

SOURCE: Fred E. Fiedler, A *Theory of Leadership Effectiveness*
(New York: McGraw-Hill Book Company, 1967), pp. 133–53.

superior where leader-member relations are good, while both task structure and leader position power are low. The reader may wish to analyze
each of the eight situations presented and attempt to explain Fiedler's
findings.

Fiedler interprets his findings as follows:

> Considerate, permissive, accepting leaders obtain optimal group per-
> formance under situations intermediate in favorableness. These are situa-
> tions in which (a) the task is structured, but the leader is disliked and
> must, therefore, be diplomatic; (b) the liked leader has an ambiguous,
> unstructured task and must, therefore, draw upon the creativity and
> cooperation of his members. . . . Where the task is highly structured
> and the leader is well-liked, nondirective behavior or permissive attitudes

(such as asking how the group ought to proceed with a missile count-
down) is neither appropriate nor beneficial. Where the situation is quite
unfavorable, e.g., where the disliked chairman of a volunteer group faces
an ambiguous task, he might as well be autocratic and directive since a
positive, nondirective leadership style under these circumstances might
result in complete inactivity on the part of the group.[13]

However one explains Fiedler's findings, it seems clear that there are
no simple, general answers to the question of preferred leadership style.
Persuasive though *Theory Y* may be, the key to the selection of an appropriate leadership style may well hinge on the many complexities within
the leader, the led, and the work structure.

SUMMARY

The leader affects the behavior of his organization in several ways.
He is a perceiver of important events, a link in the multidirectional communications network, and a decision maker who implements higher-level
decisions. At times these roles are overlooked, for typically the leader's
most visible role involves direct attempts to influence the behavior of
subordinates.

Attempts to identify leadership traits have met little success. No
single leadership "type" has been found. It is believed, rather, that the
effective leader possesses a number of important skills that can be learned.
These are technical skills (a grasp of relevant processes and techniques),
human relations skills (ability to understand and influence the behavior
of others), and conceptual skills (ability to visualize and integrate important situational relationships). Technical skills seem most important
in lower managerial positions, conceptual requirements dominate at the
summit, and human relations skills are necessary at all levels.

A leader's ability to influence the thoughts and behavior of others is
determined by his possession of several types of power. These include his
control of a reward structure (reward power, coercive power); the degree
to which others identify with him, desiring to emulate or please him
(referent power); acceptance that certain influence patterns are part of
the organization's role structure (legitimate power); and the apparent
competence or knowledge of the leader within the technical area involved

---

[13] Fred E. Fiedler, *A Contingency Model for the Prediction of Leadership Effectiveness* (Urbana, Ill.: Group Research Laboratory, Department of Psychology, University of Illinois, 1963), p. 14.

(expert power). Any leader's influence can probably be explained by his possession of some combination of these powers. Some of these are generally provided by the organization; others are generated by the leader as a person.

Among the many theories of effective leadership style is that of Douglas McGregor, who asserts that one's leadership style derives from his assumptions about the nature of man as a worker. If the worker is viewed as inherently lazy, passive, and unambitious (*Theory X*), then the managers establish a system that features economic rewards, close supervision, simple jobs, and commands. If the manager depicts the worker as potentially energetic, self-disciplined, ascendant, responsible, and innovative (*Theory Y*), then he constructs a work situation that features general supervision, participation, job enrichment, work group autonomy, and management by objectives, all designed to enlist the employees' esteem and growth needs as principal motivators.

There are many limitations to the application of integrative leadership. Not all persons are ready for great discretion or responsibilities. Many are deeply dependent because of prior conditioning, or are "stuck" at the security level. Others do not strongly identify with the organization or its management. The technology employed often requires only simple, programmed worker activities. At a point in time, therefore, individual managers may be powerless to implement integrative leadership effectively. Nor is it clear that such an approach is generally superior. Fiedler's studies indicate that the human-relations-oriented leader is effective under conditions of "intermediate favorableness," and that directive leadership is superior when conditions are extremely favorable or unfavorable. (A most favorable situation would include good leader-member relations, high task structure, and strong leader position power, according to Fiedler.) It seems clear that no simple rules exist for selecting generally preferred leadership styles.

QUESTIONS

1. The leader influences organizational goals and behavior in several ways. Discuss these.
2. What is the leader's role in implementing goals and strategies established at higher levels in the hierarchy?
3. Explain why so little success has been achieved in the search for universal leadership attributes.

4. What is leadership?

5. A comment often heard is, "My boss may not always be right, but he's always my boss." Interpret this statement in terms of the bases of leader power.

6. Might a professor possess a leader's powers? Give some examples.

7. Examine the assumptions of *Theory Y*. Do you have any reservations about them? Discuss.

8. How may the leader adapt his style to the assumptions of *Theory Y*?

9. Frederick W. Taylor is viewed as an exponent of *Theory X*, yet his system of scientific management was extremely effective at increasing worker productivity. How do you explain this?

10. How does management by objectives relate to *Theory Y*?

11. According to Fiedler, under what conditions would a "human-relations-oriented leader" be most successful? Explain the possible logic behind your answer.

12. Describe how a *Theory Y* professor might conduct a class. Contrast him with a *Theory X* professor.

case studies
for part three

Excellent Insurance Company (A)

Throughout the winter of 1952–53, Robert Jennings, a research worker from the Harvard Business School, spent several weeks studying the industrial department of the home office of the Excellent Insurance Company in Cleveland, Ohio. The home office of the company employed more than 4,000 people, 500 in the industrial department. The company had an extensive business in industrial, group, and ordinary life insurance. With more than 100 branch offices and 4,000 agents, the company had contracts for industrial insurance with more than 4,000,000 policyholders. The holders of industrial policies paid small weekly premiums as low as 10 cents. Annual dividends on these policies ranged from 5 to 10 times the weekly premium.

The service functions of the home office were organized into several departments. Three, called policy departments, handled the service transactions on existing policies, such as paying dividends and processing the

This case, Excellent Insurance Company (A) & (B), EA-A 179, was prepared by Harold F. Craig under the direction of Joseph C. Bailey of the Harvard University Graduate School of Business Administration as a basis for classroom discussion rather than to illustrate either effective or ineffective handling of administrative situations. Copyright © 1954 by the President and Fellows of Harvard College. Used by specific permission. This case also appears in *Organizational Behavior and Administration: Cases, Concepts, and Research Findings* by Paul R. Lawrence, Joseph C. Bailey, Robert L. Katz, John A. Seiler, Charles D. Orth, III, James V. Clark, Louis B. Barnes, and Arthur N. Turner (Homewood, Illinois: Richard D. Irwin, Inc., 1961).

265

transactions involved in the issue of new policies and the surrender of existing ones.

John Warner, manager of the industrial department, was responsible to Calvin Bunbury, vice-president in charge of all three policy departments.

In the dividend division of the industrial department were kept the company's records of the annual dividends on each industrial policy. The clerks in this division checked these records for accuracy and filed them. On the average, the division processed the records of 4,000,000 separate dividends a year, an average of about 15,000 each working day. There were 35 clerks in the division. The work was being converted from manual operations to a new punched-card accounting system. Jennings was studying the introduction and administration of the new system, the installation of which was nearly complete by April. From his discussions with a number of managers, Jennings became interested in some events that were only loosely related to the new accounting system. This case is a result of that interest.

On the morning of April 16, Jennings talked with Norman Homans, an administrative assistant to Bunbury. Jennings had talked to Homans on a number of previous occasions. Homans had been assigned to introduce Jennings to other members of the management of the policy departments. During the conversation, Homans mentioned a problem he had regarding Kathy O'Toole. Excerpts from the conversation follow:

Norman Homans: It all started one time when I was up having lunch with one of the personnel directors. He told me that a waitress in the executive dining room was interested in improving her position in life by getting a job as a clerk.

The girl he referred to was Kathy O'Toole. I know Kathy O'Toole quite well. She often waited on our table, and I was impressed with her efficiency, energy, and general attitude toward life. She is a married woman of about 42 who came back to work at the company after her family grew up.

Anyhow, she went to the personnel department and asked them if they had any openings in the clerical line because she didn't want to be a waitress all her life. I knew she was going to school at night studying secretarial work with a view of one day fulfilling her ambition to become a secretary, and I also knew that she was interested in getting a job in the clerical area prior to an opportunity coming up where she could use her secretarial training.

I said to the personnel director: "I may be able to do something about it. I'll look into whether we have a slot in one of the policy departments in which we could use her." I knew that we had plenty of room in the policy departments for good clerks, and I thought that here was a chance

Exhibit 1

Excellent Insurance Company.

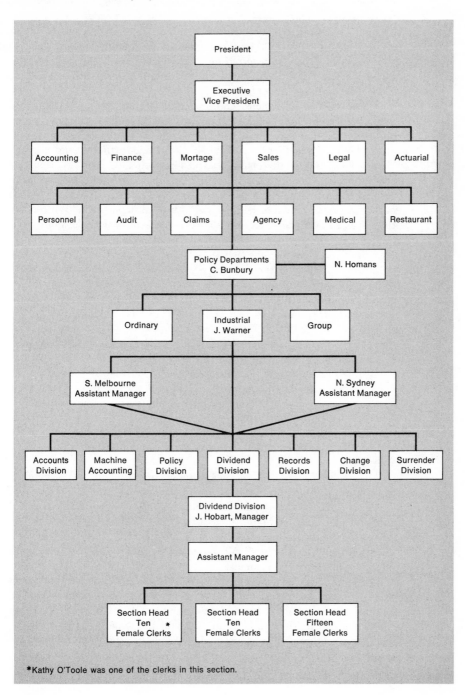

*Kathy O'Toole was one of the clerks in this section.

to get a good clerk—someone a bit above the average. You know that we are short of good clerks. We have been for some time.

That afternoon, I talk to Mr. Melbourne. He said that we could use more help in the dividend division. Then the next thing I heard was that she didn't want to be transferred until after Christmas because she wanted to get her share of the Christmas tips. We thought this was reasonable, so we transferred her in January.

There were repercussions. Quite a number of the fellows around the office here knew Kathy because she is a bright and breezy type of girl and seems to know everyone, particularly those on whom she had waited at the table. When they passed her in the corridor, they would ask her: "How is it going, Kathy? How do you like your new job?" We felt that she might have a bit of a problem in terms of transferring from waitress to clerk. We thought that perhaps some of the girls might say, "She's only a waitress," so we picked out the industrial department. We thought there was less chance of any problems there because they do more working and less talking in the industrial department than they do in some of the others, and we thought that they would get on with their work and not bother about whether she was a waitress or what she was. Anyhow, these boys asked her how things were going and how she liked it; and her report was that she hated the job, didn't like it a bit, and wanted to get out of it. Kathy continued that she didn't have enough work to do and that it was an awful job.

Then I heard that she tried to get a transfer from this department. I heard various stories about how she went about it. One was that she knew Bill Field quite well. She used to wait on his table, too, and he works in the ordinary department. According to his story, Kathy went over to see Bill and asked whether he had any vacancies in his area. He said yes, he had plenty of opportunities in his area. He needed girls in some of the accounting work where they were short of clerical help in the statistical record section, and he talked to her about an opportunity available there.

After this, Kathy went to the personnel department and wanted to know if she could be transferred to the ordinary department. The interviewer that handled this job—her name is Miss Avon—talked to Kathy and later talked to Joe Main, the assistant personnel manager, asking him what they should do about the situation. Apparently, they thought that this wasn't the way things should be done; they didn't like clerks to make their own transfer arrangements.

While all this was going on, I heard from different people that things were happening. For example, the manager of the dividend division, Mr. Hobart, heard about her making arrangements for a transfer and got annoyed about it. He said he didn't care for this type of thing going on; that she wasn't much of a clerk, anyhow; and that she wouldn't sit down and get on with her job. He said she was always hopping up and making phone calls and walking out here and there, and her general behavior wasn't good enough for him. When Kathy was asked about this, her reaction was that she never had enough work to do and she didn't know what to do with herself.

Now, I don't know who is right. If she doesn't have enough to do, there is something wrong with the way Hobart administers his division. On the other hand, it is her job to get on with her work and not be making phone calls and behaving in that manner. You see, there is a bit of a problem, in a way, because she knows so many of the people from the executive dining room on a friendly basis that she is inclined to be presumptuous.

As a matter of fact, I've got myself in a spot now because I feel I've got to justify my own action. This feeling of mine is increased by the fact that Melbourne warned us that he had heard from the grapevine that this girl liked things her own way and was inclined to put on performance if things didn't get done the way she considered was right. It is amazing what Melbourne hears on his grapevine; and it has been my experience that when he hears something, it is pretty accurate. He seems to know— I don't know how—but he just seems to find out about people. In fact, I've got to the situation now where I take his opinion against mine any time.

Anyhow, the next thing that happened on this matter was when Miss Avon talked to Bill Field. He apparently said that he didn't have an opening available. It seems that he thought about the matter in the light of some comments he heard about Kathy—such comments as the fact that she wasn't a very good clerk—and Miss Avon reported to me that he wasn't so sure he did have an opening available for her. Miss Avon told me that she thought it would be better if we didn't let Kathy make her own transfer arrangements. Miss Avon said that she had talked to Joe Main and that she had decided to tell Kathy that there was no vacancy in the ordinary department, but that there was an opening in the accounting department, and that Kathy could take a look at the job over there and, if she liked it, she could have it. Incidentally, Kathy had threatened to leave the company and said that if she had to stay in the dividend division, she would do so.

In the interview with Miss Avon, Kathy said that she was sold on the company, but she wasn't going to put up with working in the dividend division.

At the next interview, Miss Avon told Kathy that she couldn't have the job in the ordinary department but that she could have a job in the accounting department. Kathy had a look at the job in the accounting department and went back to Miss Avon and said, "No, that wasn't the type of job I wanted. I don't know what I will do, but I won't stay in the dividend division."

Next, Kathy turned up at the medical clinic, saying that she had a bad headache. She had never been in the clinic before. Following her visit, we got a call from the medical people, who said that Kathy was in a highly nervous state and that if we didn't do something about her problems, we would end up with a group insurance case on our hands and she would be out, with us paying her for some time.

We thought that it was a little silly that we should be getting ourselves into the position of having a group insurance case just for not letting the girl transfer where she wanted to, and I thought that the personnel people had really not used the right approach when they limited her transfer. I told them that it was wrong for them to be subjective about a problem and to limit this transfer just because they thought this girl was expecting too much. I thought that if there was a transfer available to the ordinary department, and the ordinary department was prepared to have her, they should let her go. After all, the ordinary policy department is under Mr. Bunbury's jurisdiction, too, and we can keep an eye on the situation. At the same time, I thought it should be made clear to her that if this job didn't suit her, she would have no complaints.

The personnel people have asked me to talk to Kathy about it; if they do arrange the transfer, they want me to tell her that this is the last time she will get any special consideration. As far as I am concerned, all I want is to be done with it. I wish I had never taken it on; and yet, she seemed like a good bet in terms of getting a good clerk.

When Jennings left Homans' office that morning, he recalled some of his impressions of the dividend division. He had spent several days in the division and had heard a number of opinions regarding the new system. Hobart, the manager, thought that the new system would be much better than the old. He remarked that it should make it easier to handle the fluctuations in the volume of work that occurred from period to period. These fluctuations, on occasion, left the girls with very little to do; on other occasions, the volume required the inventorying of work that could not be done by the normal work force. A company policy of speedy service discouraged the inventorying of work on daily transactions, and Hobart did not like to be in the position of admitting that his division could not meet its deadlines. Consequently, he was reluctant to reduce his regular work force during periods when the load was light because he anticipated difficulty in handling peak loads, which he knew would occur from time to time.

Many of the comments Jennings heard about the new punched-card system were very favorable. Several of the girls who worked in the dividend division liked the new system much better. Nevertheless, some of them commented that the fluctuating volumes of work did create slow periods and periods when the pressure was really on.

Some of the fluctuations in volume were caused through errors made by agents. The work of the dividend clerks was so organized that most of it was standardized and simplified. It was only when the agents made

errors that the job of the clerks became complicated. When an error occurred, the clerks had to ascertain its cause and fill out a form to notify
the agent and give him the reason. When no errors were made, a clerk
could process a thousand dividends in less time than was required for a
hundred dividends in an agency where errors occurred. Consequently, the
workload of the dividend division corresponded closely with the degree
of accuracy maintained by the several thousand agents operating throughout 48 states.

The section of the division to which Kathy was assigned serviced
about 100 district offices. Shortly before Kathy was assigned to the section,
12 girl clerks were doing this work. In April, 1953, the new system made
it possible for the work of one section to be done by 10 girls. Two of the
senior ones were transferred to more skilled work in other divisions of the
department. Even then, the work in the section was not sufficient to keep
the girls occupied all the time. Consequently, whenever he was in need
of temporary assistance in other divisions of the department, Melbourne,
the assistant manager, would transfer a few of the girls from the dividend
section. Some of the girls, Jennings knew, did not like being transferred
temporarily to assist another division. They felt that the harder they
worked to get their own work finished, the more chance they had of being
assigned to assist somewhere else. Consequently, the girls were inclined
to stretch out the job during slack periods and make a special effort to
look busy whenever Melbourne was about.

Excellent Insurance Company (B)

When Jennings came into the division the afternoon following his conversation with Homans, he continued his usual procedure of asking the girls
to tell him about their work and what they thought of the new punched-
card system. He stopped at Kathy's desk during his conversations and
asked her to tell him about her work.

> *Kathy O'Toole:* I don't think I'm a very good one for you to talk
> with because I haven't been here very long and I'm going to be transferred
> soon.
> *Robert Jennings:* Why are you being transferred?
> *Kathy:* Well, I don't like the work here. It is too quiet. You don't
> have enough to do. The time really drags. I like to have some work to do
> so that I can keep busy and the clock will move along. Sitting here with
> nothing to do just drives me crazy. I don't mind sorting these things

that I've go to do now because it is something to fill in time, but there are times when I could just go to sleep, and I'm not like that. Some of these young girls just seem to like to walk around very slowly and gradually get the job done. They are like my own daughter. I often tell her that she doesn't move and that she doesn't get things done, and she tells me that she gets just as far in the long run, but I can't understand these kids these days. They seem to be prepared to sit and let things go by. They just walk around very casual-like. See that one walking down there now? My goodness! I would be around there and back again in no time.

Jennings: Do you like to keep busy?

Kathy: Yes, I do. I think that is why I don't like the work here. It is just not enough for me. It depends upon what your view is, but I can't change myself at this stage. I'm too old. I'm 42, and I've always been busy doing things. I want something that is challenging and interesting. When I first started here, they said: "You know, Kathy, this needs to be done; and Kathy, that needs to be done." After I had been told a couple of times, I'd ask why, and they just wouldn't bother to tell me why. They don't tell me anything. I said to our section head: "I want to know what happens here. Why do these things come in here? I would then be a little more interested, knowing where these things go and why I am doing this." So he explained it to me. But most of these kids that come in here are prepared to sit down; and when they are told things, they do them and are not interested in who or anything else. When I came here, I didn't think anything was going to be like this, and I am just not satisfied to stay.

Jennings: You don't like this system of work, then?

Kathy: The system is all right. It is good. As a matter of fact, I think it does things pretty well. The only thing is that there is an awful waste in all the time spent here, everybody checking and sending things backwards and forwards when someone makes a silly mistake in the agency. It seems to me that it would be a good thing if they had that sort of thing checked out in the agency. Then a lot of those things could be caught before they come in here.

Jennings: They would need an extra girl in the agency to do that sort of thing, wouldn't they?

Kathy: Yes, they would, I suppose. But they could check a number of these things, and you'd think the agents could make them out a little better and correct these mistakes. Perhaps I am a little silly there; the more mistakes they make, the more clerks they need here in the office, and I could talk myself out of a job. But the point is that I am not interested in sitting here doing nothing all the time. I have to be up and doing. I've always been busy all my life, and I can't understand some of the younger people these days. They just don't want to do things. They seem to sit around. The way they dress—they come in with bobby socks and curling pins. I just can't understand it. I think it is indicative of your way of working—the way you dress. For instance, if you came in here in a pair of loafers and a sport shirt, you wouldn't give the right impression, would you? Well, I think we should look after ourselves and dress on the job, just the same as a man. We should do things properly.

Jennings: Do you think the job to which you are going to be transferred will better?

Kathy: Well, I don't know exactly where I am going to be transferred. It seems to take quite a lot to get transferred around this place; but if I am transferred where I want to go to, the work will be much better. There is more opportunity there and a chance to get ahead if you show yourself. The thing is that in this division, all the jobs are much the same. No matter how a girl works and tries, she can't get ahead here; there is nowhere to go. All they do is routine work, and that is not enough.

Jennings: What sort of work do you like?

Kathy: I'd like any work that is interesting and where there is plenty to do and you are doing different things. It is a long story, and I'll tell you how I happened to come here in the first place.

You see, my two children are grown up. My daughter is at the university now. She wanted to do clerical work at one stage, and we let her do clerical work; and then she found that she hated clerical work and wanted to go to college, so her father said: "Well, you started in doing clerical work. You can stick it out for the rest of the year and go to college next year." Anyhow, we let her go to college this year, and she is very happy there now. She is living away from home, and I think it is the best thing she could have done. I always told her what to do at home; and at least, she makes decisions for herself now, and I think she is better off for it. She is at college. My boy is grown up. He is in the Marines. Now that the children aren't at home, the place is just empty.

I like the conditions of work here, and the managers in this company are wonderful. The only thing is that I'd like to work where I can do something interesting. You know, some of these girls here are prepared to put up with anything. They just don't know any better. But I know so many of the executives that I met in the dining room that I wouldn't meet otherwise, and I know them pretty well, and I feel that I'm in a position to know better than to just put up with this type of thing here.

Jennings: Is the actual work, when you are doing it, uninteresting?

Kathy: No, that part of the work is all right. As matter of fact, I don't mind it when I've got the work to do. It is quite interesting and quite good, but you don't seem to be kept occupied. Anyhow, I just don't want to stay on this type of work. I have ambition. I want to be an executive's secretary. One of these days, I'm going to be. You know, I've got no reason to rush from here like some of these other girls who are just putting in time until they get married. I like it here, and I don't see any reason why I shouldn't make a career of it. I've got plenty of years ahead of me; and I might work here until I retire, if they give me something interesting. My husband picks me up at night and drives me in the morning; our working hours coincide very conveniently. I can handle the home without any trouble now that the children are away; and instead of just sitting at home without anything to do, I'd rather come here and work. I don't come here for the money, you know. I'm only interested in something to do. My husband wouldn't let me work for a long while. For instance, when the children were small, he wouldn't even have considered it; but nowadays, I'd just be sitting around an empty house. I just couldn't stand it. I'd much rather come here.

The following morning, Homans told Jennings that he was to talk to Kathy that afternoon.

> *Homans:* This is an interesting problem. I've got Kathy coming in to see me at 3:00 o'clock this afternoon, and I've got to know what to say to her then. I'm not sure what I'm going to do. I know one thing: I want to get something fixed and be done with it, so I'll have to think pretty carefully about what I say to her.

Claremont Instrument Company

One of the problems facing the supervisory staff of the Claremont Instrument Company in the summer of 1948 was that of "horseplay" among employees in the glass department. For some time this question had troubled the management of the company. Efforts had been made to discourage employees from throwing water-soaked waste at each other and from engaging in water fights with buckets or fire hoses. Efforts to tighten up shop discipline had also resulted in orders to cut down on "visiting" with other employees. These efforts were made on the grounds that whatever took an employee away from his regular job would interfere with production or might cause injury to the employees or the plant machinery.

Production was a matter of some concern to the officials of the

This case, Claremont Instrument Company, EA-A 108, was prepared by Harold F. Craig under the direction of Paul Lawrence and Ralph M. Hower of the Harvard University Graduate School of Business Administration as a basis for classroom discussion rather than to illustrate either effective or ineffective handling of administrative situations. Copyright © 1953 by the President and Fellows of Harvard College. Used by specific permission. This case also appears in *Organizational Behavior and Administration: Cases, Concepts, and Research Findings* by Paul R. Lawrence, Joseph C. Bailey, Robert L. Katz, John A. Seiler, Charles D. Orth, III, James V. Clark, Louis B. Barnes, and Arthur N. Turner (Homewood, Illinois: Richard D. Irwin, Inc., 1961).

company, particularly since the war. In spite of a large backlog of unfilled orders, there were indications that domestic and foreign competition in the relatively near future might begin to cut into the company's business. Anything that could help to increase the salable output of the company was welcomed by the officers; at the same time, anything that might cut down overhead operating expenses, or improve the quality of the product, or cut down on manufacturing wastage was equally encouraged.

The Claremont Instrument Company had been located for many years in a community in western Massachusetts with a population of approximately 18,000. The company employed approximately 500 people. None of these people were organized in a union for collective bargaining purposes. The company produced a varied line of laboratory equipment and supplies. Many of its products were fabricated principally from glass, and over the years the company had built up a reputation for producing products of the highest quality. To a considerable extent this reputation for quality rested upon the company's ability to produce very delicate glass components to exacting quality standard. These glass components were produced from molten glass in the glass department. Exhibit 1 presents a partial organization chart of the company.

The entire glass department was located in one wing of the company's main factory. In this department the glass components such as tubes, bottles, decanters, and glass-measuring devices were made from molten glass. Some of these glass parts were produced by hand-blowing operations, but most of them were produced on bottle-making machinery, which in effect blew the molten glass into a mold. This operation of blowing the glass by hand or by machine was the most critical operation in the department and required a high degree of skill. Immediately following the blowing operation some of the parts were "punched." The "puncher" was a mechanical apparatus into which the glass components were placed; as the machine revolved, a small gas flame melted the glass in a small area and blew a hole in the glass component. Next the parts were placed on a mechanical conveyor where they were annealed by an air-cooling process. Then the parts were picked off the conveyor by women known as packers, whose duty was to inspect them for defects of many kinds and to give them temporary packaging in cardboard cartons for transit to other parts of the factory. The final operation in the department was performed by sealers, whose job it was to seal these cardboard cartons and place them in stacks for temporary storage. Exhibit 2 is a floor plan of the glass department.

The glass department was operated on a continuous, 24-hour, 7-day-a-week basis, because of the necessity of keeping the tanks of molten

Exhibit 1

Claremont Instrument Company,
partial organization chart.

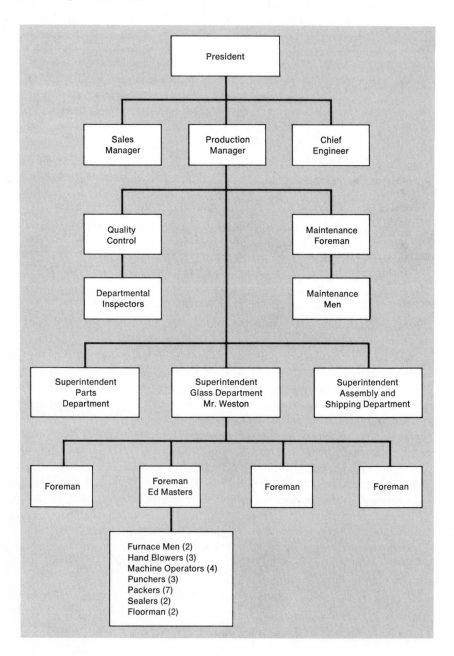

Exhibit 2

Claremont Instrument Company,
floor plan of Glass Department.

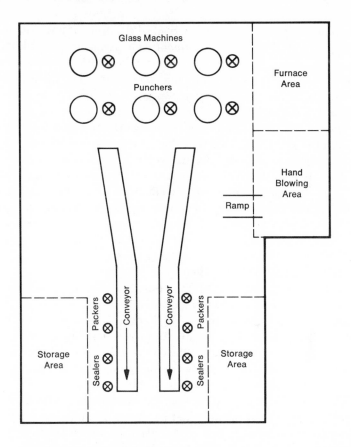

glass hot and operating all the time. Four complete shifts worked in the department. The different shifts rotated as to the hours of the day they worked. Roughly each shift spent two weeks at a time on the day shift, on the evening shift, and on the night shift. Each shift worked on the average 5 days a week, but their days off came at varying times throughout the week. The glass department was located in a separate wing of the plant and the employees of the department used a special entrance and a special time clock.

Each of the four shifts employed about 23 people. Each shift had its own foreman and assistant foreman and hourly workers as indicated in Exhibit 1. All these workers were men with the exception of the packers.

The foreman was a full-time supervisor but the assistant foreman usually operated a glass machine and only substituted for the foreman in his absence. The furnace men prepared the molten glass for the glass blowers while the floormen cleaned up broken glass and other waste and filled in on odd jobs.

An inspector from the quality-control department and a maintenance man from the maintenance department were assigned on a full-time basis to each of the four shifts. The inspector worked with the packers and was responsible for the quality of all glass components. The maintenance man was responsible for the maintenance and satisfactory operation of all machinery in the department.

Several physical conditions made work in the glass department unique in the plant. The fact that the glass furnaces were located in this department meant that the department was always unusually hot. The glass-blowing machines were run principally by compressed air, and each movement of a machine part was accompanied by the hiss of escaping air. This noise, combined with the occasional sound of breaking glass, made it impossible for the members of the department to converse in a normal tone. An oil vapor was used to coat the inside of the molds on the glass machines, and when the hot glass poured into the mold, a smoke was given off that circulated throughout the department.

In the summer of 1948, Ralph Boynton, a student at the Harvard Business School, took a summer job as a floorman on one of the shifts working in the glass department. While on this job, he made the above observations about the Claremont Instrument Company in general and the glass department in particular. In the course of the summer, Ralph became particularly interested in the practice of engaging in horseplay, and the description that follows was based on his observations.

The foreman of Boynton's shift, Ed Masters, had worked a number of years in the glass department and had been promoted to foreman from the position of operator of one of the glass machines. In Ralph's opinion the foreman was generally liked by the shift employees. One of them commented to Ralph, "If everything is going okay, you don't see Ed around. If anything goes wrong, he's right there to try to fix it up." Another one of them commented, "He pitches right in—gives us a hand—but he never says much." Frequently when a glass machine was producing glass components of unacceptable quality, Ralph noticed the foreman and the maintenance man working with a machine operator to get the machine in proper adjustment. On one occasion Ralph was assigned the job of substituting for one of the sealers. Shortly after Ralph had started his work, Ed Masters came around and asked how he was doing. Ralph replied that he was doing fine and that it was quite a trick to toss the cartons into the proper positions on the stack. Ed replied, "You keep at it, and it won't be long before you get the hang of it. You'll be tired for a while, but you'll get used to it. I found I could do it and I am a 97-pound weakling."

Ralph also picked up a variety of comments from the employees about one another. The shift maintenance man, Bert, referred to the men on the shift as "a good bunch of guys." One of the packers referred with pride to one of the machine operators, "that guy can get out more good bottles than anybody else." On one occasion, when the glass components were coming off the end of the conveyor at a very slow rate, one of the packers went around to the glass machines to find out what the trouble was. When she came back she reported to the rest of the packers, "Ollie is having trouble with his machine. It's out of adjustment but he will get it fixed in a few minutes." Ralph noticed that a record was kept of the total daily output of each shift of packers. These women seemed anxious to reach a certain minimum output on each shift. When the components were coming through slowly, he heard such comments as, "This is a bad night." If the work had been coming slowly, the packers regularly started "robbing the conveyor" toward the end of the shift. This was the practice of reaching up along the conveyor and picking off components for packaging before they reached the packer's usual work position.

A short time after Ralph started to work, the company employed another new floorman for the shift. This new man quickly picked up the nickname of "Windy." The following were some of Windy's typical comments: "My objective is the paycheck and quitting time." "I love work so much I could lay down and go to sleep right beside it." "These guys are all dopes. If we had a union in here, we would get more money." "I hate this night work. I am quitting as soon as I get another job." Most of the other employees paid little attention to Windy. One of the sealers commented about him, "If bull were snow, Windy would be a blizzard." One night Windy commented to three of the men, "This is a lousy place. They wouldn't get away with this stuff if we had a union. Why don't the four of us start one right here?" None of the group replied to this comment.

Ralph had a number of opportunities to witness the horseplay that concerned the management. At least one horseplay episode seemed to occur on every 8-hour shift. For example, one night while Ralph stood watching Ollie, one of the machine operators, at his work, Ollie called Ralph's attention to that fact that Sam, the operator of the adjacent machine, was about to get soaked.

"Watch him now," Ollie said with a grin, "last night he got Bert and now Bert is laying for him. You watch now." Ralph caught sight of Bert warily circling behind the machines with an oil can in his hand. Sam had been sitting and quietly watching the bottles come off his machine. Suddenly Bert sprang out and fired six or seven shots of water at Sam. When the water hit him, Sam immediately jumped up and fired a ball of wet waste that he had concealed for this occasion. He threw it at Bert and hit him in the chest with it. It left a large wet patch on his shirt. Bert stood his ground squirting his can until Sam started to chase him. Then he ran off. Sam wiped his face and sat down again. Then he got up and came over to Ollie and Ralph. Sam shouted, "By Jesus, I am going to give him a good soaking." Ollie and Ralph nodded in agreement. Later Ollie commented to Ralph, "It may take as long as three hours for Sam to work up a good plan to get even, but Bert is going to get it good."

Sam was ready to get back at Bert as soon as he could be lured close enough to the machine. Sam pretended to watch his machine but kept his eye out for Bert. In a little while Bert walked jauntily by Sam's machine. They grinned at each other and shouted insults and challenges. Bert went over to a bench to fix something and Sam slipped around behind his machine, pulled down the fire hose and let Bert have a full blast, chasing him up along the conveyor as Bert retreated. Sam then turned off the hose, reeled it back up, and went back to his machine.

All the other employees on the scene had stopped to watch this episode and seemed to enjoy it. They commented that it was a good soaking. Bert came back to the machines after a while, grinning, and hurling insults while he stood by Sam's machine to dry off from the heat of the machine. The other operators kidded him some, and then everyone went back to work seriously.

A little later the foreman came through the department and noticed the large puddle of water on the floor. He instructed Bert to put some sawdust on the puddle to soak up the water. Ralph was told later that Ed Masters had told Bert, "I want more work and less of this horsing around." A few minutes later Ed Masters and Bert were discussing a small repair job that had to be done that evening.

On another occasion Ralph asked Ollie what he thought of the horseplay. Ollie commented, "It's something each guy has to make up his own mind about. Personally, I don't go for it. I have got all the raises and merit increases that have come along, and I know Bert hasn't had a raise in over a year. Whenever something starts, I always look back at my machine so that I can be sure that nothing goes wrong while I am looking away. Personally, I just don't care—you have to have some fun, but personally, I don't go in for it."

Just at this point Al, one of the punchers, came down from the men's lavatory ready to take his turn on one of the punch machines. He was a moment or two early and stood talking to Sam. Ollie got up from where he had been talking to Ralph and started to holler, "Hey, Al—hey, Al." The other operators took up the chant, and all of them picked up pieces of wood or pipe and started drumming on the waste barrels near their machines. Al took up a long piece of pipe and joined in. After a minute or two, one of the operators stopped, and the drumming ended quickly. Al lit a cigarette and stepped up to take the machine for his turn.

Ralph later had an opportunity to ask Bert what he thought of the horseplay. Bert said, "You have to have some horseplay or you get rusty. You have to keep your hand in." Ralph noted that Bert's work kept him busy less than anyone else, since his duties were primarily to act as an emergency repairman and maintenance man. Ralph asked, "Why doesn't Ollie get into the horseplay?" Bert replied, "Ollie can't take it. He likes to get other people, but he can't take it when he gets it. You have got to be fair about this. If you get some guy, you are surer than hell you will get it back yourself. Now you take Sam and me. We've been playing like that for a long time. He don't lose his temper, and I don't lose mine. I knew I was going to get that hose the other night; that was why I was baiting him with a squirt gun." Ralph asked, "Does Ed Masters mind it very much?" Bert answered, "Hell, he's just like the rest of us. He knows you've got to have some of that stuff, only he gets bawled out by the superintendent if they see anything going on like that. That's why we don't play around much on the day shift. But on the night shift, that's when we have fun. The only reason we don't squirt the foreman is because he's the foreman. As far as we're concerned, he is no different from us. Besides he ain't my boss anyway. I'm maintenance. I don't care what he says."

About the middle of the summer, the superintendent of the glass department returned from his vacation and immediately thereafter an effort was made by him through the foremen to "tighten up" on the shop discipline. The men on the machines and the punchers were forbidden to walk up to the other end of the conveyor to talk to the packers and sealers and vice versa. The foreman started making occasional comments like "keep moving" when he saw a small group together in conversation. On one occasion a small group stood watching some activity outside the plant. Ed came by and quite curtly said, "Break it up." Everyone seemed quite shocked at how abrupt he was.

About this same time, the word was passed around among the employees that a big push was on to step up the output of a certain product in order to make a tight delivery schedule. Everyone seemed to be putting a little extra effort into getting this job done. Ralph thought he noticed that the foreman was getting more and more "jumpy" at this time. On one occasion Ed commented to some of the employees, "I am bitter today." One of the machine operators asked him what the trouble was, and Ed made some comment about a foremen's meeting where the superintendent was telling them that the playing around and visiting would have to stop.

One night a short time later, Ralph saw the preparations were being made for an unusually elaborate trap for soaking Jim, one of the sealers who had recently begun to take part in the water fights. A full bucket of water was tied to the ceiling with a trip rope at the bottom in such a way that the entire contents would be emptied on Jim when he least suspected it. Many of the employees made a point of being on hand when the trap was sprung. It worked perfectly, and Jim was given a complete soaking. Ralph thought Jim took it in good spirit, since he turned quickly to counterattack the people who had soaked him. Shortly after all the crew had gone back to work, Ruth, one of the packers, was coming down the ramp from the area where the hand-blowing operations were performed. She was carrying some of the glass components. Ruth slipped on some of the water that had been spilled during the recent fight and fell down. She was slightly burned by some of the hot glass she was carrying. Those who saw this happen rushed to her help. The burn, while not serious, required first-aid attention and the assistant foreman went with Ruth to the company dispensary for treatment. Ralph thought that the employees all felt rather sheepish about the accident. Ruth was one of the more popular girls in the department. The word went around among the employees that a report on the nature and cause of the accident would have to be made out and sent to higher management. Everyone was wondering what would happen.

Roger Allen

Roger Allen, an MBA graduate of a large midwestern university was visiting his alma mater about three years after graduation.[1] While on this visit, Roger went to see one of his former professors. During their conversation, Roger explained that upon completion of his MBA, he had accepted the position of sales representative in the district office of a large oil company. The professor learned in their conversation that his former student had become very dissatisfied with his work and was considering resignation of his position. Roger stated that the major reason for his desire to resign his position resulted from the procedures, meth-

[1] This case was prepared by Terry Riddle under the supervision of Dr. Irwin Weinstock.

ods, and practices used in determining service station locations and the operations of these stations. When asked to elaborate further upon his reasons for dissatisfaction, Roger explained as follows:

I am assigned to a sales territory that consists of 28 service stations. I have complete responsibility for the continuous successful operation of these stations.

Basically there are 3 main forms of service station operations. The first is called a dealer operation. In this arrangement, the oil company owns the building and usually, but not always, the land. The oil company leases the station to the dealer. The dealer is often described as an independent businessman tied to the oil company through the lease arrangement. The rental on the station is based on the potential of the station, i.e., the estimated number of gallons of gasoline and related products that can be sold each month. It should be stressed that the estimates of the sales of tires, batteries, and accessories are based, not on the history of similar stations, but on what the oil company thinks the station should sell. The company establishes ratios of tires, batteries, and accessories sales to gasoline sales. For example, for every 1000 gallons of gasoline sold, there should be 1 tire sold, 1 battery sold, $100 worth of accessories sold, $75 labor, etc. Rarely does any station meet these ratios; in fact only 1 of my 28 stations ever comes close to them. The oil company obtains the monthly rental on a per gallon basis, often with a minimum rental that must be paid. For example, a station that has a potential gallonage of 40,000 gallons per month may have a 1.5 cents per gallon rent with a stipulation that the minimum rental will be $250 per month regardless of the gallonage.

The second form of service station operation is called the manager operation. The manager does not lease the station; he is classified as a company employee and can be dismissed as any other employee. All of the products, including gasoline, tires, batteries, and accessories, in the manager-operated station are taken by the manager on consignment. The manager is responsible for the proper maintenance and operation of the station and is paid a percentage of the sales, usually with a minimum income provided.

The third type of service station is the typical "mom and pop" type of country grocery store with gasoline pumps in front of the store. There is only a gasoline contract between the company and this type of operation. The company exercises no control over these accounts and no rental is paid. The gasoline is purchased wholesale by the store and is sold at retail. Usually the oil company provides the pumps and equipment and also the maintenance on this equipment.

Practically all of my stations are of the dealer or manager type operation. My responsibility for the continuous successful operation of these stations includes the recruiting of dealers and managers, subject to the final approval of my superiors. Recruiting both managers and dealers is a major problem. Recruiting dealers, however, is far more difficult than recruiting managers, for two main reasons.

First, and most important, is the problem of locating people who are willing and able to invest substantial sums of capital in a service station operation (service stations have one of the highest management turnovers of any type of business—about one out of three change management annually). Usually the minimum amount of initial investment capital needed to open a station, new or old, is $7,500 to $10,000 (a full load of gasoline usually costs $2,500 to $3,000, with tire, battery, oil and accessory inventories often costing a similar amount. Funds must also be initially provided for payrolls, taxes, and other ordinary business expenses, as well as for tools and equipment. I always found commercial banks to be extremely reluctant to grant loans to open a service station due to the high rate of failure in this business. However, the oil company will usually provide the majority of the investment capital. In order to secure this needed capital, the dealer must sign a promissory note for the amount of capital borrowed (interest 6 to 8 percent) and also sign a deed of trust on his home or other real estate. Even with approximately $8,000 of capital provided by the oil company, the dealer is expected to provide about $1,000 cash for initial working capital. Imagine the personal tragedies that occur each time a dealer-owned station goes under.

If the prospective dealer has the necessary capital, a retail credit check is made to determine his credit history and his net worth. If this retail check proves satisfactory, the prospective dealer is granted the lease and a franchise. Sometimes the dealer is sent to the company's retailing school before he is placed in the station. At the school, he is taught the company's products and is taught basic business principles as applied to service stations. However, only about 20 percent of the prospective dealers and managers attend this school, which lasts about one month. If the prospective dealer does not possess the necessary investment capital, but his retail credit report is favorable, then the prospective dealer becomes a prospective manager.

The second important problem in locating dealers concerns the service station site itself. Most service station locations are of four basic types.

The first is the station which has been very productive over a long period of time. This type of station has a very low management turnover. In fact, turnover occurs only when the operator dies or retires. Over the years, this station attracts a steady clientele and is very prosperous. This type of station may be located anywhere—in a shopping center, in the downtown area of a town or city, or on a major highway. Locating a dealer for this type of station is very easy. Unfortunately, only a small fraction of service stations fall in this category.

The second type is the station in an old and often rundown area of a city or town. This station is often nicknamed by oil company personnel as a "dog." This station has all of the problems faced by other stations plus many others. Crime is usually very high in the areas surrounding these stations. The result is that break-ins and robberies occur with alarming regularity. Also, the general flow of traffic has usually been re-routed away from these stations. This is because many of these stations are located on once busy streets and thoroughfares that today are replaced by intra-city superhighways and expressways. The result is that service stations of this type are characterized by extremely high turnover of dealers and managers because of declining sales potential, increasing costs, and the risk of personal injury in a high-crime location.

The third type of station is typically located in close proximity to a large shopping center and/or suburban neighborhoods in towns and cities. These stations are often called "neighborhood stations" and are usually modern and recently built. Some of these stations are prosperous, but more often I find them marginal, i.e., they barely provide the dealer with a livable income.

The fourth type of service station is often called a "highway station" because it is located on a major arterial highway or interstate highway. It is, like the neighborhood station, usually new and modern. Unfortunately, these stations, again like the neighborhood stations, are often in marginal locations.

The main reasons for many of these neighborhood and highway stations being marginal is that there so often exists an oversaturation of service stations in these areas. In other words, four, five or more service stations may be trying to compete in a trading area capable of adequately supporting only two or three stations. This oversaturation occurs because the oil companies earn the bulk of their service station profits from the sale of gasoline, whereas the dealers earn the bulk of their profits from the sale of tires, batteries, oil, accessories, and the accompanying labor charges, earning very little from the sale of gasoline. An oil company will often construct a station in a saturated market area primarily to obtain the additional gallonage and additional profits for themselves.

Although the idea of constructing a new service station may originate from the sales representative himself, his immediate supervisor, or from higher levels of management, ultimate authority to construct the station must come from higher management. Usually, however, the idea to construct a new service station comes from higher management after discussions with the Director of Service Station Development, a middle manager whose sole responsibility is the development of new service stations. The Director of Service Station Development coordinates closely with state and local government officials concerning zoning regulations, new street and highway developments, proposed shopping centers, residential housing developments, traffic flow patterns, etc. He usually reports this information to the manager of the sales district. If higher management then decides to construct the station, the Director of Service Station Development may even negotiate the purchase or lease of the land for the station. Then the sales representative is "sold" on the idea of the new station by higher management, and it becomes his responsibility to locate a dealer for the new station.

As an example, my supervisors once suggested that I inquire into the possibility of constructing a station at a particular intersection along a main arterial highway in a large city. I already had two stations within two miles on both sides of this proposed station. In addition, there were ten other competitors' stations located within this two-mile span of road. I suggested that the proposed station would compete with my existing stations. In fact, my dealers in these two adjacent stations were complaining to me that they believed that another station would further saturate the market area and result in an inadequate income for everyone. My supervisor disagreed with these arguments, stating that higher management believed that this proposed station would result in higher volume for the company. Therefore, a service station proposal was formulated, which is the basis on which the station is "justified" to higher management. In this proposal, the monthly gallonage for the proposed station was estimated, and from this gallonage estimate, the sales of tires, batteries, oil, accessories, and labor were estimated, using the somewhat unrealistic ratios explained previously. Thus an estimated profit, both for the company and the dealer was computed. The key to the proposal, however, is the monthly gallonage because this is the greatest profit maker for the company.

The proposed station was constructed and two more competitors also constructed new stations in this same market area. The new station did not realize its estimated gallonage or profits and my other two stations' gallonage dropped about five per cent. I also learned through the "grapevine" that all the competitive stations' gallonage dropped likewise as a result of these three new stations. The result is that no service station in this area, either the company's or our competitors' stations, is now receiving sufficient business to provide an adequate income for the dealers in these stations.

The two problems of dealer recruitment and service station sites are actually complementary. The smart and intelligent prospective service station dealer will refuse to take a "dog" station or a station in a saturated area. The result is there are relatively few stations worthy of this prospect's consideration.

As sales representative, I am responsible for the operations of all stations in my territory, including the "dogs." I must keep these stations open and producing, either as dealer operations or manager operations, as I do not have the authority to close down a station. I can only recommend such action—only middle and top management can close down a station. However, the oil company dislikes closing down a station, even if it is a "dog," because by doing so it loses that much gallonage. As a result, I am constantly attempting to convince prospective dealers to invest up to $10,000 in hopes of trying to earn a living out of a "dog" station in an increasingly saturated market area.

I am becoming quite good at predicting the length of time it will take a dealer to go out of business. The method of predicting failure is simple. From the history of how much money the station has lost per month in the past, it can be determined how long it will take to drain the working capital out of the business, thus resulting in dissolution and often times bankruptcy on the part of the dealer. The dealer may be a fine prospective businessman, but the location and economic conditions surrounding the station prevent him from realizing his potential. The result of venturing into such a station is virtually inevitable and can be predicted with a considerable degree of certainty.

My job then necessitates finding another dealer to take his turn at ultimate bankruptcy and personal failure. After seeing approximately fifteen such failures, I find it increasingly difficult to do my job. After all, I am the guy who persuades them that this is a good investment of their efforts, hopes, and money; and I am the guy who is supposed to help them succeed after they lease the station. I feel that, if this is what business is like, I'd better find some other way to make a living.

I have given much thought recently to ways of improving the survival rate and profitability of service stations. But as long as gallonage reigns supreme in the minds of policymakers, I don't see much hope. Do you?

THE ORGANIZATION: TOWARD AN ADAPTIVE STRUCTURE

PART FOUR

the nature of
organizations

14

It was six men of Hindustan
To learning much inclined
Who went to see the Elephant
(Though all of them were blind),
That each by observation
Might satisfy his mind.

JOHN GODFREY SAXE

Although large complex organizations are visible to virtually everyone and so deeply affect our lives, they are the subject of much misunderstanding and controversy. It is not clear, in fact, what an organization is. What are its boundaries? What holds it together? Is the corporation solely a creature of the state with authority obtained from the state? Indeed, what is authority?

Because organizations have existed so long, many theories and descriptions have developed in an attempt to understand them and better manage them. It is the purpose of this chapter to probe some of the most prominent concepts of organization. Having learned from the six blind men, each examining a different part of an elephant by the Braille system, we will note that much of the disagreement results from partial observations of a complex structure. Hopefully, the insights obtained from an integrated set of partial observations can yield a meaningful picture of the whole.

The Classical View

Until the most recent few decades, formal organizations were conceived in terms of a relatively small number of executives ruling over vast numbers of subordinates. The tendency was to examine organizations from the top downward.

The organization was looked on as a single unit, with "organizational goals" and "organizational strategies." Decisions on these matters were seen to be made at the very peak of organizational hierarchies. From this summit, the objectives and plans were filtered downward to subordinate managers, whose principal task was to communicate and supervise implementation of these ends and means. Authority was seen as vested in top management, who could then delegate it downward to the other management levels as conditions dictated. Certainly there had to be upward communication of all sorts, but the flow of information concerning goals, policies, organization structure, directives, commands, and power was downward. All of this was bulwarked by a status structure and a reward structure that reinforced the willingness of subordinates to obey.

The hierarchical conception of organizations is based on two very firm foundations. One we shall term political legitimacy; the second is called the machine concept. These conceptual foundations of organizations still heavily influence thought and behavior within organizations. They demand, therefore, intensive scrutiny.

POLITICAL LEGITIMACY

The concept and role of political legitimacy are demonstrated by early corporations chartered by the Crown of England. These organizations were sanctioned as extensions of the monarchy to achieve rather specific royal objectives. Thus Latham reports:

> The charters of early corporations were not only instruments to organize the internal government of the corporation. They created what were, in effect, branches of the public government. The companies of the mercantilist period, for example, were "Charged with responsibility for commercial regulations and fiscal administration in particular spheres of foreign trade, and were equipped even with military forces and their own courts." [1]

These corporations were authorized to pursue goals compatible with those of the government and were vested with governmental powers to facilitate the process. The Crown, then, delegated some of its own powers to corporate managers, who became the chief instruments in the

---

[1] Earl Latham, "The Body Politic of the Corporation," in *The Corporation in Modern Society*, ed. E. S. Mason (Boston: Harvard University Press, 1959), pp. 218–36.

project. These early executives, bestowed with great objectives and broad authority, proceeded to create the organization's structure, strategies, operating policies, and so forth. Power had been officially vested in them from above; indeed, it was delegated by a sovereign who, by divine right, was answerable only to God. If we define legitimate power as the perceived "right" to command, then such power was clearly vested in those early corporate executives. The mandate was clear and compelling. The official powers possessed by executives were then duly delegated to subordinate managers, thus vesting in them the legitimate power to command within their assigned portion of the organization.

Although there are some differences, the process of political legitimation is still a vital aspect of modern organizations. In the United States, political legitimacy seems to flow to corporate executives as follows:

1. Society, through its representatives, has created a political-economic system. The fundamental elements of this system are incorporated in the Constitution and a set of judicial interpretations.
2. An important item in this system is the "Right of Private Property," which permits individuals and groups to own and control assets for their own benefit.
3. Owners, with rights formally legitimized, may delegate their rights to professional administrators, who are expected to pursue the best interests of the owners.
4. Top managers, then, are vested with socially accepted rights delegated by owners, and are to pursue the owners' objectives.

Thus top management, charged with the objectives and the powers of owners, possess the legitimate power to organize, command, and reward. Much as in the monarchy, the flow of authority is clearly downward. The ultimate source of legitimate authority may have shifted from divine right to socially approved ownership, but the theoretical direction of flow is unchanged.

THE MACHINE CONCEPT

The focus on the summit characteristic of the political legitimacy concept of organization is reinforced by the machine concept. Probably the best-known proponent of the machine concept is Max Weber. Writing in the early 1900s, Weber described the attributes of efficient government agencies. Although he wrote primarily of civil service, he suggested that his ideas applied to all organizations. Following are the principal characteristics of Weber's ideal bureaucracy.

The responsibilities, duties, and authorities attach to each "office" (position), and are specified by written rules and regulations. This well-defined formal structure cannot be modified by overly ambitious, covetous officials. Only those proved qualified by training, tests, and experience may be selected for each post. Objective, measurable criteria are used to make selection decisions. The authority structure is "monocratic" (governed by a single person), with a well-defined hierarchy of officials to implement the objectives and strategies established above.

Managers are thoroughly and expertly trained to perform their jobs. These duties are performed according to stable and complete written rules. The manager's knowledge of the rules is part of his expertise, his qualifications for the job. He is motivated by his desire to retain his current position and to advance up the hierarchy.

The result of this system, maintained Weber, is a rational, stable organization. Officials, objectively selected and expertly trained, administer their divisions within the boundaries represented by the stated limits of their authorities and the rules. Decisions and actions are predictable and the rules guard against subjectiveness, favoritism, and selfishness, while expertise guards against irrationality. To quote Weber:

> The decisive reason for the advance of bureaucratic organization has always been its purely technical superiority over any other form of organization. The mature bureaucracy compares with other forms exactly as does the machine with nonmechanical modes of production.
>
> Precision, speed, unambiguity, knowledge of the files, continuity, discretion, unity, strict supervision, reduction of friction and of material and personal costs—these are raised to the optimum point in the strictly bureaucratic administration, and especially in its monocratic form.[2]

Weber's view is admittedly extreme. The ideal human organization is to be composed of standardized (through selection, training, and rules) components, each of whom knows precisely his duties. Each performs his tasks in an expert manner and within explicit constraints established by superiors. Each person subordinates his immediate desires in favor of institutional requirements, so that he may receive the economic and social rewards formally provided. The organization is, in other words, completely defined.

Extreme as this system is, it has its counterparts in reality. Modern organizations have adopted many characteristics that reflect Weber's bureaucracy. American businesses, for example, do establish explicit objectives, strategies, policies, procedures, rules, organization charts, and

[2] H. H. Gerth and C. Wright Mills, *From Max Weber* (New York: Oxford University Press, 1946), p. 28.

position descriptions. Superior-subordinate linkages are clearly identified. Rewards are largely based on the nature of the position and the extent to which the incumbent reflects the traits expected for his position. Formal training is increasingly a basis for selection, as advances continue in technologies and general educational levels.

FOUNDATIONS OF RATIONAL ORGANIZATION

A further inquiry into the nature of human organizations helps to explain the pervasiveness of "bureaucratic" features. A most fundamental universal factor is *division of labor* or specialization. Where there is a large volume of standardized work to be done, great economies can be realized from breaking the complex task into subtasks and assigning these to groups of specialists. Economies result from the increased expertise of specialized workers, the full utilization of high-speed, special-purpose machinery, scientifically established operating procedures, and a host of related advantages. All lasting human organizations seem to evolve internal patterns of specialization to a greater or lesser degree. Thus even in the most primitive, smallest social unit—the aborigine family—the father may do the hunting while mother tends the infant. In the large factory, specialization may call for a worker to perform only a few motions, but thousands of times each day.

As division of labor intensifies, so does the need for *coordination* among the groups of specialists. Each specialized group becomes dependent on other groups for supplies or services. As interdependency grows, so does the value of mutual predictability. If the performance of any group is incompatible with the overall plan—in terms of product specifications, volume, or timing—the entire operation may collapse. It is not too difficult to envision the problems that arise for an automobile assembly line should carburetors arrive that do not match the engines; or should the installers fail to report for work.

In the same vein, professors amble to classes, assuming that classrooms are properly heated, lit, and cleaned. The surgeon relies heavily on the anaesthetist and other assistants. In all these cases, the specialist can be effective only if the other components have performed as expected. Those responsible for the operation of the total system, therefore, might well view it as a sociomechanical entity, each part of which must work according to its design and intent. To achieve this consistency, this predictability, the forementioned tools of bureaucracy are applied.

Machine-logic holds that control at the top is the best way to assure coordination and predictability among subunits. The larger picture can be seen best from on high. Higher officials can be readily empowered to reward compatible behavior and punish deviant activities. It is, therefore, the task of the higher-level official to plan operations and then monitor them. It is the function of lower management levels to implement the decisions of superiors and specialized operatives must perform as programmed. Again the active role of determining the direction and the productive system is seen to reside at the highest levels of organizations, while lower levels become successively more controlled and passive.

Emerging Concepts of Organization

It should not surprise the sensitive observer to hear that many once-accepted and revered social views, have been increasingly challenged during the late 1960s and early 1970s. Among these are the logics justifying exclusive control from "above." New logics are developing that challenge the classical conceptions of organizations and the managerial role. Let us first examine some current reactions to the political legitimacy model and then do the same for the machine model.

ACCEPTANCE THEORY

We have seen that, according to the concept of political legitimacy, authority is vested in organizational peaks by some higher power. Through the process of delegation, this vast initial authority is directed downward in the organization, thus permitting subordinates to assist in the achievement of organizational goals—which have also been sanctified from above.

Let us examine an alternate logic, one that has gained much recent acceptance. We will call this the *acceptance theory*.[3] This theory focuses on certain characteristics of the human individual, rather than on the organization as a whole. The individual is seen, first of all, as a decision maker.[4] Although he is constantly making decisions of all kinds, two are of special relevance to the organization: (1) Shall I join the organization,

[3] Robert Tannenbaum, "Managerial Decision Making," *Journal of Business*, XXIII (January, 1950), 22–39.

[4] It is interesting to note that many management authorities, when asked to define the nature of the managerial role, characterize the manager as a "decision maker." Yet it is clear that every human being is constantly making decisions. Perhaps this apparent inconsistency reflects machine theory, which holds that "management must manage," while the workers must follow orders.

or if a member, continue the association? (2) Assuming continued membership, to what extent should I subordinate my own behavioral preferences to those of organizational superiors?

Each individual is seen joining an organization to achieve *his goals.* He remains only so long as he perceives the association to be advantageous to him. Moreover, he follows orders, or otherwise contributes his effort and talent, only so long as such activities are compatible with his needs, abilities, and his sense of propriety. He may or may not be especially concerned with the the objectives established on high for the organization. The bombardier may intensely desire to "knock out" an enemy facility, as ordered by the high command; the professor may sincerely seek to expand the horizons or abilities of his students, as ordered; and the bank teller may well appreciate his formal role in helping clients with their financial affairs. In all too many cases, however, the relationship of the employee to the organization is a marriage of convenience. The automobile assembly-line worker may not "give a damn" whether General Motors achieves its production goals or not; the coal miner in Appalachia may wish to retain his job for lack of other opportunities, but he may not psychologically identify himself with his employer or its goals.[5] In the broadest sense of the question, the employee asks, "What's in it for me?" when deciding how to behave in the organization.

What does this mean for the nature of authority and the source of authority? The acceptance theory clearly holds that each individual possesses the ultimate control of his own behavior. No one has authority over the individual unless the individual "delegates" it. The individual, then, is the ultimate source of authority. And what he delegates, he can revoke. That is, he may choose to leave the organization rather than follow an order. Or he may decide to feign acceptance of an order, while intending never to comply. His range of possible responses to commands may be extremely wide. As one author puts it:

> The real source of the authority possessed by an individual lies in the acceptance of its exercise by those who are subject to it. It is the subordinates of an individual who determine the authority which he may wield. Formal authority is, in effect, nominal authority. It becomes real only when it is accepted. . . .
>
> An individual will accept an exercise of authority if the advantages accruing to him from *accepting* plus the disadvantages accruing to him

[5] Nor are such casual relationships limited to workers. As discussed in Chapter 1, many stockholders purchase stock for a fast profit, never really identifying with the firm. Clients may also patronize one store this week and another next week. Managers, too, are continuously making the same sort of decisions.

from *not accepting* exceed the advantages accruing to him from *not accepting* plus the disadvantages accruing to him from *accepting;* and conversely, he will not accept an exercise of authority if the latter factors exceed the former.[6]

Of course, many factors enter into an individual's behavioral decisions, when he is faced with a command or other directive (policy, quota, job description, or the like). These include the power of superiors to reward and punish, the individual's activity preferences, the norms of the work group, the intrinsic nature of the directed behavior, and so forth. Most organizations are quite stable. That is, most workers (and managers) do remain for substantial intervals and evidently do comply with directives to an extent satisfactory to superiors. This should not lead one to conclude that the downward flow of authority envisioned in the political legitimacy and machine concepts is controlling behavior at each subordinate level. It may *also* be that intelligent managers attempt to create a structure that encourages all levels to accept directives. The organization is set up to satisfy the needs, ethical codes, and other preferences of all whose contributions are required. Directives are given that, in the manager's mind, are *likely to be obeyed.* If the manager's directives are substantially influenced by the power, pressure, and preferences of those below, then who, ultimately, is "the boss"?

Perhaps then, a realistic view sees any required participant in an organization as the possessor of power. He will use his perceived power to achieve his goals, sometimes acquiescing to the directives of others, and sometimes directing others. Even the lowest operative in the organization may be saying (unheard), "I alone can ultimately control my behavior. For a price (money, status, pleasant coworkers . . .) I will permit you to direct (within limits) my behavior. This permission, which I grant (or delegate?) to you, I can revoke at any time. I will do so as soon as I deem it advantageous." The wise manager, at every level, hears this message and uses his authority accordingly.

CRITICISMS OF BUREAUCRACY— TOWARD INFORMALITY

Although the acceptance theory directly challenges the political legitimacy concept of authority, it does not deal with the notion that the view from the top is superior; that a stable, monocratic, rules-oriented, machine system is the most effective form of organization. It is true that business and government organizations resemble Weber's bureaucratic

---

[6] Robert Tannenbaum, "Managerial Decision Making," pp. 26–28.

structure in some ways. In other respects, however, modern administrators refute Weber's ideal, finding it inoperable, inferior to other approaches. Let us now examine the most common apparent weaknesses in the bureaucratic approach.

EFFECTS ON MEN.   Bureaucracy breeds conformity. The emphasis is upon obedience, predictability, continuity, strict supervision, and so forth. One looks upward—to his superiors or to rules established by his superiors—for direction. To the extent one behaves as predicted, he is considered loyal, competent, perhaps promotable. (The question of promotability involves his ability to do the same at the next level, perhaps after further development—or conditioning!) In its extreme, bureaucracy creates the "Organization Man," who lives his entire life, off and on the job, according to the preferences of his organization.

Late in life, Weber himself recognized that his system would lead to human debasement, saying:

> It is horrible to think that the world could one day be filled with nothing but those little cogs, little men clinging to little jobs and striving toward bigger ones—a state of affairs which is . . . playing an ever increasing part in the spirit of our present administrative system, and especially of its offspring, the students. This passion for bureaucracy . . . is enough to drive one to despair. It is as if in politics . . . we were deliberately to become men who need "order" and nothing but order, who become nervous and cowardly if for one moment this order wavers, and helpless if they are torn away from their total incorporation in it. That the world should know no men but these: it is such an evolution that we are already caught up in, and the great question is therefore not how we can promote and hasten it, but what can we oppose to this machinery in order to keep a portion of mankind free from this parceling-out of the soul, from this supreme mastery of the bureaucratic way of life.[7]

By constraining the use of individual imagination, information, and creativity, the bureaucratic system hinders natural human growth. Ego needs and growth needs become frustrated, leading to hostility toward the frustrating system and its administrators. The individual becomes alienated from the workplace. His work becomes meaningless; or worse, he sees his work as his sacrifice for anticipated pleasures to be experienced *off the job*. His interests and energies, therefore, focus on activities away from work. His psychological investment in the organization deteriorates, and he performs only well enough to maintain his security.

---

[7] R. Bendix, *Max Weber: An Intellectual Portrait* (Garden City, N.Y.: Doubleday & Company, Inc., 1960), p. 175.

HEADS IN THE CLOUDS. The bureacratic problems of human debasement and alienation discussed above are closely related to another negative consequence of the machine model. This model, stressing monocratic management, fails to recognize that the "view from the top" can be extremely limited and distorted. Rational decisions on rules, policies, procedures, objectives, and so forth require vast amounts of information. Most likely there is at any moment relevant information in the organization, of which even top administrators are unaware. Consider that organizations are composed of individuals and groups with widely varying skills, knowledges, perceptions, and attitudes. In an increasingly technological system, lower-level specialists could provide valuable informational inputs for rational decisions, if tapped. It is not clear that the monocratic administration will seek these inputs, for to do so is to permit lower-level personnel to influence the decisions of superiors. Indeed, subordinates may have little to gain and much to lose by too openly expressing their own views.

Not only may important information be unavailable to lofty decision makers, but information that is received may be distorted on its way upward. Great emphasis on the power of superiors to reward and punish does not promote full candidness among subordinates. Information flows will be censored by every link in the communication network, so that what arrives at the top is incomplete, even misleading. Thus the bureaucratic system, although founded upon the assumption of superior information at the summit, may render this condition almost impossible to attain. The top administrator is not encouraged to seek full participation when making his decisions; and the lower-level personnel have strong reasons to withhold or "modify" their reports. To the extent that these conditions prevail, resulting decisions will be anything but optimal. Unrealistic objectives may be established, to be achieved by ineffective procedures, inappropriate policies, and dysfunctional rules.

INABILITY TO ADAPT. The bureaucratic organization makes a great investment in formalized objectives, procedures, policies, and rules. The idea is to construct a stable, predictable system that assures the performance of routine, repetitive functions in the most rational manner. The more the operation is programmed, the better.

Such a system might work well under stable conditions: unchanging products, technology, competitive conditions, and so forth. The modern era, however, is one of accelerating change. Under such conditions, it is questionable that the fully planned and programmed system is a feasible goal. In an existing bureaucratic system, adaptation to a rapidly changing environment may be painfully slow. If all changes in organizational activity must await the official establishment of new formal procedures, policies, and so forth, adjustments in operations will be halting and costly. Immense resources will be expended to develop each new fully programmed system.

Adaptation may be further delayed by the tendency to accept the existing system as an end in itself, rather than a complex device for attaining the end, under stated conditions. Many managers and employees become conditioned to prefer, even to idolize, a long-existing policy or procedure. It becomes the "right" way. The rational foundations of the system may long since have deteriorated before concerted effort is focused on changing it. Thus the machine approach may have worked under conditions of little change. It probably takes a more flexible organizational form to survive today.

All of this has assumed that it is possible to construct a completely programmed organization, wherein each person knows (or can find complete instructions on) exactly what to do, when, where, how, and so on. Such a system is hardly conceivable. If this is true, then there must always exist alongside the formal structure of duties, responsibilities, authorities, and communication networks a parallel *informal* structure. This informal organization "fills the gaps," provides operational flexibility for all concerned, as well as providing an opportunity for social interaction that may have been ignored in the formal structure. Frequently, it is the informal structure that adapts first to important environmental or internal changes. Someone finds a new procedure that now works better than the official one; another finds that a particular policy prevents his full effectiveness, so he quietly disregards it; another finds that he can best obtain information he needs by "short-circuiting" the formal communication system. Thus human flexibility and ingenuity can be quickly imparted to the organization, perhaps despite the bureaucratic leanings of higher administrators.

INADEQUATE MUTUAL INFLUENCE. Current organization theorists visualize organizations as a complex of groups and individuals, each of which is somewhat unique. They are unique in that each has its own functions to perform, its own problems, its own flow of information, its own power position, and its own particular view of the organization. Moreover, each unit relates to others in the work flow in a specific way, receiving inputs from certain other units (purchasing, personnel, methods analysts, component fabricators, and so forth) and supplying inputs for still others.

Each group is, therefore, in a peculiar position within the system. Each has insights to problems and solutions that may not exist elsewhere.

Attempts to improve the system may well be unsuccessful if these insights are ignored by top management. Many theorists hold that the units actually involved with the operations are best able to identify their problems and to generate effective solutions. They should, at the very least, be asked to contribute such insights to higher-level decision makers; or at most, to implement their ideas at their own discretion. The point is that relevant knowledge and interest should be brought to bear on organizational problems. It is not clear that this is likely within a bureaucratic structure.

Coordination, machine theorists hold, can best be attained from above. This premise is questionable. It seems that many individuals and departments can coordinate among themselves. They can share important information, plan their related activities, and informally expedite urgent work. If it is true that higher levels have access to a broader view, then this view, too, can be shared where it is relevant.

Influence is no longer viewed as a top-down process. Rather it can (and usually does) flow in all directions. Subordinates, with their special needs and insights, do influence the decisions of superiors. In the same way, peers influence each other. One can, in fact, conceive of the organization as a mutual-influence structure. There is considerable evidence that increases in the level of *total influence* also increases the total effectiveness of the organization.[8] If this is the case, strict hierarchical control is an inferior approach to organization.

Organizations: An Overview

The views of organizations discussed in this chapter are only small indications of the complexity of the subject and the controversies associated with it. If anything is clear about organizations, it is that one must be wary of oversimplified descriptions of them and of prescriptions for running them. We will, therefore, take the approach that each view of organizations can contribute to our understanding. Every lasting organization probably contains elements of political legitimacy, acceptance, bureaucracy, and informality. The problem for the manager involves recognizing the degree to which each exists, the places where each is useful, and how these characteristics can be blended into an effective organization. Toward this end, let us reexamine the political legitimacy–

---

[8] Arnold Tannenbaum, *Control in Organizations* (New York: McGraw-Hill Book Company, Inc., 1968).

acceptance theory approaches, to see how they might relate in real organizations. The same is then done for the bueaucracy-informality approaches.

LEGITIMACY-ACCEPTANCE

It is probably quite correct to assert that durable organizations must have the approval of some "higher" authority to exist. Whether that authority rests ultimately with God, society, the "establishment," or elsewhere, such legitimizing seems a necessary condition for continued life. The power to tax is the power to destroy, as is the power to regulate. The power to grant charters, to subsidize, and to protect are elements of the state's power to help create and sustain organizations. In a private-enterprise economy, managers are delegated the authority to run organizations toward the owners' legitimate interests, within the regulations of the state. Such authority typically includes hiring, indoctrinating, training, placing, directing, rewarding, and punishing necessary personnel. Given such official powers, managers are often in a strong position to influence the behavior of subordinates. The concept of free will is admittedly attractive, but how free is the subordinate to determine his own behavior?

A variety of forces operate to restrict the behavior of the individual in organizations.[9] From birth he may be conditioned to obey authority figures: parents, teachers, preachers, and policemen. He may be taught that a system of superiors and subordinates is necessary and good. Upon becoming an employee of an organization, he is, perhaps, bombarded with the logic justifying obedience, loyalty, and productivity. This logic may be confirmed by the formal system of rewards and punishments that reinforces approved behavior and attempts to extinguish activities considered undesirable by superiors. Superiors are typically vested with clear indications of their higher status. Titles, uniforms, privileges, offices, and the like indicate clearly to subordinates the existence of an authoritative hierarchy. Thus the individual learns, to some degree, to accept the behavioral expectations of superiors. He has long been conditioned to defer to authority and he is made well aware of the satisfactions that may be provided or refused by superiors. How relevant, therefore, is the acceptance theory?

Quite relevant, it turns out. There are many real limitations to the strength of formal authority. Mobility of subordinates is a key factor.

[9] See Robert Prestus, "Toward a Theory of Organizational Behavior," *Administrative Science Quarterly*, III (June, 1958), 48–72.

Where workers are in short supply and are difficult to replace they are usually treated with "kid gloves." The more professionally mobile the individual is, the less malleable he can afford to be. Also, the better organized the work force is, the more power it possesses to participate in the creation and administration of the reward system. This is true of both informal organizations and formalized unions. In many cases, the powers of management to promote, remunerate, discharge, and so forth are severely limited by organized subordinates. Moreover, the expert power and referent power of a leader may well be challenged by informal leaders. Official powers are further reduced by growing legal restrictions and existing social mores.

In sum, it appears that in real organizations there exists a balance between the powers associated with political legitimacy and those associated with the acceptance theory. In every situation administrators enjoy certain real powers to influence subordinate behavior; and in every situation subordinates possess certain powers to influence or to resist administrators' decisions. Each set of powers constrains the other. Managers attempt to make decisions that are consistent with the total power structure; and workers attempt to do the same. Neither the political legitimacy doctrine nor the acceptance theory fully explains the phenomena of authority, influence, and behavior in organizations. Rather, they supplement each other and must be considered together.

BUREAUCRACY-INFORMALITY

A similarly balanced resolution seems indicated for the bureaucracy-informality debate. Certainly organizations require a degree of stability, a set of responsible officials, rules, records, standard procedures for repetitive activities, and some specialization among administrators and operatives. A degree of formal structuring may be required to assure that all necessary functions are performed and that linked activities are properly coordinated, all with a minimum of duplication of effort. It is difficult to imagine a large corporation without a formal hierarchy: without a board of directors answering to the stockholders, a president answering to the board, and so on. Job descriptions are unquestionably useful for hiring and training personnel. Well-thought-out policies and procedures may facilitate progress toward established objectives.

A measure of bureaucracy is inevitable in any durable organization. The question is again one of balance. Under certain circumstances, the organization may best be conceived and operated as a machine. These conditions include:

1. Stability: unchanging products, technologies, markets.
2. Managers vastly superior to subordinates in knowledge and decision-making ability.
3. Subordinates motivated by lower-level needs.
4. Relevant information more accessible and understandable to the top managers than to subordinates.
5. Need for consistency of policies and practices throughout the organization.

In contrast, a more flexible organizational form is indicated where:

1. Operations are constantly changing.
2. Subordinates are well informed and intelligent.
3. Subordinates are motivated by ego and self-actualization needs.
4. Relevant information is at least as accessible and understandable to subordinates as it is to superiors.
5. Adaptability to localized conditions is paramount to success of the organization.

It appears that the trend is toward the latter set of conditions in the developed nations. Thus we anticipate a movement toward flexible organizational form, where legitimate power defers to expert and referent power; communications and influence flow freely in all directions; and informality replaces passive subordination and obedience. Nevertheless, there are many situations that largely reflect the first set of conditions. Here the organization, over time, will probably resemble the machine model.

The manager's initial task is to ascertain the conditions that are influencing the character of the organization. He must create a structure compatible with these conditions. His tendency, however, may be to impose his preferred structure in every case, a perilous tendency. Of course, the conditions discussed above can be altered over time by the administrator. By so doing, he can alter the appropriate organizational form. Thus the autocrat may hire only dullards and condition them to obey without question. He could surely demonstrate, before long, that bureaucracy is a superior approach in his organization. The ultimate test would be the organization's ability to survive.

SUMMARY

Any object as complex as a human organization may be perceived in diverse ways. One view, of early origin, focuses on organizational summits as the centers of direction, power, and coordination. This view is based on: (1) the theory of political legitimacy, which holds that society (or some higher power) has vested in top management the authority to lead; and (2) the machine concept, which stresses formal control from the summit to assure effective progress toward socially approved objectives.

This summit orientation seems to be yielding to a growing recognition of the power and desire of subordinates to influence organizational goals and procedures. The role of "decision maker," once attributed exclusively to management, is increasingly being recognized as a function of all human beings. Benefits of organizational informality are increasingly appreciated for their salutory effects upon satisfaction, communication, adaptiveness, and mutual influence.

No single conception of organization adequately describes its nature or prescribes its most effective structure. Elements of political legitimacy, acceptance, bureaucracy, and informality exist in all organizations. The manager must understand the benefits and problems associated with each; he must be able to sense the actual existence and interplay of each within his organization; and he must adapt his preferred organizational structure to these realities.

The creation of a formal organization structure entails several categories of difficult managerial decisions. Among these are the bases for specialization within the enterprise and the problem of departmentalization. Specialization is a strategic factor that influences the "shape" of the organization. Other elements, discussed subsequently, include the proper size of departments and the amount of autonomy they enjoy.

QUESTIONS

1. What is meant by "political legitimacy"? How has the concept changed over time?
2. What are the *strengths* of bureaucracy? Under what conditions is bureaucracy an effective form of organization?
3. Relate specialization to centralized control.

4. Is delegation of authority a "downward" process? Explain.

5. It is often stated that "Power corrupts and absolute power corrupts absolutely." Comment on this statement.

6. What are the chief criticisms of the bureaucratic approach? Evaluate these criticisms.

7. Can the legitimacy and acceptance theories be combined to form a realistic theory of authority? Discuss in the context of an example.

8. Is the concept of authority changing? In what direction? What changes do you predict for the future?

9. How does your institution rate on a bureaucracy-informality scale? Illustrate with examples.

specialization and departmentalization

15

Let every man practice that art that he knows best.
CICERO

In certain respects, an organization may be looked upon as a living organism. Like any organism, it must adapt itself to its environment. It must structure itself so that it can efficiently perform the functions necessary to grow or at least to sustain itself. The power-running fullback strengthens his leg muscles through a special exercise program; the rotund young lady initiates a low-calorie diet as part of the mating game; so must the organization build itself to compete effectively with other organizations.

Whereas there may exist substantial agreement about the generally preferred structure of a young lady (at least within a given culture), the ideal "shape" for an organization is subject to widespread controversy. What is the best way to departmentalize? Should we assign to one manager the full responsibility for Product A, including design, production, marketing, and financing? Or, in contrast, should we assign to one manager the responsibility for producing *all* products in the line, while another takes responsibility for marketing all products? How large should organizational units be? Beyond what size should units be divided? How much authority should be delegated to subordinate managers throughout the hierarchy? As we shall see, these are difficult questions to answer with simple calculations. In fact, the answers take the form of guide lines, of factors to be considered in making such decisions, rather than of firm answers.[1]

This chapter examines the nature of specialization and the consequences of its application in organizations. We look first at specialization of individuals and then at the larger question of the roles of departments and organizations. Having discussed the bases for compartmentalizing organizations, we can then analyze the question of departmental size and the amount of autonomy permitted each.

Division of Labor

It is widely held that fluorides, judiciously used, are beneficial to dental health; taken in large doses, however, fluorides are poisonous. Some have used the latter fact to argue against the small amounts of fluoridic chemicals added to drinking water in many communities. Apparently, this view takes the position that if something is harmful in massive doses, it must also be harmful in lesser doses. Fortunately, the hypothesis does not possess general validity.

On the other hand, one encounters the apparent belief that more of a good thing is better than a little. Some results of this belief are painful sunburns, indigestion, personal bankruptcies, and bulging warehouses. Neither view puts much stock in the concept of balance between positive and negative effects. Both ignore the principle of diminishing marginal utility. What is bad in any amount is bad for all amounts; what is good in any amount is good in all amounts.

Such extreme positions have often influenced thinking about specialization. Early observers were quick to recognize immediate economies that could be realized through intensified division of labor, perhaps tending to ignore some negative consequences. Frederick W. Taylor held that efficient organization involved specialized managers, as well as operatives, suggesting:

> . . . dividing the work of management so that each man from the assistant superintendent down shall have as few functions as possible to

---

[1] Science advances from observation to classification to the recognition of general relationships among classes of phenomena and finally to the accurate measurement and prediction of these relationships. Administrative science has not yet progressed through the final phase. For a discussion of the development of social science theory, see George C. Homans, *Social Behavior: Its Elementary Forms* (New York: Harcourt, Brace & World, Inc., 1961), pp. 8–16.

perform. If practicable, the work of each man in the management should be confined to the performance of a single leading function.[2]

Other observers have bemoaned the undesired consequences of further specialization, while refusing to balance them against the positive effects. As we shall see, there exists a real problem of *measuring* the total impact of an increment of specialization—or its opposite, job enlargement. It is most difficult, therefore, to establish precisely the optimal degree of specialization for an organizational unit—be it one person or a department.

Specialization may be defined as training in, or concern with, a segment of knowledge, skills, or activities. The specialist, in terms of knowledge, attempts to achieve intensive understanding of a limited subject. Thus the professor of electrical engineering may know little about accounting and may care even less. The baseball pitcher may be a poor batter, feeling that the process of attaining batting skills would interfere with his efforts to become a better pitcher. He seeks to develop skills that are of great value and are most compatible with his makeup. Knowledge and skills are not the only bases for specialization. One tends to participate in activities that offer the largest probable rewards, avoiding relatively unrewarding activities regardless of whether he possesses the knowledge and skill. Rarely does a department head sweep the floor, maintaining (hopefully in truth) that his time is better spent in other activities, even if he were a better floor-sweeper than the janitor.[3]

BENEFITS OF SPECIALIZATION

There are various ways in which specialization can facilitate high productivity.[4] These include the following:

1. Less training required. Since each person requires fewer specific skills, the time and cost of training is kept low.

---

[2] Frederick W. Taylor, *Shop Management* (New York: Harper & Brothers, 1911), p. 99.

[3] The economist refers to this decision rule as the *principle of comparative advantage*, which holds that an individual who is superior at many activities will achieve his highest economic reward by utilizing his most valuable skills and allowing others to perform less valued functions, even though the others are less efficient than he is at all of the activities. See Paul A. Samuelson, *Economics* (New York: McGraw-Hill Book Company, Inc., 1961), pp. 718–24.

[4] For a classic listing of the advantages of specialization, see Charles Babbage, *On the Economy of Machinery and Manufactures* (London: Charles Knight, 1832), pp. 169–76.

2. Individual productivity reaches high levels earlier for simple, repetitive tasks.

3. The organization can hire highly productive labor at lower wages than would be commanded by the skilled generalist. This point requires elaboration, for there may be erroneous identification here. The brain surgeon is often considered to be a specialist, but only in a certain sense. He has developed certain rare and valuable skills—but he is also doctor of medicine. In effect, he has *added* an especially valuable skill to those required of the standard doctor of medicine. The skilled carpenter, likewise, may be considered a specialist—but he is much more a generalist than the worker who performs one or a few simple repetitive functions with wood. The latter woodworker may be extremely productive at his specialized task. But because he has few generally transferable skills and because others can be readily trained to perform his functions, his ability to command high wages is limited. The generally skilled carpenter—like the brain surgeon—possesses a large repertoire of valuable abilities, which can be transferred without diminution of value among competing employers, and which take years to master. He can move more readily and is more difficult to replace at low cost than is the woodworker. Thus the organization, by breaking down complex jobs into simple, standardized functions, can keep its labor costs much lower than through the use of generalists.

4. Ease of replacing employees. Since training time and cost are low, and new workers rapidly expand productivity, the specialist can be more readily replaced than one who performs a complex set of functions.

5. More intense utilization of special-purpose equipment. A generalist using several machines in sequence always leaves some idle, whereas the specialist may utilize his equipment virtually full time.

6. Ease of supervision. It is easier to supervise a group of individuals performing similar simplified tasks than it is to supervise a group of generalists. The manager's span of technical knowledge and skills can be narrow and his powers of observation less acute where subordinates perform similar, simple functions.

LIMITS TO EFFECTIVE SPECIALIZATION

As stated earlier, division of labor is a universal characteristic of human organizations, even the most primitive. The beneficial aspects of specialization are irrefutable—but only up to a point. Beyond that point, further subdivision of tasks into smaller and smaller activity cycles becomes dysfunctional. As specialization intensifies, three sets of negative consequences may grow in importance, until they may more than offset any incremental advantages. We have classified these problems as (1) diminishing efficiency, (2) coordination difficulties, and (3) motivational problems. Let us examine these developments.

DIMINISHING EFFICIENCY. One limitation to the assignment of smaller and smaller tasks to individuals is the point where there ceases to be sufficient work of a narrow nature to keep the worker busy. It may be productive, for example, to specialize the typists of a typing pool, with one handling technical manuscripts, another interoffice memos, a third outgoing mail, and so forth. But if volume of any sort of typing is sufficient to provide full-time activity for at least one typist, then the limit of efficient specialization would have been reached for full-time typists. That low-volume classification of typing would probably be added to another to compose a full-time job.

Even should the volume of each subtask be unlimited, there would still be a limit to efficient specialization. The object being processed must be transported to each successive specialist (or the specialist to it). As individuals' functions become more and more minute, transportation costs loom larger and larger in relation to work being accomplished. One can imagine a 98-cent spark plug moving to and past a thousand work stations. Suppose we then intensify specialization by a factor of two. It is unlikely that decreased costs of performing each operation would offset increased transportation costs.

As each operation performed becomes more diminutive, the relative cost per unit of simply handling each work object grows rapidly. It may be more efficient for the office worker who is manually collating 20 sheets of paper to perform the next step—stapling them together—rather than put them down for someone else to pick up and staple. Sheer technical efficiency, therefore, dictates limits to division of labor—to avoid worker idleness and unwarranted increases in transportation and handling costs.

DIFFICULTIES IN COORDINATION. Effective division of labor requires much coordination among linked specialized units. Each specialized unit becomes dependent on other units for its materials or assistance. Should the anticipated flow of output of other individuals or groups fail to materialize, then subsequent operations may be halted. Scheduling becomes extremely important, as does quality control over work done on subparts of the final product. No less important is effective communications among interdependent activities. Stability, predictability, and the sharing of relevant information become governing values, so that coordination can result among sets of specialists.

Beyond some point the incremental costs of achieving coordination may begin to grow faster than the incremental savings associated by further specialization of individuals or units. Precise scheduling may be difficult because of the nature of the work. Valuable time may be lost because of communications delays. Consider the example of a lathe operator who is shaping table legs. He is working on an order of 1,000 legs and completion time is not predictable to the minute. Upon completion, the lathe must be reset for the next order. If the machine operator is capable of setting up the machine, he need communicate with no other specialist, nor need he await the specialist's arrival. But if the lathe operator is only that, and not trained to set up the machine, then problems of coordination are possible. The possible result is enforced idleness of operators and machines, not to mention setup men who are idle at times and under great pressure at other times. The likelihood of unanticipated absences by these specialists magnifies the coordination problem. Such conditions render less predictable the delivery time of the table legs to the finishing operation, which then may experience its own scheduling problems, aggravated by imperfect arrivals of its raw materials.

There are ways of overcoming coordination problems, but they are costly. For example, extra machines may be kept on hand and the idle ones set up for subsequent orders. Also, buffer stocks of work may be kept on hand by each department to dampen the effects of late deliveries of new work. Obviously, the costs of owning and maintaining extra machinery and inventory can be significant. Beyond a point, they can be expected to offset anticipated gains of further specialization.

MOTIVATIONAL PROBLEMS. Probably the most widely recognized cause of concern with increasing specialization are problems of maintaining interest in specialized tasks. The highly simplified task, performed again and again, is unlikely to be intrinsically satisfying over a long time period. Initially, the specialized worker may find quality and quantity standards challenging. Subsequently he may retain his interest in the task only as a means to maximize his earnings and maintain his economic security. If he ascends toward the esteem and activation needs, then interest in specialized work may decline and be replaced by boredom or alienation.

The worker takes more frequent breaks from work, chats more with neighbors, daydreams, or simply "goes fishing."[5] Certainly the worker can be fitted to the job, unless so many jobs become so highly specialized

[5] An excellent discussion of worker response to simple, repetitive tasks is found in William E. Scott, "The Behavioral Consequences of Repetitive Task Design," in *Readings in Organizational Behavior and Human Performance*, ed. L. L. Cummings and W. E. Scott (Homewood, Ill.: Richard D. Irwin, Inc., 1969), pp. 42–59.

that they cannot long challenge any but the most limited intellects in the labor force.

Related to the motivational problem is that of perception. The specialist tends to be especially sensitive to information relevant to his task and his work group. Moreover, he tends to think in terms of the welfare of that group of specialists. He becomes "department bound," concerned with one set of functions and one group of associates. He loses sight of the organization's larger objectives, as well as the multiple problems faced by other specialized work groups. From this frame of reference, he may see little need to "coordinate" with outside groups. The machine set-up man may well take his time performing his task. "Let the operators cool their heels a while. Just because they are on piece work is no reason why I should hurry." The salesman (or sales manager) may be little concerned over the customer's risky financial condition. Let the credit department worry about that.

Specialization of Organization

The foregoing discussion has focused on the advantages and limitations of specialization as they relate to individuals and small groups. Much of this applies to larger organizations as well. At this level, the problem is defined as one of establishing organizational objectives and of departmentalization, the establishment of specialized departments with defined roles in the achievement of organizational goals. Management at the lower levels is concerned with the problem of devising individual tasks that elicit highest productivity; management at the higher levels must establish organization direction and develop the overall organization structure that maximizes group productivity and total productivity when group efforts are combined. It is to this larger organizational problem that we now turn.

The organization as a whole is a specialized unit. Like the individual, the viable organization focuses its energies on activities that promise a high payoff (that is, activities that are highly valued in the marketplace and are suited to that organization's capacities). Thus Aluminum Company of America is primarily engaged in the fabrication and shaping of aluminum. Even the highly diversified firm, be it the result of mergers or internal developments, does not attempt to be all things to all people. Its board of directors and executives select a set of functions and objectives and permit other organizations to handle other more-or-less specialized roles in society.

Specialization, we have seen, is practiced at the very top of the organization and at the very bottom. The organization as a whole selects a specialized role in society and individuals perform differentiated roles within the organization. Between these two levels are organizational units (divisions, departments, plants, section, and so on) that are also specialized. Specialization, therefore, pervades the entire organization. But on what basis should work be divided? What are the consequences of differentiating departments by function, such as stamping, grinding, finishing, and assembly? Or by product, with formal departments responsible for all functions performed upon its product? Figure 15-1 demonstrates structuring by function and product. Product and function are not the only bases for departmentalization. Other bases include division by client, by geographical territory, and by time (as in work shifts). Because departmentalization by product and function are probably the most ubiquitous, let us now compare the consequences of these two approaches to organization.[6]

FUNCTIONAL DEPARTMENTALIZATION

The functional basis of specialization probably exists in all lasting organizations. Even in the smallest retail outlet, one person probably does virtually all of the ordering from wholesalers; another, with an artistic bent, may prepare point-of-purchase displays or price signs. Suppose this retail outlet is so successful that the decision is made to open a second one similar to the first. At this juncture another decision must be made. Should each store be treated as a separate entity, doing its own ordering, interior styling, hiring, and so on? Or should one specialist perform each function for both stores? As the firm develops into a large chain of stores, should it organize functionally, on a store basis, or some combination of these?

By the same token, what administrative units should be established as a one-product manufacturing firm diversifies? Should there be one unit responsible for product *A*, and another for product *B*? Or should one person be responsible for manufacturing products *A* and *B*, while another unit markets both? The latter approach, based on differentiation by kind of work done, is termed functional departmentalization. This is probably the most common basis for departmentalizing small firms, as well as the lower levels of large organizations.

---

[6] Much of the following is influenced by the excellent discussion in Joseph Litterer, *Analysis of Organizations* (New York: John Wiley & Sons, Inc., 1965), pp. 176–85.

Figure 15-1

Hypothetical illustrations of functional
and product departmentalization.

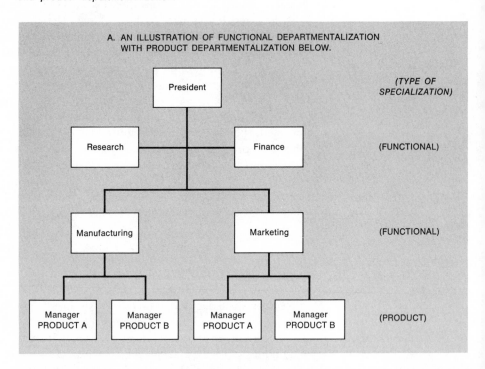

A. AN ILLUSTRATION OF FUNCTIONAL DEPARTMENTALIZATION
WITH PRODUCT DEPARTMENTALIZATION BELOW.

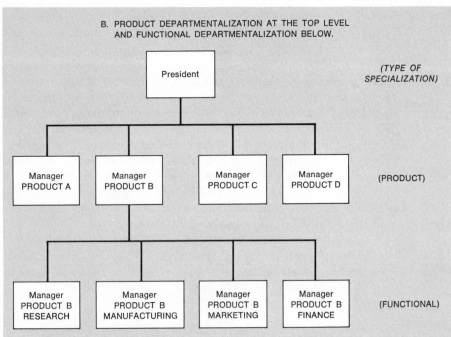

B. PRODUCT DEPARTMENTALIZATION AT THE TOP LEVEL
AND FUNCTIONAL DEPARTMENTALIZATION BELOW.

ADVANTAGES OF FUNCTIONAL DEPARTMENTS. Functional organization enables individuals and work teams to develop great proficiency at their specialized tasks. Insights gained while working one product may be transferable to ease subsequent efforts on other products. Process innovations may well be shared among the members of a functional unit. Such transfers might not occur as readily where product A is processed in a completely separate unit—perhaps hundreds of miles distant—from product B. It is even less likely to be shared if the product A unit feels it is competing for rewards and resources against the product B unit.

The functional approach may also facilitate the professional development and personal satisfaction of unit members. Here one's efforts and competence are judged by fellow specialists, by professionals in the same discipline. Technical prowess and assistance is close at hand. In a product-oriented unit, he is judged by individuals who may be less qualified to evaluate the technical merit of his work and who are less concerned with technical merit than they are with the success of the project. Moreover, the similar career and technical interests of a homogeneous group of specialists may provide for more comfortable informal relationships.

These values of the functional approach are demonstrated by a study of an advertising agency that shifted from a functional form (copy department, art department, research department, and so on) to a client-centered organization. Each discipline was now mixed into composite groups who produced integrated advertising campaigns for specific clients. There were several positive consequences of this change; but there also resulted some loss of satisfactions that had been derived from the old functional structure. Thus one market research specialist stated:

> I feel lonely since we have moved offices. There's nobody to talk to except about business. You know, before this happened we used to have other research people look over our work and we used to talk about all sorts of other things. I don't know why it is, but I can't seem to warm up to this other group.
> And another thing, what do these people know about research? I can't talk to them about what I do. So what *do* I talk about—sales figures? [7]

PROBLEMS OF FUNCTIONAL DEPARTMENTALIZATION. Departmentalization by function can also have offsetting drawbacks. For example, a group of specialists may become increasingly absorbed with their technical processes and professional relationships to the degree that the objectives of the larger organization are disregarded. Satisfactions become increas-

[7] Arthur J. Kover, "Reorganizing in an Advertising Agency: A Case Study of a Decrease in Integration," *Human Organization*, XXII, no. 4 (Winter, 1963–1964), p. 257.

ingly tied to that department, that technology, and that group of specialists. Information not directly related to that function is ignored, so that
the lack of concern with organizational matters is compounded by ignorance of those matters.

As discussed earlier, specialization increases the need for coordination. Coordination usually requires that the different groups respect each
other's organizational role and needs. Effective communications are also
extremely important among coordinating groups. To the extent that functional specialists are looking "inward," stressing their own problems, technology, and peer recognition, there is diminution of concern about other
groups. Thus while the need for coordination may be greatest because of
functional specialization, the desire for coordination may be lacking and
the interdepartmental communication may be insufficient.

Another possible problem associated with functional departmentalization is the narrow scope of personnel development within specialized
units. The advertising copywriter may be exposed almost exclusively to
the problems and procedures involved with generating good copy. His
knowledge of the related functions would be extremely limited, as would
his group of coordination mechanisms. This functional structure may,
therefore, fail to develop him for those managerial positions that require
that he integrate and coordinate the efforts of various specialized groups.

PRODUCT DEPARTMENTALIZATION

Organizational growth may be measured along several dimensions,
including total sales, assets, profits, and number of employees. One may
also include the extension of organizational capabilities to an increasing
number of product lines as an indicator of growth. These lines may be
elaborations of a previously single-phased line. For example, a quality
shoe manufacturer may decide to establish a lower-priced line, perhaps
under a new brand name. The manufacturer of "medium-priced" automobiles may develop a smaller version of its product, such as the Buick
Special or the Pontiac *Tempest*. The organization may add related products to its already established lines, as Gillette added shaving cream to
its razor and blade line, and then introduced other personal products
(shampoos, deodorants, and so on). As the organization's product line
grows more diverse, the pressure to shift away from a functional structure to a product structure grows with it. Since the processes involved in
the production of shampoo differ so substantially from those for razor
blades, the advantages of functional departmentalization with the production part of the organization are lost. Product plants will probably be
established for each product line, or for sets of compatible lines, under

the direction of a general plant manager. *Within* each plant, however, there will probably be a functional departmentalization.

By the same token, some forms of diversification lead to product departmentalization within the marketing department. A new production process may yield new by-products that are marketable, but in different markets from the primary product. A petroleum-processing firm may well establish product divisions within its marketing department to distribute its various chemical outputs.

STRENGTHS OF PRODUCT DEPARTMENTALIZATION.   Like any other bases for departmentalization, the product basis has both positive and negative consequences. On the favorable side, product departmentalization can yield an overall focus on the final objective being sought, rather than emphasis on local processes and concerns of functional units. Stress is placed on the integration of specialized services toward the achievement of volume and quality objectives. Operational goals, coordination, and mutual assistance may replace narrow provincial interests.

Product-oriented divisions are generally self-contained units, possessing the capacities required to attain objectives. These units must be internally coordinated, but may require little coordination with outside units. The coordination among specialists with a product orientation is more readily achieved than coordination among functionally oriented personnel.

With a product orientation, the role of individuals and groups in the attainment of departmental and organizational goals may be more discernible than under functional differentiation. Whereas a functional orientation may stress the technical capacity of an individual or group, product orientation leads to emphasis on actual contributions toward desired output. A unit that knows it is identified with the volume and quality of its output is more likely to seek high achievement levels, whereas the functional unit may feel that it is but one of a large number of units who influence final output and that it is not identified with any particular product.

Finally, the integrative concern of product-organized teams is said to facilitate managerial development. Personnel are conditioned to view the overall system, with an emphasis upon balance, timing, and coordination. One's interests and knowledge base are likely to be broader in scope, a perspective frequently valued in higher managerial positions.

PROBLEMS OF PRODUCT DEPARTMENTALIZATION.   The drawbacks of product departmentalization can be severe. For example, unless the volume of work associated with a product is great, the demands on individual functional groups may be insufficient to warrant the use of the most productive equipment. Other potential economies may be foregone, such as discounts for quantity purchases and the ability to keep specialists busy full-time at their most productive tasks. It is one thing to separate out the Chevrolet Division as a product-based department, but such a basis for departmentalization might be unfeasible were only a few thousand Chevrolets produced per year, instead of millions.

A second serious problem with product departmentalization is possible duplication of effort and investment. Each unit, for example, may be doing its own research, with a large staff and expensive equipment engaged in improving its product or its processes. Each unit may be incurring huge expenses working up computer programs for the solution of various problems that may be common to all other product units.

Since each product unit is self-contained, there may be little communication among them. As a result, insights, shortcuts, and superior systems may not be shared. In fact, each unit may wish to conceal its innovations from other units to gain a competitive advantage over them. Product units are frequently expected to compete with each other. It would not be surprising to find that the Pontiac Division of General Motors is secreting important improvements from the Oldsmobile and Buick Divisions. Such competition can prove to be a great motivator, but the costs of hoarding information and insights may offset this advantage.

OTHER BASES FOR DEPARTMENTALIZATION

Although function and product are probably the two most widely applied bases for departmentalization, other bases are also important. For example, companies with widespread markets utilize geographic divisions. Some find that they can service different types of customers by departmentalizing on a customer basis. An automobile firm may well have separate divisions for sales to dealers, to large industrial purchasers, to auto leasing firms, and to governments. Then there are organizational groupings based on time, as in shifts; or based on the use of a common facility, such as a computer. As with the product-function comparison, each approach to organization has strengths and weaknesses when compared to all other alternatives. Pointing out all of these poses too great a task to be fully treated here.

COMBINED STRUCTURES

The typical organization utilizes some combination of product, function, facility, consumer, geography, and other bases for departmentalization. For example, a gas and electric utility may be functionally organized at the vice-president's level, with specialists in electrical generation, transmission, marketing, and so on, as in Figure 15-2. Within the marketing division, there may be product-based departments, specializing in natural gas on the one hand and in electricity on the other hand, perhaps competing vigorously for the same consumers. Although the overall plans and major policy decisions are established at these top levels, actual implementation is left to lower levels. This implementation and day-to-day administration of programs conducted over extended *geographic* regions is the major concern of the territorial managers. Were we to develop the

Figure 15-2

A simplified version of the organization chart of a utility company.

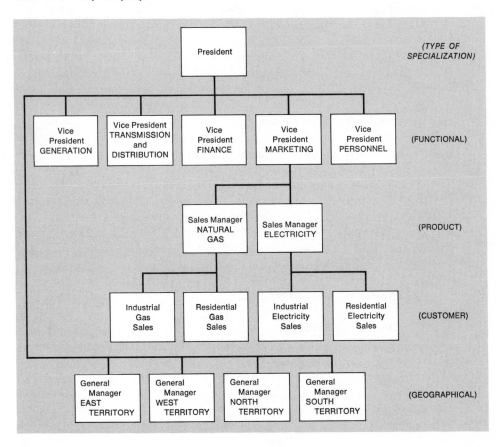

organization chart farther downward, we would encounter all the forms of departmentalization discussed above, including time shifts and repair groups organized around specific pieces of equipment.

TEMPORARY GROUPINGS: PROJECT ORGANIZATION

Like many individual organisms, the organization can modify its configuration to meet its challenges. Thus, although the organization structure of departments based on function, product, territory, facility, or time may be more or less stable, certain temporary departures from this stable structure may be necessary. Task teams may be created to perform a short-term assignment requiring an integrated effort. The individuals so assigned may be temporarily relieved of their normal duties and hierarchical accountability or they may be asked to contribute their efforts to the teams while carrying on some level of normal duties.

Receiving increasing attention is the project organization. Heavily used by defense contractors in the design and early production of expensive, complex weapons systems, the project organization seems to be a hybrid of the functional and product forms. Picture a large organization made up primarily of functional divisions. Each major functional division may be subdivided into more narrowly defined departments (the research division, for example, might include separate departments for research on propulsion systems, aerodynamics, structural testing, and the like).

Now the firm receives a multibillion-dollar contract to design and construct a new plane or space vehicle. Because the contract spans a period of years, a semipermanent team, with a formal project leader, is established to take full responsibility for contract fulfillment. Essentially, a product form of organization is superimposed upon a functional organization for the period of the project, perhaps several years.

The project team may be composed of specialists drawn from the various functional departments, as well as individuals hired specifically for this project. Jobs are not necessarily held open for any project members after the project is completed. The project group may be granted broad responsibilities, including:

1. Product definition.
2. Control over funds allocations and team member assignments.
3. Make-or-buy decisions.
4. Scheduling.
5. Progress review systems.

6. Identification and solution of subproblems.

7. Customer and subcontractor relations.

8. Development of market potentials.[8]

Internal problems over the respective authorities of the project manager and functional managers are not unlikely. Individual firms vary in their attempts to work out the best formal authority structure. The project manager may be delegated the authority only to issue time-quality-volume orders to functional divisions, with no supervision of or direct contact with functional operations. On the other extreme, he might be authorized to take temporary command of functional divisions or components thereof until they have completed project work. As yet there are no general decision rules for establishing the limits of a project manager's authority.[9]

There are compelling reasons for the use of project organization. It assures high-level attention and a coordinated team approach to important projects. It provides a communications center for maintaining contact with all of the important participants in the project, including the client, subcontractors, suppliers, and functional divisions within the organization. Like the product structure, it trains individuals to perform various management roles in integrating diverse needs and specialties.

Despite these advantages, the project form must be used with care. It can (both apparently and actually) undermine the authority of functional managers, and this, plus differing points of view, may result in conflict rather than the required cooperation. Individuals may hesitate to accept assignments to project teams, perhaps feeling that their permanent functional positions will be jeopardized. Functional managers may be reluctant to release valuable personnel from other important assignments. Specialists working part-time with project teams may find themselves with two direct superiors, perhaps with contradictory demands. Long-range organizational planning may be sacrificed as emphasis shifts to project commitments. Insights gained from one project may not be transferred to other teams on other projects.

Despite the potential problems, it does appear that project organization is a viable approach to very large, complex commitments. Used sparingly, it can combine the advantages of product and functional organization. Used too freely, the project approach can splinter the organization into uncohesive, conflicting, short-term-oriented groups.

[8] After C. J. Middleton, "How to Set up a Project Organization," *Harvard Business Review*, XLV, no. 2 (April, 1967), 73–82.

[9] Ibid., p. 76.

An understanding of the potential strengths and limitations of alternative organization structures provides an initial framework for evaluation. A second step involves the statement of the conditions that help to determine which alternative is likely to be superior. It is not yet possible to construct a realistic general mathematical model for departmentalization decisions. It is possible, however, to suggest some guides for making organizational decisions. Let us examine some of the factors that might affect rational decisions concerning departmental structures.

PRODUCT SIMILARITY. Where an organization's products lend themselves to common production processes and a common distribution system, many economies could be obtained from a functional form of departmentalization. Specialized skills, equipment, and techniques could be applied to all the products and needless duplication of effort and investment could be avoided. In contrast, a truly diverse product line seems more consistent with product departmentalization. For example, a firm that produces school furniture, surgical equipment, and fishing rods would probably establish product departments at a high level, with functional departments below to service those products exclusively. The production problems would differ markedly for each, as would the marketing processes.

ECONOMIC SIZE AND VOLUME. With a given technology, there are limits to the efficient size of a production operation. Unless a certain minimum volume of work is assured, investment in the most economical (lowest cost per unit) system may be unfeasible. Beyond a certain maximum volume level, however, cost per unit may not fall further with additional volume. In fact, such costs may well increase. For low-volume operations, therefore, a product organization might prove too costly. Every attempt would be made to use common facilities in the processing of all products. As volume expands, however, a point will be reached where differentiation by product becomes economical. Should volume for any product expand to the point where one shift cannot handle it, then shifts may be added (differentiation by time); and further volume will probably result in additional departments or plants being added (differentiation by physical space or territory).

FLUCTUATIONS IN VOLUME. Not only the typical magnitude of volume, but also the stability or variations in volume, affect departmentalization decisions. Consider the case of a series of one-secretary offices. Demand for the services of each secretary may fluctuate independently of that for the others. This would result in idle intervals for some secretaries while others were swamped with work. If secretarial work (telephone calls, typing, duplicating, and so on) arrives randomly, then a secretarial pool may be advisable. The peaks and lulls in work emanating from some of the offices will offset those for others, assuming that the demand for secretarial work in each office is independent of the demand in each other office. As the number of secretaries grows larger and the scope of office workloads expands, the law of large numbers should apply: that is, the total workload arriving each day should more closely approximate the mean daily workload than would be the case if there were one secretary in each office.

Wide fluctuations in workloads for a small group, then, may be corrected by combining that group (and its workload) with others. The nature of the combination would be determined by a judgment concerning the best pooling of skills and, perhaps, personalities. Frequently, as with the secretarial pool, the combination will take the functional form. Here skills, technology, and personal orientations seem more likely to overlap than would be the case if individuals and specialized groups were to perform new sets of functions in a small product group. Should the volume of work be stable, as well as sufficient for economic operation, there would be no pressure to consolidate the small functional groups within product lines into larger functional departments encompassing more than one product.

GEOGRAPHICAL FACTORS. In many cases the performance of the major functions cannot be economically concentrated within one plant or even one geographic area. For example, the company that produces and sells bottled chilled orange juice may find it most economical to extract the juice in Florida and ship the juice in bulk to bottling plants near its major markets. Such a situation may well call for functional divisions of extraction and bottling, not to mention other possible functional departments concerned with purchasing and transportation. If, on the other hand, all major processes involved in the production and sales of the each product can be economically centered in one plant, then a product organization becomes more feasible.

HUMAN FACTORS. Decisions on workable organization structures must consider the probability that particular human groupings provide the required mix of skills and are socially compatible. Chemists may prefer to work closely with other chemists, rather than accountants and industrial engineers. Where strong professional orientations exist, a forced integration of several diverse backgrounds and interests may result in insurmountable communications barriers and conflict. The values and perspectives of such professions may be too divergent to permit a close, harmonious, integrated effort. Much would depend also on the personalities involved. The ability to tolerate differences in others varies widely within human beings. Therefore a product structure might work well (1) where the professional orientations among the groups included are compatible or (2) where tolerance levels among those with divergent orientations are high.

Should it appear that these professional orientations are incongruent and tolerance levels of some groups are low, then functional structuring seems indicated. Such coordination as is required among functional groups could then be achieved by representatives of the groups, who are kept aware of overall objectives and who are readiest to objectively consider the viewpoints of other groups. Such coordination may be achieved informally or through officially established committees of such representatives. A second much-used mechanism for coordinating functional divisions is the external department assigned the coordinating function. A scheduling department, for example, may attempt to assure the smooth flow of work from one department to another, specifying the routing and timing of all jobs. A quality-control department may have the assignment of assuring that specifications are met for each portion of the total task before that component moves to the next step.

Bass provides an interesting discussion of productive group composition, presenting conditions that favor groups composed of homogeneous persons and those favoring heterogeneous groupings.[10] In brief, he states that groups of workers with similar backgrounds and interests can more readily influence each other's behavior and tend to achieve greater mutual acceptance and social satisfaction within the group. Such groups may be highly productive where tasks are simple, that is, where the group possesses all of the required skills. Because of the group's positive social relationships, high productivity is also possible where tasks require closely coordinated efforts within the group. Functional organization, with resulting homogeneous groups, can, therefore, induce greater mutual influence, more social satisfaction, and high output for simple tasks or those requiring cooperative effort.

On the other hand, heterogeneous groupings are said to be superior where tasks are complex and a diverse set of skills is needed. Diverse backgrounds may also facilitate the generation of creative approaches to old and new problems. Group decisions may be improved where diverse viewpoints provoke wide-ranging analyses of issues, alternatives, and

[10] Bernard M. Bass, *Organizational Psychology* (Boston: Allyn & Bacon, Inc., 1965), pp. 204–9.

consequences. As the nature of the task shifts from routine and simple to complex and creative, the case for the heterogeneous group grows. As Bass puts it:

> For simple, routine assignments, the optimum mix is of fairly similar types of men. For complex tasks with creative demands, the optimum becomes a more diversified assemblage. For assignments requiring easy, cooperative interaction, the optimum is again of similar men. But when such cooperation is less important, the men can differ more.[11]

SUMMARY

A fundamental advantage of human organizations over unorganized individual effort is the opportunity to realize the benefits of specialization. Prudent division of labor can enhance productivity by: (1) minimizing training requirements, (2) facilitating rapid progress toward job mastery, (3) reducing labor costs associated with employing skilled generalists, (4) easing replacement of employees, (5) permitting intensive utilization of special purpose equipment, and (6) simplifying supervision.

Like many good things, however, specialization may be overdone. As specialization intensifies, problems multiply in the areas of employee idleness and costs of product transportation and handling. Coordination becomes more difficult. A worker's enthusiasm for his job may decline, as his interests contract to a few functions and associates.

Decisions must also be made concerning the nature of the specialization among whole departments or divisions. Functional departmentalization tends to encourage process innovation and proficiency, while facilitating personal development and satisfaction. Product departmentalization tends to increase as organizations grow and diversify. This structure stresses team effort among diverse specialists toward the achievement of complex objectives. The need for intradepartmental coordination increases, while interdepartmental coordination diminishes in importance. Emphasis on integrated output replaces the narrow functional viewpoint. Individuals may be judged on their contribution to goal attainment, rather than pure functional excellence. Because the product approach stresses the integration of functions, it is believed to develop potential managers more effectively than the functional structure. Although both approaches also bear serious drawbacks, they dominate most organizations.

[11] Ibid., p. 204.

Other bases for organizing, used in conjunction with function and product, are geography, customer, time, and project. The project form draws on permanent departments for personnel to man a team that is assigned to a long-range, intricate problem. In essence, an additional product department is superimposed on the existing structure, but the product is a one-time achievement. The project approach assures high-level attention and coordination on significant projects, but it can undermine the permanent structure if used too freely.

Decisions concerning the appropriate bases for department differentiation should be based on the following pivotal factors: (1) product similarity, (2) economic size and volume, (3) fluctuations in volume, (4) geographical factors, and (5) human factors. Although no comprehensive model exists for easy decisions, these factors can provide strong clues to the appropriate structure.

The bases for departmental differentiation help the manager to decide the *kinds* of departments to create. Closely related are his decisions concerning how large operating departments should be. If productivity is found to be related to department size, then the manager must sometimes separate groups performing the same function. We next turn to these decisions of proper department size.

QUESTIONS

1. What are the most important values and the limitations of specialization?

2. What is the relationship between specialization and the need for coordination? Cite an example.

3. How does specialization affect the perceptions of workers?

4. Why is departmentalization by function so universal?

5. What might a "concerned" top management do to avoid the problems of functional departmentalization, while utilizing its advantages?

6. Under what circumstances is departmentalization by product or service preferable to the functional structure?

7. Describe the product form of organization. Where is it best utilized? What are its advantages?

8. Discuss the key factors to be considered in making departmentalization decisions.

9. Why departmentalize at all?

department size

16

What shall their number be?
Of what shall they have charge,
and what shall be their duration?

ARISTOTLE

Decisions regarding the kinds of departments best suited to an enterprise must be supplemented by further decisions concerning the proper size of each unit. The technology employed may well dictate the number of operatives and their work-flow relationships. Human factors also seem to be an important consideration here. As we shall see, the number of members in the group can influence such variables as group cohesiveness, communications, and productivity.

Of course, the organizational units established must be manageable. There are limits to the energies and leadership capabilities of any man. If the desire is to create units that are readily managed by one man, perhaps aided by staff assistants, then departmental size must be somewhat limited. Accordingly, we must examine the classical management concept of span of control, seeking to understand what determines the number of subordinates a manager can effectively handle.

Effects of Group Size

In a recent work, Rensis Likert attempts to explain why many past studies show little consistency among such variables as leadership style, employee attitudes, and employee productivity. Other factors, he maintains, also influence these variables, thus at times obscuring the effects of leadership style on employee attitudes and the effects of attitudes on output. One such external variable is group size, as Likert states:

> . . . Other factors, such as variations in the size of the department . . . , can also affect the relationships. . . . Size tends to affect adversely the intervening and end result variables, the larger the department, the less favorable the attitude and the poorer the performance.[1]

This conclusion is based on his own studies, which corroborate findings from still other studies.[2] Likert found that the most effective units of one organization ranged from 15 to 20 members. Optimal group size probably varies with such factors as the nature of the group's work, the technology employed, and the characteristics of individual members. But given these factors, management may, through experimentation, estimate the most appropriate group size. Should the work load and work force expand within a department, managers may well establish a cut-off point beyond which the department will be split into two separate work units. Studies indicate, for example, that the optimal size of a group whose task is to solve problems is 5 to 7 members. Evidently larger problem-solving groups experience more inhibition by individuals, insufficient time for expression of everyone's views, and a tendency toward disorder. Extremely small problem-solving groups may lack the required variety of knowledge and skills useful in solving complex problems. They may also face an unwillingness by individuals to freely express their views, for fear of alienating others in a close-knit team.[3]

The factors limiting effective group size are probably similar for groups performing functions other than problem solving. It appears that lower limits will typically be set by the skill and volume requirements of the technology employed, as well as the social needs of group members. Upper limits to effective group size are determined by increasing coordination problems, probably caused by increasing communication difficulty as the group grows. These difficulties may be compounded by the tendency of individuals to identify with small primary groups, which develop their own goals and behavior patterns. One study, conducted among girls

[1] Rensis Likert, *The Human Organization* (New York: McGraw-Hill Book Company, Inc., 1967), p. 97.

[2] Rensis Likert, *New Patterns of Management* (New York: McGraw-Hill Book Company, Inc., 1961), pp. 38, 157–61.

[3] Donald E. Porter and Philip B. Applewhite, *Organizational Behavior* (Englewood Cliffs, N.J.: Prentice-Hall, Inc., 1964), p. 81.

in an industrial training school, concluded that 12 close relationships was a typical limit per girl. Where larger groups existed, there was a tendency for closely knit subgroups to evolve.[4] Studies of military performance indicate that the fighting man's willingness to fight and die is associated with his loyalty to his buddies. His motivation is tied to the small primary group, to those to whom he is emotionally bound.[5] He identifies in decreasing degrees to larger entities. Several studies have found an inverse relationship between group size and member satisfaction.[6] Depending on the technology employed, therefore, the manager may well consciously limit the size of work units to permit the coordinated, motivated effort that may result from effective communication, personal commitment to the group, and the group stability resulting from member satisfaction.

Span of Control

The "principle" of span of control is said to be one of four "pillars" of classical organization theory.[7] The term is alternately used to signify (1) the number of subordinates directly answering to one superior, or (2) the number of subordinates that a superior can effectively handle. We shall use the first definition. The span of control concept is surrounded by controversy, largely because early theorists attempted to demonstrate that large numbers of subordinates led to ineffective management. Thus Lyndall Urwich, a noted management theorist and consultant, held that the optimal span of control for high-level executives was 4, while that for the lowest level of management was 8 to 12.[8] Another management consultant, V. A. Graicunas, developed a mathematical equation for

[4] Helen Jennings, *Leadership and Isolation* (New York: Longmans, Green & Co., Ltd., 1950).

[5] Edward A. Skills, "Primary Groups in the American Army," in *Continuities in Social Research: Studies in the Scope and Method of "The American Soldier,"* ed. R. K. Morton and P. F. Lazarsfeld (New York: Free Press of Glencoe, 1950), pp. 16–39.

[6] R. J. House and J. B. Miner, "Merging Management and Behavioral Theory: The Interaction Between Span of Control and Group Size," *Administrative Science Quarterly*, XIII, no. 3 (September, 1969), 451–64.

[7] According to William G. Scott, the other three "pillars" are division of labor, scales and functional processes, and structure. See his "Organization Theory: An Overview and Appraisal," *Academy of Management Journal*, IV, no. 1 (April, 1961), 7–26.

[8] Lyndall Urwich, "Axions of Organization," *Public Administration Magazine* (October, 1955), pp. 348–49.

determining the number of "relationships" between a manager and his subordinates as the number of subordinates varies.[9] His central theme was that the total number of possible relationships between the manager and individual subordinates, between the manager and various combinations of subordinates, and between subordinates themselves increase geometrically with each addition to the work group. According to his equation, the total number of relationships may be calculated as:

$$n(\frac{2n}{2} + n - 1)$$

This yields 18 relationships where n equals 3 subordinates, 100 relationships for 5 subordinates, and 5,210 relationships for 10 subordinates.[10] The point is clear: the number of *possible* relationships within the department mushrooms as the department grows. At some point in this growth, we are told, the manager's ability to comprehend and manage these relationships is exceeded by their sheer volume.

For all of its apparent precision and sophistication, the Graicunas approach has had little impact on current management practice. That there is truth to the relationships' growth and possible managerial limitations in handling them there is no question. But there may be a vast difference between the relationships that *can* exist and those that *do* exist. Moreover, it appears that the *nature* of these relationships is a key determinant of a manager's span of control limits. Let us examine, therefore, some factors that can affect the number and nature of the relationships with which the manager must cope. Basically, we are examining the contacts or interactions within a department and the variables that can influence them.[11]

ABILITIES OF SUBORDINATES

Human abilities cover a wide range. Where a group of subordinates lacks the intelligence, experience, or formal training to perform independently, the manager may find himself continually involved in assisting

[9] V. A. Graicunas, "Relationship in Organization," in *Papers on the Science of Administration,* ed. L. Gulick and L. Urwich (New York: Institute of Public Administration, 1937), pp. 181–87.

[10] For an excellent analysis of Graicunas' ideas, see H. Koontz and C. O'Donnell, *Principles of Management* (New York: McGraw-Hill Book Company, Inc., 1968), pp. 245–47.

[11] The literature on span of control is voluminous. For an excellent analysis of some determinants and a recent bibliography, see L. R. Pondy, "Effects of Size, Complexity, and Ownership on Administrative Intensity," *Administrative Science Quarterly,* XIV, no. 1 (March, 1969), 47–60.

and developing them. In contrast, the manager may be brought very few problems where his operatives are properly selected, trained, and experienced. The continuous, intensive involvement in the first instance converts to occasional concern with unique conditions in the second.

Nor is this true solely for individuals performing their own tasks. Even where the total task requires close coordination within a work team, the manager's involvement will vary with the group's capacity for self-coordination. This capacity is a function of the personal relationships within the group, the effectiveness of the group's internal communications system, the length of time that the group has worked together, and the informal leadership patterns that have developed. These interrelated factors help to determine whether a group can integrate its own internal efforts, or will require the "external" coordination of the manager. That manager who finds that he can rely on effective "horizontal" coordination, as well as competence among individual subordinates can handle, perhaps, several times the number of less capable and more disorganized subordinates.

MOTIVATION OF SUBORDINATES

It should be obvious that the work group whose objectives are compatible with those of the manager will require less supervision than the work group with deviant goals. Many managers spend much of their time in close supervision, not because they question the competency of individual workers or of the group as a whole, but because these managers suspect that individuals' values and group norms deviate from the manager's desires. This condition probably is most extreme among forced laborers in prisons and prisoner-of-war camps. It is not wholly absent from the industrial scene, however. Work is often uninteresting and unpleasant and perhaps hinders social activities preferred by operatives. Workers may also feel that the volume of available work is limited and that its quick completion may jeopardize their economic security.

Compounding the manager's problem is the fact that individual output may not be readily measurable, except at great cost. Under these conditions, the manager is likely to stress close supervision to assure that subordinates remain at their stations and *appear* hard at work. In contrast, the manager who feels that he has competent subordinates who share his goals probably feels less need for supervision. His span of control, then, is partially determined by the relationships between subordinate need structures and the satisfactions achieved by subordinates through productive effort. The greater the commitment to assigned tasks, the smaller the need for supervision and the greater the manageable span of control.

Just as the capacities of operatives vary, so do those of managers. Some can foresee potential problems and act to avoid them. By effective planning, they avoid "fighting fires" later. Some are true leaders, able to gain the support of their work group toward mutual goals. Some have the knack for developing subordinates rapidly, so that they quickly learn the skills and generate the self-confidence to perform without constant assistance. Some managers possess intellects so comprehensive and keen that they can quickly grasp the core of problems and generate superior solutions. Some are blessed with extremely high levels of energy and endurance, as well as stable temperaments.

To the extent the manager possesses these attributes, he can handle large numbers of subordinates. It is probably not uncommon, for example, to find a manager who is an inspiring leader, but a poor planner; or one who plans well, but "rattles" easily when events do not conform to plans; or one who is extremely intelligent, but technically naive. Clearly any calculation of the appropriate number of subordinates must encompass this variable, unless all managers are to be considered as standard inputs.

COMPLEXITY OF WORK

Among the limitations of a manager to handle effectively large numbers of subordinates is his ability to help solve problems as they arise. Should these be simple problems with quick solutions, this may be an unimportant constraint. As the work takes on greater and greater complexity, so that problems are not as quickly grasped, alternatives more obscure, and the consequences of each alternative tougher to evaluate, then the limits of manageability may be a relatively small number of subordinates.

In the same vein, the span of control should probably be smaller where the work is highly diverse. Where all subordinates are performing similar tasks, planning is simplified; problems are likely to be standard and repetitive, so that new solutions to unique problems are less frequently needed. The processes of selection, training, and establishing reward structures are simplified. The technical knowledge required of supervisors is narrowed. It should not be surprising, therefore, to encounter large spans of control at the foreman level of a functional unit or a product unit where the functions are simple and few.

As discussed earlier work-group stability facilitates coordination among its members. Often it also permits greater mutual understanding and predictability between the work group and its manager. Another aspect of stability is the work process. Radical changes in the work system

334

decrease this predictability and the conditions basic to coordination. In addition, planning, motivating, and training become more burdensome for the manager. In effect, great changes mean more diverse, complex problems, indicating a smaller span of control than would the stable or gradually evolving system.

FORMALIZED CONTROLS

Until now, we have implicitly assumed that supervision is a direct and personal activity. This is a gross simplification of the supervision process. As indicated in Chapter 5, managers typically develop a series of standing plans (such as stated goals, policies, procedures, standards, and decision rules) to assist subordinates in the solution of problems without recourse to the manager. Measurement of performance, moreover, can frequently be objectively measured by clerical and inspection personnel and succinctly reported to managers. Standardized charts and computerized analyses are often available to help the manager ascertain at a glance the level of operations at various points within his department.

Not only is the manager relieved of physical supervision and personal analysis of many operative problems. He may also have available another set of programs to help him solve technical problems at his level. Thus computer programs are available to help him determine the proper inventory levels for all raw materials, the number of lathes necessary for various production schedules, and the least costly approach to machine maintenance. Official policies and procedures may well simplify his decision process further by eliminating some potential solutions and favoring others. A collective bargaining contract may, for example, require that promotions be decided on the basis of seniority. The job goes to the man most senior among those qualified for it. Thus the manager need not select the *most* qualified man, which could be difficult and embarrassing. He need only consider those who meet stated qualifications and select the senior man. The contract may also prescribe wage levels for all covered employees, thus relieving the supervisor of the need to decide the wage level for each individual. It is not uncommon for a manager to state that collective bargaining has, in many respects, simplified his job. All of this does not guarantee that subordinates or the manager will make "better" decisions. It does, however, permit a larger span of control by simplifying the manager's job.

Related to simplification of the manager's role by formalizing procedures is the help of staff personnel. The manager may have allocated to him one or more staff assistants, who may be specialists in particular functions, such as inventory control, personnel, or accounting. Others may be general trouble-shooters or may assume some of the simpler, more routine (but time-consuming) activities performed by managers. Staff personnel may assist in creating policies and procedures, help to measure and analyze performance within departments, take a role in hiring and training personnel, provide valuable inputs toward solving problems that arise, and so on. If effectively used, then, staff assistance can magnify the manageable number of subordinates in a given situation.

MANAGERIAL PHILOSOPHY

In addition to a set of skills, intellect, and energy, a manager usually brings with him a philosophy of management. This conceptual framework may heavily influence his management style. For example, if he internally emphasizes the growth potential and self-control characteristics of subordinates, then he may tend toward permissive leadership. Should his past leadership experiences have persuaded him to favor close supervision and vertical control of work-group activities, then he may initially carry this approach to the new situation.

Hopefully, the new manager soon adjusts his leadership style to the conditions (this work, these subordinates, and so on) that exist, unless he can alter them. As suggested earlier, no leadership philosophy or style has been demonstrated superior under all conditions. Nevertheless, it is not unlike many people to transfer the lessons learned under one set of conditions to a new, and possibly dissimilar, situation. Initially, then, one can expect many managers to adopt a managerial style (based on a philosophy) that influences the number of subordinates he can manage. A permissive or laissez-faire leader can presumably "handle" greater numbers of subordinates than his *Theory* X colleague, but the consequences of these two styles of leadership will vary with the circumstances.

Effects of Various Spans

Early treatises on span of control typically focused on the negative effects on performance where managers—from top executives down to foremen—supervised "too many" subordinates. It was widely believed that industry and government were running inefficiently due partially to violation of span of control "principles." Occasionally one encounters this logic today. In any case, the problem of ideal unit size remains a key aspect of the organizational structure challenge that faces all managers. There are obvious values associated with small administrative units, but there are also serious drawbacks.

PRESUMED MANAGERIAL CONSTRAINTS

The chief argument for small administrative units is its presumed advantage in internal efficiency. The manager is better able to comprehend the social and technical variables and therefore can better direct his unit toward established objectives. He has more time for planning and a less complex unit for which to plan. The managerial challenges remain well within his capacity to deal with them quickly and judiciously. Not only are his plans and his operating decisions better, but he can also take an active role in developing, just getting to know, and indoctrinating subordinates. Of course, he can also closely supervise activities to assure that they conform with plans. Such managerial activities, it is held, are of great value in achieving a productive, stable work unit.

The preceding logic, which dominated span of control literature in the early 1900s, focuses on the manager as organizer, developer, coordinator, and general decision maker within his domain. Little attention is given to the potential activities of the work group as an alternative or a participant in performing such functions. Management was to manage; subordinates were to obey. Under such an arrangement, a large number of subordinates would pose too great a managerial challenge, thus the emphasis on limiting spans of control.

Or would it? One possible reaction to an overburdening number of subordinates is to permit them a greater role in performing their functions. It is universally recognized that work groups do generate informal organization structures, that they can coordinate their own efforts toward common goals, that they do develop and otherwise assist accepted co-workers, and that they often contain the knowledge and skills to solve many of their own problems. Perhaps the adaptable manager, faced with an overwhelming number of subordinates and *forced* to adjust his style, delegates more authority and removes himself from detailed control of operations. Earlier analyses either ignore this adaptation or assume that this style is inferior to close supervision, a questionable assumption.

The classic study relating span of control to leadership style was conducted at Sears, Roebuck. Among the conclusions derived from this study was the following:

> An organization with few layers of supervision and a minimum of formal controls places a premium on ability to stimulate and lead. The driver type of executive, who functions through maintaining constant

pressure and whose chief sanction is fear cannot operate as effectively in such an organization. In the more simple types of organization structures, where management has been effectively decentralized, an executive accomplishes results and moves to higher levels of responsibility chiefly to the extent that he is able to secure the willing, enthusiastic support of his colleagues and subordinates; he does not have the "tools" . . . to accomplish the result in any other manner.[12]

Worthy notes that the doctrine of limited span of control is frequently and *purposely* violated, stating:

A number of highly successful organizations have not only paid little heed but have gone directly counter to one of the favorite tenets of modern management theory, the so-called "span of control," which holds that the number of subordinate executives or supervisors reporting to a single individual be severely limited to enable that individual to exercise the detailed direction and control which is generally considered necessary. On the contrary, these organizations often deliberately give each key executive so many subordinates that it is impossible for him to exercise too close supervision over their activities.[13]

Span of control, then, is not purely a dependent variable. One can see the span as directly influencing overall management style, the degree of formalized controls employed, the development of subordinates, and so on. These relationships appear circular and interdependent. No simple, rudimentary statement can comprehend these complex interrelationships. The optimal span of control within a particular situation may well depend on the leadership style and so on that higher management deems superior in that situation. Top management may choose to cultivate that style by (among other measures) manipulating the number of subordinates reporting to each manager. Which, then, is the dependent variable?

ORGANIZATIONAL HEIGHT

Where small administrative groups are established throughout the organization, one result is a large number of *levels* in the hierarchy. For simplicity's sake, let us assume that each manager, at every level, has only three subordinates, as in Figure 16-1A. It would take four levels of managers (40 in all) to administer, directly or indirectly, 51 operative employees. Should the span of control be increased to 8 subordinates at every level (Figure 16-1B), it takes only 2 levels of managers and 9 total

---

[12] James C. Worthy, "Organizational Structure and Employee Morale," *American Sociological Review*, XV, no. 2 (April, 1950), 168.
[13] Ibid., p. 168.

Figure 16-1

A comparison of a "tall" organization structure (smaller span of control) and a "flat" organization structure (larger span of control).

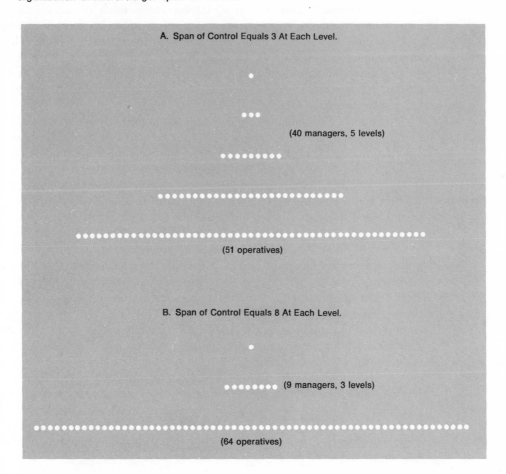

A. Span of Control Equals 3 At Each Level.

(40 managers, 5 levels)

(51 operatives)

B. Span of Control Equals 8 At Each Level.

(9 managers, 3 levels)

(64 operatives)

managers to administer 64 operatives. Possible savings in administrative costs with large spans seem obvious, although they may well be offset by the need for better trained subordinates and the like.

A further result of the "tall" structure (small spans of control, thus more levels) is the increased number of vertical links in the communication network. Communications from top management must pass through more managerial levels on their way to the operatives. At each level, the

339

intended message may be interpreted, supplemented, or digested before being relayed to the next level. The process consumes time and increases the risk that messages finally received at the bottom of the hierarchy differ materially from those transmitted at the top. A similar process occurs for information on the way up the hierarchy. Each manager screens information, summarizes the significant portions, adds his interpretation, and transmits the product to his superior, who then does the same. This large communication distance between the top and bottom can cause the organization to adapt slowly, and perhaps irrationally, to changing conditions. Its nervous system transmits messages upward and downward too slowly and inaccurately.[14]

The preceding logic undergirds opposition to small spans of control, stressing faster, more direct communications networks. It should be recognized, however, that a policy of large numbers of subordinates per manager also involves potential communication problems. Individual subordinates may experience difficulty in getting to see their superior. He becomes remote, so tied up with "important" matters that subordinates hesitate to disturb him. In consequence, the manager may lose his awareness of the difficulties existing within his operation, as well as potential ideas for its improvement. His reports to superiors may unintentionally reflect a distorted image of reality. Superiors, themselves burdened with large spans, may compound these distortions in their own reports. Thus the "flat" organization structure may also experience communication problems, those associated with an insufficient number of information-collecting centers. These problems can be alleviated by such devices as the use of staff assistants as communications links, by programmed reporting procedures, or by communicating with informal group leaders. None of these techniques eliminates the sense of managerial remoteness. Programmed reports typically include only the information specifically requested, ignoring other potentially important topics. Moreover, staff and informal leader networks add links between the manager and his operating subordinates, introducing time lags and possible distortions, much as in the tall structure.

NO MAGIC FORMULA

As a recent study of top corporate management indicates, no equation yet defines the optimal number of subordinates for a manager. The authors state:

[14] Communication is discussed more fully in Chapter 15.

> If corporate practice . . . may be accepted as a criterion, there most assuredly is no magic or immutable number of subordinates that should report to an immediate superior.[15]

The span of control for chief corporate executives is found to range from 1 to 14, with a mean of 10. It is found to vary during the history of the same company, in one case from a low of 3 to a high of 15; and in another from 5 to 20.[16]

This is not meant to discourage careful study and analysis of the factors that underlie span of control decisions. By recognizing these factors and their relative importance within a specific organizational context, intelligent (if not optimal) decisions can be made regarding unit size. The Lockheed Missiles and Space Company has devised such an analytical system, which appears to be working well.[17] The system identifies and assigns weights to a set of factors similar to those discussed herein. For example, the factor "Similarity of Functions" may be weighted from 1 (all functions of the unit are identical) to 5 (the functions are fundamentally distinct and varied). The weighted total for all variables indicates the appropriate number of subordinates. The Lockheed approach, although admittedly based on approximations and judgments, is a step in the right direction. It attempts to identify the important factors and to give them proper weight. Such an approach may benefit any organization.

SUMMARY

Several studies indicate that group size is an important determinant of group productivity. For problem-solving groups, optimal size may be 5 to 7 members. Larger groups (perhaps 15–20) may be optimal for most routine tasks. The lower limits probably relate to the skill and volume requirements of the technology employed, as well as the need for social fulfillment. Upper limits involve coordination problems, the tendency for large groups to split into cliques, and difficulties in identifying with the goals of very large entities.

[15] Paul E. Holden, et al., *Top Management* (New York: McGraw-Hill Book Company, Inc., 1968), p. 60.
[16] Ibid., p. 61.
[17] See Harold Koontz, "Making Theory Operational: The Span of Management," *Journal of Management Studies*, III, no. 3 (October, 1966), 229–43.

An important consideration is the manager's capacity to handle extremely large groups of subordinates. Important variables underlying this capacity are: (1) abilities of subordinates, (2) motivation of subordinates, (3) managerial abilities, (4) complexity of work, (5) formalized controls, and (6) managerial philosophy.

Traditional logic usually concludes that a small span of control is advisable. This logic is founded on the assumption of active control by superiors of subordinates' activities. Real delegation, however, can expand the span of control many times without any necessary loss of operational efficiency. Managerial style may be partially a *dependent* variable, shifting toward more emphasis on subordinate selection, training, motivation, and authority as the number of direct subordinates increases.

Large spans of control result in the "flat" organization, with possible savings in administrative costs. This advantage may be more than offset if subordinates do not perform well without vertical assistance or supervision. The "tall" structure may suffer from long vertical communication networks, high administrative costs, a tendency of managers to over-supervise, and a sense of executive remoteness from operations. Beyond the rather tentative numerical and qualitative guides stated above, there are no firm, universal decision rules for establishing optimum department size. The problem is as yet much too complex for either arm-chair or computer solutions.

QUESTIONS

1. What social factors seem to limit the size of effective work groups?
2. Evaluate the Graicunas approach to understanding the effects of group size. What does it stress and what does it ignore?
3. How would the following conditions affect appropriate spans of control?
   a. Simplification of the product line.
   b. A shift from authoritative to permissive management.
   c. An increase in formalized controls.
   d. A general economic recession or depression.
   e. An increase in employee turnover.
   f. A change from functional departments to product departments.
4. Discuss the relationships between span of control and organizational communications.

5. Relate the arguments for a small span of control to assumptions about the proper role of a manager.

6. Explain the statement, "Span of control is not a purely dependent variable."

7. How does the nature of a group's activities affect "optimal" group size?

8. From your own experience, does it appear that the typical person prefers to interact with a limited number of associates? How would you explain your conclusions?

distribution of authority

Theirs not to reason why,
Theirs but to do and die.
Into the valley of Death
Rode the six hundred.

ALFRED, LORD TENNYSON
The Charge of the Light Brigade

Assume now that decisions have been made establishing both the bases for departmentalization and the appropriate size of departments. These decisions might be depicted in an organizational manual and organization chart, which together indicate the nature of operations for which each manager is responsible and to whom he is accountable. They do not necessarily indicate, however, the authority relationships among different levels of management or how much autonomy and discretion has been delegated from superior to subordinate. In the centralized organization, little managerial authority is likely to be delegated. Important decisions are made at the summit and communicated downward for implementation. Even questions concerning techniques of implementation may be directed upward for resolution and detailed instructions. In the decentralized organization, the reverse is likely to be true.

As with departmentalization and unit size decisions, there is no simple method for calculating the ideal distribution of authority and responsibility. The concept and operational characteristics of decentralization are often misunderstood. Much work has been done, however, to identify conditions most compatible with various degrees of centralization

344

or decentralization. We shall examine these matters, preceding them with a discussion of the delegation process.

Delegation and Role Theory

An old management shibboleth states that "authority can be delegated, but responsibility cannot." The point is that the delegating manager retains his reponsibilities, regardless of his delegations to subordinates. To put it another way, the manager can delegate, but he cannot abdicate (and still retain his position). Still another management proverb holds that "authority must equal responsibility." Put more lucidly, one should possess as much authority as is required to fulfill the responsibilities assigned to him. These rules for organizing provide partial insights into the nature of the delegation process, but they fail to provide a comprehensive understanding of the topic. A useful framework for gaining perspective into the overall picture of delegation is role theory.[1]

Departmentalization and delegation are the processes by which the formal roles of individuals and larger units are defined. A formal role may be defined as the set of behavioral expectations officially associated with an office and its incumbent. The dimensions of the role include duties, obligations, activities, objectives, interactions, and authority. An organization may be conceived as an interdependent system of roles designed to achieve certain objectives. Through rational delegation, the manager hopes to create an effective formal structure of roles. This implies that the structure of role expectations is:

1. Appropriate for existing personnel and technologies employed.
2. Clear to all participants.
3. Internally consistent, so that all needed roles are performed without conflict over role boundaries.

The superior is a "role sender," transmitting to subordinates his expectations of their roles as individuals and as members of a working team. He also sends his expectations regarding the working relationships between his subordinates and himself. It is important to remember that the direct superior is only one role sender, others being the peers of the

[1] An excellent discussion of role theory appears in D. Katz and R. L. Kahn, *The Social Psychology of Organizations* (New York: John Wiley & Sons, Inc., 1966), pp. 171–98.

subordinates, their own subordinates, and managers at even higher levels.[2] All of these role senders can influence the role concept of each person in the organization. Then there is the individual's own concept of his role. A discussion of delegation focuses on the superior-subordinate relationship as role sender and receiver—with each playing both parts. The role of the manager whose position is one notch higher on the organization chart may be profoundly affected by the role transmissions from below. Role structuring is a dynamic process of mutual influence among participants at various interconnected points within the organization.

If role expectations are not compatible, then the individual finds himself faced with conflicting demands from role senders. To satisfy one sender, he must risk alienating another. Mr. C, a subordinate manager, requests a "free hand" in running his department. Mr. B, C's direct superior, has no objections in principle, for he is basically a democratic manager; but he suspects that his own superior, Mr. A, prefers authoritarian leadership. Moreover, it is not clear that C is sufficiently competent to succeed without constant guidance. B thus is receiving incompatible role expectations from himself, from A, and from C, and he experiences the frustration of role conflict.

In the above example, B seems to be aware of the behavioral expectations of his superior, although they may conflict with his own role concept. In other cases, subordinates may receive insufficient or contradictory cues from superiors or other role senders. This can happen under various circumstances, but is most likely for a person in a newly created or altered position or wherever a new subordinate-superior relationship is formed. There results a "feeling around" atmosphere in which each attempts to define his role and those of persons adjacent either vertically or horizontally in the organization. This condition of uncertainty and testing is termed role ambiguity and is a tense, uncomfortable position for all involved.

The manager charged with the job of creating an effective, harmonious group will generally attempt to avoid or resolve role conflict and role ambiguity. He can start by assigning responsibilities and delegating authority appropriately, clearly, and consistently. This is only one step toward role compatibility. Changes in technologies employed, in market conditions, or in the role incumbents themselves underlie continuing role evolution, with the associated risk of role conflict and ambiguity. Organization, therefore, is a continuing task for the manager.

---

[2] Not to mention the role senders who are usually thought of as external to the organization. These include clients, government officials, union leaders, suppliers, one's church, family, and so on, all of whom may attempt to influence the role concepts of organization members.

The Act of Delegation

The formal act of delegating authority is usually preceded by some understanding between the superior and subordinate of the duties and objectives for which that subordinate is to be responsible. Let us, then, examine the concept of formal responsibility. Perhaps the best place to begin is with the objectives of the organization, as established by its top management. For these objectives to be achieved, certain work must be performed in the appropriate magnitudes, qualities, and time intervals. The functions to be performed are then organized into rational sets and assigned to specific organizational units: divisions, departments, sections, and so on. The responsibility for fulfilling a unit's part of the program is assigned to that unit's manager. Within his sphere of responsibility, he may assign further, more detailed responsibilities to subordinates.

The term, "assign" may be misleading, for it implies that the action is taken by the superior, while the subordinate is the passive recipient of responsibility. This is far from true. The complete act of creating formal responsibility involves:

1. Communication by the superior of the duties and objectives he wishes the subordinates to include in his role.
2. A communication by the subordinate that he commits himself to those duties and objectives.

This commitment by the subordinate may *precede* the formal assignment by the superior, as in the case of the alert, ambitious manager who sees an opportunity, seizes it, and then (if successful) informs the boss of what he has accomplished. Perhaps he finds a new use and a new clientele for an old product. Having profitably served this new market, he suggests that he be permitted to continue doing so. His superior must now decide how this new responsibility should be assigned. In any case, responsibility involves a dual assignment, for both superior and subordinate must agree on their interconnected roles or no real responsibility exists.

The delegation of formal authority is closely tied to the assignment of responsibility. We shall define formal authority as the formal right to act or command within specified boundaries. Such rights are buttressed by the legitimate power (title, office, salary, privileges, and so on) attached to each office and a portfolio of formal sanctions (promotions, wage increases, suspension, discharge, and so on) available to each officer. Hopefully, the manager will also possess sufficient expert power and referent power to obtain the cooperation of his subordinates.

Although the preceding discussion centers on managerial authority, it must be made clear that *every person employed by the organization must possess authority*. The operative may possess no rights of command, but he must be *authorized* to be in certain places and to do certain things, or he is of no value to the organization. The janitor patrolling the "halls of ivy" possesses keys to both the offices and the broom closet. These keys are both symbols of his authority and the mechanisms with which he fulfills his responsibility. So, too, for the machinist, bookkeeper, and professor. Each plays a role that includes specific responsibilities and requires appropriate authority. Noncommand authority may be termed *operative authority* or staff authority, as contrasted to *managerial authority*.

Extent of Delegation

We have seen that the manager—with the assistance of his subordinate—attempts to determine how much authority is required by the subordinate to fulfill his responsibilities. At times these authority boundaries are only vaguely defined; at other times they are clearly stated. For example, a plant manager may be authorized to spend up to $5,000 on any piece of needed equipment. Beyond that amount, he must receive the approval of some higher office or committee. A department foreman may be authorized to *recommend* the discharge of a subordinate, but he is not empowered to discharge an employee on his own. Such boundaries are often precisely understood. In contrast, the level is frequently disputed. A commonly cited example are the disputes between the production manager and sales manager over production schedules. Production desires long runs and limited product variety. Sales pushes for expanded variety and instant availability of each line, color, and size. The formal role of each officer in the determination of product lines and production schedules is often unclear. Similar vagueness in authority relationships may exist between staff officers and line managers, as is discussed in Chapter 18. Thus the role of the position incumbent may well be precisely defined in some areas and indefinite in other areas.

Even recognizing the instances of indefinite authority boundaries, it still can be said that more authority will probably be delegated under certain conditions than under others.[3] As has been suggested several times

[3] Thus there may be vast differences in the degree of delegation at different managerial levels in the same organization. Moreover, the conditions within each functional or product division may call for variations in the magnitude of delegation. Here perceptions are sometimes distorted by the reports of unsophisticated observers, who

earlier, the viable organization (and each part of it) must adapt its structure to existing conditions. Over time, the organization that is vigorous and growing in a competitive industry must be doing some things right. Success may be explained in terms of superior products, lower costs, or effective sales programs; but underlying these visible characteristics may be a superior organizational structure, one that is suited to the internal and external conditions faced by the firm. Let us examine some of the factors that may help to indicate the degree to which authority and responsibility can be usefully retained at the summit or shared through the lowest levels: the determinants of centralization and decentralization.

NEED FOR CONSISTENCY AND COORDINATION

Under some circumstances, there is great value in establishing operations that are virtually identical. Thus F. W. Woolworth or A & P retail outlets are centrally designed for quick recognition by customers. Their internal layouts and operating policies vary little from store to store within a region, again as a result of centralized decisions. The organization's positive image is thereby readily transferred from store to store. The customer feels confident of his ability to find what he wants; he feels a comfortable sense of familiarity with product lines, price policies, check-out procedures, and so on. Because top-level managers highly value this consistency, they do not delegate to store managers the authority over these matters.

The need for consistency pervades many facets of organizational operations. Employment procedures, for example, must conform to civil rights laws and customs. Sales practices must abide by statutes prohibiting price discrimination. Insurance companies may prescribe certain procedures and conditions for lowest premiums on industrial health and accident policies. Such broad constraints force top management to retain operational controls at high levels of the organization. The discretion accorded to subordinate managers declines as such constraints multiply.

In contrast to the Woolworth and A & P chain operations are highly diversified firms whose units sell in different markets and involve altogether unrelated technologies. The Brunswick Corporation does not need to stress marketing consistency among its divisions selling surgical supplies, bowling lanes, schoolroom furniture, yachts, and defense products. Nor is its top management likely to prescribe consistent production

---

may incorrectly assume that authority patterns at the point observed apply equally to the rest of the organization.

techniques for each line. Moreover, each division may negotiate with a different union and may be subject to different government regulations. Under such circumstances, there is small need for consistency and little impetus toward central control.

The hardware department in a Sears Roebuck store operates quite independently of the cosmetics department. That is, the operations of one do not depend in substantial measure on the prior or concurrent operations of the other. There is probably some value in consistency between these departments, but there is little need for coordination. Department managers may well be delegated broad powers to run their units as they see fit, subject to minimal consistency requirements. In contrast, consider the requirements for close coordination among naval, air, and ground units when an invasion from the sea is planned. Because success hinges so directly on the synchronized efforts of all contributing units, it is probable that a central control point will be established. In general, there is probably a greater tendency to centralize where units are highly interdependent and to decentralize where units are substantially independent.

Even in the interdependent situation, there may be substantial decentralization. As noted earlier, coordination can be achieved among peers working closely toward common objectives. Control from higher levels, then, may not be the most effective means for achieving synchronized operations. The minimal requirements for horizontal coordination are: (1) goals that are shared, so that each unit, in helping to achieve the larger objective, is also achieving its own objective, and (2) effective horizontal communications, so that all concerned understand their respective roles and can predict the relevant actions of the others. Where top managers perceive the goals of subunits to be incompatible or where horizontal communications are inadequate, there will probably exist a strong tendency to centralize operations.

LEVELS OF COMPETENCY

It is widely held that such firms as General Motors and General Electric are decentralized organizations. Other firms, such as large retail chains, appear to retain more control at the higher levels. Although many factors may help to account for this organizational difference, one major influence may be the caliber of managers at each level. General Motors and General Electric may be able to recruit a more select group of management trainees than can the typical large retailer, because of differences in "glamour," salaries (both initial and potential), and other factors. Both manufacturers, for example, can boast of intensive management development programs. The organization that can attract superior managerial raw material and then develop it internally may well delegate authority to low management levels. In fact, the relationship is circular. That is, recruitment and development programs affect the tendency to decentralize; and the decision to decentralize influences the willingness to employ higher-caliber trainees and then to develop them intensively.

At a given point in time, the superior who feels more knowledgeable and intelligent than his subordinate managers will probably retain control over important decisions at his level. He who feels that his subordinates are at least as intelligent and as informed on relevant matters will probably tend to delegate authority to them and to hold them responsible for results. Many managers complain of the inadequacies of their subordinates, basing a centralized operation upon this problem. The problem may well be the employment and development program that must undergird effective decentralization.

MOTIVATION OF SUBORDINATES

The perceived competency of subordinates must be accompanied by the belief that they are motivated to strive toward the goals considered important by the superior, or he is unlikely to relinquish direct control. There is a natural tendency among managers to give first priority to their own desires, as in the case of empire builders. Moreover, the departmental manager wants to be identified with a successful operation and he may become sincerely concerned about the welfare of that department's members. This localized focus may cause the departmental manager to make decisions that overlook the organization's best interests. To lower departmental costs, he may neglect needed maintenance of machines, postpone costly training programs, or cut corners on product quality. To assure continuous operations, he may hoard raw materials. Such actions may maximize current departmental efficiency ratings, but they suboptimize for the overall organization.

The foregoing are examples of covert efforts at suboptimization. In many cases, the disagreement between managers at different levels is overt and recognized by both. They may disagree on objectives as well as on strategies and procedures. The superior who perceives either great inconsistencies in stated objectives or a strong tendency to suboptimize covertly may well hesitate to delegate authority over key matters.

FEEDBACK MECHANISMS

It should not be concluded from the above statements that overt disagreements or a tendency toward covert suboptimization exclude the possibility of decentralization. Even where superior-subordinate views and goals appear to be incompatible, the subordinate may find it in his interest to adapt in the desired direction. This can be accomplished through a structure of sanctions that rewards contributions to organizational goal achievement and punishes the tendency to place personal or group gratification above the organization's interest.

Such a reward system requires the specification of approved objectives for every important phase of subunit operations. In addition, progress toward approved objectives must be measured frequently and compared with expectations. Where (1) objectives can be specified encompassing the paramount functions of each unit, and (2) progress toward objectives is easily and accurately measured, then higher-level managers may feel sufficiently certain of subordinate managers' conformity to delegate operational authority. Should results deviate from expectations, then corrective action may be taken before great harm is done. Lacking such feedback, however, top managers may insist on an active role in the management of the several units for which they are responsible.

INFORMATION FLOWS

One stated advantage of decentralization is that local managers can make better decisions because of their intense grasp of relevant local conditions. Thus the individual store manager in a large chain may be delegated substantial control over the merchandise carried for his clientele. The factory foreman (or college dean) may enjoy the right to assign his men where they are most useful and happiest. The assumption is that the unit manager possesses information that higher-level officials lack. He must be permitted to decide where his information—his "feel" for the situation—is superior.

This informational justification for delegation oversimplifies the delegation decision. With accelerating technological improvements, information can be transferred more rapidly, accurately, and inexpensively than ever before. With direct telephone connections, closed-circuit television networks, computer-to-computer transmissions, and so on, information is becoming less and less the personal property of the unit manager; it is increasingly incorporated into the data banks of central offices. In brief, the degree of delegation may rest on communication efficacy (speed, cost, and precision). As pertinent data are more readily communicated to central processing points and as resulting decisions can be more readily returned, centralized operations become more feasible and decentralization less of a necessity.

It should be further noted that superior knowledge of local conditions is, in itself, an insufficient basis for decentralization. Conditions elsewhere in the organization or external to it may be quite as relevant as those within the unit. The question arises concerning where in the organization the required mix of local and environmental sets of information can best be compiled for decision purposes. The analysis must include the needs for and volume of each kind of information; and the cost, speed, and accuracy of transmission for each.

MANAGERIAL PHILOSOPHY

The readiness of any manager to delegate is heavily influenced by his general beliefs concerning the best way to run an organization. A manager who has been successful in the past with centralized operations may well believe that structure to be best in general. A preference for centralization may also result from a lifetime within a culture where authority is accepted as resting with superiors, calling for unquestioning obedience by the lower classes. Many a manager has been heard to say, "A happy ship is a taut ship," "If you want something done right, do it yourself," or "Management must manage." Such statements are reflections of a preference for rule from the top.

Other managers, perhaps reared in democratic participative environments or trained by other managers so inclined, seem to prefer greater amounts of delegation throughout the organization. Their general propensity is in the direction of decentralization. The *Theory Y* executive, believing that great capacity, drive, and self-control can be cultivated among subordinates, may well attempt to utilize these resources through delegation. The *Theory X* executive may believe it unwise to assign important matters to subordinates he views as lazy, security-minded, and intellectually limited. The point is that every manager carries with him certain beliefs about the general nature of human beings. These beliefs are important in determining the authority structure with which he feels most comfortable. Thus the manager is himself one of the variables that contribute to the shape of the organization.

SUBORDINATE ACCEPTANCE

As discussed earlier, the subordinate plays a vital part in determining his role within the organization. If he is self-confident and ambitious, he may acquire heightened responsibilities officially or informally. If he lacks these attributes, he may fear added responsibility. The superior's attempts to delegate may well be fruitless when faced with such a barrier. William Newman proposes five reasons why a subordinate may shrink from increases in responsibility. These are:

1. He finds it easier to take orders than to make decisions.
2. He fears the criticism associated with his mistakes.
3. He feels that he lacks the information or resources required to fulfill the added responsibility.
4. He feels already overburdened.
5. He lacks self-confidence.[4]

In time these barriers can be overcome by a sensitive manager. He can help subordinates to develop self-confidence by coaching them and otherwise developing their talents, all the while openly noting their progress and achievements. He must consider mistakes as part of the process of learning, growth, and the transfer of fulfillment of high responsibilities. He can develop a reward system that encourages the acceptance of greater responsibilities. He can relieve the individual who accepts new and more difficult challenges of some unimportant and time-consuming functions of his prior role. Much of this takes time to accomplish. Meanwhile, the organization may remain highly centralized, as attempts at delegation are frustrated by unresponsive subordinates.

Operational Decentralization

Many disastrous errors have been made in the name of decentralization, for the concept is often misunderstood or applied under inappropriate circumstances. Decentralization does not mean treating subsidiary units as independent businesses. It does not mean giving subordinate managers "enough rope to hang themselves." Rather, decentralization as practiced by leading corporations features important central controls relating to objectives, policies, programs, required reports, and executive staffing. Through a careful blend of central controls with operational delegation, top management can attain the direction and coordination desired, as well as the operational motivation flexibility and growth associated with delegation.

[4] William H. Newman, "Overcoming Obstacles to Effective Delegation," *Management Review*, January, 1956, pp. 36–41.

The role that each unit is to play within the total organization is rarely determined solely by that unit. More frequently, top management—with inputs from unit managers—establishes a set of organizational goals and assigns appropriate subgoals to each unit. Questions concerning the product line, quality levels, investment to expand production capacity, movement into new markets, and so on, are jointly decided through dialogues between superior and subordinate managers. Peter Drucker describes one role of central management in General Motors as follows:

> Central Management not only delimits the divisions against each other, it fits them into a general pattern as part of a unified corporation. It establishes the general overall aim and allots to each division its role on the team. It establishes a total production goal on the basis of an analysis of the economic situation and assigns to each division its minimum quota. It determines how much capital to allow to each division.
>
> Above all, central management thinks ahead for the whole corporation. . . . A good division manager is fully as much concerned with the future as with the present; . . . But it is not his responsibility to decide in what direction his division should develop; that is the responsibility of central management, however much it may rely on the advice of divisional management.[5]

Thus divisions are tied to headquarters by the central decisions establishing overall organizational goals and the contributions to be made by each division.

POLICY CONSTRAINTS

Centralized influence over division objectives provides direction for organizational parts. Further constraints upon divisional discretion take the form of policies, the boundaries delineating the limits of acceptable behavior in the pursuit of established objectives. Major policies may be centrally developed to help guide managerial decisions in every phase of operations. As discussed earlier, policies leave the manager substantial freedom to run their operations. It is, nevertheless, necessary to assure that each division will perform its functions in a manner compatible with the health of the overall organization. The more sensitive the matter, the greater will be the need for central guidance.

[5] Peter Drucker, *The Concept of the Corporation* (Boston: Beacon Press, 1946), p. 51.

The decentralized unit is typically dependent on the central organization for investment capital. Any desire to expand substantially the capital invested in the unit must be approved as part of the total financial plan of the parent organization.[6] Uncontrolled attempts by subsidiary companies or organizational divisions to expand capacity could result in severe financial problems for the organization. Each demand for additional investment capital is weighed against all other such demands to determine the best expected returns on investment. Next these demands are related to the parent's financial capabilities. It is clear, where such a process of investment evaluation prevails, that such decisions are purposefully centralized—even in firms characterized as decentralized.

BUDGETING AND REPORTING

As part of the process of establishing objectives, forecasts are formulated, constituting a schedule of anticipated costs and results. Such forecasts may be highly detailed, covering every important measurable facet of the unit's operations. Each unit manager is then expected to report at stated intervals the actual progress achieved for each aspect of operations and to explain significant deviations from the forecast. How the desired results are achieved is the business of the subordinate manager, so long as he abides by corporate policies. This is the very essence of decentralization. At the same time, the parent organization is protected from extensive long-term deviations from expectations by frequent detailed reports.

Illustrative of the inclusiveness of budgets and the role of operating divisions in establishing their own budgets are these statements by Ralph Cordiner, then president of General Electric Company:

> . . . The operating budget of the General Electric Company is not a document prepared by the Executive Offices in New York. It is an addition of the budgets by the Operating Department Managers, with the concurrence of the Division General Managers and Group Executives. These budgets include planned sales volume, product development plans, expenditures for plant and equipment, market targets, turnover of investment, net earnings, projected organization structure, and other related items.[7]

[6] See, for example, W. M. Jarman and B. H. Willingham, "The Decentralized Organization of a Diversified Manufacturer and Retailer—Genesco," in *A Management Sourcebook,* ed. F. G. Moore (New York: Harper & Row, Publishers, 1964), pp. 268–76.

[7] Ralph Cordiner, *New Frontiers for Professional Managers* (New York: Columbia University Press, 1956), pp. 59–60.

These budgets then serve as an elaborate set of goals for the operating departments. At frequent intervals, each department head must report actual progress toward the budgeted goals, goals that he played the key role in setting. His motivation to attain these goals goes far beyond the need for economic security. He is betting his ego and his reputation as a planner on this operating forecast.

STAFFING

As stressed earlier, true decentralization is neither likely nor effective without clearly competent subordinates to fulfill great responsibilities. The decentralized organization, therefore, must put forth great efforts to select potential managers for all positions receiving substantial authority and to develop managerial potentials to handle increasing responsibilities as the organization grows or higher-level positions open by reason of normal turnover. It is no surprise, then, to find highly decentralized corporations supporting high salary structures and extensive management development programs.

Such a policy provides top executives with a superior pool of managerial potential from which to select individuals for important positions. Nevertheless, the success of a promising manager is never guaranteed. At a given point in time, a manager may be found unable to meet the challenge that he has been assigned and that he has accepted. His deficiencies may be remediable through further training, including short periods of intensive coaching by his superior. Should he not respond satisfactorily to development efforts, he may be quickly replaced. The concept of decentralization requires a minimum of direct involvement of superiors in departmental or subsidiary operations. Staffing with strong, capable subordinates is imperative. The corporate situation is probably analogous to the relationship between a college president and his football coach. The coach is made aware of the objectives expected of his team, of policies within which he must operate, and of the resources available to him. It is most improbable that the president will provide substantial operational assistance should football results prove less than satisfactory. Rather, the unsuccessful football coach will "resign," to be replaced by one deemed worthy of the confidence of the college president (not to mention the alumni, students, legislators, and so on, whose pressure cannot long be ignored).

Decentralization, it is seen, is not to be equated with complete freedom among operating managers. Rather it is a vigorous, challenging form of organization, designed to achieve overall organizational goals by utilizing to the fullest the knowledge, skills, and motivations of well-trained subordinate managers. It requires close interactions for establishing shared objectives, policies, resource allocation, and reporting systems. It is a tough, "hardnosed" managerial system. The payoffs to all participants can be great in economic, ego, and growth terms; but so can the costs of failure.

SUMMARY

Decisions regarding division of labor and optimal group size determine the organization's departmental structure. Complementing these decisions is another concerning the locus of control—the question of local autonomy versus central control.

Delegation includes: (1) a communication by the superior of the duties, authority, and objectives he wishes included in the subordinate's role; and (2) a parallel commitment by the subordinate. The relationships among these roles is probably the best way to depict the true organization structure. To avoid conflicts, these roles must be appropriate for personnel and technologies employed, clear, and internally consistent.

The appropriate degree of delegation rests on a number of key variables. These are: (1) the need for consistency and coordination, (2) levels of competency, (3) motivation of subordinates, (4) feedback mechanisms, (5) information flows, (6) managerial philosophy, and (7) subordinate acceptance.

The term decentralization has often been taken to mean complete freedom for subsidiary units. Such an approach may have disastrous consequences. In most modern organizations, decentralization features central controls over objectives, policies, programs, and executive staffing. Periodic reports on strategic operating results are required. Local management is given substantial discretion within these constraints and is then held accountable for results. This system may provide managerial challenges and recognition for performance at every managerial level.

QUESTIONS

1. What is a role? A role sender? Role conflict? Role ambiguity?
2. Describe the process of delegation in terms of role theory.

3. Under what conditions is a firm likely to be highly decentralized?

4. What social, technological, and economic changes are likely to affect the distribution of authority in the organization of tomorrow?

5. Comment on the description of decentralization as "giving the manager the ball and letting him run with it."

6. It has been said that decentralization approaches the status of a religion, to be devoutly and unquestioningly pursued. Might this be accurate? Why?

7. Is fast feedback really consistent with the concept of decentralization? Explain.

8. Relate information flows to the proper locus for decisions.

9. What can the manager do to overcome subordinate resistance to increased responsibilities?

10. "Every person employed by the organization must possess authority." Discuss this statement.

the role of staff

18

*The final irony of this whole situation
is that it is the staff and not the line
which is beginning to represent
the real power in the modern
industrial corporation.*

Douglas McGregor

As discussed earlier, not all authority is command authority. Authority is defined as the formal power *to act or command*. Many officials holding high organizational office do not possess formal command powers. For example, a firm's legal counsel, Mr. S, may be delegated the task of examining the legal implications of various company policies and making recommendations to higher line officers. He is, in essence, a technical advisor or an internal consultant. Mr. S may heavily influence the decisions of top managers through his expertise and persuasive powers, but his legitimate formal role excludes command. His is a clear illustration of staff authority as traditionally conceived.

The staff concept has been changing, however. Thus it is necessary to examine the evolving staff role, so as to understand its effects on the line and on line-staff relationships. We now turn to this topic, first defining common authority types, then noting some effects of changing authority concepts, and finally forwarding some suggestions for the effective blending of line-staff contributions.

Some Definitions

We have noted the traditional concept of staff as an advisor to superior line officers. In contrast, a staff officer might be delegated the authority to control certain aspects of operations within a plant or firm, even though there is a manager in charge of each. Mr. S, for example, may possess the authority to veto certain practices as legally hazardous. The comptroller may require that records be kept in a prescribed form, with reports due periodically. The scheduling department may be empowered to issue firm directives concerning the timing and sequencing of production activities. Although often labeled staff officers, these men possess *command authority*. They can issue orders, but solely within the scope of their functional specialties, thus the term *functional authority*. We will view this as a hybrid form of authority, involving command power over a particular area of expertise. Let us more clearly demarcate these forms of authority.

> *Line Authority:* The formal power to act and to command. Command powers cover all operations and functions within a specified physical dimension of the organization, such as the section, department, or firm.
>
> *Staff Authority:* The formal power to advise line management or otherwise to facilitate the performance of line functions.
>
> *Functional Authority:* The formal power to command, limited to a specified area of expertise, such as accounting, law, maintenance, or the like; may be directed across departmental boundaries.

The large modern organization makes extensive use of line, staff, and functional authorities. Each has its valuable applications and its potential problems, all of which must be recognized if sound organizations are to be constructed.

Structural Forms

One way to examine the impacts of these authority forms is to build them into hypothetical organizational structures. Let us begin with the pure line structure and then add the staff and functional roles.

LINE ORGANIZATION

The pure line organization is the simplest organization structure. Each subordinate has only one superior, and each line officer has complete charge over his unit. Roles are more readily defined by all participants than is the case where the structure becomes more elaborate. The manager responsible for achievement possesses the unchallenged authority to fulfill those responsibilities. Promotional paths are clearly defined, not cluttered with various nonline positions and nonline competitors.

STAFF AUGMENTATION

The simplicity of the pure line structure is accompanied by severe limitations, evidently so weighty as to force important staff and functional variations from this structure. The merits of staff offices are next presented, along with their possible drawbacks.

THE EXPERT. A major force leading to the introduction and elaboration of staff positions is the increasing complexity of organizational life. The line officer once ruled supreme over a relatively simple technical operation, leading rather passive work groups in a legally permissive environment. Change was slow and gradual, adding the advantage of stability to that of simplicity.

With the introduction of scientific management, increasingly complex mechanization, unionization, spreading government controls, better-educated and more mobile workers, and an accelerating rate of change in products, processes, and moves, the ability of the line officer to cope deteriorated. He could not be equally expert in every important phase of operations. Increasingly he needed assistance in sophisticated disciplines and systems. This assistance often came in the form of staff officers, who were to advise line officers in their fields of expertise. The "line and staff" organization predominated.

Unity of command was preserved, for staff assistance came in the form of advice that was directed *upward* to line superiors. Resulting commands still originated from line superiors and were the result of the applications of expertise, fortified by the manager's day-to-day pragmatism. Thus a major force leading toward organizational elaboration was the increasing complexity of managing and the resulting need for the inputs of experts into the managerial decision process.

THE ADMINISTRATIVE ASSISTANT. In many instances, the demand for staff assistance results from an increase in the sheer volume of the manager's work. Some of his functions are routine and repetitive, occupying much time and energy and diverting him from other pressing matters. One solution is to assign an assistant to the manager, one who will perform the least challenging, though important, parts of the managerial jobs. A college dean may be assigned an assistant to evaluate transcripts of incoming transfer students, to arrange for deviations from regular exam schedules, to counsel with students having academic problems, and so on. The corporate president may select an assistant to perform special studies of his firm's operations and opportunities, to generate the data for speeches, and to represent him at meetings that he cannot attend himself.

Such assistants are not chosen for their intense knowledge in a specialized area. Rather they are valuable for the *general* assistance they provide. Not infrequently the "assistant-to" position is used as a training ground for future line officers. Its primary reason for being, however, is the manager's need for relief from detail and routine, so that he can focus his energies on matters that require his personal efforts.

THE MONITOR.   A third kind of service performed by the staff assistant is the monitoring of operations within his superior's area of responsibility. The staff assistant may serve as supplementary eyes and ears for the line officer. Some staff men are hired specifically to perform this supervisory function, auditors being the prime example. All staff assistants, however, may do some observing and reporting of line operations as part of their normal duties. Thus the "expert-type" staff assistant may closely observe operating practices related to his specialty, reporting upward any apparent deviations from his expectations. The "assistant-to," in the course of his assignments, may be expected to report his observations and his ideas for improving performance.

As we shall note shortly, this monitoring function may cause as many problems as it solves. Such activities may interfere with the performance of the other two staff functions. It is difficult to be, at the same time, a known spy and a trusted consultant.

FUNCTIONAL ORGANIZATION

The ultimate in direct control of operations by specialists is the functional organization. This form of authority can pervade the entire organization, from top to bottom. Probably the earliest to develop a general scheme for functional management at the foreman level was Frederick W. Taylor.[1] It should be recalled that Taylor expected his foremen to assume the managerial tasks that had been forfeited to the workers, including methods analysis, time study, training, motivating,

[1] Frederick W. Taylor, *Shop Management* (New York: Harper & Brothers, 1919), pp. 91–112.

scheduling, and so on. He went so far as to name eight types of functional foreman, four of whom were to operate in the shop (gang boss, speed boss, inspector, and repair boss), while the other four were located primarily in the planning room (order of work and route clerk, instruction card clerk, time and cost clerk, and shop disciplinarian).

> The greatest good resulting from this change is that it becomes possible in a comparatively short time to train bosses who can really and fully perform the functions demanded of them, while under the old system it took years to train men who were after all able to thoroughly perform only a portion of their duties. . . . The special knowledge which each functional foreman must acquire forms only a small part of that needed by the old style gang boss.[2]

Management at the supervisory level was to be performed by specialists or experts, each of whom exercised control over a specific facet of the work, an example of pure functional foremanship. Few men, it was proposed, could adequately master all the expertise required to run a department. The management task had to be divided into its components, which were to be assigned to specialists, who were to be delegated command authority within their functional spheres of responsibility.

Functional foremanship was never generally accepted in industry. A modification of it has, however, gained widespread usage. The line foreman still remains. Above him, however, typically reside a group of "staff" offices, which exercise, in effect, functional control over the foreman's department. The difference from Taylor's system is that directives from these functional departments are channeled through the foreman, rather than directly to the operatives. Again, the idea is to maintain "unity of command" at the operative level, if not at the foreman level. The foreman receives directives concerning production schedules, work methods, accounting procedures, personnel policies, and so on, from these several "staff" offices. Note the use of the term "directives," as opposed to "advice" or "command," for messages transmitted may have an intent and effect anywhere between these two extremes.

A modern electric utility, which we will call the Eastern Power Corporation, provides a clear application of functional organization at the top. Eastern Power maintains two sets of vice-presidencies. One set is housed in the company's headquarters building; each of the second set of four vice-presidents is officed in the service territory for which he generally is responsible. This latter group of vice-presidents are considered line officers; they possess command authority over all operations within their respective territories.

[2] Ibid., p. 104.

The headquarters vice-presidents are functional officers, specialists in their respective functions. Thus the vice-president of production is *the* authority on the generation of electricity; the vice-president of transmission and distribution is *the* authority on the transportation of electric power from generation to consumer; and the office of the vice-president of sales establishes the sales program for the entire company. Decisions regarding technical and commercial operations of the company are made in the central offices and then communicated to the territorial vice-presidents, whose job it is to implement those decisions. The degree of participation by the territorial vice-presidents in these major decisions varies with the nature of the problem, their perceived knowledge, the personal relationships between the executives, and so on. The key point, again, is the desire of the company's board of directors and president to make the utmost use of the expertise available in a situation where technical sophistication is believed to be the paramount attribute of the successful firm. Serious organizational problems accompany this functional structure, but they are assigned less weight than the technical advantages of the system.

Evolution of Staff-Functional Authority

We have noted that the role of staff covers a rather wide spectrum. Let us now examine some of these gradations in staff authority and then probe the problems associated with them.

To begin with, staff positions were created to provide the line officer with subordinates who would fill in the specialized expertise that he lacked or would perform his more mundane, routine activities. The staff man was one to lean on, as the term staff implies. Staff assistance, then, was directed *upward*, in the form of information and advice, as requested. A program of action might be recommended to a line superior, who, if he approved, would sign it and send it to line subordinates for implementation. His signature legitimated the program, stamped it as his will.

Now suppose this line officer finds himself extremely busy and is perhaps absent from the office for long time intervals. Suppose further that he has developed a deep respect for the knowledge and abilities of a staff officer. The temptation becomes strong to change the communication and authority structure. Why not authorize Mr. Staff to communicate his recommendations directly to the subordinate line managers, who can then implement them or not as they deem proper? These are to be recommendations, not commands; there must be no pressure, only persuasion based on expert power and referent power. The line structure, accordingly, retains its integrity and its command structure is unchanged. Meanwhile, the expertise has been made directly available to a larger segment of the organization. Communications lines are shorter and more direct; and the harried executive has been somewhat unburdened.

Mr. Staff is now more fully utilized. He now deals directly with line officers "below him" on the organization chart. Are there now forces that will change the nature of his messages from recommendations and advice to insistence and pressure? For one thing, both Mr. Staff and the line subordinates may become accustomed to acquiescence by the line to Mr. Staff's recommendations. They have been aware of the origins of prior programs in that area, no matter that the programs were first signed by their superior and then sent downward.

These line subordinates are well aware, furthermore, of their superior's high regard for Mr. Staff. It is also noted that the office of Mr. Staff is located next door to the boss (perhaps hundreds of miles away from the offices at the next lower level). Who is in the best position to influence the boss, to "get his ear"? Did not the superior delegate to Mr. Staff the authority to initiate downward?

Even under these circumstances, the staff role might remain advisory, characterized by the "soft sell," if Mr. Staff thinks highly of the line subordinates and if he does not seek power for himself. There is substantial evidence, however, that many staff members do not approve of line approaches to mutual problems. Staff men tend to stress technical correctness and the "scientific" approach, whereas line officers are more interested in reduced costs, immediate results, and minimal interference with normal operations. Mr. Staff, then, might well become impatient with the intransigence and "resistance to change."

Not only may Mr. Staff differ from line officers in operational values and perspectives; he may also be competing for power. Mr. Staff may perceive his best route to promotion to lie within the line structure. Advancement through the constricted structure of his staff unit may appear slow, with a relatively low ceiling. He may decide, accordingly, to display a capacity for "leadership" by going beyond pure advice toward higher-pressure forms of influence. He may feel that "visibility" to higher management is essential if he is to be recognized and singled out for advancement. The objective, soft-sell, detached approach may be perceived as incompatible with visibility, recognition, and rapid advancement.

Given busy top managers who stress values of technical expertise, a dab of conditioning toward compliance or reliance among line officials, and a competent, ambitious staff official, we may have the ingredients for a gradual evolution toward functional organization. Advice, persuasion, pressure, and command are all devices for influencing the behavior of others. Not all staff-line relationships will evolve toward functional control; but conditions such as those described, which are not uncommon, probably underlie a trend toward increasingly positive acts of influence by "staff" officers.

The extreme of formal functional authority results when the superior line officer delegates to technical specialists command authority over operations in his domain. This may involve official legitimation of informally evolved functional relationships as line officers rely increasingly on technical assistance or acquiesce to staff pressures. Functional organization may also result from a conscious analysis by top management, wherein the decision is made to magnify the role of specialists through a change in organization structure.

In making this decision, top managers may realize that they are rendering subordinates accountable to more than one superior. Subordinate managers may interpret the change as a loss of power and status; their roles as *subordinates* are elaborated, while their independence as policy makers is constrained by closer supervision. They may feel that they carry as much responsibility as before, but less authority. There is increased likelihood of conflicts among functional officers or between line and functional officers, some of which will be based on conflicting commands. More chronic symptoms of conflict may result in continuing struggles for control, power, and status.

The chief benefits of line-and-functional organization are:

1. The maximum application of available expertise.
2. The objectivity that functional control may bring to line problems.
3. Consistency of policy and practice throughout the organization.

It would appear that the costs of functional authority are high in terms of role clarity, relations between line officers and specialists, and the personal commitment of line officers to organizational goals. The use of functional authority may be beneficially limited to those parts of the organization where exotic technology is used or where interdepartmental consistency is necessary (as in standardizing accounting systems, avoiding violations of law, and synchronizing of sales programs).

Line-Staff Conflict

As the role of staff personnel has evolved from upward-directed assistance toward the monitoring and control of subordinate officials, so has the incidence of line-staff conflict. The detrimental effects of such conflict can be extremely serious, neutralizing the potential contributions of staff personnel. Conflict often leads to mutual avoidance by the parties, with a cessation of communication, and a weakening in the ability of each to understand the other's problems, perspectives, and potential contributions. Energies are expended to win power and status struggles, at the expense of productive effort. Frustrations develop on both sides as line officers fail to receive needed assistance and staff personnel find their talents wasted.

Conflict is probably as natural a consequence of organized activity as is cooperation and harmony. Each interest group within any complex organization has its own set of objectives, some of which are bound to conflict with those of other groups. Each group develops its own somewhat unique perspectives, logics, and preferred solutions to organizational problems.[3] These differences in goals and frames of reference are universal causes of conflict in organizations, not to mention the problems caused by personality incompatibilities. Let us examine how such factors relate to the struggles between line and staff. The classic study of this conflict was done by Melville Dalton.[4] He found three broad reasons for conflict among line and staff officials: (1) ambitious staff personnel, (2) social differences, and (3) staff desires to gain acceptance of its contributions. Let us examine these problem areas and then refer again to role theory for an understanding of line-staff conflict.

STAFF AMBITIONS

Dalton described the staff personnel in the plants he studied as "markedly ambitious, restless, and individualistic." They tended to be younger and better educated than their line counterparts. They derived from higher socioeconomic status groups. Their youth, education, and social status led them to strive for early promotion. This ambition, not objectionable in itself to line officers, was complicated by the relatively small number of higher staff positions. Staff officers found themselves competing with the very managers they were attempting to assist. Man-

---

[3] The universality of role conflict and intergroup conflict are discussed further in T. M. Newcomb, et al., *Social Psychology* (New York: Holt, Rinehart and Winston, Inc., 1965), pp. 393–462.

[4] Melville Dalton, "Conflicts between Staff and Line Managerial Officers," *American Sociological Review*, XV (June, 1950), 342–51.

agers were, therefore, suspicious of the intentions of staff personnel and not especially eager to provide them the opportunities to impress higher line officers.

SOCIAL DIFFERENCES

The social differences between line and staff officers may have contributed an additional obstacle to harmony. Staff personnel tended to be more meticulously dressed and groomed. They spoke and wrote more correctly and articulately. They stressed status, frequently dining with higher-level line officers. Thus the conflict arising from the competitive atmosphere was intensified by differences of values and life styles.

THE DRIVE TO CONTRIBUTE

Staff personnel often found themselves unwelcome in line departments. Line officers feared that staff "assistance" involved a loss of autonomy and an intrusion by another authority figure into his domain. The desire to remain the sole official leader in the eyes of his subordinates was probably accompanied by other fears:

> . . . Every time staff consultants come around with their new concepts and new approaches, he [the line officer] runs the risk that the very foundation on which he has built his career will be eroded. He fears that the familiar body of knowledge and experience which has given him a sense of confidence may no longer be as relevant. The manager may also be concerned lest he not really fathom the new approaches and thus reveal a fatal weakness to the staff experts or to his associates. He may worry that the consultants, while nosing around, may "uncover" fundamental ills in the way he is managing his job. Perhaps the staff-introduced innovations will require him to operate in new ways for which he has not been trained or which he cannot follow with skill and confidence. Perhaps his reliance on staff help will appear to be a sign of weakness; or possibly the staff will get the credit for improved results.[5]

Confronted with the resistance and defensiveness of line officers, staff personnel drove even harder to demonstrate to the organization their value and their mastery of their fields. The results were staff pressure

[5] J. K. Baker and R. H. Schaffer, "Making Staff Consulting More Effective," *Harvard Business Review* (January–February, 1969), p. 62.

and insistence, which only served to further antagonize wary line officers. Each group, then, posed a threat to the other: the staff jeopardized the line's authority and confidence and the line interfered with the staff's desire to prove its worth.

ROLE CONFLICT

In the discussion of delegation, role conflict was defined as the simultaneous occurrence of two (or more) role sendings such that compliance with one would make compliance with the other more difficult. Conflicting expectations may come from a single sender or from multiple senders. It appears that line-staff conflict results, at least in part, from the incompatible role expectations of superior line officers and staff personnel.

As discussed earlier, the role sendings to staff from superior line officers have often evolved from advice upward, to advice downward, to monitoring subordinates, to commands downward. It is not uncommon for a staff officer's role to include all of these expectations simultaneously. Thus he is expected to advise upward on certain matters, downward on others, and so on. A question arises concerning the probable reactions of subordinate line officers to a staff officer who advises them on certain matters, reports to their common superior on the effectiveness of line operations, and issues commands in other matters.

Can staff serve the three roles of assistant, monitor, and superior? How likely is a departmental manager to seek the help of an individual who serves also as an intelligence agent and a boss? The situation is not unlike a business owner asking an agent for the Bureau of Internal Revenue to keep his books for him. Although the agent's advice might be of great value, his external identification would impede the free flow of information necessary for the full utilization of his knowledge. Management, in expanding the staff role from advice to control and command, may have increased the defensiveness of line subordinates and decreased their willingness to request staff assistance.

Staff experts are themselves subject to intense internal conflict. They have been trained to strive for certain values and to utilize preferred procedures. Simultaneously, they must fit into the organizational structure and the pragmatic perspectives of line officials. Scientific exactness conflicts, at times, with ingrained organizational practices; political considerations conflict with solutions considered optimal; identification with the profession (industrial engineering, personnel, marketing research, and so forth) conflicts with identification with the organization.

The staff officer, himself, then is a source of role conflict. His preferred recommendations as a method analyst may well be compromised by his desire to avoid upsetting the positive line relationships required for early promotion. That is, his perceived role as a professional is incompatible with his role as a member of the management team, one who will advance through the line structure.

Some companies have attempted to strengthen the professional role and image of staff groups, providing advancement up the staff hierarchy, giving recognition to sophisticated approaches to problems, and locating groups of experts together in strong, cohesive units. This approach may well reduce the specialist's internal conflict; but it may intensify line-staff conflict, as Webber indicates in his discussion of industrial engineering roles.

> Contemporary Industrial Engineers may be confused as to where their futures lie and whom they want to impress. The problem, however, may be resolved by the movement towards professionalism. The future Industrial Engineer may see his future in Industrial Engineering. . . . Accordingly, schizophrenia in the Industrial Engineer's aspirations may be eliminated. But such professionalism will aggravate the conflict between line and staff. The social and organizational gap will widen; the attempts of staff to control line will increase; and greater emphasis on professional development and sophisticated techniques will diminish the engineer's interest in assisting the production manager to solve the latter's mundane problems.[6]

Toward Productive Harmony

The obstacles in the path of harmonious and effective use of staff expertise are great. They include the economic, social, ego, and growth needs of both line and staff officials. Struggles for control, power, autonomy, status, advancement, stability, change, and so on seem intertwined with the efforts to utilize the talents of staff specialists within line departments. Perhaps the most obvious step toward effective line-staff relationships is the development of a heightened awareness on the part of each: an awareness of his own motives and perspectives and a heightened sensitivity to the motives and perspectives of the other fellow. There are ways to develop such an awareness, including sensitivity training laboratories, role playing

[6] R. A. Webber, "Innovation and Conflict in Industrial Engineering," *Journal of Industrial Engineering*, XVIII (May, 1967), 310.

(perhaps reversing the positions of line and staff personnel), and human relations case discussions, all, perhaps, augmented by readings and lectures on human behavior.

COMPATIBLE ROLES

Awareness and sensitivity may help to avoid misunderstandings, but they do not remove the structural causes of line-staff conflict. This challenge lies with top management, the designers of the organization. It may be advisable, for example, to avoid combining the advising and monitoring functions in one position. Some suggest that the staff-line relationship should approximate that for medical doctors and their patients. In assisting the patient toward good health, the doctor is sworn to treat his patient's medical file as confidential, to be communicated typically only at the request of the patient. Similar obligations of confidentiality are accepted by lawyers, tax consultants, and other private consultants. Given such a professional-client bond between staff experts and managers, the latter's services might be much more welcome and the information given them more complete.

In line with the professional-client relationship of staff and line is the policy of providing staff assistance only when it is requested by the operating line officers. Staff departments or personnel may be considered as internal consultants. Their services are not to be forced on managers, but should rather be sought by managers as technical needs are recognized. As with external consultants, the operating department may be charged for its use of staff personnel, so that such services go where needed. The burden is on the staff, then, to demonstrate its value to line managers, so that they are willing to bear the economic costs of calling for this assistance. Staff officials are placed in the position of educating line officers on the potential services available. The responsibility for requesting staff assistance and then implementing staff recommendations lies solely with operating line officers.

A closely related approach to smoother line-staff relationships is the provision of a staff organization and a reward structure that can satisfy the needs of staff personnel without forcing them to compete for their satisfactions with line officers. With the expansion of staff services that has accompanied technological development, the staff hierarchical structure has grown, permitting more promotions within the professional unit. Monetary, social, and ego rewards may be based on one's professional achievements, as evaluated, at least partially, by professionals within the same discipline. Evaluations may well include the ability of staff personnel to gain the confidence of appropriate line officers, as well as sheer technical competence. Thus the organization supports staff efforts to "sell" their services to the line, but evaluations are performed by one's staff colleagues and his own staff superior. This approach somewhat lessens his dependency on the line structure for approval and advancement.

When considering the implementation of such a system, top management is faced with a tradeoff of values. The functional approach to staff carries with it the most immediately aggressive and authoritative applications of technical expertise. It opens the door, however, to line-staff conflict, with line managers fearing, avoiding, and circumventing the numerous "superiors" directing them. The use of staff divisions as internal professional consultants may *initially* dampen the potential technical specialists, as line officers pursue procedures with which they are most comfortable. Given true technical competency, however, and an ability to gain the trust and respect of operating managers, the ultimate effect could be an even greater implementation of technical progress than is probable with the functional and/or the monitor approach.

STAFF BEHAVIORAL GUIDELINES

The problem of the reluctant line officer is widely recognized by top managers and staff personnel. Even given the organizational modifications suggested above, the line officer may still hesitate to invite the technical specialist into his department. Perhaps, it is suggested, the personal behavior of staff personnel can further encourage a warmer welcome and fuller cooperation from line officers. The suggestions of a high Union Carbide Corporation staff officer may be enlightening here.[7] Five guides to staff effectiveness are offered, as follows:

1. *Begin each consulting assignment where the line managers are ready to begin.* Note carefully how the manager sees the problem, what assistance he wants, how much effort he is willing to expend, and when he needs the answers. Frank discussions about what is feasible, the time and expense involved, and the possible compromises can do much to avoid later disappointments on both sides, thus building mutual trust and confidence.

2. *Build on success in the first project in order to make more ambitious projects feasible later on.* Small projects successfully completed can provide a firm foundation for future collaboration. Gradually line

[7] See Baker and Schaffer, "Making Staff Consulting More Effective," pp. 67–71.

officers learn what the staff can do for them in reducing costs, improving systems, avoiding problems, and so on. Staff personnel, meanwhile, can learn about the line problems and personalities, perhaps gaining sufficient understanding to suggest how they may be of further assistance.

3. *Share control with line management.* It is important that the concerned line managers play an active role in the staff studies that are to affect their operations. Staff personnel may tend to "take the ball and run with it," making little effort to gain continual management involvement. Line officers, preoccupied with current operations, may be all too willing to forego active participation in staff studies. Without line involvement in the study, the staff recommendations may fall on unsympathetic ears. By working together, however, both groups should become aware of the pertinent facts, constraints, alternative approaches, and so on. Moreover, each can influence the other's frame of reference. Recommendations will more likely reflect the varied backgrounds and interests of the participants; and the suggestions will come as no surprise to line managers, who, after all, will decide whether to implement them. Hopefully, successful cooperation in each study will improve the mutual respect and empathy of each group, leading to a mutual desire to collaborate on future projects.

4. *Share knowledge with line management.* The consultant view of the staff role stresses the development of line talent through education, as well as assistance in the solution of individual line problems. Each function assists in the performance of the other: knowledgeable line officers can better determine where staff help is needed and can better contribute to the staff analysis; and the very process of joint problem solving is educational. It is not uncommon, however, for the educational staff function to be underemphasized in favor of individual departmental staff studies. Such an approach fails to develop the technical competence and interests of the line in general, obscures the potential services of staff departments, and encourages the belief that each related line problem is completely unique. In contrast, technical information can be disseminated and interest created through periodic reports and line-staff workshops. For example:

> An effort to help Union Carbide make use of some modern approaches to controlling maintenance costs began with a two-day workshop on managing the maintenance function. The participants were two-man teams— i.e., the plant manager and chief engineer—from a number of manufacturing plants. Talks on several new concepts and tools for controlling maintenance costs were presented. In addition, each [team] took some time to develop their own work plans for improving maintenance costs.
>
> One important result of this workshop was decisions by several plants

to test some of the concepts presented in the sessions. . . . Now, based on the success of the first plants, some additional plants are preparing to introduce similar approaches.[8]

5. *Unify internal staff consulting efforts.* Some problems require the collaboration of diverse staff specialists, along with the line contribution. The task of bringing the required staff specialists together and integrating their efforts often falls on the line. It is suggested that staff departments should ascertain the potential contributions of other staff groups. A complex problem in systems analysis might well encompass the expertise of industrial engineers, cost accountants, personnel specialists, and maintenance men. Recognition of the limits of one's own expertise and the location of the other valuable talents can substantially ease the problem of aggregating the required team, which may once have been a pure line responsibility.

STRESSING CONTRIBUTIONS

The distinction between line and staff departments is not as clear as was once thought. It is probably not very functional to refer to the line as performing the "organic functions," while the staff performs a supporting role. It is not clear what the organic functions are;[9] nor is it certain that actions facilitating the performance of those functions are so different that they should be distinguished from the line functions. Rather than labeling a person or a department as line or staff, the emphasis should be on the contributions they can make toward the achievement of organizational goals. Labels can rarely help one understand the nature of even well-defined, stable objects. Given the immense variability in the roles of line and staff officials, it seems doubtful that either term adequately describes or predicts the role or the behavior of either.

Skills, resources, and roles can be defined, however, formally or otherwise. It would appear to be the responsibility of departmental managers to determine where required assistance resides and how it may best be utilized. Complementing this responsibility is the active role of technical specialists in publicizing their skills and availability, exciting thought about potential improvements in operations, and then working effectively with operating managers to realize fully the combined potentials of all.

[8] Baker and Schaffer, "Making Staff Consulting More Effective," p. 70.
[9] For example, try to classify the following functions as line or staff: research and development, finance, equipment maintenance, purchasing.

SUMMARY

The concept of "staff" has evolved over many years from: (1) upward advice, to (2) downward advice, to (3) downward persuasion and pressure, to (4) downward commands. Thus the staff officer, originally the personal assistant of the line officer, has emerged as an additional superior.

Among typical forms of staff assistants are the technical expert, the general administrative assistant, and the "monitor." At various times, one staff assistant may play all of these roles. The ultimate in formal power for staff is termed "functional authority," the right to command within one's area of expertise. As technology intensifies, there appears to be a trend toward increased functional authority in organizations in an attempt to maximize the influence of technical specialists.

The expanding role of staff officials has occasionally increased conflict between line and staff officers. Four specific reasons for this conflict are: (1) staff ambitions for higher line positions, so that line and staff officers are competing for the same jobs, (2) social differences, (3) the desire of staff personnel to contribute, in spite of the "obstinacy" of line officials, who are regarded as obstacles to progress, and (4) the inconsistencies among the various roles expected of staff men (such as advising and monitoring).

Suggestions for improving line-staff relationships include providing human relations training for both, restructuring the staff role to be internally consistent, and establishing a staff reward structure that provides a full range of possible satisfactions without requiring invasion of the line. Some suggest setting up a client-professional relationship, with rewards to both line and staff officers based partially on their effectiveness in their respective roles.

In addition, it appears that staff personnel might benefit from the advice of a Union Carbide staff executive. He presents a series of behavioral guide lines, beginning with initial line-staff efforts and developing with each successful project to the point where, hopefully, line managers seek and enjoy staff participation within their domains.

QUESTIONS

1. Distinguish between line and functional authority. Between staff and functional authority.

2. What roles may a "staff" officer be performing in an organization?

3. What is the logic underlying the use of functional authority in organizations?

4. Do you believe that the use of functional authority will increase or decrease in the United States? Explain your answer.

5. What seem to be the key factors leading toward an evolution from advisory to functional relationships?

6. Is line-staff conflict inevitable? Explain.

7. Is role conflict more of a problem for the staff expert than for the typical line officer? Why?

8. What problems do you see associated with the use of staff personnel as "internal consultants"?

9. How would the role of staff change as a company decentralizes?

10. Dalton's study on line-staff conflict was published in 1950. To what extent may his findings reflect current conditions in industry?

communication

19

"When I use a word," Humpty Dumpty said,
in a rather scornful tone,
"it means just what I choose it to mean—
neither more nor less."
"The question is," said Alice, "whether you can
make words mean so many different things."
"The question is," said Humpty Dumpty,
"which is to be master—that's all."

LEWIS CARROLL

Communication is central to the activities of man. It is through communication that one man can establish a relationship with a second. The very survival of cultures and societies intimates communication, for if there were none, there would be no means to pass on a history from one generation to another and all learning would be lost with the death of the individual. It is also through the process of communication that men's actions are coordinated.

Just as communication is important to the survival of man and his cultures, so it is critical to the survival of an organization. An organization is a group of individuals banded together for the achievement of certain common goals. The recognition of mutual interests and the establishment of common goals result from communications. In order to achieve these goals, the actions of these people must be coordinated. Imagine 11 men on a football team all trying to score a touchdown by using 11 different plays at the same time. Communication is necessary if common goals are to be achieved through the concerted efforts of all persons within the organization. It is mainly through communication that we can attempt to mold the attitudes of the persons within the organization, motivate subordinates to carry out certain functions, fulfill a leadership role, and coordinate the efforts of the people within the organization. Consequently, communication is central to the operation of the organization.

378

There are many different definitions of communication. However, the definition we will use as a basis for our discussion is: "Communication is the transfer of information and understanding from person to person."[1] It is essential that one realize that the transmission of information does not constitute communication. In order for true communication to take place, information must be transferred and the message must be understood. Consequently, the mere act of speaking words does not qualify as communication until those words are received and understood.

The aspect of understanding is quite important when we think about the different functions of communication mentioned above. It was noted that communication is critical to the motivation of subordinates to carry out certain duties. In other words, concerted goal-directed behavior requires effective communication. The clarity (or ambiguity) of a person's role within the organization is related to the degree of mutual understanding that is present. The greater the understanding, the lower will be the ambiguity of the receiver's role. The more clearly one understands his organizational role, the greater the probability that he will develop appropriate behaviors and attitudes.

The Communication Process

Communication involves an apparently simple procedure consisting of only a few steps. Berlo has provided one technical model for understanding the communication process.[2] His model contains the following elements:

1. A communication source.
2. The encoder.
3. The message.
4. The channel.
5. The decoder.
6. The communication receiver.[3]

---

[1] Dale S. Beach, *Personnel: The Management of People at Work* (2d ed.) (New York: The Macmillan Company, 1970), p. 581.

[2] David K. Berlo, *The Process of Communication* (New York: Holt, Rinehart and Winston, Inc., 1960), p. 32.

[3] These elements are not necessarily always separated, since a person can send a message to himself, and, therefore, he would be both the source and the receiver and do both encoding and decoding. Furthermore, the elements are not restricted to people, since machines may be used in the communication process.

The elements are not very difficult to understand. The source conceives an idea that it wishes to send to the receiver. Before it can be sent, however, the idea must be encoded into a message that can be transmitted. The brain is an encoder of spoken or oral messages as is the part of your telephone that encodes your words into transmittible signals. The message is then sent through some channel or pathway to the receiver who, in turn, decodes the message or signal. If every step is performed well, the intended communication will occur. As we shall see, however, there are numerous pitfalls along the way.

Thus far, the model or process has been discussed in terms of oral communication. However, the definition of communication does not restrict itself to the transfer of oral or written messages. In reality, the concept is rather broad and includes the transfer of any type of information. Facial expressions can be considered communication—a frown tells you that the person does not understand what you have said or a yawn depicts boredom. A pay increase may communicate to a subordinate the approval of his efforts by superiors.

Determinants of Meaning

The process of communication appears rather simple, yet we frequently have difficulties in transferring information and understanding to each other. These difficulties arise due to certain determinants of meaning, which include words and semantics, emotions, one's general frame of reference, and situational contexts.

WORDS AND SEMANTICS. Words are symbols and do not have meaning in and of themselves.[4] These symbols derive their meaning from their continual use in a given culture. Meaning, then, is the cultural heritage of a symbol. Words refer to ideas or objects outside themselves. For instance, the word "tree" has no meaning in itself. "English-speaking" societies use the word to refer to a wooded plant. In like fashion, different cultures and societies have given different meanings to the same words.

We have said that communication is a process and the term process connotes a dynamic phenomenon. Communication involves the interaction of at least two minds, which are influencing each other. Moreover, the symbols we use for communication are not static. Being able to put

---

[4] David K. Steward, *The Psychology of Communication* (New York: Funk and Wagnalls Company, 1968), pp. 3–4.

symbols in correct order to spell a word is not sufficient. One must know the probable meaning attached to the word, and this tends to change. This fact becomes evident if you look in a dictionary for 1920 and one for 1970. Not only has the number of words grown, but the number of definitions for each word has also increased. In order to communicate with another person we must be aware of the words and the different meanings associated with those words.

"Semantics is the systematic study of the meaning of words."[5] As noted above, the meaning of a word is formulated by the society and culture in which it is used. Yet we are not familiar with all of the different cultures in the world and how they interpret words. Many times when we are talking with another person we have a problem in semantics in that the receiver does not decode the message the same way as we have encoded it. This problem is not restricted to communication between distinct cultures, but takes place within an organization. One's family background, religious teachings, and so on influence his interpretation of the words being used. Consequently, the problem of word meaning is an everyday occurrence.

The study of semantics relates closely to the study of perception. As discussed earlier, people may interpret the same stimulus in different ways, depending on their background and past experience. Take, for instance, the worker who invents a new time-saving way of doing a job. His peer group may perceive this as an attempt to "beat the system" and increase his production; furthermore, they might see this as a threat to the norms and values the group has formulated. Therefore, they label the worker a rate-buster and ostracize him from the group. His boss, on the other hand, views this same worker as being innovative and creative. The same stimulus evokes different attitudes due to the way each person perceives the stimulus. Note that words are "events"—environmental stimuli perceived by an individual. All events go through the overall process of perception. In fact, hearing and reading words are only special cases of perception. Again, the problem is that decoding is not identical among all recipients of the stimuli.

EMOTIONS. The emotions of the sender will influence the encoding of the message, just as the emotions of the receiver affect the decoding. A person will decode an identical message in different ways depending on his emotions at the time the message is received. A study done by Opinion Research Corporation found that the employees reacted differently to words or phrases that in essence "meant" the same thing. For

[5] Dalton E. McFarland, *Management: Principles and Practices* (3d ed.) (New York: The Macmillan Company, 1970), p. 572.

instance, the term "union shop" evoked a favorable reaction, although employees disliked the phrase "compulsory union membership." [6] Emotions affect our understanding and influence the decoding process.

Since many times people do not think solely with their minds, but also with their emotions, it is rather difficult to eliminate entirely the effects of emotions on communication. There are means available, however, that will allow the sender to reduce the dysfunctional consequences of emotions. We will discuss these later in this chapter.

FRAME OF REFERENCE.   The term frame of reference is a concept that encompasses one's background, attitudes, prior knowledge, and experience accumulated since birth. One's frame of reference influences to a great extent how he perceives words and other stimuli. Thus we cannot ignore or discard events in our life once they have occurred; rather, they remain in our minds to influence the interpretation of future events. Consequently, our frame of reference will influence the encoding and decoding process.

As mentioned above, we must be aware of semantic differences when we communicate with others. Semantics is influenced by the person's frame of reference, as are emotions and perception. This is one of the reasons for the "communication gap" between different generations. A person who has endured the depression has a different frame of reference than a person who has only known the affluent period of the 1950s and 1960s. The words they use will be the same, but their different frames of reference will result in different interpretations or responses to stimuli.

SITUATIONAL CONTEXT.   "That is not what I meant. They took that out of context." How many times have you heard someone make such a comment, especially a politician? What has happened is that someone has picked a sentence or two out of a longer message. When one does not know what preceded or what followed, one may well experience difficulty in ascertaining the exact meaning of the message. It is very rare that one or two sentences carry a full message; rather they receive some of their meaning from the preceding portion of the communication and are explained further in that which follows. The same can be said of single words or phrases. For example, if we mention that "we need more cases," you can envision many different things. However, if we precede this with a message about a party, you immediately think of a case of soft drinks or beer. If we have been talking about lawyers and court sessions, the message would connote the need for more clients. If we had been

[6] Verne Burnett, "Management's Tower of Babel," *Management Review,* L, no. 6 (June, 1961), 4–11.

conversing about a management course in college, one might think about the case study approach to classroom presentation.[7] We do not wish to restrict the concept of situational context to only those words that precede and follow the message in question. The environment in which the message is sent also constitutes part of the context, for words seen or heard form only a part of the stream of events being perceived at that moment. Each perceived stimulus may be influencing the meaning attached to the other stimuli.

Barriers to Communication

The failure to communicate effectively can destroy an organization. Recognition of this fact has caused increasing attention in management theory to the causes of communication breakdowns. Some of the chief barriers to precise and complete communications are discussed below, followed by some ways to surmount these barriers.

NOISE. The channels we use to transmit messages are not perfect. Disturbances may occur that will distort or even block the transmission of information and, therefore, create interference. Such interference is referred to as *noise* and includes anything moving in the channel other than the signal desired by the sender.[8] A simple example of noise is the static disturbance received on a radio, usually created by an electrical storm or the presence of high-voltage wires. The manager must be cognizant of noise when he attempts to communicate either with his employees or with persons outside the organization. Communication does not take place in a vacuum; the receiver is being bombarded with more than one signal at a time. For instance, during a business conference noise will be produced by the secretary typing in the next room, the sound of traffic on the street, and the shuffling of papers by those present at the meeting.

The receiver may also be the source of noise. According to some studies, Americans talk at about one hundred twenty-five words per minute in everyday communication situations and slow down to around one hundred words per minute when speaking informally to a group. The receivers, on the other hand, can think at about four to five hundred words

---

[7] Berlo, *The Process of Communication,* pp. 207–8.
[8] Colin Cherry, *On Human Communication* (New York: Science Edition, 1961), p. 42.

per minute.[9] Since the mind is capable of working faster than the signals are being received, there is idle capacity. The mind does not remain idle, however, and will attempt to fill the gaps. Unless the receiver concentrates on the message, he will send messages to himself. Some of these thoughts may be entirely irrelevant to the discussion. Others may take the form of internal responses to the message or plans to react to the message. In any case, the receiver's own mind is interfering with the receipt of the signal.

THE MESSAGE. Many times the message content creates a barrier to communication. If the information is too complex for the receiver, he may ignore or reject the entire message. How many times has the professor's lecture been so complex that the student has completely shut him off and allowed his mind to wander? Conversely, the message may be rejected as unworthy of attention by the receiver if he perceives it to be too simple or ambiguous. In either case, his interest in the message will be lost and communication will not take place: the receiver has been "turned off." [10]

PERSONAL TRUST. Another barrier to communication is the absence of personal trust. If the receiver does not trust the sender, he may distort or ignore the message. Rather than attempt to decode the message as it was encoded, the receiver may distort the signal in such a way as to reinforce his present feelings toward the sender. The worker may completely ignore or distort a message from a boss he dislikes, even though the communication is intended to benefit him. An example would be the worker who receives praise from his superior, but perceives the boss as attempting to "butter him up" in order to ask for a favor. If the sender does not establish an atmosphere of trust and confidence, the communication process will be burdened with distortion and rejection.

EVALUATION. Listeners have the natural tendency to evaluate, judge, approve, or disapprove the statements or messages of other people or senders. The tendency to evaluate these messages increase with the amount of emotion and feeling associated with the content of the message. Of course, the receiver makes the evaluation in accordance with his own frame of reference rather than the sender's. The evaluation may be pre-

[9] Ralph G. Nichols, "Personnel Management: New Perspectives," in *Human Relations in Management* (2d ed.), ed. S. G. Huneryager and I. L. Heckmann (Chicago, Ill.: South-Western Publishing Company, 1967), pp. 558–59.

[10] Bertram M. Gross, *The Managing of Organization*, II (Glencoe, Ill.: The Free Press of Glencoe; London: Collier-Macmillan, Ltd., 1964), p. 768.

mature in that the listener makes his judgment before the entire message is received. This is particularly harmful if the evaluation results in disapproval, since the receiver will usually not receive the rest of the message. Instead, he is formulating a rebuttal to communicate as soon as the present sender is finished. Many times have two people argued heatedly until one or both finally stop long enough to ascertain they were both supporting the same point of view. Perhaps the problem was that neither one took the time to listen and to decode the entire message being sent by the other. Evaluations were performed on partial messages with regard to one's own frame of reference, including his assumptions about the sender.[11]

SELECTIVE LISTENING. The manner in which we select messages to decode presents another barrier to communication. We all attempt to arrange our perceptions of the environment in an orderly, consistent manner; and once this arrangement is achieved, we strive to select only that information that reinforces our position. We go to great pains to protect and retain this cognitive organization of our world, hesitating to recognize phenomena that threaten it. Consequently, we perceive selectively. We accept all those messages that support our position, since this increases our cognitive security, and we reject those that demand cognitive change. We strive to avoid "cognitive dissonance," a condition in which current perceptions are incompatible with our existing structure of reality.[12] This resistance is particularly strong when the dissonant information threatens positive aspects of our self-image, or our self-esteem. When dissonant information is received, it is human nature for a person to reject it, distort it, or reinterpret it.[13]

Improving the Communication Process

Thus far we have illustrated barriers to good communications without explaining how they may be overcome. In this section we will discuss

[11] Carl R. Rogers and F. J. Roethlisberger, "Barriers and Gateways to Communication," *Harvard Business Review*, XXX, no. 4 (July–August, 1952), 46–52.

[12] L. A. Festinger, *A Theory of Cognitive Dissonance* (Evanston, Ill.: Row, Peterson and Company, 1957).

[13] Mason Haire, *Psychology in Management* (2d ed.) (New York: McGraw-Hill Book Company, Inc., 1964), Chapter 4.

three different means of improving the communication process: feedback, redundancy, and empathy.

FEEDBACK. The concept of feedback involves nothing more than allowing for two-way communication. After the receiver has decoded a message, he is allowed to send a message back to the original sender. This does not necessarily mean that the return message must be verbal. As pointed out earlier in this chapter, messages may be sent via facial expressions or by various other actions. A may send a message to B and, by observing B's expression or return message, determine if B understood the original message. If B lets it be known that he is confused (that the decoding does not make sense or is not understood), A can attempt to convey his idea by using a different encoding system, by using synonyms, or possibly by changing to a graphic explanation.

The teacher attempts to use feedback in the classroom by observing his students. If he has stressed an important and complex point and observes many frowns and blank stares, the teacher will usually attempt to reword his message. Or if the students look drowsy and are staring out the windows, the instructor realizes that the students are bored with the topic and might try to liven the message up.

The manager also attempts to use feedback by encouraging the subordinate to ask questions or otherwise to respond to the messages received. This is especially necessary if it is suspected that the sender and receiver may not have similar frames of reference. If the manager does not receive immediate feedback from his subordinates, he cannot ascertain if the message was received and understood. His feedback may come later in the form of poor production, high waste, or low morale. The manager who desires functional feedback may well work toward an atmosphere of mutual acceptance and respect. Differences in formal rank are deemphasized, while contributions from all toward common goals are stressed.

Leavitt and Mueller did a study to ascertain the effects of feedback on accuracy of communication. Four groups were asked to reproduce by use of paper and pencil certain geometric patterns after receiving verbal descriptions. The first group was not allowed any verbal feedback and they could not be seen by the instructor (i.e., visual feedback was also eliminated); the second group was permitted no verbal feedback to the instructor, but there was visual contact; the third group was allowed to respond to questions of the instructor strictly on a yes-no basis; and the last group was permitted free feedback in that they could ask the instructor any type of question and there was visual contact. The last group (free feedback) obtained the highest score on accuracy; the first group (zero feedback) scored the lowest. It must be pointed out also that the time of instruction was longest with the free feedback.[14]

Several conclusions can be drawn after considering the Leavitt and Mueller study and other experiments that have been performed. First, two-way communication is more accurate in developing understanding than is one-way communication (zero feedback). Furthermore, with two-way communication the receivers of the original message are more certain of the correctness of their decoding of the message and, hence, of the appropriateness of their response to the stimulus.

If feedback is so beneficial, why is it not used more often? People do not allow feedback for any of several reasons. First, the use of feedback consumes time and time might be scarce. In an emergency situation, there may not be time for feedback. When the assembly line breaks down, the foreman may not be able to allow feedback, but will have to revert to the use of direct and uninterrupted orders. Other people do not allow feedback because they view questions from subordinates as a threat to their status and power. They do not feel that a subordinate has the right to question any message sent by the superior. This is a rather sad situation for the organization, since the ideas transmitted by the superior may not be very sound; the concepts held by the subordinates may be better, but the organization will not be able to benefit from them. Other superiors (and teachers) feel that questions may expose their superficiality, their lack of a sound position.

The responsibility for good feedback lies mostly with the superior. He is the one who must produce a receptive atmosphere that will encourage the subordinates to ask questions and make suggestions. As Carl Rogers suggests, one thing the superior must learn to be is a good listener.[15] Although there is great stress on learning the art of transmitting, insufficient emphasis is probably given to developing the skill of listening, a most important managerial attribute. Even less attention is devoted to the creation of an environment free of communication inhibitors.

Figure 19-1 depicts how feedback is related to the other elements of the communication process.

REDUNDANCY. A second means of coping with the barriers of communication is through redundancy of the message. It is hoped that messages containing the same information will either reinforce one another

[14] Harold J. Leavitt and Ronald A. H. Mueller, "Some Effects of Feedback on Communication," *Human Relations*, IV (1951), 401–10.
[15] Rogers and Roethlisberger, "Barriers and Gateways to Communication," p. 47.

Figure 19-1

The communication process with feedback.

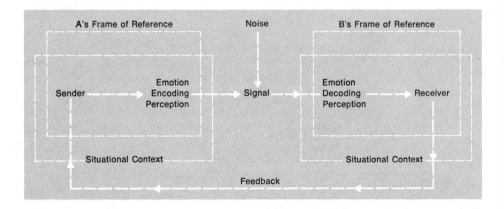

or clarify the possible ambiguities that each signal may contain. For instance, the instructor uses redundancy when he explains a topic to the students verbally, graphically, and mathematically.

Redundancy is used in the industrial organization also. Many times when top management wants to get information to a great many people at one time, they will use different channels to send the same message. They may pass the information downward through the formal chain of command while they also publish the same announcement in the company newspaper. A third channel top management may use would be letters mailed directly to employees' homes. However, redundancy may be expensive and should be used sparingly. Consequently, a balance must be achieved between the costs of such a program and the benefits that will accrue from increments of understanding. If the message content is important, redundancy may be a necessary cost. It will be recalled that one of the barriers to communication is distrust or dislike of the source, since it results in distortion or rejection of the message. Using multiple channels helps to solve or overcome this type of barrier. Moreover, redundancy can be used to indicate the importance attached to the message by the sender. It is one means of achieving desired emphasis.

EMPATHY. Empathy may be defined as the ability of a person to imagine or perceive himself in the situation of another. In other words, it is the ability to view the environment as others see it. Another term that is used is "social sensitivity." It is a technique the sender or receiver should use in order to understand the other's personality and his frame of reference. Without empathy, the sender cannot accurately predict how the other interprets various symbols. We mentioned earlier that communication is necessary in order to motivate and direct the behavior of others. However, if we do not make an effort to perceive the situation as it is viewed by the respondent, the stimulus sent may evoke behavior contrary to what was desired. If one mistakenly assumes that his and the receiver's perceptions and frames of reference are identical, then the risk is high that unanticipated behavior will be evoked. It is believed that social sensitivity can be learned, as indicated by widespread acceptance of "sensitivity training" in industry and government.

Upward and Downward Communication

As stated earlier, communication is necessary for the organization to attain its objectives. There must be good communication not only downward from superior to subordinate, but also upward from subordinate to superior. A problem exists, however, in that personal motivation affects the flow of communication within the organization. In other words, the way the sender perceives how the information will affect him when it is received by a second person determines the amount and types of information he is willing to release.

Looking first at the subordinate and his motivation to communicate upward, we find that he will communicate with his superior if one of three factors are present. First, he will transmit information upward to his superior if the transmission of such information will have pleasant or favorable consequences for him. At the very least, he must perceive the information as not being harmful to his ego, job security, promotional aspirations, and so on. Second, the subordinate will transmit information upward if he knows that his superior will shortly receive the information anyway from some other source. (The subordinate may reason that it would be better for him to tell his boss first.) Think of a small boy, for example, who has committed some questionable deed during the day. He meets his dad in the driveway and summarizes his activities, giving the tale his own slant before his mother can relate the story. So it is in industry: if we know the information will be sent through other channels, we prefer to give "our side" of the story to our superior first. Third, the subordinate will communicate information upward if he realizes that his superior needs the information in order to work and communicate with his own superior. The subordinate realizes that if his superior is criticized by his own boss for not having certain information, he will, in turn, criticize the subordinate for withholding that information. A problem occurs when the subordinate does not know what information his superior needs and, consequently, may transmit irrelevant data.[16]

Read studied executives in business organizations in order to ascertain the variables affecting upward communications.[17] He found that the mobility aspiration, that is, the desire and hope for advancement, among subordinate executives was related in a negative manner to the accuracy of upward communication. In other words, the more the person aspired for promotion, the more he was likely to alter his messages in order to increase the probability of promotion. If a person wants to be promoted, he surely will not send information that will indicate that he is incompetent. Consequently, the information is screened before it is sent and only selected pieces of data are allowed to move higher in the industrial hierarchy.

Because the screening or filtering of information is a natural occurrence, it can cause widespread problems for the organization. The transmission of information upward in the organization is necessary for rational decision making by those persons at the head of the firm. One can imagine the difficulties encountered in attempting to make decisions using information that has been filtered. The problem increases, of course, as the number of levels within the organization through which the information must flow also increases. As discussed earlier, this is one argument often used for a short and wide type of organization structure.

Communication downward in the organization is not without its problems. There are two major reasons why there may be bottlenecks in the flow of information downward. First, the superior may withhold communication from a subordinate in order to maintain a power position. As one can imagine, this type of behavior is not very constructive in terms of the functioning of the organization. According to Simon, this type of retention of information is usually a symptom of a tyrannical or insecure manager.[18] The manager will restrict the downward flow of communication in order that the subordinate will be dependent on him for decisions and direction. The superior fears that the release of all the information will allow the subordinate to make decisions affecting his role within the organization. As such, this person may make decisions that prove superior

[16] Herbert A. Simon, *Administrative Behavior* (2d ed.) (New York: The Macmillan Company, 1957), pp. 162–63.

[17] William H. Read, "Upward Communication in Industrial Hierarchies," *Human Relations*, XV (February, 1962), 3–15.

[18] Simon, *Administrative Behavior*, p. 163.

to those made by his boss. Consequently, the superior, in order to protect his job and maintain authority over his subordinate, retains much of the information that his subordinate needs in order to operate efficiently.

Equally as unfortunate for the organization, but more easily resolved, is failure to share information because the superior does not realize that his subordinate needs it. This is due to a lack of a clear understanding of the subordinate's role within the organization. The superior often feels that transmission of orders is sufficient to allow the subordinate to function. The remedy is frequent discussion of the appropriate roles of each and of the types of information necessary for the successful completion of those roles. This should not be difficult, since, unlike the first reason stated above, the problems of personality, power, and insecurity are not present, but merely a lack of common understanding.

The screening process is as relevant to downward as to upward communication. As mentioned earlier in this chapter, we are neither perfect senders nor perfect receivers. Consequently, it is very difficult for us to receive a message and replicate it perfectly when we send it to another person. We filter out certain portions of the message and consciously or unconsciously add our own bias. So it is with downward communication in the business organization. One report claims that as information is passed from the board of directors through the vice-president, to the general manager, to the plant manager, to the general foreman, and finally to the worker, the communication has lost 80 percent of its informational content.[19] Such a loss of information makes it rather difficult for an organization to operate efficiently.

It should be realized that downward communication fits the traditional concepts of management, whereas upward communication runs somewhat counter to these ideas. As discussed earlier, authority was traditionally viewed as vested with those at the top of the organization, who, in turn, could delegate this authority. Consequently, the important communications were directed from those at the top downward to their subordinates. The superior had to decide what information was necessary for the subordinate to carry out his authority. Upward communication has always been requested, but often at a very minimal level. Subordinates have been required to submit reports as to work progress, problems, and so on—little more than a means of feedback and the minimum requirement for the successful operation of the organization. It is currently believed that if the organization is going to obtain the maximum value from its employees, the upward communication channels must be utilized to a greater extent. As McGregor pointed out with his *Theory Y*, creative

[19] Ralph G. Nichols, "Personnel Management," pp. 547–48.

ability is widely distributed in the population.[20] Great treasures of skills, knowledge, and interest may lie at the lower organizational levels, needing only a secure, sensitive manager to tap them. However, the organization will not be able to tap this immense potential resource unless the upward communication channels are built to carry this type of information.

Lateral Communication

Some of the traditional theorists found exceptions to the rule that communication should follow the chain of command. Both Henri Fayol and Frederick Taylor were aware of the fact that it is sometimes necessary to bypass the chain of command. Fayol, for example, formulated the idea of "Fayol's Bridge."

Fayol recognized that sometimes lateral communication would be necessary in order for interdependent functions to be coordinated. If the organization adhered strictly to the concept of unity of command, the communication process would consume too much time. Referring to Figure 19-2, suppose the supervisor in charge of producing product A wants to contact the sales manager in charge of product A. By the strict law of unity of command the supervisor would communicate upward through his superior until he reached the president and then the message would proceed downward to the sales manager. Two problems exist. First, by the time the communication loop had been completed the environment might have changed enough to render the information contained in the communication valueless or incorrect. Second, the communication had to go through five intermediaries before reaching the desired receiver. How much noise would enter the system? Fayol claimed that the two persons directly involved, the supervisor and the sales manager, should be allowed to communicate directly. However, he was not willing to completely discard the law of unity of command. Fayol insisted that in order for this direct communication to work, the subordinates must keep their immediate superiors fully advised of their deliberations. Consequently, the hierarchy relationship would be maintained.[21]

[20] Douglas McGregor, *The Human Side of Enterprise* (New York: McGraw-Hill Book Company, Inc., 1960), Chapter 4.

[21] Henri Fayol, *General and Industrial Management*, trans. Constance Storrs (London: Sir Isaac Pitman & Sons, Ltd., 1963), pp. 34–35. The interested reader should also refer to Henry A. Landsberger, "The Horizontal Dimension in Bureaucracy," *Administrative Science Quarterly*, VI (December, 1961), 299–332; and Melville Dalton, *Men Who Manage* (New York: John Wiley & Sons, Inc., 1959) for recent analyses of lateral communication.

Figure 19-2

Illustration of Fayol's bridge.

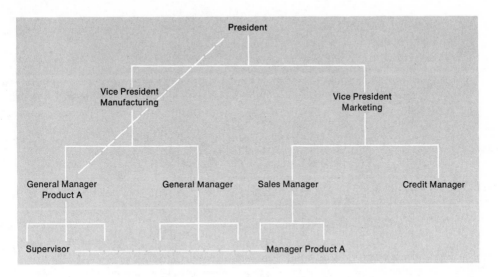

Where are the functional and dysfunctional consequences associated with vertical "short circuiting"? With reference to Figure 19-2, what happens if and when the president communicates directly with the general manager of the production of product *A*? Such communication may be quite desirable if the president needs information quickly about this portion of the operation in order to make some decision. We have already mentioned that the presence of an intermediary in the channels slows down the flow of information. Direct communication also allows higher officials to become more familiar with lower-level subordinates. This in turn aids in making decisions and helps satisfy the esteem needs of the subordinates. However, as with horizontal bridging, the manager in the middle should be informed of such communications. If this is not done, the intermediary, in this case the vice-president for manufacturing, may perceive his position as being undermined and consequently look on his subordinate and superior with distrust. Moreover, he may be unable to maintain a general "feel" for the matters of concern affecting his subordinates and superiors.

Upward short-circuiting is also common and involves consequences similar to those discussed above. The subordinate may need quickly information that he knows his immediate supervisior does not possess. Upward short-circuiting must be done with care and with the knowledge of the immediate superior or he may perceive the communicants as attempting to bypass the chain of command and undermine his position.

The Grapevine

The communication system of the informal organization is usually referred to as the *grapevine*. Such a channel of communication is inevitable, since the people constituting the organization will form both work groups and social groups. One would not expect people to work together all day without the transfer of information, some of which is not essential to the task they are performing at the time. Furthermore, when the employees go on coffee breaks they can be expected to exchange information on any topics of mutual interest. (When the housewife does this over the back fence we call it gossip, but in the business organization we label it an informational exchange.)

Many managers become disturbed at the presence of a grapevine, since much of the information it transmits is fallacious. Furthermore, the speed of informational exchange is sometimes much quicker through the grapevine than through the formal channels of communication, since the former is not restricted by concern about the unity of command or any strictly established channels. In essence, the grapevine institutes the concept of Fayol's bridge to the utmost. Since rumors do travel so quickly and are many times incorrect, they can be detrimental to employee attitudes and behavior. For example, the rumor starts on Monday morning that company sales are falling and there is going to be a 30 percent layoff. By Monday afternoon both the morale of the work force and their production have slumped, as everyone wonders if he will still be working next Monday. For this reason managers must be concerned about what the grapevine is transmitting, even though they cannot eliminate it.

Since management cannot eliminate the natural occurrence of a grapevine, they should attempt to increase its contributions to efficiency and to minimize its dysfunctional effects. The best way to do this is to supply the employees with the maximum amount of useful information feasible. Rumors survive best in a confused atmosphere or in an informational vacuum. However, if the employees have official information about events and policies that directly affect them or if they can readily obtain it, they will not be as likely to seek and spread rumors. The information the manager dispenses has an advantage in that it originates from a source of authority, whereas the source of a rumor is very difficult to identify. Consequently, if the employees are kept informed of where they stand and what they can expect in the future, the dysfunctional consequences of the grapevine will be greatly reduced.

Thus far we have stressed the dysfunctional consequences of the grapevine. Like everything else, however, the grapevine also has its merits. First, as mentioned above, the grapevine transmits information very quickly. Therefore, if manager desires to "get the word around quickly," the grapevine may be the best channel available. Second, the grapevine is very flexible in that it does not have to maintain a given channel of communication, but can change quite easily to include those persons most concerned with the information. Third, this type of inter-action among employees helps to satisfy their social needs. Fourth, the grapevine helps fill the gaps in information transmitted through formal channels. Last, the manager may desire to transmit information informally to the worker, perhaps preferring that the information not be attributed to his office. The grapevine is made to order for this need.

SUMMARY

Communication is so central to organization that some would define the organization by its communications network and content. Important though it is, there are many instances of failure to communicate effectively.

For one thing, there is the problem of meaning. Our interpretation of a word, a gesture, a deed, and so on is influenced by many factors—our backgrounds, perceptual precision, emotions, and the situational context being primary ones. Beyond the broad problem of semantics, there are the problems of "noise," the tendency to ignore overly complex or unpleasant messages, and the tendency to distort or ignore messages from untrusted communicators. Human beings are rarely passive receivers. They generally evaluate message content while they are receiving. Unfortunately this process introduces noise into the channel and also the possibility of unconscious but purposeful message distortion. Finally, we tend to listen and interpret so as to confirm our existing structure of reality. Any of these mechanisms can make true communication very difficult.

A number of techniques may be used to counter these communication pitfalls. A leading method is the use of feedback: the two-way communication process. Feedback may increase communicating time, expense, and the risk of embarrassment for high-status communicators.

It does improve communication precision, as well as confidence that true communication has resulted.

Redundancy—repetition of the message in different symbols and media—may also help overcome communication barriers. Again, however, there are associated costs. A most effective aid to communication is empathy, a high degree of understanding between communicators. This can alleviate semantic pitfalls, but not the others.

Several factors are found to limit vertical communication within organizations. Screening, the systematic filtering out of information detrimental to the sender, is a chief culprit limiting the upward flow. Many managers fail to request or systematically ignore upward communication. Information hoarding by superiors for status or power reasons constricts the downward flow. Information may be withheld because the possessor believes it to be unimportant to the others.

Modern organization theory stresses the importance of *lateral* and *informal* networks within organizations. Both can improve coordination among the diverse members of the enterprise; and they help to create an informed, empathetic atmosphere. The manager's task is not to impede such information flows, but rather to help assure that information so transmitted is accurate and relevant to organizational success.

QUESTIONS

1. What does the term "mean" mean?

2. Relate general perception theory to the process of receiving a communication.

3. Why do attempts to communicate fail so frequently?

4. How can we improve communication within an organization?

5. It is said that vertical communication in organizations were stressed by classical management theorists to the virtual exclusion of diagonal communication. Why might this have been so? And why is there now a shift in emphasis to the latter paths?

6. Does one's status in the formal or informal organizational structure influence his patterns of communication? In what way?

7. The communication process involves several elements. At each point in the process, there are potential pitfalls. Describe some pitfalls to be considered in each of the following steps:

    a. Encoding.

    b. Transmission.

    c. Reception.

    d. Decoding.

8. Does meaning reside with the word (or other symbol)? Where does meaning derive from?

9. Discuss as fully as you can the role of communication in the initiation and operation of an organization.

10. It is said that no description of a real object can be absolutely complete. Thus all attempts to describe reality are, at best, partial. Discuss. (You may wish to select a simple object, such as a pan, a table, or a football, and attempt to describe it.)

case studies
for part four

Non-Linear Systems

During the 1960s a small, rapidly growing firm, Non-Linear Systems, became renowned among management theorists and practitioners. In 1960 Non-Linear converted from an assembly-line production system to a system long thought outmoded and inefficient: assembly of the entire product by individual operators.

JOB ENLARGEMENT AND ENRICHMENT

Under the new system, an operator's functions typically included blueprint and diagram reading, setting up the work area, planning the sequence of assembly operations, actual assembly, quality testing, and trouble shooting on units performing improperly. Assembly was not a short or simple process but involved hundreds of steps and required a variety of skills. The basic product, an electric voltmeter, was built in several sizes and complexities. A large, complex unit might take three weeks to complete. Production employees who were asked to make the conversion from the single-function task of an assembly line to the multifunction task of individual assembly were of various backgrounds, including many with less than high school educations.

This program of job enlargement and enrichment was one prominent feature of the new system at Non-Linear. Other important characteristics of the system were small work teams, work group autonomy, and individual responsibility.

AUTONOMOUS WORK TEAMS

Non-Linear reorganized its production personnel into teams averaging about seven members. Each team was headed by a technician with the title, Assistant Assembly Manager. These teams enjoyed virtual freedom from external controls. They established their own operating procedures and their own work pace. As one observer noted:

> Each team runs its own little business. Each has its own rooms, for which it decides the decor; its own door to the outside. There are no time clocks. Everyone receives a weekly salary, with no docking for sickness or lateness. There are no scheduled coffee-breaks—anyone can get coffee whenever he feels like it.
>
> A gray-haired woman near me was smoking as she busily laid out a pattern of wire circuits. . . . Propped up in front of her were several pages of diagrams and notes. "This woman has done all her own planning and programming," my guide said. "She tests as she goes along. When she finishes this instrument she will sign her name to it. If a customer develops trouble with it, the instrument will come back to her for correction.[1]

Non-Linear emphasized both formal training programs and informal intra-team training. Management established as a primary goal the development of individuals and teams to permit utmost flexibility and mutual assistance.

Commenting upon the discretion permitted work teams, vice president Arthur Kuriloff stated:

> There is no formal planning. By mutual agreement the team members decide who will do what and in what sequence. They pace themselves at their own rhythm. They know each other's strengths and generally do a better job of planning than if directed by some external authority.[2]

---

[1] Vance Packard, "A Chance for Everyone to Grow," *Readers Digest*, LXXXIII (November, 1963), 115.

[2] Arthur H. Kuriloff, "An Experiment in Management: Putting Theory Y to the Test," *Personnel*, XL (November–December, 1963), 14.

INDIVIDUAL RESPONSIBILITY

Although Non-Linear's management believed that autonomous work teams would prove to be productive and socially satisfying, the factor of individual motivation was not ignored. Each voltmeter assembled was the responsibility of a single operator, whether he did the entire job himself or received substantial assistance. As far as was feasible, the individual was permitted the satisfaction (and the challenge) of performing "the whole job." When he signed his name to the job completion form, he knew that he was personally accountable for the machine's performance.

MANAGEMENT'S LOGIC

The management of Non-Linear Systems was admittedly strongly influenced by the ideas of Abraham Maslow and Douglas McGregor. It was believed that judicious application of the theories of these men could foster high output and high employee satisfaction simultaneously. It was felt, furthermore, that human motivation and productivity required more than appropriate leadership styles. Also necessary were an organizational structure and a formal reward system compatible with ascending human aspirations. Management, therefore, created a production system with the following characteristics:

1. job enlargement (more complex work cycles)
2. job enrichment (increased discretion and responsibility)
3. small work teams
4. work group autonomy
5. individual accountability
6. high, stable salaries (well above comparable community employers)

The results of this industrial experiment were very gratifying to management. By 1963 productivity per employee was 30 percent above the best prior period in the firm's history. Customer complaints about product performance had declined by 70 percent from 1960. Employee turnover had decreased, and the absenteeism rate was less than half that for comparable firms in the area.

Mr. Kuriloff expanded on the Non-Linear philosophy in a talk given to the Industrial Engineering Institute.[3] Some of his comments are presented below.

[3] Mr. Kuriloff's comments are reproduced by permission of the Industrial Engineering Institute.

The business enterprise is a *group of people* banded together for the sake of an economic purpose. It is clear that the organizational structure and operational style must stem from management's view of the people who form the organization. The philosophical assumptions management makes about the behavior and nature of its people determine these patterns directly.

The covert traditional philosophy says that the employee is a pair of "hands." In fact, when industrial organizations hire people, they very often talk about hiring "hands." These hands are considered homogeneous and interchangeable. They may be substituted readily for one another on the production line. Since production line tasks are usually cut down to a minimum number of small repetitive motions, no great skills are required. The tasks may be learned by the new worker with negligible training.

In addition, the average hand is thought to be really not very bright and essentially unmodifiable. He is inherently lazy, will shun work whenever possible, lacks sound judgment, is shortsighted and prone to error. On top of all this, he is probably a little dishonest. He must be watched closely if he is to give an honest measure of work for a day's pay. To sum up all these statements, we may say that he cannot be trusted. Therefore, the pattern and operational style of the organization are structured to detect and correct error. The kind of organization that results is very common in our conventional enterprise. It is often called the "accounting" model, displaying a complex pyramidal network of authority relationships with many layers of organization. The attendant difficulties in communication, the distortions in content, as directives and information flow up and down the communication ladder, are well known to all of us.

On the other hand, what kind of organization emerges if management views the individual in a different fashion? Suppose we were to say that people are not "hands"; they are individual human beings. Each has a discrete and different complement of traits and talents. Suppose we assume that people are not lazy; work is a normal part of the business of living. Suppose we say that people are capable of being trained; their skills may be enlarged by adequate and proper coaching. They can do a bigger and better job if we make it possible for them to do so, if we assume that training is a major part of management's job. In addition, suppose we say that people are fundamentally honest; they can be trusted. We can tolerate error as a normal part of human endeavor so long as it remains within reasonable bounds. We can accept a mistake providing it isn't repeated. If we make these assumptions, then we can organize our enterprise completely differently. We find then that we do not need time clocks to assure the worker is doing a full day's work. We can eliminate many layers of authority in the organization structure. We can improve our communications by shortening and paralleling the channels. We can adopt something closely resembling the organizational structure we are trying in our experiment at Non-Linear Systems, Inc.

Significant in our experimental approach to management is the way individuals are organized into working groups. We use the group method in every department in our company. Groups range in size from three to nine people. As an instance of how the group works, we might look at our engineering operation. The engineering group is known as a project team. It is under the management of a project manager. He is a highly skilled, competent, experienced electronic engineer. He has working with him in the minimum size group of three, a product designer and an electronic technician. Each project group works in its own rooms; sometimes two, sometimes three rooms. The project manager occupies a private office. His product designer has a private office and his technician works in a development laboratory next to the other two rooms. When a new product is started, the project manager receives from the Executive Council a specification for the instrument. The specification consists of a small sketch plus inputs, outputs, and tolerances. There may be some explanatory notes. An indication of the approximate sales price of the instrument tells the project manager how much he can spend for parts in the production instrument. He studies the specification and comes back with his recommendations. After consultation with the Executive Council, the changes that seem reasonable or desirable are made in the specification. The manager is told to go ahead with his work. He may now proceed in his individual fashion with the development of the instrument. He can buy any item he needs without counter-signature so long as the amount does not exceed $2,500. He develops the instrument. In time he comes up with an engineering prototype. His product designer and his technician have worked closely with him through all phases of the job.

When the prototype is ready, the Executive Council examines it. If we find that it meets its specifications and looks satisfactory generally, we proceed into production. If there are deficiencies, we may ask that further development work be done. When we consider the item ready for production, we assign one or two people from an instrument assembly department to help build several prototypes. This is usually done in the project manager's quarters. We use the prototypes for sales, reserving one for a production model. Meanwhile the project manager and his little group have produced the necessary drawings and technical data needed for production.

We believe that the project manager should develop the original instrument, help build the production prototypes, consult with the people in our assembly department who must put it together, stay cognizant of technical and production problems throughout the active life of the instrument. The project manager has authority in technical matters as long as the instrument is made. No one may make a change in the design without his approval.

Now let us look at an instrument assembly department as an example of how a manufacturing group works. The average group in instrument assembly has seven people. One of the seven is an expert electronic technician. He has had years of experience and is extremely competent technically. He is known as an assistant assembly department manager. The group itself is made up of all kinds of people. When we made the switch from our old assembly lines two and one-half years ago to the present group method, we did not fire anyone. We simply reorganized the available people into groups of seven each.

Each group in the instrument assembly department is self-contained. By this I mean they do the whole job. They put complete instruments together from kits of parts, electrical components and hardware. They place components on the etched circuit boards, do the soldering, fabricate harnessing. They build up the hardware from the pieces delivered with the kits and assemble the total instrument. They then run the machines in, calibrate them, troubleshoot and repair if necessary. When they get all through, they sign the quality assurance tag on the instrument and place it in its shipping box.

There is no formal planning. The members of the group decide who will do what by mutual consent and decision. They know each other's strengths and weaknesses and will generally do a far better job of planning when left alone than if directed by some kind of authority.

There are some very interesting things happening in these groups. The capabilities of the people have been developed in two and one-half years to the point where they were able to write their own instructions for procedure in assembly. They write their own troubleshooting instructions. They help each other; they help members of other groups; they help write the service manuals we require for each instrument. They have acquired the skills and knowledge to build half a dozen or so different kinds of instruments in each group. By the way, as a company we manufacture over forty different kinds of standard instruments. It is very interesting to walk through the rooms where these groups are operating. You will see some groups building several different kinds of instruments, for example. They seem able to adjust readily and to accommodate to changes from one kind of an instrument to another with no apparent disorganization. It seems very clear to us that the experiment is showing markedly improved performance of the people in the instrument assembly groups since the change in the organization of two and one-half years ago. In fact, production figures now show performance 30 percent better than any time in the company's history.

I said that there is no formal planning in the procedures in these departments. By that I mean we do not have a formal planning office in our company. The planning done within the groups result from the groups' ideas of what should be done and when things should be done. However, the total work of the instrument assembly departments must be planned from week to week. We accomplish this kind of planning by what we call our reservoir system of operation. The Executive Council establishes maximum and minimum quantities for each kind of instrument we build. We change the mix from time to time as conditions in the sales areas change. Now all the instrument assembly managers have to do to find what kinds of instruments to build next is to count the number of instruments in each stack in the storeroom, check against maximum and minimum quantities, and thus determine what instruments to stop and start building during the next few weeks. Additional data come from weekly meetings of the instrument assembly department managers with managers of several other departments. Among these are representatives from the materials department, which is responsible for buying parts and components, and the distribution department, which has inputs from the sales regions all over the country. The managers thus receive some notion of what sales prospects are for the next few weeks and even months. The instrument assembly department managers use this data in making calculated decisions to adjust their product mix.

The reservoir concept as I have described it for instrument assembly represents an idea we are experimenting with throughout the whole company. We believe that it is possible to develop reservoirs in all areas of operation in the company. These reservoirs produce what might be called feedback in a servosystem. Operations of the department are adjusted in accordance with the command signals of feedback from the reservoirs. For example, in our components department which makes precision wire wound resistors, stepping switch assemblies, and cable harnesses, a reservoir system similar to that in instrument assembly becomes readily workable. In the distribution department the reservoir consists of backlog of orders as yet unfilled. In the sales regions we have an idea that the reservoir concept can be developed in terms of potential for making sales and for creating new customers.

The Fibers Department

Part A

The King Chemical Corporation, a medium-sized chemical company, operated several plants in the midwestern United States.[1] In one of these plants, a serious quality control problem had developed, which threatened the loss of several very large and profitable accounts. The product receiving the most serious quality complaints was a line of filtering materials that were sold to other manufacturers who fabricated various kinds of filters from them. The market for filter materials was highly competitive, although prices tended to be quite stable. Competition was based upon service to the customer and product quality. Total demand for this product was expanding, but so was the industry's capacity. As a result, there continued a vigorous struggle among suppliers to maintain or expand their market shares.

When the quality variations became critical, the plant manager, Al Benton, requested the superintendent of the Fibers Department, Ron Collins, to report the nature of the problem and a program of action designed to eliminate it. Ron reflected upon the complex situation that seemed to underlie the deterioration in his department's performance.

The fibers production process required that quality faults be detected and corrected promptly. In fact, it was necessary to catch quality defects during actual production, for the product was packed and shipped immediately. No additional in-plant processing provided an opportunity

---

[1] This case was prepared by William K. Martin, under the supervision of Dr. Irwin Weinstock.

to cull defective fibers. Consequently, constant alertness of production employees was essential to high quality output.

The Fibers Department was constituted of two sections (See Exhibit A-1), which we will call Sections X and Y. These sections performed distinct, but closely related, functions. Both sections operated around the clock, seven days a week, with four rotating shifts, plus a relief shift. Each shift of Section X had two foremen, who jointly supervised 28 operators.

Section Y was separated into two parts, one processing a filters product, while the second processed an insulating product. Nine operators and a foreman performed the insulation production functions. The filters process was handled by twenty operators under the joint supervision of two foremen. Because of union insistence, the operators in Section Y were rotated weekly between filters and insulation operations. Union leaders asserted that this rotation was equitable in view of the fact that the work in insulation was easier and the working conditions more pleasant. Ron felt that this rotation policy might be contributing to low-quality output.

Exhibit A-1

Organization of the Fibers Department.

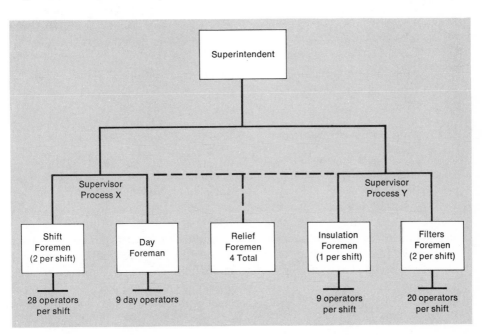

There was no team spirit, because team content and function were constantly changing; and the usual bond between foremen and their operators could not develop because operators transferred from one unit to the other.

It was believed that two foremen were necessary on each filters shift because their duties included making certain delicate equipment adjustments, at times even replacing defective equipment. This task, plus the functions of general supervision, were considered too burdensome for a single foreman to perform effectively.

Ron reflected on other relationships that seemed to be affecting his department's output. The processing was continuous, with the termination of Process X and the starting of Process Y occurring at a series of machines called the crammers (Exhibit A-2). Ron knew of several incidents when a Section Y foreman decided to replace a crammer to improve output quality. In almost every case, a conflict arose between the foremen in Sections X and Y, for the replacement of crammers created substantial additional work for Section X hourly and supervisory personnel.

On other occasions, violent arguments erupted among hourly personnel, foremen, and, at times, the supervisors, over the causes and the proposed cures for severe quality defects. Hostilities intensified as each attempted to defend his own position. Lasting hostility seemed extremely detrimental, for close communication between and within the sections was necessary for customer satisfaction. When low product quality was detected in Process X, the operators were to transmit appropriate information to operators in Process Y, thus assuring that the final product was downgraded. Marketing feedback revealed that severe quality problems were going unattended, indicating either a lack of attention by all concerned or a failure in communications between Process X and Y.

THE QUALITY INSPECTORS

The visual inspections by production operators and foremen were augmented by periodic product examinations by quality inspectors. These inspectors were employees of the Quality Control Department and reported to a supervisor in that department. Inspectors' reports of product defects to the section foreman triggered process adjustments in either Process X or Y, or both. When a product fault was borderline between passable and reject, the inspectors and foremen engaged in serious arguments. Ron knew of several instances where foremen had refused to adjust the process when confronted with alleged quality deficiencies. He sensed a growing mutual hostility between process foremen and quality inspectors.

Exhibit A-2

Diagram of the Fibers Department.

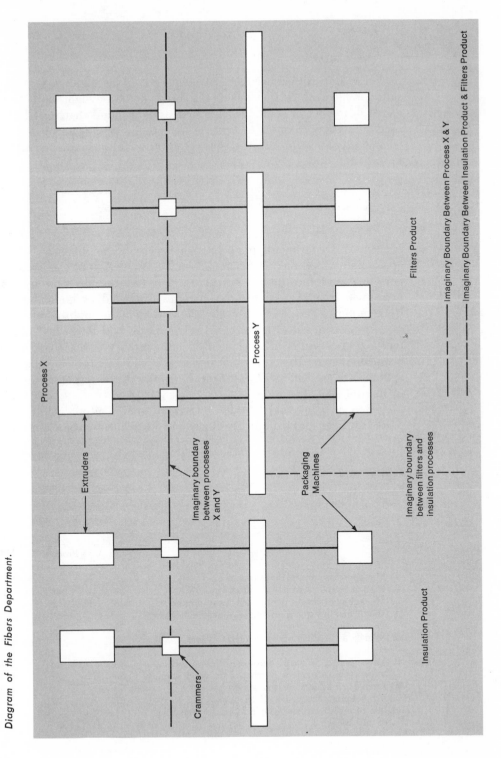

The only direct contact between Ron or his supervisors and his shift foremen occurred when they rotated to the daylight shift or were called in to special meetings. Ron increasingly found that shift foremen used these opportunities to criticize the other shifts. It seemed to be a common practice for a shift to leave certain quality hazards uncorrected, to "pass the buck" to the next shift.

WHAT TO DO?

It seemed to Ron that conflict was the dominant characteristic in his Fibers Department, pervading the relationships between (1) the operators and foremen in Sections X and Sections Y, (2) the production personnel and the quality inspectors, and (3) the shifts of operating personnel. It appeared that the energies expended on these hostilities were seriously detracting from the effort to maintain high quality ouput.

Ron's concern with personnel relationships was intensified when he received the results of a plant-wide opinion survey that had recently been conducted. The report revealed serious morale problems among the operators in the Fibers Department. Examples of the responses are given in Exhibit A-3.

Ron now felt that he was "under the gun." Output in his department had been singled out by clients and his plant manager as being of

Exhibit A-3

OPINION SURVEY RESULTS

Question	% AGREEING WITH STATEMENT		
	Process X	*Process Y*	*Plant*
1. Machines are more important than people.	75	75	50
2. I get a lot of satisfaction out of my job.	54	46	71
3. Management thinks people are really important.	43	59	63
4. When making decisions, management considers the employees' interests.	31	25	37
5. Management does not give credit where credit is due.	92	71	60
6. Management is really interested in our ideas.	35	34	43
7. Supervisor recognizes it when I do good work.	50	37	64
8. I have confidence in my supervisor.	50	59	73
9. My foreman treats us all the same	27	21	46
10. My foreman explains the reasons for rejection of my ideas.	39	33	52

unsatisfactory quality. And now it was general knowledge that his employees were deeply dissatisfied. Ron felt that he must solve his dual problem soon, but he was not sure what action to take.

The Fibers Department

Part B

Ron Collins believed that the quality control problem in his department was not caused by a lack of skills or by a defective technical system. He felt certain that his men and machines could produce consistently high quality materials if they were properly organized. For about a week, Ron discussed the overall problem with his foremen, the quality control superintendent, specialists in the Personnel Department, his superiors, and himself. The result was a comprehensive reorganization of the Fibers Department.

THE NEW ORGANIZATION

The following major changes were recommended in the Fibers Department structure (Exhibit B-1).

1. A supervisor position was created for each shift, to be generally responsible for the coordinated operations of Sections X and Y.
2. The technical aspects of each shift's operation were assigned to two manufacturing specialists, who were jointly responsible for the technical side of operations. These men were accountable directly to the shift supervisor.
3. Two foremen were assigned to each shift, one for Section X and one for Section Y. These men were primarily responsible for the supervision and administrative duties of the hourly personnel. The technical (equipment adjustment, etc.) responsibilities, once part of their jobs, were now the primary concern of the manufacturing specialists. Foremen were directly accountable to their shift supervisor.
4. The quality control inspectors were reassigned to the manufacturing organization, reporting to the shift supervisor.

By having the foremen, the manufacturing specialists, and the quality inspectors report to the shift supervisor, Ron hoped to eliminate the problems associated with the boundaries within each shift. Squabbles

Exhibit B-1

The Fibers Department after reorganization.

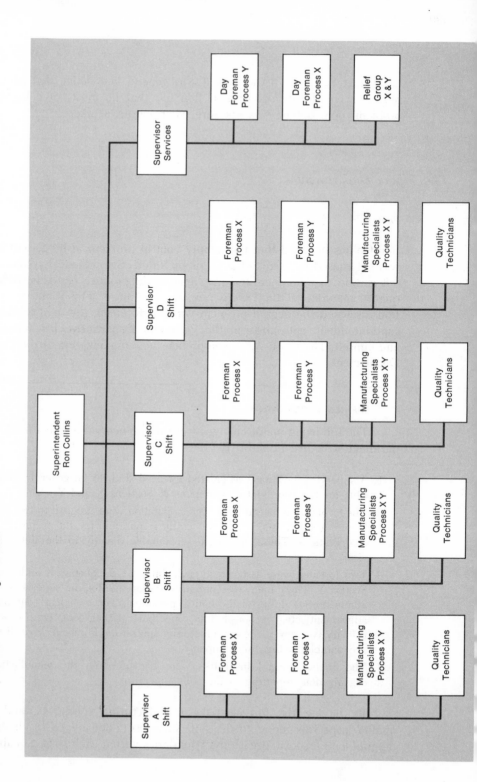

between inspectors and foremen, between X and Y foremen, or between manufacturing specialists could be settled quickly by the supervisor, avoiding the lengthy, heated arguments that developed before. Serious operational decisions, which might earlier have been left for the second level of management on the day shift, could now be made whenever the problems arose.

Ron believed that the presence of an overall shift supervisor would reorient his foremen and operators toward the overall functioning of the shift, rather than exclusive concern for their own individual process or function. The shift supervisor was to stress the final quality product and the team effort required to achieve it. Ron hoped, also, that the shift supervisor's presence would add an element of status and personal attention to shift operations. The shift supervisor could now assist in solving personal problems once handled by the day supervisor. Ron had always thought that second-level management was too remote, too impersonal, under the old system.

By assigning only one foreman to Section X and one to Section Y on each shift, Ron hoped to clarify the prior fuzzy lines of authority. The manufacturing specialists were to play the role of technical experts, handling equipment corrections and production records. The foreman was to be freer to focus his energies on the human inputs in his section. Ron selected his foremen by their ability to gain enthusiasm and cooperation from subordinates. He then assigned his remaining best technical experts to manufacturing specialist posts. Foremen and manufacturing specialists were to receive similar salaries. All had been foremen under the old structure.

The assignment of quality inspectors to the shift supervisors was seriously questioned by several manufacturing and quality control officials. Their logic questioned the objectivity of inspectors who were now working for the man responsible for output. Would not the production-oriented supervisor allow the shipment of inferior material in order to meet volume goals? The quality control function is almost always separated from production operations, serving as a judge of the suitability of output. Ron believed that an integrated, coordinated, face-to-face approach to quality control might prove superior to the old setup, particularly if shift supervision were sufficiently oriented toward quality.

Ron presented his proposals to all who would be directly affected. There were many objections and debates, as well as many compliments by foremen, quality inspectors, and operators. In the end, a concensus was attained that approved a trial for the new structure. Ron drove to work the next Monday morning having slept little the night before. Had he made the right decisions? Had he been too forceful in selling them?

Today the new structure would be implemented. That recurring tightness in his stomach told him it had better work.

The Fibers Department

Part C

EVALUATING THE NEW STRUCTURE

Several techniques were used to evaluate the effectiveness of the reorganization, including:

1. An opinion survey conducted among the 22 first line supervision; i.e., foremen and manufacturing specialists.
2. An interview with first and second level supervision by an unbiased third party.
3. Quantitative measurements in marketing, labor relations, production efficiency, and economics.

ATTITUDE SURVEY—FOREMEN

Immediately prior to the reorganization, a company-sponsored attitude survey was conducted to identify major problem areas within the plant. Twenty-two Fibers Department foremen participated in this survey. The survey provided before-reorganization data that were used to help to measure the effectiveness of the organizational change. Forty-four questions of the 89 in the study were selected because these questions were believed to be most relevant to the organizational change. These questions were divided into seven general categories, representing the foremen's evaluations of, and attitudes toward:

Category	Number of Questions
1. Management Practices	(18)
2. Confidence in Management	(2)
3. Pay and Benefits	(2)
4. Supervisory-Employee Relationships	(13)
5. Job Pressures	(3)
6. Communications	(5)
7. Opportunity for Growth	(1)

Pay-and-benefits questions, which are not closely related to the structural effectiveness, were included as a measure of communications effectiveness. Shift supervisors had engaged in a thorough discussion of corporate pay policies shortly after the reorganization. The opportunity-for-growth question was included to measure the group's feeling about including two college-trained individuals in the reorganized structure.

INTERVIEW

Because opinion surveys do not provide the participants with the opportunity for full expression of their opinions, a company behavioral service consultant was asked to interview the five supervisors and twelve randomly selected foremen and manufacturing specialists and form his opinion as to the effect of the new organization on morale, communication, and hence, human relations. The results of these interviews and the opinion of the company psychologist were presented to plant and department management.

QUANTITATIVE MEASURES

Certain quantitative measures that related to organizational effectiveness or ineffectiveness were available. These measures pertained to marketing, labor relations, and production efficiencies.

In the area of marketing information, the company's quality image was judged by a customer complaint scoring system. This complaint system consisted of four major categories with points assigned according to the level of severity. The categories, points, and explanation of the magnitude of the complaint severity were as follows:

Grade	Points	Magnitude of Quality Problem
1. Critical	100	Extensive quality deficiency causing immediate threat to major sales. Probable claim of $5,000 or more, return of 10,000 pounds of product.
2. Major	50	Severe deficiency of short duration resulting in loss of quality image. Claim of $2,000–$5,000, return of 5,000–10,000 pounds of product.
3. Important	10	Product problems representing hazards to processing by customer. Claim of $100–$2,000, return of 100–5,000 pounds of product.
4. Minor	1	Single occurrence of minor problem. Claim of less than $100, return of less than 100 pounds of product.

There were many different classifications of customer complaints, but the one that reflected most upon the personnel of the organization was one termed *workmanship*. Workmanship complaints were defined as "those complaints controllable by the operators or supervision, either because they caused the condition by doing something or not doing something, or failing to reject defective material." Another measure of market information was the sales volume of the product.

Labor relations, the quality of interactions between management and labor, was measured by the total number of grievances initiated during appropriate time intervals. Production efficiency and economic effects of organizations were determined through production and accounting control records.

All the foregoing measures were used to compare the old organization with the new. The period of time selected represented a twelve-month period prior to reorganization and a twelve-month period after reorganization, as well as a nine-month period commencing six months after the organizational change. The last interval was used to offset any early "resistance to the change" and to reflect the personal and interpersonal adaptations that might occur over time.

ATTITUDE SURVEY RESULTS

The results of the attitude survey are contained in Exhibit C-1. The results show a definite improvement in the attitudes of the foremen-manufacturing specialists group, with the possible exception of "Confidence in Management." Ron believed that this category was actually a

Exhibit C-1

RESULTS OF ATTITUDE STUDIES AMONG FOREMEN

	PERCENT FAVORABLE RESPONSES		
Category	*Before Reorg.*	*After Reorg.*	*% Change*
Management Practices	47.8	61.7	13.9
Confidence in Management	40.0	41.0	1.0
Pay and Benefits	55.0	61.0	6.0
Supervisory-Employee Relationships	51.9	77.6	25.7
Job Pressures	23.3	48.0	21.7
Communications	43.0	66.4	23.4
Opportunity for Growth	20.0	27.0	7.0
Average all Statements	45.7	63.4	17.7

measure of top plant level management, having little or no bearing on the specific organizational change. The question regarding growth opportunity, as previously mentioned, was included to measure the attitudes regarding the inclusion of two college-trained persons in the shift supervisor job. As expected, this group perceived this move as reducing their ability to receive additional promotions, although the improvement in favorable responses was gratifying.

The anticipated salutary effects of the organizational change seemed confirmed by these attitude changes. It had been anticipated that the addition of the shift supervisor would improve supervisory-employee relationships and would also improve communications. The restructuring of foremen's duties and the creation of the manufacturing specialist jobs did substantially reduce perceived job pressures, Ron believed.

INTERVIEW FINDINGS

The interviews were conducted by a company psychologist who specialized in behavioral sciences applications within the multi-plant company. The technique used was a semi-structured approach; i.e., certain key areas were probed in the interview but each interviewee had ample opportunity to elaborate on his own views or to bring out additional material. In addition to questioning members of the Fibers Department, the interviewer also discussed the organizational change with marketing personnel to determine their perception of the effect of change on client satisfaction.

There were two areas in which widespread agreement existed among the staff of the Fibers Department: (1) communications among the hourly, foremen/specialist and supervisory levels had improved noticeably, and (2) "team spirit" had risen.

Interviewees agreed that information was being received much more rapidly and with less distortion than prior to the reorganization. Face-to-face communications were much more frequent, both vertically and horizontally. The improvement in communication seemed to strengthen the perceived contribution of all employees toward company goals. Supervisors were now conducting informal meetings to give information regarding product quality, plant management changes, sales volumes, and so on, which had not previously been the practice. The result was widespread association of each employee with the final product and with company goals. A sense of common interests, plus improved communications, seemed to have promoted mutual trust and confidence among the various levels of workers and to have strengthened the relationships among the various groups.

The presence of a second management level on each shift facilitated decisive action regarding problems that were previously left until the daylight shift. Two comments from foremen are worthy of mentioning:

> My boss is right here, so I tell him what is going on. He can come and see for himself, and he can get action from the superintendent faster because he really understands my problems.
>
> My shift supervisor really takes the monkey off our backs because he knows right now if there is a problem and can make the decisions if we can't.

The interviewer found that many foremen and specialists had been initially unhappy regarding the changes made. However, most confided that after three to four months they realized the changes were for the better and that the reorganization was good. They now felt better about their jobs. Several foremen admitted that frank and open discussions with supervisors had helped to change their feeling about the change.

Thus interview data supported the survey information that morale was improved and that the organization change was working in the best interest of the company. Regarding the severe quality problems, several interviewees' remarks indicated the general beliefs regarding product quality:

> I feel like I really work for the customer, to see that he gets a real good product.
>
> The best thing to come out of the reorganization was better quality— a whole lot better quality, and better morale.

The discussions with marketing company representatives, those people who actually sold filters, indicated marked improvement in product quality. Marketing representatives were obviously encouraged by the reactions of customers.

> Customer unrest is at a low ebb and has been for more than six months. They are pleased with our product.
>
> We are building a quality image. Our quality is now probably a little better in some ways than the competition's.

The key to the improvement noted was the ability of the Fibers Department to detect poor quality before the materials were packaged. Although marketing personnel recognized the importance of the Quality Control Department, they commented:

> Quality control does a first class job but couldn't begin to if manufacturing wasn't functioning at a pretty high level.

Of course, you can track this improvement right back to the (hourly) operators, so something has changed pretty drastically.

From the information collected, the interviewer concluded that performance was much improved and that elements of job satisfaction heretofore missing were now motivating employees to higher performance levels.

OBJECTIVE MEASURES

Product quality complaint scoring for the fibers line reflected a dramatic improvement in product quality after reorganization, as indicated in Exhibit C-2.

Exhibit C-2

QUALITY COMPLAINTS TO FIBERS DEPARTMENT

Complaint Category	Points	12 Mos. Prior to Reorganization	12 Mos. After Reorganization	Latest 9 Mos.
Critical	100	22	6	0
Major	60	8	4	2
Important	10	23	23	9
Minor	1	73	81	54
Total Complaints		126	114	65
Total Complaint Score		2903	1111	244
Average Points/Complaints		23.0	9.7	3.8
Workmanship Complaints		14	11	2

It is also noteworthy that a significant increase in sales volume occurred during the latest twelve month period. Ron believed that these sales increases could be directly attributed to improved product quality, image, and performance.

Effects of the change on labor relations were difficult to pin down because of changes in union representation. Ron decided to use three periods for his analysis: the twelve-month period prior to reorganization when the hourly employees were represented by ABC Union, the eight-month period after reorganization when union representation was ABC Union, and the latest eight-month period with XYZ union representation. Data from the personnel department indicated that a sharp drop in the number of grievances had occurred since the reorganization (Exhibit C-3).

Exhibit C-3

NUMBER OF GRIEVANCES INITIATED IN FIBERS DEPARTMENT

1. Twelve months prior to reorganization (ABC Union)	27
2. Eight months after reorganization (ABC Union)	6
3. Latest eight months under XYZ Union	9

Since reorganization (16 months earlier) only 15 grievances had been filed by the same 250 hourly employees in the Fibers Department, compared with 27 for the twelve-month period prior to reorganization. Since reorganization four major reductions in operating personnel had occurred in the department. These four reductions were responsible for 5 of the 15 grievances received. In the twelve-month period prior to reorganization no labor reduction projects were initiated. The sharp reduction in grievances was interpreted by Ron Collins as indicating a definite improvement in the relationships between management and labor since the organizational change.

Although product quality actually shipped had definitely improved, there was no increase in the volume of defective material rejected in process. Furthermore, labor expenses were within 0.1 percent of budget for the period. With a strong sense of satisfaction, Ron noted that these improvements in operations had been achieved with no increase in department personnel. A position that had been eliminated on each shift was now filled by the supervisor, thereby maintaining the same headcount. The addition of the quality technicians in the manufacturing organization did not constitute a headcount increase because transfer of these men from another department reduced one headcount while increasing another.

CONTROL: THE ASSURANCE OF PROGRESS

PART FIVE

the role of staff

20

*The superior man, when he sees what
is good, moves toward it;
and when he sees his errors, he
turns from them.*

THE BOOK OF CHANGES
(China, c. 1200 B.C.)

All the functions of management involve decision making and action for the future. Under ideal conditions, the planning, organizing, and motivating functions, once completed, would guarantee the efficient and effective achievement of objectives. However, in real life, there are discrepancies between plans and results. Because planning focuses on the future, decisions are frequently made by the manager under conditions of uncertainty. Consequently, some decisions and actions may seem inappropriate later, when more is known about the external environment surrounding the planned system. In response to newly acquired information or an ever-changing environment, the manager may modify his objectives, restructure the organization, hire or reassign personnel, or employ different leadership methods. For example, a major corporation once established an industrial facility to manufacture stereo tape cartridges. Plans were based on a forecast that in the near future approximately 30 to 40 percent of automobiles built in this country would be equipped with tape players. Later, when the actual demand proved to be significantly less than had been predicted, the size of the manufacturing work force was reduced and equipment acquisition was curtailed. At the same time, some of the advertising efforts were shifted to create a demand for tape players in the home. Thus the uncertainty of customer

421

demand at one point in time *later* caused the need for a *new* management cycle of planning, staffing, and directing.

Results may also deviate from planned accomplishments because of factors within the business system, either due to faulty action by management or improper performance by some component of the system. Even with adequate knowledge, the manager may not develop the necessary objectives and plans or organize and staff his area of operations properly. Or, even if plans and directives are not amiss, subordinates may make or cause errors or fail to carry out activities according to plans. Consequently, machines may not be adjusted properly, materials may arrive late, blueprints may be misplaced, production orders may be misread, and the foreman may take five coffee breaks a day instead of two. It is these conditions, caused by internal factors within the system, that make the *control* function so important.

Because we do not live under utopian conditions, we must employ managerial control in all business systems and at all organizational levels to keep the actual results from each venture in line with planned achievements. The control function of management must address itself to the following questions:

1. How well is the business system achieving the objectives and plans developed by management?
2. When is corrective action necessary and what specific action is needed?

Thus control is the managerial function of measuring and, if necessary, correcting the performance of all systems and subsystems in a business venture so that objectives and activities are accomplished as planned.

The Basic Control Mechanism

The following sequence of activities is usually found in the control function or control system:

1. *Determine performance measures* that will ascertain the degree of success of personnel, projects, operations, or systems of interest.
2. *Set standard levels of performance* for each performance measure selected.
3. *Measure actual performance* of individuals or systems as they attempt to achieve planned results.

4. *Compare standard and actual performance and report the results* of the comparison to those individuals and managers who can take corrective action.

5. *Take corrective action,* when necessary, to diminish any discrepancy between planned and actual activities or results.

Regardless of what is being controlled, these activities are always involved in the control system. The control system, together with the business system being controlled, then forms a *feedback model.*

THE FEEDBACK MODEL

Many so-called "control" systems measure actual performance and compare it against desired standard levels quite well, but proceed no further. However, the control function does *not* terminate with the report of a difference between actual and planned results. This comparison is extremely important, but is a waste of time and effort unless the cause of any discrepancy is determined and corrective action taken if necessary. Consequently, the heart of any major control system is the feedback portion, where information is reported, the sources of undesired performance found, and corrections made. As we will see later, substandard performance may either be present today or occurring in the future.

To understand the feedback control model, it is helpful to mention the concept of *open-loop* and *closed-loop* systems. An open-loop system is one that either needs no further control or cannot be further controlled once it is activated. The system is guided by a predetermined set of fixed instructions or laws that are *not* affected by any comparison between actual and planned conditions. Thus, "the die is cast" once the system is activated and will run its course regardless of what is happening (Figure 20-1A). For example, if a motorist falls asleep and his vehicle leaves the road, the man-machine system may unfortunately become an open-loop system. The actual condition (heading for the ditch) is not sensed and compared to a standard (staying on the road). Consequently, the result of such a comparison is not fed back to the controller (the driver) to correct the situation. Sometimes actual performance (output) of an open-loop system is compared with a standard, but the feedback information cannot be used for further control (Figure 20-1B). This would be the case if the motorist in our example woke up in time to recognize the situation, but too late to change the course of events. In this situation, the feedback information would probably do more harm than good. On the other hand, if the motorist were lucky, the change in terrain would startle

Figure 20-1

Open-loop systems.

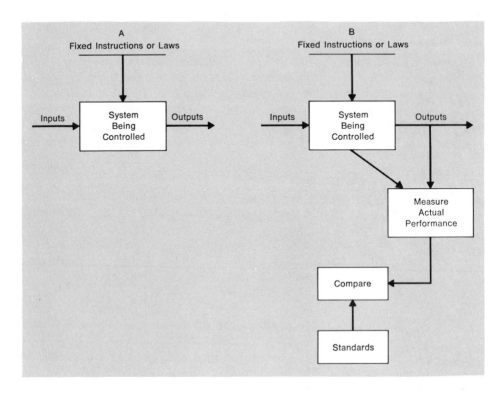

him out of his dreams in time to return the vehicle to the road, thus forming a closed-loop system.

A closed-loop system provides for both the comparison of actual conditions to standards *and* corrective action when deemed necessary. Attached to the system being controlled is the control system, which includes the feedback loop, denoted by the heavier arrows in Figure 20-2. This system is the previously described mechanism used to control the majority of business systems.

From our discussion so far, one could assume the controlled system to be of a physical or mechanical nature. This assumption may be true if the system being controlled is a machine or an automated production process. However, if our view of these systems is expanded to include the plans for the mechanical systems—the designs, operating schedules, and maintenance procedures—then the human component becomes an im-

Figure 20-2
Closed-loop systems.

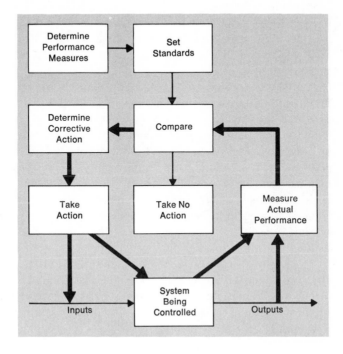

portant part of the system being controlled. Also, as the system becomes larger and more complex, the human element becomes more and more involved in the control system in order to handle the increasing number of factors influencing performance. As a result, requirements for closed-loop or feedback control systems increase.

Confusion often results when one attempts to classify a system in the business world as either an open-loop or a closed-loop system. In its *pure* form, open-loop control provides no completed feedback mechanism or corrective action and closed-loop control implies *continuous* monitoring and correction. Systems with continuous feedback information and correction are sometimes found in actual practice. Examples include highly automated machines and processes, as well as other self-adaptive mechanisms. However, in most business and industrial situations, the measurement of actual performance and corrective action does *not* take place continuously. Also, it is probably safe to say that in a business venture a system may have an open-loop status only for a given period of time. For example, an open-loop lighting system in an industrial parking lot may be programmed so the lights come on at 7:30 P.M. and go off at 5:30 A.M. every day during the summer months. However, as winter approaches, the system may be corrected in response to the shorter number of daylight hours per day. In addition, the lighting system may be turned off on weekends and holidays when the plant is not operating. Thus the system loses its open-loop classification during the time when these modifications are made. Another example would be a manufacturing process governed by a set of fixed controls, where the output of the process is only checked at the end of every week. At the time of inspection, the controls may or may not be adjusted. In this situation, the system during the week is acting as an open-loop system, but when viewed over a longer time span, it occasionally has the characteristics of a closed-loop system. Consequently, it seems reasonable to say that all systems *eventually* have a feedback loop, even though a system may appear to be controlled by an open-loop process. Therefore, rather than attempting to classify systems either as open-loop or closed-loop, it would be less confusing to differentiate control systems on the basis of the occurrence of actual performance measurements and corrective actions.

SYSTEMS TO BE CONTROLLED

The word "system" has been used frequently in the preceding discussion without definition. The word is not new; it is used both in everyday language and by specialists,[1] and perhaps it is too often used without definition. If one attempts to establish an operational definition of "system" by observing how the word is currently employed, one finds the task difficult and frustrating. Warren E. Alberts, Vice-President of Management Services at United Airlines, has stated: "As you can probably guess, a system can be anything you want it to be." [2] For our purposes, a system can be considered to be an assemblage of components or constituent parts with an interactive effect. Systems may include hardware, as does a production line, or they may be more procedural in nature, as

---

[1] Howard L. Tims and Michael F. Pohlen, *The Production Function in Business: Decision Systems for Production and Operations Management* (3d ed.) (Homewood, Ill.: Richard D. Irwin, Inc., 1970), p. 99.

[2] *Report of System Simulation Symposium* (New York: American Institute of Industrial Engineers, May, 1957), p. 3.

is an accounting process. In any case, the notion of a system includes input variables, an operating environment, and output results—the purpose of the system. With this in mind, a discussion of each step in the control function is in order.

Performance Measures and Standards

The functions of management discussed earlier—planning, organizing, and directing—always result in systems that must be controlled. The manager must find out whether or not the plans he has developed, the organization he has structured, and the directives and guidance he has given are satisfactorily achieving the objectives of the business venture. Also, he needs to know if his plans and directives are being followed and if the personnel he has hired and placed in various jobs are performing as expected. To obtain these facts, he requires feedback information about actual performance. This information must be compared to some set of guidelines before the manager can determine *when* and *where* to take corrective action, as well as *what* correction is needed. These important guidelines are the performance measures and their corresponding standards.

Performance measures are information about the system variables that the manager chooses to keep track of and control. For example, sales volume and worker output are system variables that can be measured in terms of the performance indices of *dollars* and *parts per hour*, respectively. If the variables and the corresponding performance measures or indices can be controlled satisfactorily, the manager assumes that the entire system will function properly. Even though this assumption is a very practical one, it sometimes fails the manager, as we will see later. Once the variables and the performance measures are selected, then the manager is still faced with the problem of setting standards. These standards are the levels of achievement that management desire of each performance measure. Using a highly repetitive industrial task as an example, productivity and workmanship may be selected as variables to control. Once these have been identified as characteristics of good performance, the performance measures of units per hour and percent of rejects may be used, with standards set at 200 parts per hour and a maximum of five percent rejected parts.

Theoretically, one could argue that the selection of performance measures and standards is really not a part of the control function, because the managerial function of planning is always a prerequisite for control. Thus setting objectives and planning should make the first two steps of the control process unnecessary. But in practice this is rarely true. As adequately stated by one group of authors, the reason for determination of performance measures and standards in the control function is:

> The needs of workable control almost always call for refining and clarifying objectives and duties. Without fail, though, we should start with the plans that have already been developed. Then the process of developing [performance measures and] standards from these plans for purposes of control is really a matter of refinement.[3]

MEASURES

As we have mentioned before, the fundamental purpose of control is to make sure that the objectives and corresponding plans of a system are accomplished properly. The system under the direction of a manager consists of many subsystems, and the system and subsystems have multiple objectives. Each objective is usually influenced by a wealth of variables within the system and subsystems. Consequently, multiple measures of performance are required for effective control. For example, when examining the performance of a plant manager, the vice-president may want to keep track of the plant operating costs on a monthly or even on a weekly basis. In addition, the plant manager is usually evaluated on the basis of quantity and quality of output, as well as his ability to meet production deadlines. The utilization of capital investments and other resources, such as machinery, plant facilities, and the human work force, are variables that may also be investigated. Other, more subjective performance measures may cover such variables as the plant's reputation, community-plant relations, and employee morale. Additional information may be desired in order to pinpoint more precisely any performance inadequacies that may be found. Further, the vice-president may use measures for other variables that are outside the plant manager's control, but that may be influencing the plant's performance. For example, adverse economic conditions, increased competition from other local industries for skilled workers and managers, and delays in deliveries of raw materials are just a sample of many causes possibly contributing to negative trends in the plant's and the plant manager's performance. It is also important to note here that the vice-president may use several different performance

---

[3] William H. Newman, Charles E. Summer, and E. Kirby Warren, *The Process of Management: Concepts, Behavior, and Practice* (2d ed.) (Englewood Cliffs, N.J.: Prentice-Hall, Inc., 1967), p. 679.

measures to control a single system variable. The plant's financial variable may be measured in terms of total variable costs, total fixed costs, costs per unit, total profit, or profit per unit, for example. On the other hand, several system variables may be involved in influencing a single performance measure. If dollar profit is used as a measure, the list of variables is probably endless.

In every organizational structure, a hierarchy of systems exists. In an industrial plant organization, the plant manager has authority over the entire plant system, the assistant plant manager has a smaller area of authority, the production foreman has an even smaller area, and so on. Independent performance measures must be developed for *each* of these areas of authority, because measures are most effective when they are related to the performance of a specific individual or a specific system. Consequently, when actual performance is later compared with the standard in terms of various performance measures, both the man himself and his supervisors will know if he and the system he has authority over should be praised or blamed. Koontz and O'Donnell expressed this idea as the principle of organizational suitability when they stated that:

> The more controls are designed to reflect the place in the organization structure where responsibility for action lies, the more they will facilitate correction of deviation of events from plans.[4]

Thus fitting performance measures in a control system to the organizational design will aid in pinpointing *where* corrective action is needed, as well as frequently helping to determine *what* action may be required. Employing the principle of organizational suitability is not always easy to do. Often no one individual or organizational group is solely accountable for a particular performance measure. A classic example is the inventory policy of a business, where the performance measure may be the quantity of, or dollar investment in, inventory.

> The production department is interested in long uninterrupted production runs, because such runs reduce setup costs and hence minimize manufacturing costs, but such long runs may result in large inventories of in-process and finished goods in relatively few product lines. Marketing wants to give immediate delivery over a wide variety of products. Hence it wants a more diverse but still large inventory. It would also like a flexible productive department that can fill small special orders on short notice. Finance wants to minimize inventory because it wants to minimize capital investments that tie up assets for indeterminate periods. Personnel

[4] Harold Koontz and Cyril O'Donnell, *Principles of Management* (4th ed.) (New York: McGraw-Hill Book Co., Inc., 1968), p. 733.

wants to stabilize labor and this can only be accomplished when goods are produced for inventory during slack periods, etc.[5]

In some companies, one person has the task of meshing these different viewpoints and setting inventory levels. Usually, however, the task is divided. The production manager schedules production, the purchasing manager makes decisions that determine raw-material inventory levels, the marketing manager forecasts sales, and decisions of other managers have an influence on the total quantity and mix of inventory. In such situations, the principle of organizational suitability can be followed by developing performance measures for each step that is performed by different individuals or organizational units. Then management can determine where corrective action is needed if the inventory system is in trouble.

In the preceding discussion, we have often implied that a strong correspondence exists between the system variables to be controlled and the performance measures selected by the manager. Usually this is the case, but not always. If a manager is careless, the correspondence may be weak or nonexistent. Consequently, a great deal of thought must be devoted to developing strong performance measures that are responsive to significant changes in the variables being controlled. Unfortunately, in some instances, very precise performance data are collected and evaluated, but the data are independent of the system variables being controlled and perhaps are even being used to monitor the wrong variables. In addition, control systems often contain performance measures pertaining to variables, but the variables do not affect system output. In either case, this is likely to lead to wrong corrective action being taken or to corrective action that is not necessary. Thus the manager must ask himself frequently, "Does this performance measure reflect what I want to know about the system, subsystem, or particular variable?" If it does not, then the performance measure should not be used, even though it is easy to measure and/or some other manager or company is commonly using it. Performance measures must fit the situation at hand, rather than the dictates of convenience or tradition.

Although emphasizing the need for strong performance measures, we do not suggest that it is generally possible for a measure of performance to *perfectly* reflect the variable or variables being controlled. For example, a staff manager who is responsible for training employees wants to control the "learning" variable. Unfortunately, no performance measure

---

[5] C. West Churchman, Russell L. Ackoff, and E. Leonard Arnoff, *Introduction to Operations Research* (New York: John Wiley & Sons, Inc., 1957), p. 4.

known to man can perfectly indicate the learning phenomenon. At best, the training supervisor can use measures such as the increase in quantity of output (parts per hour) or the improvement in quality (percent of rejects or percent accepted). But the employee may have learned more (or less) than these performance measures indicate. The same condition is true in the classroom, where test scores are used to evaluate how much the student has "learned." The student who has received a score of 62 percent may inform the professor that he has really learned the subject matter better than his test has indicated and he may be right! However, even though the correspondence between the variable and performance measure is never perfect, this fact should not prevent a manager from seeking and using the *best practical* measure available. Hesitation at this point would certainly prevent effective control.

If a manager were able to control all system variables, the overall system would be guaranteed to succeed in adhering to planned objectives. However, to attempt to control *all* system variables would be burdensome and extremely costly. In order to overcome the problem of excessive control costs, while at the same time providing for adequate control, managers must direct their attention to *key* system variables. Only *key* performance measures are monitored in the control process in order to strike a balance between absolute control and a reasonable cost for controlling the system or individual subordinates. The degree of control probably does not suffer much, if at all, when minor performance measures are dropped from the control system. Many variables contribute very little to the overall performance of a particular system and would not convince anyone to take corrective action even if they were evaluated. Whether a variable is considered a key variable or not, of course, will depend on the system and the particular situation under consideration. If emphasis shifts from one variable to another, or if attention is also directed to a new variable, the set of *key* performance measures will also change.

One additional aspect of performance measures should be mentioned before moving on to the next step in the control process. First of all, when we think of the control function, we normally picture a supervisor looking at the *final* results of his previous decisions. This is necessary to avoid the recurrence of mistakes—of making the same error a second time and a third. But control can, and often must, occur before the final results are in. Performance measures can be developed to direct management's attention to *potential* problem areas so that the manager, by taking early corrective action, can prevent the occurrence of serious deviations from plans. For example, a statistical control chart (which will be discussed in the next chapter) may be used to detect a shift in some characteristic of product quality. If the trend can be detected in time and if corrective action is taken, the permissible tolerances for that characteristic may not be exceeded and the product may not have to be discarded or reworked.

STANDARDS

Having identified the characteristics of good performance and having developed performance measures, the manager must determine the level of achievement or standard in each measure that is a reasonable expectation for good performance. This is similar to the frustrating game of golf, where par has been set for each hole on the course.

To set standards, management has used various techniques, some of which are far more successful in the control process than others. Consequently, it will be advantageous to mention the major ones. *Historical* standards are those based on past performance figures of a particular system. If the factors influencing the performance of the key system variables are stable, then the manager may use past performance data as standards for the future, or he may feel that his organization can better the past by a certain amount. For example, the total time spent on modifying design drawing in an engineering group has stabilized over the past two years at about 10 percent of total man-hours. The engineering manager may use the 10 percent value for a standard next year or he may try to improve performance by setting an 8 percent goal. Of course, these standards would be meaningless if the department were larger or smaller next year than during the last two years, since the total man-hours would be changing. Historical standards can be set in nonstable situations, however, once adjustments have been made to dynamic variables. In our example then, the 10 percent standard could be adjusted to 5 percent if the engineering work force for next year is to be doubled. If the type of engineering-design work is expected to be somewhat different next year, another modification to the standard may be needed.

Another technique, similar to the use of historical standards, is to examine the past performance of similar and compatible systems. Management in a steel fabrication plant, for example, may examine past data from other plants in the same company or from other firms in the industry. These *comparative* standards also may be used directly or modified to fit the system and the purposes of the management involved.

Even when data on stable or predictable variables have been used to set historically based standards or comparative standards, caution must still be taken. For one thing, the good manager would not want to use his own or someone else's poor performance as a future standard for his own organization. However, many managers have and will continue to fall into the trap of setting standards on the basis of the inadequate performance of the past. Since performance measures and standards are really extensions or refinements of managerial plans, what we have just said about standards also applies to the more general ends and means formulated by the manager.

Rather than basing future plans and resulting standards on present and past performance, it may be to the advantage of the manager to use the "ideals" concept.[6] Basically, this concept advocates that a manager should develop ideal plans and standards, even if they are impossible to attain. Then, because of technological and real-life restrictions, the manager backs away from the ideal to arrive at a recommended system. Various techniques are employed to minimize the difference between the ideal and recommended systems. This concept introduces the idea of looking forward, rather than looking backward, in developing plans and standards. Consequently, the manager should ask himself, "Where should we be in the future in terms of performance?" or "What are we really capable of doing?" instead of relying strictly on past events.

Also, even if past performance levels have been adequate, they still may lead to suboptimum decisions regarding performance standards. There is often a tendency for individuals to set future standards that are not too dissimilar to past performance, even though new plans for the future have been formulated. This tendency prohibits the manager from tapping the maximum capability of his organization. Thus, the ideals concept can provide a new managerial viewpoint that will result in very progressive standards and outstanding accomplishments in the future.

One of the real-life restrictions that can prevent standards from being as ideal as they could be is the aspiration level of the individual or system being controlled. Some individuals have higher personal goals than others. These "aspiration levels"[7] are conditioned to a large extent by the individual's past levels of performance. If standards are set that are below a person's aspiration level, he will not be challenged or motivated to improve his future performance. On the other hand, if the standards seem too difficult to achieve, the individual may become discouraged and give up trying.

In a manufacturing plant of a major electronics firm, one department produced an experimental product in a pilot-plant operation for one year. At the end of this period, marketing felt the product had a great potential and a new manufacturing facility was built. During the pilot-plant year,

---

[6] Gerald Nadler, *Work Systems Design: The Ideals Concept* (Homewood, Ill.: Richard D. Irwin, Inc., 1967), Chapter 3.

[7] Forrest W. Fryer, *An Evaluation of Level of Aspiration as a Training Procedure* (Englewood Cliffs, N.J.: Prentice-Hall, Inc., 1964) provides a survey of aspiration level research, especially as applied to the training function.

very loose time standards had been set for each task. Also, only 5 percent of the work force had been informed of the production standards and very little effort was made to correct substandard performance. However, for the new manufacturing facility, accurate time standards had been developed. Unfortunately, the actual performance level in the pilot plant had been less than 50 percent of the productivity levels required by the new standards. Because the poor performance level of the past had become the expected standard or aspiration level in the minds of the employees, they considered the new standards ridiculous. Performance as usual continued in spite of the new standards and the efforts of management. Consequently, revised standards that were closer to the aspiration level of the present organization had to be implemented.

The Feedback Control System

Once adequate performance measures and standards have been established, it is necessary to design a feedback control system in which the following steps can be carried out on a routine basis during the life of the system being controlled:

1. Measure actual performance.
2. Compare actual and standard performance.
3. Take corrective action when necessary.

Control will be of little value unless there is an element of action—of doing something positive and corrective. It is the feedback system that permits this corrective activity. The feedback system and corrective function must be meshed into the everyday affairs of the organization.

MEASURING PERFORMANCE

The actual data corresponding to performance measures will tell the manager different things about the system. Some of the data will reflect the performance of individual components of the system; others will represent larger amounts of the system's overall performance. However, the data measured through a *formal* structure of performance measures can only begin to inform us about all of the important aspects relating to how a system is performing. For example, two supervisors may both have met their production-schedule deadline satisfactorily. But

435

if their manager knew that one of the departments had been besieged with
illness, poor quality of raw materials, and an influx of inexperienced personnel, then he would rate the supervisor of that department higher than
the other supervisor. Thus the additional information was critical, even
though it probably was not derived from *formal* control structure.

In most systems, there are some work activities on which practical
standards are difficult to develop and overall performance is hard to
measure accurately. Activities such as the reworking of production parts,
maintenance trouble-shooting, development of engineering designs, and
other nonroutine tasks fall into this category. Consequently, when attempting to measure the performance of such activities, the manager
usually can not rely exclusively on a specific reporting system. Instead,
he may use a combination of qualitative information, personal observations and discussions, and the quantitative data that is to be made available, in order to subjectively appraise the overall performance of the
system. For example, a manager may want to check the performance of
a department charged with the responsibility for pinpointing and correcting mechanical problems in manufacturing equipment. The manager
may note that no complaints have been heard about the department's
performance. Also, the employees of this maintenance group appear to
be good workers, based on the positive comments from the manufacturing
supervisors. In addition, machine down-time figures have recently reached
an all-time low. Based on these different sources and types of information,
the manager should be able to evaluate the department's performance
better than if he only compared machine-down-time data to a downtime
standard whose accuracy was highly questionable. An accurate downtime
standard, in terms of the maximum time a machine should be nonpro-
ductive before it is completely repaired and functioning again, would
depend on numerous factors, such as the type of machine, the source or
sources of trouble, the availability of replacement parts, and the number
of other machines needing repair. No practical standard could be developed to handle all these factors in the many unique situations that
might occur. Even if it were possible to set such a flexible standard, the
excessive down-time may also be the fault of the preventive maintenance
group and/or of the manufacturing personnel, as well as of the department having the responsibility for making the nonpreventive repairs.
Therefore, when standards are hard to develop and overall performance
data is not easy to measure, the manager must employ ingenuity in seeking
bits of informance from various sources before making a subjective measurement of performance.

We have just looked at a situation where exact standards and performance measurements were hard to come by because of the numerous

qualitative factors involved. The same condition could also occur because of the *vague* performance measures that must be developed for some activities. For example, evaluation of a plant manager or a personnel manager may hinge on the attitude of labor unions and the enthusiasm and loyalty of subordinates, as well as other measures. Standards on such performance measures could only be very vague. What *specific* standard could be set for loyalty of subordinates? What piece of information could be collected that measures the actual loyalty in the present organization? Thus as a person moves upward away from the lower levels of a system or organization, the task of measuring his actual performance becomes more complex. More and more *direct* means of measurement, such as observations of a system and discussions with individuals being measured, must be used, rather than relying only on *indirect* measurements found in control reports. For example, measurements of *procedures* used by individuals and systems to achieve results may be more beneficial to the manager than vague measurements of *results*. Thus a manufacturing supervisor may ask, "Do my foremen spend time in communicating with their people?" instead of seeking ways to measure the *degree* of communication skills of each foremen or the employees' knowledge of current conditions within the plant. In addition, information from unique sources in the organization may be gathered and combined in order to measure the performance of complex systems or the managers who direct them, instead of utilizing routine reports.

When discussing performance measures, we mentioned the fact that only *key* measures should be monitored. It is not enough, however, merely to determine which measures are key ones. The manager must then decide how frequently the actual measurements should be made. The cost of not knowing the condition of a system and of not taking corrective action, of course, will be a major factor in determining the measurement frequency. For example, the severity of being out of control for even a short period of time is extremely great in many chemical processes and they are monitored continuously. In most cases in the industrial and business world, however, measurement of performance occurs much less frequently. Another factor that may or may not influence the specified time between individual measurements is the frequency of corrective action permitted. If adjustments to a manufacturing process can only be made once every two weeks, it may not be useful to measure the performance of the process continuously or every hour. Also, the frequency of measurements is usually influenced by past successes or failures. If a system has caused problems in the past due to its sporadic behavior, more frequent observations may be desired in the future. On the other hand, infrequent measurements may be adequate on systems that rarely deviate from plans. However, without this knowledge of past performance, the important factor of uncertainty often emerges. For example, when an employee is new in a job, his boss is usually uncertain about his ability and will want to watch his work more closely than that of an experienced subordinate.

In addition to considering how often measurements of performance should be conducted, the manager must also investigate the life span of a system or a program, in order to determine critical points where performance should be measured. This "critical point" concept has been used briefly in previous discussions and a more thorough treatment is now warranted. First of all, measurements of *final* results are needed to evaluate previous plans so that past mistakes will not be repeated. A football coach makes such measurements when he looks at the final score and the films of last Saturday's game. These observations may help in future encounters, but unfortunately they will never correct past history. Thus the after-game measurements are critical only for future games. More critical points are found during the game, however, where the coach can use two types of control. He may *detect* substandard performance and make corrections before the game is completed or he may use various types of measurements to *predict* poor performance in the future if action is not taken now. The prediction and prevention of poor performance—"forward-looking" control—is certainly more effective than detection control. Consequently, these observations for predictions and the times at which they are made are more critical from the standpoint of control than those used to detect errors. In either type of control, it is also critical to make the measurements at early stages of the football game so that the corrective action has a chance to work. If a new quarterback is put into the game too late, he may not have enough time to move the ball down the field. Or he may not have enough time to undo the poor performance of the man he has replaced, especially if the score is 52 to 14.

The most critical point for performance measurements to take place, of course, occurs before the game. If one or more players lack various skills during the practice sessions, they probably won't be much better in Saturday's game. Corrective action in terms of training or changing the line-up of the first string often holds more promise than any action that could be taken during the football game. In our example, then, we have illustrated the fact that optimum or near-optimum control is possible if performance measurements are taken at critical points, where the most good can be made of the data. The same fact is true at all levels in the business world.

As stated before, developing performance measures and standards and gathering data are a waste of managerial time and effort if corrective action is never taken. Management can not live with an open-loop control system forever. Prior to the time when control action is warranted, however, some mechanism is usually needed to accumulate, store, process, and transmit standard values and performance data to managers. This mechanism is the control-information system. Some say that data is not "information" until it reaches the manager.[8] However, the term "information" means much more than this. According to the concepts of information theory, data only becomes information when there is a reduction in uncertainty, in other words, when the data tells the person receiving it something he did not already know.[9] For example, the statement that two times two equals four conveys no information to most of us. However, for those who have not studied elementary mathematics, the statement may be informative. And the statement that $2^7 = 128$ may reduce uncertainty for a large segment of the human population. Using this concept of information, one might say that the most effective information system is that which conveys only "information" to each manager. Each manager would then be freed from searching through data he already knows about and could direct his full attention to new items.

It is true that managers would like to develop information systems for themselves and their subordinates that would reduce uncertainty as much as possible. But in practice, an information system can not be designed to convey 100 percent information, as we have defined it, to each and every manager. What one person already knows about the business is always different from what another person knows. Thus, if control reports were to transmit only *new* data, a unique report would have to be designed for each manager. Our problem does not end there. What each manager already knows about the organization under his direction is never known exactly. Moreover, his knowledge changes continuously with time. Consequently, practical information systems will provide some new information and some data that is already known. Therefore, the value of any information system in reducing uncertainty will vary with respect to the person using it and the time when output is received.

Redundancy in an information system is not undesirable for control purposes, however. A manager may know, for example, that the productivity of his department has been 20 percent below standard for several

[8] Leonard J. Garrett and Milton Silver, *Production Management Analysis* (New York: Harcourt, Brace & World, Inc., 1966), p. 680.

[9] Paul M. Fitts and Michael I. Posner, *Human Performance* (Belmont, California: Brooks/Cole Publishing Company, 1967), p. 86.

months. The latest control report, which conveys the same identical data, *may* convey no information but does serve to increase the priority for taking corrective action. If the manager has attempted to solve the problem in the past, he may now know or suspect that his past efforts did not work and that new control actions are needed. In this case, the identical data would be information. In either case, the data has served a control purpose. Thus, the major function of a control-information system is to increase the chance of *identifying* and/or *correcting* the most important actual or potential problems that might arise, regardless of the system's "informational value."

"Any change in the nature of the problems . . . managers must face or in the methods they use to solve them, inevitably affects the requirements of an information system. The reverse is also true; any change in the information system influences the means by which managers solve their problems." [10] Thus the degree to which the control report affects the probability of recognizing and correcting problems depends on the many and varied components making up the information system. As we have previously noted, the performance measures and standards that are selected for the control report are very important, as are the factors governing the actual data that are fed into the report. Beyond the quality of these inputs, we must consider how the inputs are combined and presented to the manager and his subordinates. In addition, decisions must be made about who should receive what data, the accuracy and timing of the report, and the cost of data processing.

Often, *formal* data-collection techniques and reports are not needed to control small and simple systems. The manager may observe the functioning system directly and discuss performance matters with his subordinates. The condition of the simple system and the factors affecting its performance may be well known to everyone within that system. But as the organization grows and becomes more complex, the opportunity for direct observation diminishes rapidly. Even more critical is the fact that the number of necessary standards and the amount of performance data that must be handled become too great for any informal information system. This is also true as one goes up the hierarchy of system levels— common knowledge of the facts is no longer possible, because people become farther removed from the source of these facts. Consequently, *formal* control reports are needed to summarize and communicate the comparisons between standards and actual performance data.

The control information should always be sent to the person whose work or organization is being controlled, regardless of his position in the

---

[10] Garrett and Silver, *Production Management Analysis*, p. 680.

organization. He is the one who is most likely to do something about substandard performance. Even individuals who are merely carrying out specific instructions can and should take action to improve their own performance. In addition, the control-report information should go to the person's immediate supervisor. Usually, this information is received by the superior in summary form and at a later date. This gives the subordinate the opportunity to exert *self-control* over his area of responsibility and to have a feeling of participation. The employee, motivated and experienced by participation, becomes skilled in predicting and preventing potential problems, as well as in solving existing ones. In a majority of situations, self-control also frees the supervisor from the task of determining the corrective action needed. Control actions by the subordinate *may* also be more effective than those by managers who are farther removed from the problem at hand.

In addition to meeting the primary need for promoting corrective action or informing the man and his boss that "all is well," the control report may be routed to interested staff groups, who may use the information for special studies and reports. If the information is needed by other line managers in order to adjust the activities of their respective organizations, the control report may also be directed to them.

The control data must be pertinent to the possible control actions that the person receiving it may undertake. The idea here is to increase the probability of recognizing the more important problems that may arise now or in the future, and at the same time, not to overburden the individual with control data. One way of relieving the manager from an excessive amount of data, of course, would be to transmit only information, thus reducing his uncertainty. Then the manager would not be bothered with data he already knows about. As previously mentioned, this type of control feedback is not *completely* feasible for practical reasons. Even if it were practical, however, the information transmitted may not be pertinent to the area or system for which the manager has responsibility. If some of the data is unnecessary for controlling his operation, the supervisor's time is wasted in excessive search for the relevant. Also, the probability of overlooking relevant data will increase as the search task becomes more complex. Consequently, control reports must be as informative as possible, but more important, they should contain only pertinent data.

Before the report can be considered pertinent, it must include feedback data related to the variables over which the person has control, but the manager or his subordinates also need information concerning uncontrollable variables that directly or indirectly influence the system to be controlled. For example, if a foreman is notified of low productivity among his workers, he should probably delay any corrective action until he has checked the quality and rate of supply of raw materials, the amount of operator experience on the job, and other influential factors that may be beyond his control. If his organization is presently staffed with newly hired workers and production deadlines are critical, the manager may borrow temporary manpower or work his present staff overtime. If his employees' machines have received poor maintenance, he must exert pressure on the department at fault. Consequently, data on variables not under his control are important to save the manager from making inappropriate control decisions.

Having control reports tailored to the responsibilities and performance of each organizational unit at one system level also aids management at the next higher level. If higher management receives summary feedback data that is segregated by lower organizational groups, the departments responsible for poor performance and high costs can easily be pinpointed.

The format of the control feedback is also critical, because data presented in one manner may permit more rapid and more accurate decision making. Unfortunately, too many examples exist of control reports that are ignored because they are not readily understandable. Worse yet, some reports are misinterpreted and cause grave errors. To avoid these problems, the designer of control reports has the very difficult task of anticipating the various ways the recipients may input and process the data. This requires a substantial knowledge of the behavior and background of the different individuals receiving the report, as well the effects of various kinds of data formats on humans in general.

In addition to indicating where and when corrective action is needed, the control report may provide an insight into which corrective action is most appropriate. In the final analysis, however, the human must make the decision. Unfortunately, the person making control decisions may be overloaded with feedback material. Therefore, as a control system becomes more complex, there is a tendency to issue control reports less frequently. Another often-used solution to "overloading," called "management by exception," is to report only the exceptional cases, where performance levels are outside some predetermined limits. The major disadvantage of this method, however, is the fact that it is strong on detection but very weak on prevention. One can not follow performance trends that may indicate what problems will arise in the future unless corrective action is taken now.

Probably the best way to provide "forward-looking" control and at the same time reduce "overloading" is to use a two-stage feedback system. This idea has been discussed before, but is important enough to be repeated. In this reporting system, the manager frequently reviews the performance trends of a small number of generalized, but critical, performance measures. Only if potential problems are anticipated or if actual trouble is detected in the first stage does the manager need to review additional and more detailed data to determine the underlying factors influencing the general performance measures. Consequently, the lower levels of the performance-measure hierarchy are used only occasionally, when the second stage is employed.

The success of the feedback portion of control depends not only on the type of data used and its accuracy, but also on the *timing* of the feedback information. One aspect of feedback timing involves the frequency of measurements and the "critical points" in the productive system's life cycle where measurements are most important. The other aspect of feedback timing involves the time lag between the performance at the time of measurement and the time when the system is brought back into control. The various components making up this lag are the times needed for the following steps and functions:

1. Collecting and compiling the control data and sending it to the appropriate individual.
2. Determining if corrective action is necessary.
3. Determining where, what, and when corrective action can best be applied.
4. Implementing the control action.
5. Evaluating the response of the system to the control action.
6. Returning to step 3 if previous actions do not bring the system into control.

Obviously, management would like to reduce the duration of these time components as much as possible, as long as the benefits of doing so outweigh the cost. As we have seen, the frequency of data collection, the number of performance measures, and the control-report format can be manipulated somewhat to cut down the feedback lag time, notably in the on-going activities of steps 1 and 2 above. These variables also can eliminate some time spent on steps 3 and 6. In addition, the increasing use of automatic data-processing techniques have been beneficial. The physical portions of the controlled system in some cases may also be quickly monitored and corrected by automatic control mechanisms.

Unfortunately, much of the feedback function does not lend itself to mechanical or automatic procedures. A great deal of human effort and time may be needed to evaluate control information and to select the corrective action to be taken. Consequently, where promptness in control reports is critical, the accuracy of the data, the evaluation, and the control action may suffer. Then the system may remain out of control that much longer, and finally, additional time may be needed to find a better method of correction. As a result, management is usually forced into a trade-off between feedback speed and accuracy.

CORRECTIVE ACTION

Control reports only call attention to past, present, and, it is hoped, future deviations of performance from planned results or procedures. Management must then evaluate these symptoms to find the real problems causing them. That costs are out of line is not the real problem, but just a symptom of a problem. Of course, the control report can be designed to narrow the search for symptom causes, but the manager must complete that task. Then he must decide how to overcome the difficulties and transform his decisions into action.

If one searches for the causes of poor performance long enough, one will eventually find that the outcome of all plans, physical or procedural, is influenced by people. In order to reduce or eliminate poor results or procedures, one must change the *future* activities of the responsible individual or group of individuals. There are two basic ways of modifying future performance. Koontz and O'Donnell have termed these methods as "indirect control" and "direct control." [11]

Most of the tools and procedures that have been and are being used in the control process are indirect. Even though it is often successful, the indirect control method is sometimes costly or inaccurate or results in excessive feedback time. In this method, the underlying causes of poor performance symptoms are sought and eventually traced back to the person (or organization) responsible. Once responsibility is fixed, corrective action supposedly will follow. Several problems exist with this method, however. For one thing, poor performance may have resulted because previous decisions were made under conditions of uncertainty. Unfortunately, errors caused by unforeseen events can not be corrected. On the other hand, if human inadequacy or lack of motivation on the part of the responsible party was the problem, then corrective action may be taken. Individuals may be given further guidance or training, removed from their present jobs, or corrected in some other manner. The critical question of whether or not corrective action will or can be taken still remains, however, even after spending the time and effort to pinpoint causes and responsible individuals. In a particular manufacturing plant, for instance,

[11] Koontz and O'Donnell, *Principles of Management,* pp. 715–31.

each line supervisor was notified of the workers' performance levels every day, as well as each week and month. Even with this elaborate and expensive labor control system, a number of trained assembly operators were found to be working at very substandard levels for weeks and even months without any control action being taken. For many and often undetermined reasons, corrective action may be delayed or never implemented. Probably some managers lack the time or the desire to select and implement a course of action. Or the cost of investigating the symptoms may outweigh any benefits that could be derived.

In some cases, corrective action may not be possible, because the control report arrives too late or the decision to take action is delayed too long. Another problem arises when no one person or group within the organization is responsible for poor results. Factors outside the company may be directly responsible, such as the condition of the industry or of the general economy or actions taken by various government units. Consequently, it would be wasteful to search either internally or externally for causes of poor performance that are completely out of one's control.

It should be stated, then, that indirect control can be successful, but only for certain situations. We have just mentioned a few places where this control method is not very helpful, despite being time-consuming and costly. Unfortunately, one usually can not determine in advance where it will or will not be useful. One of the major complaints about indirect control is its negative approach. Present problems, and less frequently, potential problems must exist and be recognized before any control action can be planned and initiated. As we have seen before, planning and replanning certainly slow down the feedback response. If sufficient time is not permitted, then the control action may be dropped. To relieve these and other problems of indirect control, direct control is recommended.

The basic idea behind direct control is that if managers and their subordinates are qualified, well trained, and highly motivated from the time they begin a job, they will make fewer mistakes and the need for indirect control will diminish. This method is the ultimate limit of "foreward-looking" control. During periods of satisfactory system performance, managers are checked on their application of management principles and corrective action taken if needed. Nonsupervisory personnel are also evaluated on the basis of their work methods and procedures. The frequency of out-of-control system performance is significantly reduced because potential problems are prevented. When system problems do arise, however, advanced corrective action on procedures probably has already been initiated and has yielded some improvements. Thus direct control provides more time for making accurate corrections, since the feedback control mechanism is called into play prior to the time when the system might go out of control. Also, the time needed to bring the system back into control is greatly reduced.

By it nature, direct control only emphasizes performance measures over which the individual has complete control. Thus the advantages of self-control are present in this method. Much of the wasteful time spent in ferreting out causes of poor results by indirect control methods can be avoided. Managers can then be evaluated on the basis of their adherence to proven managerial principles or standards of planning, organizing, staffing, directing, and controlling.

SUMMARY

The control function is necessary to insure that actual results conform to planned results. In order to establish and maintain a control system, performance measures are necessary, standards of performance have to be established, actual performance has to be measured and compared to the standard that has been established, and finally, corrective action must be taken when necessary to reduce or eliminate any discrepancy between planned and actual results. The control system requires a feedback model, in which a measure of actual performance is "fed back" for comparison purposes. This may be done continuously or at discrete intervals. If, after comparison with the standard that has been established, corrective action is taken either on the input to the system or on the system itself, a *closed-loop* feedback control system may be said to exist. If no such corrective action is taken, an *open-loop* system exists. In this latter case, we do not actually have a control model.

The proper identification of performance measures and the correct establishment of performance standards is a necessary requirement of the control system. The performance measures should relate to the objectives of the organization. They should also be related to the system variables that are under the control of the manager. The development of standards will depend on the definition of good performance or achievement. *Historical* information and/or *comparative* information may be of assistance in establishing these standards. Alternatively, and perhaps ideally, the manager should assess the capability of the department or firm and establish standards that are near the capacity of the organization.

After the measures and standards have been established, the feedback control system requires the measurement of actual performance, the comparison to the standard of performance, and the taking of corrective action when necessary. The measurements should be made on the significant system variables and they should be accurate. The frequency of measurement will be influenced by both the likelihood of the system going out of control and the significance or cost of the out-of-control condition. The control reports should be readily understandable and should facilitate the taking of corrective action when necessary.

In the next chapter the control system will be described in terms of its life cycle. Some general control systems will be introduced and some specific control systems will be described.

QUESTIONS

1. Define "control."

2. List the steps or events that are necessary to establish a control function.

3. What is an open-loop system? A closed-loop system?

4. Give an example of a continuous closed-loop system. An intermittent closed-loop system.

5. Why are multiple measures of performance likely to be needed to effect control?

6. In regard to performance measures, what is the "principle of organizational suitability"?

7. Why do we usually focus on *key* rather than *all* performance measures?

8. How might one set standards of performance?

9. Why is qualitative as well as quantitative information needed to measure performance?

10. How might we measure the information content in a report?

11. What factors influence the time needed to maintain system control?

12. What is "indirect control"? "Direct control"?

13. What is involved in the last step in the control function—taking corrective action?

some control systems

Anyone can hold the helm when the sea is calm.

PUBLILIUS SYRUS

In the previous chapter, the various steps involved in the control function were discussed. In this chapter, we will direct our attention to the application of controls to a system's life cycle. Then some commonly used and specific control techniques will be presented.

Life-Cycle Controls

In the study of systems, we quickly find that all systems have certain general characteristics. For example, each system must have input variables and output results (or purpose), as well as a means for transforming inputs into desired output. Systems differ from each other on the basis of output, degree of mechanical or procedural nature, size, and complexity. In addition, each system, regardless of other properties, has a *life cycle*. The cycle begins when the need for a system arises and ends when the system is modified, replaced, or eliminated completely. During its life cycle, a system is designed, installed, and utilized in hopes of accomplishing an intended purpose. Whether or not the necessary steps in the life cycle are conducted, and how well they are performed, will depend on the

447

quality of the managerial functions of planning, organizing, directing, and controlling.

The time span of a system's life cycle may be short, intermediate, or long, depending on the need for the particular system. The need for a particular system arises when other systems require its output to serve as one of their inputs. For example, a particular production system can only exist as long as the marketing system and the customers have a need for the items it produces.

The life cycle of a system is really a sequence of three distinct stages —development, implementation, and operation. These stages have inputs and outputs and are subsystems of the main system (see Figure 21-1). The inputs to each stage are either external (i.e., outputs from other systems), outputs from preceding stages, or both. This is illustrated in Figure 21-1, as is the flow pattern of outputs. The sum of the individual time spans of the various stages equals the duration of the entire life cycle $(t_d + t_i + t_o = T)$, which depends on how long there is a need for the

Figure 21-1

Stages of a system's life cycle.

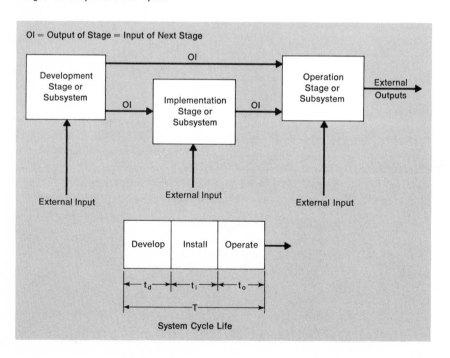

system. Because the overall time, T, is to some degree fixed, management usually attempts to lengthen the operational time, t_o, by reducing the time spans of the two preceding stages as much as possible. It is for this reason that deadlines exist. How much time is allocated to each stage hinges on a number of factors. The time allocation in a manufacturing system, for example, will depend on the potential unit volume, expected profitability, available capital, complexity of the production process, the use of the outgoing product, and so on. If a low-volume, relatively inexpensive product is to be made, management will probably not waste time in developing and installing an assembly-line process, but will use an already existing job shop. On the other hand, if a highly specialized item is to be made for the missile industry, the time for development may be quite long, regardless of the anticipated sales volume.

Another point that could be made about these stages or subsystems is that each one consists in turn of a number of smaller systems, with respective time spans and interacting inputs and outputs. The managerial control function is involved in each stage of the overall system's life cycle. Controls are needed to guide the various systems in every stage so that deadlines are met and the major system is developed, installed, and used according to plans. The number and types of control systems employed in each stage will depend on the complexity, cost, and time span of the system stages. Some control techniques (general controls) are applicable in all three stages; more specialized or specific controls are suited to only one or two parts of the life cycle. Some of these general and specific control techniques will be discussed later in the chapter, after we review the work involved in each stage of a system's life cycle. This review will help us determine what controls are necessary for each stage.

The work content involved in the various stages of a system's life cycle differs from one system to another. In the life cycle of a particular aircraft system, for example, the development stage includes the activities from general planning to flight testing. The production of the aircraft is the implementation stage and the functional life of the aircraft becomes the operation stage. On the other hand, if only the aircraft production system is of importance to management, then the development stage will involve designing the production processes, sequence, equipment, and arrangement. The acquisition of equipment, the actual layout of facilities, and the hiring and training of personnel would be needed to implement the production system. The operation stage would then begin when manufacturing commenced. One should notice that a system like manufacturing may fall in the implementation stage of one system (aircraft) but in the operation stage of another system (production) as a result of changing the maximum system of interest (see Figure 21-2).

Figure 21-2

Work content in stages of different systems of interest.

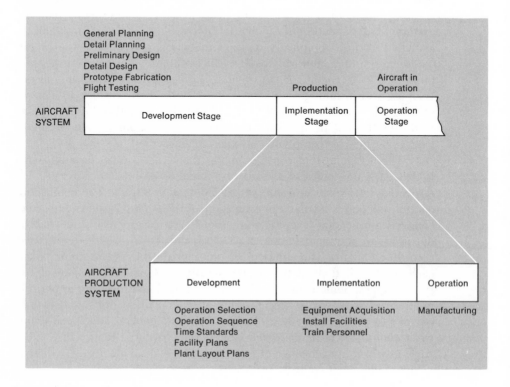

DEVELOPMENT STAGE

Development begins when a present or anticipated need for a particular system is recognized. During this stage, management formulates the plans and the organization for the system in its forthcoming operating stage. Various alternative designs for the system are usually proposed and evaluated and, eventually, a specific design is chosen.

The critical point that should be made here is that the development of the system's plans and organizational structure will require all of the managerial functions that have been discussed throughout this book. The manager must set objectives and make plans for the design process and organize, staff, and direct the activities of the design group. Of course, the manager must also control the performance of design activities and personnel in order to meet time deadlines, design standards, and budget

450

ceilings for research and development. Thus all functions of management, from planning through controlling, must be performed during the development stage to achieve the purpose of this stage—the planning and organizing of the ultimate system of interest.

IMPLEMENTATION STAGE

Management in the implementation stage determines *how* and *when* the system can best be installed. If, for example, a new accounting system has been proposed, plans must be drawn up concerning the sequence of steps required to introduce the new system and to phase out the present system without excessive costs or damaging interruptions to the business. A special task force or temporary organizational unit might also be needed to direct and control a smooth transition between the present and proposed systems. Thus some or all of the management functions may be called into play during the implementation stage, depending on the complexity of the system being installed. Controls are required to insure adequate planning and performance in carrying out these plans of installation. Time schedules must be set and met in this stage as they were in the development stage. Controls are also needed to monitor the activities of hiring or reassigning personnel and training them for the new system.

Unfortunately, sometimes the manager fails to employ the necessary managerial skills in this stage of the system's life cycle. One reason for this oversight is that a manager may be working under a severe deadline to get the system into operation as soon as possible, if not sooner! The implementation process may also be slighted if the manager is extremely impressed with the design of the proposed system. Because the benefits are so "outstanding," the manager often acts as if the system will install itself in the most efficient manner. As a result of these situations, many worthwhile systems never start out "on the right foot," and expected operating performance never materializes.

OPERATION STAGE

During the operation stage, the last phase of the life cycle, the fruits of development and implementation either ripen or turn sour, resulting in profit or loss. Poor performance here may be the result of the outputs of the previous stages, poor operating management, or some combination of both. If the system is adequate and profitable, however, it will remain in operation until it is replaced by another, improved system in the future.

While in the operating phase, the functions of staffing, directing, and controlling of the system occur on a more or less continuous basis.

Most of the discussion of controls normally found in books on management tend to be centered around the operating stage of a system's life cycle. One reason for this is that the operating stage usually covers the major portion of the life cycle. However, this condition is changing, due to the recent advent of more complex systems and more frequent technological changes. Another reason for the heavy emphasis on operational controls is the greater ease of establishing standard performance measures and evaluating actual performance in the operating stage than in the development and implementation stages. However, an attempt has been made here to indicate that the control function is necessary in all three stages of a system's life cycle.

General Controls

The function of control, as we have seen, is needed in all stages of a system's life cycle. Some of the commonly used control procedures are employed in one form or another in every stage; we have referred to these as general controls. Budgets, standard costs, and time controls are examples of general controls.

BUDGETS AND COST CONTROLS

Early in the development stage, certain decisions are made that influence the minimum possible cost of the system throughout its three stages. For example, management decides what the system should do and how well the system should function. These and other basic decisions determine the minimum time and effort, as well as quality of performance needed to develop, implement, and operate the overall system. The result of these initial and basic decisions form the minimum threshold for success.[1] This threshold is the minimum amount of money that must be spent for development, installation, and operating expense in order for the system to succeed in meeting its intended purpose. If management is unwilling or unable to reach this financial threshold, the desired system cannot be achieved. Anything less than this minimum amount of capital will result in failure. Unfortunately, systems often fail or fall short of

[1] H. G. Thuesen and W. J. Fabrycky, *Engineering Economy* (3d ed.) (Englewood Cliffs, N.J.: Prentice-Hall, Inc., 1964), p. 37.

their objectives because of inadequate funding and the blame is usually placed inaccurately on the idea or design of the system. Even though this minimum threshold for success can not be determined exactly, management must make an effort to estimate its magnitude as carefully as possible. If this minimum level of financial funding cannot be met, the system should not be attempted. For example, if a man who is shopping for a car can only accumulate $600, he should have enough sense not to purchase a car that will not meet his needs. If a $600 used car will not be satisfactory because of a lack of dependability, it would be a mistake to purchase it simply because it is all he can afford. Experience in and out of the business world sometimes reveals neglect of this "minimum threshold for success" concept.

Of course, management usually finds it wise to invest more than the minimum monetary threshold for a system. The incremental benefit or gain from each additional dollar spent may justify a higher level of expense, at least over a given range. Thus the man who wants a new automobile may purchase a Cadillac instead of a lower-priced car because he feels the increased personal "benefits" are worth the extra cost, even though either car would provide adequate transportation.

Another financial estimate that management must make is the worth of the project or system. The estimated worth represents the maximum possible cost that the venture can incur without the company taking a loss on the investment. Without such an estimate, systems' costs often exceed this value, even though management may have elaborate plans and controls to minimize capital and operating expenses. Consequently, the value or worth of the system helps to determine the sophistication of the system's objectives and design. It becomes a constraint on decision making and activities throughout the system's life cycle. A system may have to be pared down until estimated expenses are equal to or below the system's worth in monetary terms. If the resulting system is not then desirable, it should be dropped from consideration.

In order for a system to have a chance for success and also to be economically feasible, the costs incurred throughout its life cycle must remain somewhere between the system's worth level and its minimum threshold (see Figure 21-3A). However, something more is likely to be desired. In almost all cases, management wants to achieve at least a minimum profit. Consequently, a cost standard or actual budget is set far enough below the worth level to achieve a minimum or a reasonable profit, as illustrated in Figure 21-3B. Detailed plans and controls are then needed to achieve or better this actual budget.

Budgets are predictions of the results, usually expressed in monetary terms, of activities anticipated in the future. If the predictions do

Figure 21-3

Costing standard of a system.

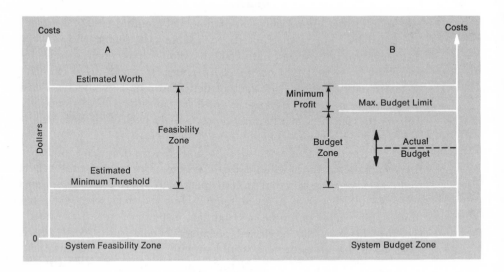

not fall in the budget zone (Figure 21-3B), then modifications or new activities are planned until a satisfactory system design-budget combination is found. Once plans are approved, budgets are useful in making sure that adequate monetary and nonfinancial resources are available when needed. Thus, budgets are predetermined plans that are used as a guide for decision making and scheduling activities in the development, implementation, and operation of a system.

Regardless of the time span and complexity of each stage of a system's life cycle, management should establish an upper limit on the monetary funds and other resources that can be used. Then the activities of subordinates must be controlled so budgets are not exceeded. Consequently, budgets also serve as standards against which actual performance is evaluated in the control process.

A large number of different kinds of budgets are usually used in companies. Some budgets are used for detailed planning for the future; others serve as controls. Specialized budgets are often designed for research and development activities, installation work, and operation management. Some are short-range budgets; others are long-ranged. In addition, unique budgets are found for each organizational unit or department and at each level of the business organization. These differences are mentioned in more detail in other books and will not be discussed further here.[2] What is important here is that all line and staff managers are subject to one or more budgets, which must be coordinated into a well-balanced program.

Budgets should be administered only by the managers who are responsible for the systems or programs budgeted. Planning and taking corrective control actions with respect to the budget must be performed by the manager involved, rather than by a budget committee or a budget coordinator. Top management must actively support the concept of budgeting and encourage each manager to participate in budget making for his area of responsibility. The authority of management at all levels can also be maintained if managers are allowed to change the allocation of funds within their budgets somewhat in response to changing conditions.

With each manager preparing his own budget, a great deal of coordination is necessary to ensure that the individual budgets are mutually consistent and feasible. All budgets must fit together and must be directed toward the achievement of the firm's overall objectives. Budgets must be reviewed and periodically examined to check their objective-orientation characteristics. During the coordinating process, budget requests are often pared down, usually because available resources cannot cover every request for monetary support. As a result, managers learn to ask for much more than they need. In order to control this tendency, the plans of each manager, as well as his calculations and estimates, must be carefully evaluated. The budget coordinator and top executives should avoid giving dictatorial orders to cut the request by a certain amount. It is better to conduct a systematic investigation and to modify or eliminate those plans of lesser priority. Managers will then have more respect for the budgeting process and will remain more alert to ways of improving activities under their control. In other words, a successful budget acts as a catalyst for other good management practices.

For control purposes, budgets should be designed so the manager is held responsible only for those costs that he can influence. For example, one company set a dollar ceiling on materials to be used by a manufacturing department, but because material prices fluctuated greatly, the dollar budget was meaningless. It would have been better to have had a nonfinancial budget phrased in terms of material quantity. Another approach would have been to price all material at a fixed rate, and then use this price as a reference to assess material utilization, over which the manager has control. For this reason, control budgets are tailor-made to fit the area of responsibility and are not identical to conventional cost

[2] See Harold Koontz and Cyril O'Donnell, *Principles of Management* (4th ed.) (New York: McGraw-Hill Book Co., 1968), p. 652–54.

accounts. The only similarity between cost accounting and budgeting is that both attempt to establish responsibility for controlling costs at the point where costs originate.

Budgets usually make the ongoing job of control easier for the superior as well as for his subordinate. Rather than checking performance against numerous and detailed performance-measure standards, one can evaluate adherence to the total budget instead. The budget's common denominator for many diverse activities—the dollar—lends itself quite well to summaries and comparisons. This advantage, however, may be accompanied by some difficulties.

When cost control is strongly emphasized, as in preparing and administering budgets, other important factors may be neglected. For example, excellent cost control is often achieved at the expense of poor quality of service, because budgets usually hide the symptoms of inadequate service from management's eyes. If certain variances from budget standards are treated as basic problems, the result may be dictatorial action. Overtime payments bothered the management of a mining company, for example. An order was issued that no overtime would be budgeted or allowed in the future. As a result, every department hired many more employees, because the work activities had to be performed by crews. After adding additional crews of men, the cost of excess man-hours were far greater than previous overtime hours. Hiring and training costs skyrocketed, and morale among the work force reached an all-time low. Managers were deprived of the needed freedom to operate their departments because of overemphasis on minor expenses. And budget goals were allowed to supersede the objectives of the firm.

Another danger of budgets is that of inflexibility. A budget, or any other standard, is developed for a fixed set of conditions. The budget indicates what costs should be, if these conditions exist. However, unchanging conditions rarely exist for long periods of time in a dynamic economy. A partial solution to this problem is the use of variable budgets. These can be designed to change as the volume of sales or level of production varies. Usually a detailed analysis must be made to determine how each individual cost item should vary with volume changes. Then a composite model of all cost items is used as the variable budget. Based on volume forecasts for the future, managers can readily determine their budgets for the periods ahead. Several drawbacks of this concept may be found, however.

If the budget is varied too frequently in response to short-term variations in volume, managers should cease to use the budget as a planning and control aid. For example, a manufacturing organization gained a reputation for firing and hiring direct-labor personnel, as well as managers, staff engineers, and sales people, in direct response to seasonal sales forecasts. As a result, the high cost of training, lack of skilled and experienced personnel, and poor employee loyalty and morale marked the end of an otherwise successful company. Consequently, variable budgets work better when reasonably accurate long-range forecasts can be made. Then changes, such as in employment levels, can be made in a gradual and efficient manner.

If a variable budget deals only with changes in volume, then adjustments probably neglect other changes over which the manager has no influence. For example, changes in the product or service mix can cause difficulties when a common variable budget is used. One approach to this problem is budgeting by standard costs. Here cost parameters are individually specified for materials, each operation, and appropriate overhead expenses for each product on a per unit basis. With volume forecasts for each product or product class, budgets for different product mixes can be formed. However, the increased flexibility with standard costs may bring with it some weaknesses. The costs per unit are not likely to be identical and independent of the volume. A far more serious problem exists if the manager's costs are improperly evaluated. If standard cost items are monitored, item by item, by higher management, the manager's hands may be tied more than necessary. Cost standards should be used only to develop total budgets and to help the manager make corrective decisions. If held responsible for total expenses over which he has control, then the manager should be free to control the *critical* cost variables and to disregard the others.

Reasonable budgets can be useful for purposes of control and adjustment of plans. They must be developed far enough in advance so that any necessary control action can be completed satisfactorily. Corrective action requires time and ingenuity on the part of management, and budgeting procedures must permit this time and effort.

TIME CONTROLS

In addition to being evaluated on the basis of budget performance, managers are also rated against time standards. Because of the relationship between the time to complete an activity and the cost involved, it might be argued that time controls are really unnecessary when adequate budget control is present. However, cost and time goals are sometimes at odds with one another. A manager may be able to meet a particular deadline only because he was willing to violate a few budgetary standards. Often the ideal of never keeping the customer waiting is so strong a motivation that high labor and machine costs are necessary for lower time requirements, no matter how ridiculous they may seem. In more normal situations, time standards have so many uses in planning, organizing, and controlling that the list seems endless. At best, only a sample of these standards can be mentioned here.

Historically, time standards and controls were initiated and widely used in the operation stage, notably on highly repetitive task in manufacturing. In recent years, the use of time control has branched out to cover the activities of the increasing numbers of white-collar workers and indirect-labor personnel. This expansion in all three stages of the system's life cycle has required new methods of setting and using time standards for planning and control purposes. More frequent changes in technology and designs have reduced the life of many systems. This, in turn, has changed the ways of developing many time standards.

Even the best-developed time standard is still only an approximation of how long it should take to complete an activity. Like budgets, time standards are valid only for a standard set of conditions. However, numerous chance (unassignable) and assignable causes are always at work upsetting standard conditions. Human activity times vary throughout the day, for example, as a result of such factors as fatigue, boredom, ambient environment, and so on. Elaborate time standards are neither feasible nor practical in many work situations, but these situations should not be used as an excuse for having no time controls. Schedules still must be planned and deadlines met for activities such as those found in development and implementation stages.

Time standards can be developed from estimates, historical records, and work-measurement procedures. Both historical records and work-measurement techniques will give much more accurate values than judgment estimates alone.[3] For untried design activities, however, only management estimates may be possible. Time estimates need not be wild guesses, however, and certain procedures can be employed to improve their accuracy. Overall estimates, for example, will usually be more accurate if they are based on a composite of estimates of underlying variables than if overall estimates are made directly. For example, in estimating the volume of an object, it is usually better to estimate the several dimensions of the object and then to calculate the volume as the product of these dimensions. The same approach applies to estimating activity time standards. Large jobs can be broken down into smaller tasks to the point where the resulting time estimates are more manageable and accurate.

[3] Benjamin W. Niebel, *Motion and Time Study* (4th ed.) (Homewood, Ill.: Richard D. Irwin, Inc., 1967), p. 238.

If similar activities have been performed on other systems, historical time records can provide the data needed to calculate time standards. This is often a practical approach for activities that recur in the development and implementation stages, as well as for certain managerial and indirect labor tasks in the operation stage. One danger with historically based standards is that they may tell us how long it once took to do a job, but not how long it *should* have taken. This problem can be partially controlled if management keeps records of activities and makes an estimate of their efficiencies as they are performed.

On semirepetitive and highly repetitive tasks, most frequently found in operation stages, work-measurement techniques represent a better way to establish accurate time standards. These techniques—stop-watch time study, predetermined time systems, standard data, work sampling, and so on—are thoroughly discussed elsewhere.[4] Basically, two major steps are required to derive work measurement standards. First, a "normal" time is found for a particular job, representing the time required by a "normal" employee who is working at a "normal" pace to complete a given task. Judging what is "normal" has been troublesome when using some of the work-measurement techniques, but not with others. In the second step, allowances for legitimate interruptions, such as personal time, rest periods, and unavoidable delays, are determined. The standard time then becomes the normal time plus allowance times.

Regardless of what work measurement technique is used, the cost of determining allowances for a particular job is the same. But the cost of finding normal-time values varies greatly with the measurement technique used. Consequently, care must be taken when developing time standards, so that the costs of controlling do not overshadow the benefits of these controls. Unfortunately, this concern for economic controls is often ignored.

Allowances may be another source of problems for the control function. If allowances are arbitrarily determined, the time standards are usually in error or not consistent. Some companies use the same allowance values for every job, even when this practice is not justified. Therefore, inequities in the control standards occur. Allowances are used by some managers to hide inefficiencies in their operations. For example, a manager may gradually, but forcefully, negotiate for allowances to cover such things as time to rework poor-quality items made by his department. If successful, his department's performance will always be

---

[4] See Niebel, *Motion and Time Study;* Ralph M. Barnes, *Motion and Time Study* (5th ed.) (New York: John Wiley & Sons, Inc., 1963); and Marvin E. Mundel, *Motion and Time Study* (4th ed.) (Englewood Cliffs, N.J.: Prentice-Hall, Inc., 1970).

inflated on control reports and the need for corrective action may never be recognized. In such situations, the "squeaky wheel shouldn't get the grease" if effective controls are to prevail.

One important work-measurement technique is *work sampling*.[5] It can be used in all three stages of a system's life cycle, and has many other advantages as well.[6] This technique makes use of random observations rather than direct time measurements. The percentage *number* of observations recording a particular activity is assumed to be a reliable measure of the percentage *time* for that activity. As an oversimplified example, we might say that 2,000 observations were made on a product-design team over a two-week period. An analysis of the observations revealed that the team was working during 1,700 observations and that legitimate interruptions accounted for another 100 observations. During the two-week period, two design projects were started and completed. The approximate time per design project was 36 hours per team.[7] This standard could be used to schedule future design work and could be updated as more work-sampling studies were made later. More detailed information would also be possible if observations had been recorded on the different types of working activities.

Besides easily determining standards in nonrepetitive activities, work sampling is an important tool for measuring actual performance and taking corrective action. Table 21-1 shows the results of a work-sampling study of an engineering design group and compares it with a distribution pattern that management felt desirable.[8] Without work sampling, this study probably would not have been conducted because of economic reasons. Trouble areas are pinpointed, indicating the need for corrective action. After the control action is implemented, future work-sampling studies could be used to evaluate the effectiveness of the action, as well as to initiate other corrective measures, if needed.

---

[5] Also referred to as ratio delay, activity sampling, and performance sampling.

[6] Barnes, *Motion and Time Study*, pp. 552–53, provides a list of the advantages of work sampling.

[7] Working   1,700 observations
Allowances   100 observations
Unrelated Activities   200 observations
Total Time (hrs) = (2 weeks)(40 hours/week) = 80 hours
Time (hours)/project/team = $\dfrac{1,800 \ (80 \ \text{hours})}{2,000 \ (2 \ \text{projects})}$ = 36 hours

[8] The example is modified from Louis M. Kuh, "Work Criteria for Engineers," in *Industrial Engineering Handbook*, ed. H. B. Maynard (2d ed.) (New York: McGraw-Hill Book Co., Inc., 1963), Section 10, p. 117.

Table 21-1

WORK DISTRIBUTION STUDY (ENGINEERING DESIGN GROUP)

		PERCENTAGE OF TIME	
Activity	*Desired*	*Actual* *	*Difference*
1. Engineering work at desk	45%	27%	−18%
2. Discussion with other engineers	20	10	−10
3. Telephone calls	5	3	− 2
4. Field trips	10	31	+21
5. Meetings	7	9	+ 2
6. Search files	4	13	+ 9
7. Personal	6	5	− 1
8. Miscellaneous	3	2	− 1

* From work-sampling study.

Specific Controls

In this section, attention is directed toward specific control techniques that are only used in one or two life-cycle stages or are only successful in specialized situations. PERT/CPM, production-control, and statistical-control models are examples of controls of a specific nature.

PROJECT CONTROL: PERT AND CPM

Project-control techniques are normally reserved for large-scale, one-time projects. Research and design work in the development stage, as well as the installation of systems, are certainly unique one-time projects. Consequently, project-control methods may be applied economically to these projects individually, provided each is complex or large in scale. Sometimes these individual projects are not very complex, but if management considers them only as components of a much larger project or system, this enlarged system of interest may require some form of project control. A strong emphasis on completing the project on time must be present if project-control techniques are to fulfill their usefulness. Thus, timing is often primary and expense control is of secondary concern.

Numerous activities must be done in a proper sequence if a major project is to be completed on time. The deadline may have been contracted with the "customer" or it may be the minimum expected completion date. Often contracted cost penalties are involved if projects are late, and in rare situations, financial incentives are given for projects to be finished before the deadline. In order to perform activities on schedule, plans must be made to properly allocate resources to the total project. Within timing constraints, efforts are directed toward minimizing total costs. Because of the size of these projects, close attention is only given to the larger and more important activities and to the interactions between them. Careful analysis of minute details can not be justified.

Some common examples of project or network control methods are PERT (Performance Evaluation and Review Technique) and CPM (Critical Path Methods). PERT initially was developed by the U.S. Navy to plan and control the Polaris missile program; the DuPont Company developed CPM to control maintenance and engineering functions. The PERT technique was credited with helping to shorten the originally estimated development time on the Polaris system by two years. Similar outstanding contributions have been exhibited by these techniques since their development. PERT and CPM are based on the same concepts, but differ in some details. Both are based on a network plan that determines the most critical activities to be controlled so as to meet completion dates. Originally, PERT methods were based on probabilistic estimates of activity times, whereas CPM methods assumed constant or deterministic activity times. The initial designs of these methods also differed in the way the graphical network was prepared. Actually, either the probabilistic or deterministic model, as well as either network scheme, can be equally applied to PERT or CPM. In fact, many recent PERT applications have dropped the use of probabilistic activity times for the sake of convenience.[9]

The basic concepts underlying such methods as PERT can be illustrated by highly simplified examples, as we will do shortly. However, it should be remembered that project-control techniques are applied in practice to projects of such magnitude that a computer is often required to handle large amounts of data. The reader who is interested in the detailed methods used to handle complex project problems should refer to other sources.[10]

Several major steps are necessary to design and utilize project-control methods. These steps are activity analysis, network diagram construction, network time analysis, and the control of critical activities. In large projects, care must be taken not to overlook anything when fore-

---

[9] Elwood S. Buffa, *Modern Production Management* (3d ed.) (New York: John Wiley & Sons, Inc., 1969), pp. 195–96.

[10] See Buffa, *Modern Production Management*, pp. 194–218; and Jerome D. Weist and Ferdinand K. Levy, *A Management Guide to PERT and CPM* (Englewood Cliffs, N.J.: Prentice-Hall, Inc., 1969).

casting what major activities will be required to complete the project. Besides this careful listing of necessary activities, the precedence relationships among activities must be specified in activity analysis. The result of this initial analysis is a list of required activities, such as the one in Table 21-2, which shows the basic activities required to design and

Table 21-2

ACTIVITY LIST

Activity	Description	Immediate Predecessors
A	Design product	
B	Determine process and equipment specifications	A
C	Design package	A
D	Order product materials	A
E	Make equipment ready	B
F	Order package materials	C
G	Fabricate products	D, E
H	Fabricate package	F
I	Package product	G, H
J	Distribute product	I

manufacture a product. For reasons of simplicity, the many activities involved in forecasting sales, advertising, and hiring and training of personnel have been omitted.

With the results from the activity analysis, the project network diagram can be constructed. Care must be taken here to prevent any violations of the precedence relationships among the activities. In the diagram in Figure 21-4, the activities are represented by arrows. The length of these arrows has no significance. The numbered circles indicate the beginning and ending points (or events) of activities and are called nodes.[11] The direction of the arrows indicate the precedence requirements of the project. For example, in Figure 21-4, activities D and E must be completed before activity G can begin. On the other hand, activities B, C, and D may all proceed simultaneously, once activity A is finished.

Time values must be estimated for each activity in the network diagram. Either deterministic or probabilistic time values may be used. If a probabilistic model is used, the activity times are more realistically represented by probability distributions, based on *three* time values for each activity. The optimistic time value, T_o, is the shortest possible time to

---

[11] In original PERT designs, arrows = activities and nodes = events, whereas in CPM, arrows = events and nodes = activities. Either method may be used, however.

Figure 21-4

PERT network diagram and time analysis.

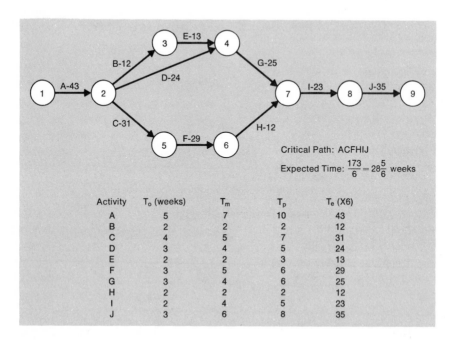

Critical Path: ACFHIJ

Expected Time: $\dfrac{173}{6} = 28\dfrac{5}{6}$ weeks

Activity	T_o (weeks)	T_m	T_p	T_e (X6)
A	5	7	10	43
B	2	2	2	12
C	4	5	7	31
D	3	4	5	24
E	2	2	3	13
F	3	5	6	29
G	3	4	6	25
H	2	2	2	12
I	2	4	5	23
J	3	6	8	35

complete the activity if no problems arise. The pessimistic time, T_p, is the longest time to finish the activity under adverse situations. The other time value, T_m, is the one most likely to occur. Individuals who are familiar with the work involved in the activities and prevailing environmental conditions usually estimate these three time values for each activity. The expected or mean time value of each activity is calculated by the following formula:

$$T_e = \frac{T_o + T_p + 4T_m}{6}$$

The expected time values can then be used to find the project's critical activities.[12] In Figure 21-4, the following paths through the network and their expected times are found:

[12] Normally, it is more convenient to find critical activities using $(T_o + T_p + 4T_m)$ values rather than T_e values.

1. *ABEGIJ* ⅙ (43 + 12 + 13 + 25 + 23 + 35) = 151/6 = 25-⅙ weeks
2. *ADGIJ*   ⅙ (43 + 24 + 25 + 23 + 35) = 150/6 = 25 weeks
3. *ACFHIJ* ⅙ (43 + 31 + 29 + 12 + 23 + 35) = 173/6 = 28-⅚ weeks

The *critical* path (3) is the longest time path through the network diagram, and each activity on this particular path is critical. If our project is expected to be completed in 28-⅚ weeks, controls are usually used to insure that each *critical* activity is started and ended approximately on time. The noncritical activities (*B,D,E,* and *G*) have some *slack* time available. That is, they can be started somewhat late or performed more slowly than their expected times without delaying the overall project. Therefore, management will devote more attention to the critical-path activities than to the others.

Because activity times are rarely constant, the progress of the network activities must be monitored and a rapid feedback of information is required so that performance may be brought back in line, if necessary. If the project's target time is the total *expected* time of the critical path (28-⅚ weeks in our example), then the cumulative time along this path must not significantly deviate from the expected or standard cumulative time. The job of controlling the project, of course, will be easier if the contracted completion time is greater than the critical path's expected time. In our example, if the contracted time was 32 weeks, the critical activities would have (32 − 28-⅚) or 3-⅙ weeks of slack time.

With probabilistic models, it is possible to develop additional information important to managerial decisions when controlling the project. The variance of the distribution of each activity is often helpful and can be easily computed as follows:

$$S^2 = \frac{1}{36} (T_p - T_o)^2$$

The activities with the higher variances often should be monitored more closely than those with low variances, regardless of whether the activities are critical or not. For example, if slack times are low and noncritical activities have high variance values, noncritical paths may frequently extend beyond the slack time and thus become critical. In this situation, management probably should pay more attention to noncritical activities than to critical ones, especially when the time variances of the critical path are low.

Control is not completed until corrective action is taken when it is needed. Thus when activities may be or are delayed to the point of causing the project to fall behind schedule, managers should be able to *shift* resources from noncritical activities to critical ones or to *add* more resources to the project. Of course, the expansion or reallocation of resources will cost money and management must take this into account. It may be cheaper to delay the project somewhat. A similar problem also arises when the contracted project time is less than the expected time of the critical path. Finally, in some projects the available resources are inadequate to do the job on schedule. Problems such as these may be solved by one of the following groups of control techniques:

1. Load-leveling models.
2. Limited-resource models.
3. Least-costing models.

Load-leveling models are used to modify PERT/CPM schedules in order to reduce idle labor costs, hiring and separation costs, or the cost of any resource that may be affected by fluctuations in the demand for its use throughout the long duration of the project. *Limited-resource models* are used to allocate scarce resources to the most critical activities in the order of changing priorities so as to meet the schedule deadline. *Least-costing techniques* attempt to determine if it is economically worthwhile to shorten the critical path by adding more resources. Where the resources should be expanded, these models also select the least-cost activities. Since we are on the subject, the reader should be aware of the fact that if the critical path is shortened, eventually a new critical path will be created. Thus, at that point, it may be desirable to shift any additional resources and control procedures to different activities. For a more thorough coverage of these resource deployment models, the reader should check other references.[13]

In summary, the concepts of networks and critical-path controls can be applied to many situations where we are interested in getting a job done on time. PERT/CPM methods are useful in planning and controlling the progress of highly complex projects or nonrepetitive operations.

PRODUCTION CONTROL

In manufacturing operations, production planning and control are dynamic managerial processes designed to strike a balance between several objectives or goals. Plans are made to have the system operate economically and complete customers' demands on time. Uncertainty plays a large role in production planning. In continuous production

---

[13] Buffa, *Modern Production Management*, pp. 212–17.

systems, where items are manufactured before actual sales are transacted, decisions must be made in advance about how many of each product to make and when. Even in job-shop operations, where items are produced only in response to customers' orders, forecasts must be made concerning some future requirements, such as total man-hours, types of equipment, and total machine-hours. Since it is impossible to forecast perfectly what events the future will bring, production plans are made at several levels in hopes of being able to meet demands economically. At the broadest level, plans deal with various initial design aspects of the production system, such as plant location, general modes of production, and plant layout. These plans, made under a great deal of uncertainty, may set basic patterns for years to come. More frequent year-to-year, month-to-month, and day-to-day plans must also be made to meet the short-range or immediate, less uncertain demands. Over the short term, managers must plan raw material needs, determine how each item will be made, specify in-process inventory levels, and schedule equipment and manpower for all products so that men, materials, and machines are available at the right time and in the amounts needed. Of course, these plans must take into account budget and plant capacity limitations.

At this point, the reader probably is questioning why there is a discussion of production *planning* in a chapter on *control*. The point we are making here is that the problems facing production planning also make the task of production control very difficult. First of all, we have just seen that more detailed preliminary plans and replanning later are necessary to respond to increased knowledge about the future, such as revised sales forecasts. Recognizing the need for more plans and revisions as uncertainty diminishes is not really a control process, but the continuing development of a new system. However, with numerous new plans and frequent modifications, production *control* standards and actions must be changed. Obviously, this becomes a burden for those in charge of production control.

Control of production does occur, however, when management must spot and correct poor performance in production planning. But the problems do not end here. Well-designed plans are always interrupted by numerous unplanned situations. Union strikes against suppliers, customers, or the company itself, absenteeism, machine breakdowns, poor workmanship, rush orders, design changes, lost and stolen materials, and inventory spoilage are just a few things that play havoc with production plans. Here again, control is needed to correct some of these factors or at least to minimize their effect on production plans.

Summing up then, we see that production control has two general goals—economical operations, including low inventory costs, and meeting customers' demand. But the plans needed to achieve these objectives are frequently changed due to the fluctuations in numerous external factors. For example, product or order priorities may vary significantly in a short period of time. Consequently, attempts must be made to keep production in control with varying standards. In addition, with a given set of standards, controls are needed to cope with managerial errors and disrupting internal events, such as design changes and lost inventory. Adequate feedback of information about actual production performance and flow of materials through the factory is also needed to enable management to take corrective action.

To discuss, or even mention, all of the various facets of production control would be impossible here, because of the vastness and complexity of the subject. However, we will discuss several control techniques, in the hope that they will be illustrative samples of the vast domain of production control.[14]

LINE OF BALANCE. Often management needs techniques to compare actual and planned progress in production operations and elsewhere. One such method makes this comparison through the use of "line-of-balance" (LOB) charts.[15] LOB charts make it easy to see if production is falling behind schedule or getting ahead. These charts are economical for long-term production lasting several weeks or months and for products made from at least several components. The following example will illustrate the LOB concept.

A company has contracted to ship electronic assemblies to a customer over a period of 28 working days, according to the schedule in Table 21-3. Management did not want to start working on this order too soon and have a lot of money tied up in inventory. Nor did they want to be late on any of the shipments. Therefore a PERT type analysis was conducted to determine critical activities. The assembly consisted of 22 parts, some of which were purchased and the others manufactured by the company. Even though there were many activities involved in making or buying and assembling these parts, only six activities were on the critical path of the PERT network. Attention was then directed only to these critical activities.

The critical activity times and lead times are given in Table 21-4. Lead times are defined here as the minimum number of working days that

---

[14] Excellent discussions of production control may be found in such sources as: Franklin G. Moore and Ronald Jablonski, *Production Control* (3d ed.) (New York: McGraw-Hill, Book Co., 1969); and Elwood S. Buffa, *Production-Inventory Systems: Planning and Control* (Homewood, Ill.: Richard D. Irwin, Inc., 1968).

[15] Efraim Turban, "The Line of Balance—A Management by Expection Tool," *The Journal of Industrial Engineering*, XIV, no. 9 (September, 1968), pp. 440–48.

Table 21-3

REQUIRED SHIPMENT SCHEDULE OF COMPLETED UNITS

Day	Quantity	Cumulative Quantity	Day	Quantity	Cumulative Quantity
2	10	10	16	18	186
4	18	28	18	14	200
6	24	52	20	14	214
8	36	88	22	11	225
10	30	118	24	9	234
12	27	145	26	8	242
14	23	168	28	3	245

Table 21-4

ACTIVITY AND LEAD TIMES

Critical Activity	Activity Time	Lead Time
A	6 days	17 days
B	3	17
C	2	15
D	9	7
E (Assembly)	6	5
F (Packing)	1	0

a critical activity on a part must be completed prior to the date when the assembly containing that particular part is shipped. For example, a part must pass through activity C no less than 15 days before an electronic assembly is ready for shipment. In addition, if the activity times are correct, the part must arrive at activity C at least 17 days before the date of shipping.

To make a line-of-balance chart, we first construct a *cumulative-output-time* or *objective chart* as shown in Figure 21-5a. This chart is a *permanent* chart, as long as the shipment schedule (Table 21-3) remains fixed. Because management is interested ultimately in meeting the *required* shipment output, this cumulative output is plotted on the objective chart.

The line-of-balance (LOB) chart is not permanent; it changes every time management wants to evaluate the production progress being made on each critical activity. Once a new LOB chart has been drawn, it becomes the performance standard at that particular review point. Let

Figure 21-5

Line-of-balance graphical method.

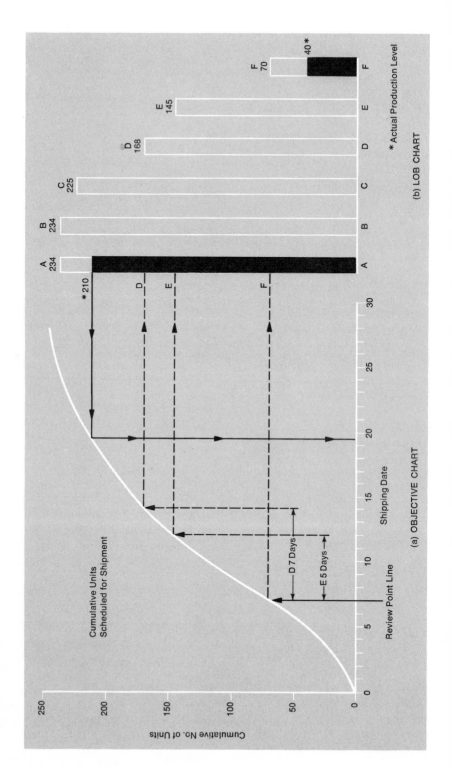

(a) OBJECTIVE CHART

(b) LOB CHART

* Actual Production Level

us now assume that the company, for example, is presently producing the electronic assembly, and management wants to review performance at the end of the *seventh day* of the 28-day shipping period. A review-point line is then placed on the objective chart (Figure 21-5a) before determining the LOB standard chart for that point. Extending this line to the objective curve, we can see that a cumulative number of 70 assembly units should have been packed (activity *F*) and ready for shipment up to this review point. This fact could also be found in Table 21-3 by interpolation. Thus, the cumulative production or LOB standard for activity *F* is 70 units, which is shown on the LOB bar chart in Figure 21-5b.

The cumulative production standards for the other critical activities are found by using the objective chart (or Table 21-3) and the respective lead-time values. For example, activity *E* has a lead time of five days (Table 21-4). This means that on our review date of seven days, the cumulative production through activity *E* must be equivalent to the cumulative amount for the twelfth day on the objective chart (Figure 21-5a) or in Table 21-3. Therefore, the present standard for *E* is 145 units in order to meet the required shipping schedule five days from now (see Figure 21-5). Likewise, the cumulative production for *D* should be 168 units. The LOB standards for the remaining activities are determined in the same way.

After management measured actual cumulative production at the end of the seventh day, it was compared with the LOB standard in Table 21-5. From the unit variance column, we can readily see that ac-

Table 21-5

ACTUAL VERSUS REQUIRED PERFORMANCE (END OF THE SEVENTH DAY)

Activity	Actual Cumulation	Standard LOB Cumulation	Unit Variance	Time Variance
A	210 units	234	−24	−4.5 days
B	245	234	+11	+4.0
C	230	225	+ 5	+1.0
D	175	168	+ 7	+1.0
E	160	145	+15	+1.5
F	40	70	−30	−2.0

tivities *A* and *F* have fallen seriously behind schedule, and corrective action seems in order. How many days are *A* and *F* behind? (Management may need this additional bit of information.) To find it, the actual production values can be represented on the LOB chart (see shaded area in Figure 21-5b). Projecting the actual volume back to the objective chart, the standard time when this volume *should* have been completed is determined. For example, 210 units have been finished at activity A. From the objective chart, we see that the 210 units will cover the shipping schedule through 19.5 days. However, at the end of 7 days, the LOB standard for A (or 234 units) should have been completed, covering the shipping schedule through 24 days.[16] Consequently, activity A is 4.5 days behind, based on the *future* shipping schedule. This means that the finished assembly schedule will be behind in the future unless corrective action is taken now.

The time variance information is more important than unit variance figures. This fact is illustrated in Table 21-5. Based on the unit variance criterion, activity F appears to need more corrective action than A. But this is not the case as shown by the time variance column. Also, if personnel or other resources are to be temporarily shifted to a faltering activity, the loan should probably come from B rather than E.

The line-of-balance method is a simple, but dynamic, tool for controlling production-scheduling problems. Control actions can be made while the project or operation is ongoing, thus providing a forward-looking control process.

CRITICAL PATH SCHEDULING. Assigning various work requests to employees and/or machines can often become a managerial headache in an intermittent or job-shop production system. A manager may be faced with a number of work orders that must be processed by a limited number of available machines or personnel. In order to get all the work out on time, decisions must be made as to which orders should be processed first. When faced with this situation, the manager needs to have dispatching decision rules or policies covering job priorities. Then, after initial decisions are reached and assignments made, more problems can arise. For example, raw materials for some jobs may arrive late or a job may require more production debugging than expected. These difficulties often mean a reshuffling in the sequence of jobs processed, requiring more decisions from the manager.

Numerous computer simulation studies have been conducted to see which dispatching rules are best to follow.[17] Some of the policies that have been tested are: first-come-first-served, "shortest-operating-time" jobs first, "maximum-operating-time" jobs first, and oldest jobs first. Un-

---

[16] The 24 days could be found from Table 21-3 or by adding the review date to the activity lead time (7 + 17 = 24).

[17] J. M. Moore and R. C. Wilson, "A Review of Simulation Research in Job Shop Scheduling," *Production and Inventory Management,* January, 1967, pp. 1–10.

fortunately, none of these methods or any others has been superior in all situations. However, in a sizeable number of cases, the "shortest-operating-time" rule has been best. This policy often results in the fewest delayed orders. Of course, rules of this type do not help much when actual processing times are not the same as expected. For control purposes, more dynamic tools are needed, such as the *critical-ratio scheduling* methods.

Critical-ratio techniques are used in production-control systems to:

1. Establish relative priorities among jobs on a common basis, regardless of whether the jobs are continuous (make to stock) or intermittent (make to order).
2. Automatically adjust priorities as changes in demand and job progress occur.[18]

The general critical-ratio model is:

$$\text{Critical Ratio (CR)} = \frac{\text{Date Required} - \text{Today}}{\text{Days Required to Finish Job}}$$

Other models have also been developed for specific purposes and can be found elsewhere in the literature referenced. But the principles remain the same. If the critical ratio (CR) for a job is greater than unity, the job is ahead of schedule. If $CR = 1.0$, the job is on time and with $CR < 1.0$, the job has fallen behind the schedule and is considered critical. The *lower* the critical ratio, the more critical the job is.

Periodic reviews, often daily, are made on each job in operation to update their individual CR value. On any particular working day, a few jobs may become critical, and hopefully a few will be dropped from the previous critical list. If the manufacturing process happens to be flexible and responsive, then resources can be easily shifted from high-CR jobs to low-CR tasks, in order to meet all or many of the deadlines. On the other hand, if it is costly and time-consuming to make physical changes from one job to another, corrective action can not be as frequent. In this latter situation, control limits on the critical-ratio values could be used. For example, the policy might be as follows:

> Slow down or temporarily stop work on jobs with $CR > 1.10$. Start or speed up operations on jobs with $CR < 0.90$. Otherwise, continue at the present operational rate.

Such a policy would prevent managers from overreacting when job priorities vary sporadically.

---

[18] *Critical Ratio Scheduling*, APICS Training Aid #2, American Production & Inventory Control Society. G. W. Plossl and O. W. Wight, *Production and Inventory Control* (Englewood Cliffs, N.J.: Prentice-Hall, Inc., 1967), pp. 296–300.

The primary advantage of the critical-ratio method is its forward-looking control feature. *Potential* problems can be pinpointed and corrective action started while the jobs are in production and while enough time is still available to bring the operations into control. This prevention of future problems, of course, is the ultimate goal of any control process.

STATISTICAL CONTROL

Even in an age of standardization, of mass production, and allegedly of conformity, we see extremes, we note differences and we recognize that variability is inevitable. No two snowflakes are alike and no two fingerprints are identical. So, also, two successive charges of steel will not contain exactly the same proportion of ingredients and the resulting products will not have the exact same characteristics. With the possible exception of those properties that may be reduced to counting, variation is inherent in all objects, states, or events. Variation will occur in the quality of incoming materials, in the time required to complete a work cycle, in the dimensions of a finished product, in the time-to-failure of equipment, in the number of workers absent on Monday and then on Tuesday, in the number of defectives produced by the first, second, and third shifts, and in the number of arrivals per time period into a queuing situation.

The concept of statistical control is based on the existence of *a stable system of chance causes*—a pattern of variation that is consistent and controllable over time. One specific unit may be different from the second, the third, and so forth, but if the statistical distribution describing the characteristic in question is stable, then we have a state of statistical control.

Consider the successive rolls of a six-sided die such as might be used in a game of *Monopoly*. The first roll yields a three, perhaps the second roll is a one, the third is a five, and the fourth roll is another three. It is not unlikely nor unexpected that successive outcomes may be different; however, these outcomes will all be the result of tossing the same die—a die that is assumed not to be changing over time. The die should produce a stable system of chance causes. With enough data, and using the relative frequency definition of probability, we could plot the appropriate distribution, which would be in the shape of a rectangle ranging from one to six. This distribution is our stable system of chance causes.

Now assume that someone changes our die (without telling us) by converting the one to a four, the two to a five, and the three to a six. In effect, we now have a die with two fours, two fives, and two sixes. We are unaware of the change, but we do have the opportunity of continuing to observe the results of successive tosses. Assume we toss a four, then a six, another four, and a five. After four tosses, would we know that the die has been modified—that we no longer have the original stable system of chance causes? Not likely! Eventually we might become suspicious, but it might take a few more tosses before we realize we have not recently seen a one, a two, or a three. On the other hand, had the die been modified by adding two dots to each side, giving us a die reading from three to eight, we would be decidedly suspicious the first time we observed a seven or an eight. We would claim that the process has changed!

A probabilistic steady-state or stable pattern of variation exists when the parameters of the statistical distribution describing the system of chance causes remains constant over time. Such a pattern exists, if only for the first day, in Figure 21-6. Assume that we are honing pistons. At 15-minute intervals through the 8-hour day, a unit is selected, the

Figure 21-6

A stable and some unstable patterns of variation.

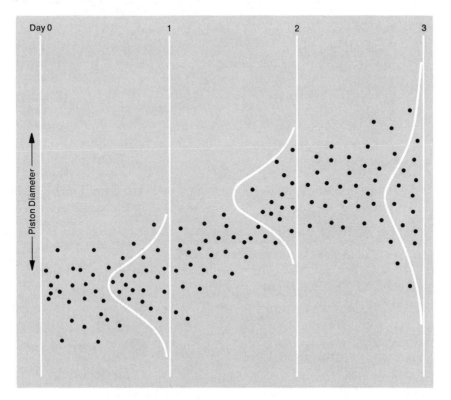

diameter measured and plotted as in Figure 21-6. The statistical distribution at the end of that day describes the process—the system of chance causes, at that point in time. During the first day, the process is stable and *in control*. During the second day, however, a trend is evident. The central tendency is increasing and the diameters are becoming larger. By the end of the day, the average has shifted noticeably upward. The process may be said to be *out of control* during the second day. Another form of instability can be seen during the third day, when the dispersion increases over time. In each of these two cases, the changes were gradual. In another instance, the shift might be more severe and erratic. In any case, we would like to know when a shift is occurring. We would like to know when the stable system of chance causes no longer exists.

Control limits are often placed about the initial stable pattern of variation to insure stability or detect subsequent changes. This can be seen in Figure 21-7. Samples are taken and the appropriate dimensions, e.g., the diameter, noted in comparison to the control limits. If the sample falls within the control limits, the process is said to be *in control*. If the sample falls outside the limits, the process is deemed to have changed and is said to be *out of control*. With each inference, an error is possible. Perhaps the process has not changed, but a value falls outside the control limits (the shaded area of Distribution A, Figure 21-7). We would incorrectly assume that the process has changed and would seek to take some corrective action when none was necessary. On the other hand, the process may have actually changed, but our sample falls within the control limits (the shaded area of Distribution B, Figure 21-7). Again, we would be in error, this time in not seeking an assignable cause in variation when one exists.

Other means exist for detecting shifts in the basic process. For example, a run test may be used. "Grounds exist for suspicion that the process average has shifted . . . whenever in 11 successive points on the control chart, at least 10 are on the same side of the central line." [19] Alternatively, a finite sequence of increasing (or decreasing) values may result in the inference that the process is changing. In any case, we never know for certain that the initial stable pattern is changing, we can only observe some values and draw an inference.

The first and most fundamental problem in statistical control is to detect changes from the stable system of chance causes, to detect them as quickly and as economically as possible, and not to be in error too

[19] Eugene L. Grant, *Statistical Quality Control* (3d ed.) (New York: McGraw-Hill Book Co., Inc., 1964), p. 95.

often by inferring that the process has changed when in fact it has not. The second problem is to seek the cause of variation and take the appro-

Figure 21-7

A stable and an unstable pattern of variation and appropriate control limits.

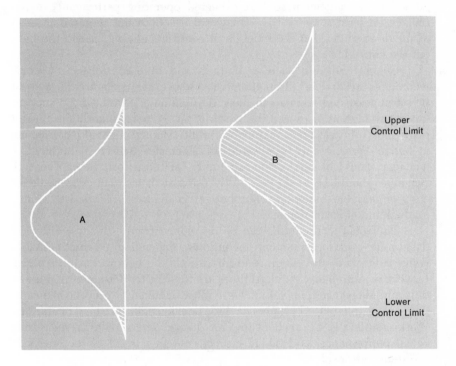

priate corrective action. However, this is primarily a function of the technology involved in the process. For example, some mechanical equipment adjustments could be made to bring the average diameter of the pistons back down to the initial condition. If the time to complete a work cycle is becoming excessive, appropriate corrective action would have to be identified. If the time-to-failure of some production equipment is becoming significantly less, again, some assignable reason would have to be noted and corrective action taken. In each case, the detection step must be followed by corrective action to close the control function loop.

SUMMARY

Regardless of the nature and complexity of a business system, three stages —development, implementation, and operation—make up its life cycle. This cycle begins when design work is started and ends when the system is modified or terminated. In the development stage, attention is directed toward the plans and organization of the ultimate system. Later, management must determine how and when the system can best be installed. (Unfortunately, this step is often neglected.) Then the system must be guided by management so that expected operating performance materializes. At least some of the managerial functions are required in each of the three stages, but the function of control is always needed throughout the entire life cycle.

General controls, such as budgets and time controls, are specific techniques needed in all stages of a system's life cycle. Budgets must be set at least high enough to meet the minimum threshold for success, but not so high as to exceed the worth of the system. In addition, budget plans must provide for a reasonable profit. Managers should participate in budget making and be allowed to administer their own budgets. A manager should be held responsible only for those costs he can control. A budget should be made flexible by using such techniques as standard costs or variable budgeting, but budget changes should be made in a gradual and efficient manner.

Time-control standards can be developed from estimates, historical data, and work-measurement techniques, depending on the activities being controlled, the accuracy desired, and the control costs involved. In work measurement, standard times are found after determining normal-time and allowance-time values. Care must be taken to prevent managers from using inflated allowances to hide inefficiencies in their operations. Work-sampling is an excellent tool for determining standards, measuring actual performance, and taking corrective action in all of the stages of a system's life cycle.

Specific controls, such as PERT/CPM, production, and statistical controls, are normally used in only one or two life-cycle stages. PERT/CPM models are economically used on large-scale, one-time projects to insure that these projects are completed as soon as possible or within a specified time limit. Project-control methods usually require an activity analysis, graphical network, network analysis, and control of critical activities. Either probabilistic or deterministic time values can be employed to pinpoint critical activities that have zero or minimum slack time in the precedence network. With probabilistic models, activities with relatively high time variance can also be carefully controlled. When action becomes necessary, various deployment methods are available to correct different project-control problems.

The objective of production planning and control is to achieve an adequate trade-off between operating a system economically and meeting customers' demands on time. Uncertainty and constant interruptions to the operating system require rapid information feedback and corrective actions, as well as changing standards of production performance. At best, production-control techniques that are forward-looking should be used, such as line-of-balance (LOB) and critical-ratio scheduling methods. These types of models allow management to pinpoint *potential* problems before they occur and to take corrective action soon enough to avert their birth.

Variability of performance is inevitable. At best, we can try to achieve a pattern of variation that is consistent and controllable over time. Hopefully, this stable system of chance or random causes will fall near the standards set by management and customers. Statistical control procedures are employed to detect changes in the stable system as quickly as possible. At the same time, efforts are made to prevent overreactions to sporadic variations. Consequently, control charts are designed to strike a balance between these goals. In addition, the charts should spot potential problems before they happen. Then corrective actions can satisfactorily close the feedback-control loop.

QUESTIONS AND PROBLEMS

1. What major stages are found in the life cycle of a system?

2. The manager of a manufacturing plant wants a safety program (or system) in his organization. List the activities needed in each stage of the program's life cycle.

3. How does the *relative* time span of each stage of an intermittent production system compare to a continuous system?

4. Why do managers often fail to plan and control the *installation* of a system?

5. Why are controls necessary for the planning function? Suggest some controls that might be used.

6. What is the minimum threshold for success? Why is it important?

7. What is a budget?

8. Costs may exceed the worth of a project, even though management has elaborate controls to hold capital and operating expenses in line. Why?

9. Who should administer budgets?

10. Discuss the problems that may arise if all managers are ordered to cut their budgets by 10 percent during an economic slump.

11. Should standard costs be used by top management to control subordinate managers? Why?

12. Give reasons why historically-based time standards may be invalid.

13. Two major steps are taken to determine work-measurement standards. What are these steps?

14. Give some specific applications for work sampling.

15. What corrective actions might you propose as a result of the study given in Table 21-1?

16. PERT/CPM models can be used profitably on projects having what characteristics?

17. What is a critical path? Slack time? Expected time?

18. Discuss some examples where PERT/CPM load-leveling models may be used. Limited-resource models. Least-costing models.

19. What are the main goals of production control? What conflicting factors may need to be considered in meeting these goals?

20. What components of the LOB and critical-ratio models make them forward-looking controls?

21. If a process or operation is statistically in control, is it "in control" with specifications or standards set by management? Why?

22. When rolling a single die, what is the expected outcome value? What is the probability of tossing a *four* each time in three successive rolls? What application does this have to control charts?

23. A work-sampling study was conducted on a maintenance crew in a machine shop, resulting in the following data.

Activtiy	Number of Observations
Inspect machines	50
Repair machines	1,500
Get tools and materials	150
Personal time (allowed)	150
Rest Breaks (allowed)	100
"Horseplay" (*not allowed*)	50
Total	2,000

If each man in the crew can service 5 machines per 8-hour shift, on the average, what is the *standard time* in hours per machine?

24. In the PERT example given in the chapter, trouble arises with activity D (see Figure 21-4). Therefore, the expected time for D will be revised upward to 9 weeks, if the normal work-shift of 8 hours per day is maintained. How many *hours* of overtime should be scheduled for D in order to meet the original deadline?

25. What activity has the largest time variance in the PERT example?

26. If the *actual* performance in Table 21-7 applied to the tenth shipping day instead of the seventh day in the LOB example, find the following for each activity:

   a. Standard LOB value
   b. Unit variance
   c. Time variance

What corrective actions would you propose, in order of priority?

APPENDIX

COMPOUND INTEREST FACTOR $(1 + i)^n$

n	½%	1%	2%	3%	4%	5%	6%	7%	8%	10%
1	1.005	1.010	1.020	1.030	1.040	1.050	1.060	1.070	1.080	1.100
2	1.010	1.020	1.040	1.061	1.082	1.103	1.124	1.145	1.166	1.210
3	1.015	1.030	1.061	1.093	1.125	1.158	1.191	1.225	1.260	1.331
4	1.020	1.041	1.082	1.126	1.170	1.216	1.262	1.311	1.360	1.464
5	1.025	1.051	1.104	1.159	1.217	1.276	1.338	1.403	1.469	1.611
6	1.030	1.062	1.126	1.194	1.265	1.340	1.419	1.501	1.587	1.772
7	1.036	1.072	1.149	1.230	1.316	1.407	1.504	1.606	1.714	1.949
8	1.041	1.083	1.172	1.267	1.369	1.477	1.594	1.718	1.851	2.144
9	1.046	1.094	1.195	1.305	1.423	1.551	1.689	1.838	1.999	2.358
10	1.051	1.105	1.219	1.344	1.480	1.629	1.791	1.967	2.159	2.594
11	1.056	1.116	1.243	1.384	1.539	1.710	1.898	2.105	2.332	2.853
12	1.062	1.127	1.268	1.426	1.601	1.796	2.012	2.252	2.518	3.138
13	1.067	1.138	1.294	1.469	1.665	1.886	2.133	2.410	2.720	3.452
14	1.072	1.149	1.319	1.513	1.732	1.980	2.261	2.579	2.937	3.797
15	1.078	1.161	1.346	1.558	1.801	2.079	2.397	2.759	3.172	4.177
16	1.083	1.173	1.373	1.605	1.873	2.183	2.540	2.952	3.426	4.595
17	1.088	1.184	1.400	1.653	1.948	2.292	2.693	3.159	3.700	5.054
18	1.094	1.196	1.428	1.702	2.026	2.407	2.854	3.380	3.996	5.560
19	1.099	1.208	1.457	1.754	2.107	2.527	3.026	3.617	4.316	6.116
20	1.105	1.220	1.486	1.806	2.191	2.653	3.207	3.870	4.661	6.727
21	1.110	1.232	1.516	1.860	2.279	2.786	3.400	4.141	5.034	7.400
22	1.116	1.245	1.546	1.916	2.370	2.925	3.604	4.430	5.437	8.140
23	1.122	1.257	1.577	1.974	2.465	3.072	3.820	4.741	5.871	8.954
24	1.127	1.270	1.608	2.033	2.563	3.225	4.049	5.072	6.341	9.850
25	1.133	1.282	1.641	2.094	2.666	3.386	4.292	5.427	6.848	10.835

n	½%	1%	2%	3%	4%	5%	6%	7%	8%	10%
26	1.138	1.295	1.673	2.157	2.772	3.556	4.549	5.807	7.396	11.918
27	1.144	1.308	1.707	2.221	2.883	3.733	4.822	6.214	7.988	13.110
28	1.150	1.321	1.741	2.288	2.999	3.920	5.112	6.649	8.627	14.421
29	1.156	1.335	1.776	2.357	3.119	4.116	5.418	7.114	9.317	15.863
30	1.161	1.348	1.811	2.427	3.243	4.322	5.743	7.612	10.063	17.449
31	1.167	1.361	1.848	2.500	3.373	4.538	6.088	8.145	10.868	19.194
32	1.173	1.375	1.885	2.575	3.508	4.765	6.453	8.715	11.737	21.114
33	1.179	1.389	1.922	2.652	3.648	5.003	6.841	9.325	12.676	23.225
34	1.185	1.403	1.961	2.732	3.794	5.253	7.251	9.978	13.690	25.548
35	1.191	1.417	2.000	2.814	3.946	5.516	7.686	10.677	14.785	28.102
40	1.221	1.489	2.208	3.262	4.801	7.040	10.286	14.974	21.725	45.259
45	1.252	1.565	2.438	3.782	5.841	8.985	13.765	21.002	31.920	72.890
50	1.283	1.645	2.692	4.384	7.107	11.467	18.420	29.457	46.902	117.391
55	1.316	1.729	2.972	5.082	8.646	14.636	24.650	41.315	68.914	189.059
60	1.349	1.817	3.281	5.892	10.520	18.679	32.988	57.946	101.257	304.482
65	1.383	1.909	3.623	6.830	12.799	23.840	44.145	81.273	148.780	490.371
70	1.418	2.007	4.000	7.918	15.572	30.426	59.076	113.989	218.606	789.747
75	1.454	2.109	4.416	9.179	18.945	38.833	79.057	159.876	321.205	1271.895
80	1.490	2.217	4.875	10.641	23.050	49.561	105.796	224.234	471.955	2048.400
85	1.528	2.330	5.383	12.336	28.044	63.254	141.579	314.500	693.456	3298.969
90	1.567	2.449	5.943	14.300	34.119	80.730	189.465	441.103	1018.915	5313.023
95	1.606	2.575	6.562	16.578	41.511	103.035	253.546	618.670	1497.121	8556.676
100	1.647	2.705	7.245	19.219	50.505	131.501	339.302	867.716	2199.761	13780.612

index